Qshell for iSeries

Qshell for iSeries

Ted Holt and Fred A. Kulack

Qshell for iSeries
Ted Holt & Fred Kulack

First Edition

First Printing—January 2004
Second Printing—April 2006

MC Press offers excellent discounts on this book when ordered in quantity for bulk purchases or special sales, which may include custom covers and content particular to your business, training goals, marketing focus, and branding interest.

For information regarding permissions or special orders, please contact:
    MC Press
    Corporate Offices
    125 N. Woodland Trail
    Lewisville, TX 75077 USA

For information regarding sales and/or customer service, please contact:
    MC Press
    P.O. Box 4300
    Big Sandy, TX 75755-4300 USA

ISBN: 1-58347-046-8

Contents

Preface

In 1981, I entered the world of computing as a third-shift operator of IBM mainframe computers. I barely knew the difference between hardware and software, but I found information processing fascinating, and I devoted almost every spare hour to learning about and advancing in my new career. I took classes in RPG II programming at a local community college. I taught myself COBOL and S/360 Assembler language at work during idle hours. I wrote RPG II programs on an IBM System/34 for an orphanage at no charge.

Two years after I began my operator job, I entered college to get a degree in computer science. Suddenly, I was exposed to scientific and mathematical computing. Pascal, FORTRAN, and C were quite a change from RPG II and COBOL. The world of stacks and queues, linked lists, pointers, and so forth was quite different from file processing and report generation, but I was eager to learn and I enjoyed exploring new territory. I never lost contact with my data-processing roots, however; I paid my way through college by programming a S/34 for a home-health agency.

After completing my computer science degree, I returned to the IBM midrange world full-time, taking jobs in S/36, S/38, and AS/400 shops. Mathematical and scientific programming was fun, but when it came time to make a living, business programming was more practical, at least in small-town America. I never forgot, though, what was on the other side of the programming fence. I remembered how Unix programmers created tools to help them in their work, and I would write utilities to help me in the business-programming world.

When IBM introduced Qshell, I was hopeful that I would be able to use Unix tools like grep, tr, sed, and perl to help me with everyday drudgery. I quickly discovered, however, that there was not much information available about Qshell, either on the Web or in print. And what was available was not complete. That's why I decided to write this book—I realized that iSeries programmers and system administrators needed to know more about Qshell than IBM's Web site and manual will tell them.

THE AUDIENCE

Since this book has two authors, it is written from two angles. My angle is that of an IBM midrange programmer. As I have worked on this book, I have kept in mind the traditional AS/400 professionals, who are accustomed to things like CL and RPG.

On the other hand, my co-author, Fred Kulack, comes from a different background. The poor soul doesn't know RPG, DDS, and such ancient and esoteric things, but he's a whiz when it comes to newer things like C and Java. (Well, C's not new, but it's new to the iSeries.) For this I am indeed grateful, because Fred can relate to people who are coming to Qshell and the iSeries after using Unix and Unix shells on other machines.

RELEASES

When this book was written, V5R2 was the current release of OS/400. Most examples have been tested under V5R2 Qshell. Some were also tested under V5R1 and/or AT&T's Korn shell. Some were tested only under V5R1.

Because V5R2 is the current release, we point out V5R2 features throughout the text. We did not go back to previous releases to indicate what works with each release and what doesn't. If you want or need to know if a particular feature is supported under a certain release of OS/400, see appendix B.

GUARANTEES (OR RATHER, THE LACK THEREOF)

Fred and I have included a lot (and I do mean a lot!) of code examples, so you won't have to waste a lot of time trying to figure out how the Qshell commands work. Please bear in mind that the code examples in this book are just that—examples. This book is not intended to provide production code. We have made every effort to provide accurate information, but there is no way we could have tested the code in all situations. There might be bugs and/or typos and/or wrong information, but there aren't any lies.

Before you run a Qshell command or script, therefore, use the following precautions:

- Do not modify important data without a backup.

- Do not modify important data until you have thoroughly tested the command or script you intend to run.

- Do not assume that the code in this book is reliable.

Please understand also that this book is not exhaustive. To cover all the parameters of all utilities, for instance, would require a book in itself. This book is intended to be a complement to, not a replacement of, IBM's Qshell reference manual.

CONVENTIONS

In giving syntax, this book uses the same conventions as IBM uses in its Qshell manual:

- Boldface indicates that the text is to be typed as-is.
- Italicized text is to be replaced with a value.
- Brackets indicate optional elements.
- Ellipses indicate that an element may be repeated.

For example, here is the syntax diagram for the sort utility:

```
sort [-cmubdfinr] [-t char] [-T char] [-k keydef ...] [-o output] [file] ...
```

The name of the utility is sort, so the word *sort* must be typed. The permitted options are b, c, d, f, i, k, m, n, o, r, t, T, and u. If you use the t, T, k, or o options, you must follow them with an argument. The k option may have one or more instances of a key definition. You may repeat the file parameter.

When a terminal session is shown in a figure, input to Qshell (the commands typed by the human) is shown in bold, and output is shown in italics. This convention is illustrated in the following figure.

```
> ls *.csv
  cust.csv          two.csv           uuu.csv
  /home/JSMITH $
> ls *.txt
  cvthex.txt       filestar.txt      output.txt        readdata4.txt
  demo.txt         ftpin.txt         parm2.txt         serr.txt
  dirlist.txt      ftpmodel.txt      readdata.txt      sout.txt
  errorlog.txt     grepout.txt       readdata2.txt     tabdelimf.txt
  filedot.txt      mylsout.txt       readdata3.txt
  /home/JSMITH $
```

This is an example of a terminal session.

OUR GOAL

Fred and I trust that this book will help you do your job well. We plan to update it as long as IBM continues to enhance Qshell, to cover new features as they become available, and to add more and better examples. In short, we plan to serve you if you work with Qshell. Please help us serve you more effectively by sending feedback (whether positive or negative) and corrections to me at the following email address:

tholt@mcpressonline.com

Ted Holt

Chapter 1
Introduction to Qshell

A *shell* is a program that allows a human to interact with an operating system in a conversational way. The QCMD program that runs on the IBM iSeries 400 computer is a shell of sorts. DOS, the original operating system of the IBM PC, boots up to a shell called Command.com.

UNIX AND LINUX SHELLS

Unix systems also have shell interfaces, but in the Unix world, there are several shells from which to choose. The Bourne shell, introduced in 1979, is the standard Unix shell, primarily used for system administration. It lacks many of the features of other, more recently developed shells, but is available on all Unix systems.

The C shell, which was developed at the University of California at Berkeley, is based on the C programming language. It is more powerful than the Bourne shell, and many programmers were quick to adopt it when it became available.

All other Unix shells are descendents of the Bourne and C shells. For example, David Korn developed the Korn shell in the mid-1980s as a superset of the Bourne shell. That is, the Korn shell is able to run scripts written for the Bourne shell, but the Bourne shell cannot run all scripts written for the Korn shell.

The invention of the Linux operating system brought about many new shells, but the two primary Linux shells are the Bourne-again shell (known as "bash"), based on the Bourne shell, and the TC shell, based on the C shell. These shells are now included with some Unix systems.

To facilitate the use of technology across platforms, two organizations have established standards for Unix shells. In 1986, the Institute of Electrical and Electronics Engineers (IEEE) released the Portable Operating System Interface (POSIX) standard for Unix systems. The POSIX standard is based on the Korn shell. The Open Group, a consortium of information-technology suppliers, created the X/Open standard as a superset of the POSIX standard. Qshell is based on both POSIX and X/Open standards.

```
                         QSH Command Entry
   _

      /home/SMITH $


















   ===>  _____
         _____
         _____
         _____

      F3==Exit   F6=Print F9=Retrieve F12=Disconnect
      F13=Clear  F17=Top  F18=Bottom  F21=CL command entry
```

Figure 1.1: The interactive shell resembles the QCMD display.

QSHELL

Qshell is a Unix-like interface to the IBM iSeries. It is a Bourne-like shell, with many features from the Korn shell. Qshell began as a port of the ash shell, a Bourne-like shell from Berkeley Software Design (BSD). After the porting team had dealt with iSeries-specific issues like translation between ASCII and EBCDIC, they began adding features from other Unix shells. When a feature was implemented differently in different shells, the team followed POSIX standards.

Qshell consists of a command-line interpreter and a collection of utilities. The interpreter may be run in either interactive or batch mode. In interactive mode, it looks similar to the QCMD interface to OS/400.

The Need for Qshell

OS/400 already has the QCMD interface, a menu-driven interface, and iSeries Navigator (previously known as Operations Navigator). You might wonder, then, why there is a need for the Qshell interface. The answer lies in its unique benefits:

- Qshell includes commands that are not found in QCMD or iSeries Navigator, so it complements the other interfaces; it does not replace them.

- Qshell is well suited for working with the Integrated File System (the IFS), because the IFS is a hierarchical file system similar to those used on Unix systems.

- Qshell can run shell scripts from Unix platforms with little or no modification, so programmers from Unix systems can do productive work on the iSeries.

- Qshell handles multithreaded programming.

- Qshell is a good environment for creating Java applications.

Installing Qshell

Qshell is a licensed-program product that ships with OS/400. However, it is not mandatory that you install Qshell for OS/400 to operate.

To determine whether or not you have Qshell, use option 10 of the LICPGM menu. Look for an entry for the Qshell Interpreter, as shown in Figure 1.2.

```
                    Display Installed Licensed Programs
                                                    System: SOME400
     Licensed  Installed
     Program   Status       Description
     5722SS1   *INSTALLED   OS/400 - Library QGPL
     5722SS1   *INSTALLED   OS/400 - Library QUSRSYS
     5722SS1   *INSTALLED   Operating System/400
     5722SS1   *INSTALLED   OS/400 - Extended Base Support
     5722SS1   *INSTALLED   OS/400 - Online Information
     5722SS1   *INSTALLED   OS/400 - Extended Base Directory Support
     5722SS1   *INSTALLED   OS/400 - *PRV CL Compiler Support
     5722SS1   *INSTALLED   OS/400 - Host Servers
     5722SS1   *INSTALLED   OS/400 - System Openness Includes
     5722SS1   *INSTALLED   OS/400 - GDDM
     5722SS1   *INSTALLED   OS/400 - ObjectConnect
     5722SS1   *INSTALLED   OS/400 - OptiConnect
     5722SS1   *INSTALLED   OS/400 - QShell Interpreter
     5722SS1   *INSTALLED   OS/400 - Domain Name System
                                                              More...
     Press Enter to continue.               _


     F3=Exit   F11=Display release   F12=Cancel   F19=Display trademarks

     (C) COPYRIGHT IBM CORP. 1980, 2002.
```

Figure 1.2: Verify the installed status of the Qshell Interpreter.

If the Qshell interpreter is not listed as an installed program, load the system installation media and use option 11 to install Qshell. Page through the list of licensed programs until you see product option 30 (OS/400-Qshell Interpreter). Type *1* in the Option column of the Qshell Interpreter line as shown in Figure 1.3, and press Enter.

The system will ask you to confirm that you wish to install Qshell. Press the Enter key. You will see the Install Options display, pictured in Figure 1.4.

```
                        Install Licensed Programs
    _                                               System: SOME400
 Type options, press Enter.
   1=Install

         Licensed  Product
 Option  Program   Option   Description

    _     5722SS1    12      OS/400 - Host Servers
    _     5722SS1    13      OS/400 - System Openness Includes
    _     5722SS1    14      OS/400 - GDDM
    _     5722SS1    16      OS/400 - Ultimedia System Facilities
    _     5722SS1    18      OS/400 - Media and Storage Extensions
    _     5722SS1    21      OS/400 - Extended NLS Support
    _     5722SS1    22      OS/400 - ObjectConnect
    _     5722SS1    23      OS/400 - OptiConnect
    _     5722SS1    25      OS/400 - NetWare Enhanced Integration
    _     5722SS1    26      OS/400 - DB2 Symmetric Multiprocessing
    _     5722SS1    27      OS/400 - DB2 Multisystem
    1     5722SS1    30      OS/400 - QShell Interpreter
                                                           More...
 F3=Exit   F11=Display status/release   F12=Cancel   F19=Display trademarks
```

Figure 1.3: Start the install of the Qshell Interpreter.

```
    _                       Install Options
                                                System: SOME400
   Type choices, press Enter.

     Installation device  . . .  OPT01      Name

     Objects to install . . . .  1          1=Programs and language objects
                                            2=Programs
                                            3=Language objects

     Automatic IPL  . . . . . .  N          Y=Yes
                                            N=No



   F3=Exit   F12=Cancel
```

Figure 1.4: Specify installation options on the Install Options display.

Ensure that your installation device is specified correctly depending on which CD or DVD drive you're using. Specify option 1 to install both programs and languages. Rebooting your iSeries is not required when installing Qshell, so specify an automatic IPL option of N. Press Enter to start the installation, and the system will begin installing Qshell.

```
  _                    Installing Licensed Programs
                                                   System: SOME400


 Licensed programs processed . . . . . . . . . . :      0 of 1


                 Licensed program install in progress
```

Figure 1.5: Wait for the system to finish the installation of Qshell.

You will know you are finished when you get the confirmation message shown in Figure 1.6. The Qshell interpreter is now ready for use.

```
 _LICPGM                    Work with Licensed Programs
                                                        System: SOME400
   Select one of the following:

     Manual Install
        1. Install all

     Preparation
        5. Prepare for install

     Licensed Programs
        10. Display installed licensed programs
        11. Install licensed programs
        12. Delete licensed programs
        13. Save licensed programs


                                                         More...
   Selection or command
   ===>

   F3=Exit   F4=Prompt   F9=Retrieve   F12=Cancel   F13=Information Assistant
   F16=AS/400 Main menu
   Work with licensed programs function complete.
```

Figure 1.6: Installation of Qshell is completed.

SUMMARY

Qshell adds a Unix-like interface to the iSeries. It is especially helpful for developing in Java and for working with the IFS. Once you have verified that Qshell is installed, you are ready to run it, which is the subject of the next chapter.

Chapter 2
Running Qshell

Use the "Start Qshell" CL command (STRQSH or QSH) to enter the Qshell environment. STRQSH has one parameter, CMD. The default value for CMD is *NONE, which means that no Qshell command is to be executed.

What happens when you run STRQSH depends on three things:

- Whether Qshell is running in a batch job or an interactive job
- Whether the CMD parameter specifies a Qshell command
- Whether Qshell is already active in an interactive job

The rest of this chapter examines these variations on STRQSH.

QSHELL IN AN INTERACTIVE JOB

If you start Qshell in an interactive job, and do not put a Qshell command in the CMD parameter, Qshell opens an interactive terminal session, as shown in Figure 2.1. If you use terminal services under Java, you will find this terminal session very familiar, since Qshell and Java use the same terminal support.

```
                              QSH Command Entry
      ▬
       /home/SMITH $




       ===>  _____
             _____
             _____
             _____

       F3==Exit   F6=Print F9=Retrieve F12=Disconnect
       F13=Clear  F17=Top  F18=Bottom  F21=CL command entry
```

Figure 2.1: Both Java and Qshell use the same interactive terminal support.

The Output Area

Below the panel title is the output area. When a Qshell session begins, the output area is blank except for the Qshell primary prompt string, which in Figure 2.1 is the value */home/SMITH $*.

The dollar sign is a prompt character. Qshell uses four prompt characters, shown in Table 2.1, to indicate that it needs input. In chapter 9, you will learn how to change the values of these prompt characters. For example, you will be able to use a percent sign (%) instead of a dollar sign for the PS1 prompt character.

In the output area, Qshell lists the commands you give it and the response to those commands. Figure 2.2 shows part of the output area of an interactive Qshell session. First, the *ls* command tells Qshell to display a list of files whose names end with a period and the characters *csv*. Qshell responds with a list of three file names and the Qshell prompt, which in this session is set to the

Table 2.1: Qshell Prompt Characters

Prompt Character	Description	Default Value	New in Release V5R2?
PS1	Primary prompt string. Qshell is ready for a command.	$	No
PS2	Secondary prompt string. Part of a command has been entered. Qshell is waiting for the remainder of the command.	>	No
PS3	Select command prompt. Qshell is waiting for the user to choose an option presented with the select compound command.	#?	Yes
PS4	Debug prompt string. Qshell is displaying data in debug mode.	+	No

current directory followed by a dollar sign. The prompt informs the user that Qshell has completed the request and is ready for work.

```
> ls *.csv
  cust.csv          two.csv            uuu.csv
  /home/SMITH $
> rm -f *.csv
  /home/SMITH $
> ls *.txt
  cvthex.txt        filestar.txt       output.txt        readdata4.txt
  demo.txt          ftpin.txt          parm2.txt         serr.txt
  dirlist.txt       ftpmodel.txt       readdata.txt      sout.txt
  errorlog.txt      grepout.txt        readdata2.txt     tabdelimf.txt
  filedot.txt       mylsout.txt        readdata3.txt
  /home/SMITH $
```

Figure 2.2: The Qshell output area holds commands and responses.

The next command in Figure 2.2 is the *rm*, which removes directory entries. In this example, it deletes all CSV (comma-separated value) files.

11

The second *ls* command in Figure 2.2 lists files that end with *.txt*. Qshell responds with the appropriate list of file names and another Qshell prompt.

The Command Line

Below the output area is the command line, where you type the commands you want Qshell to carry out. Do not confuse this command line with a CL command line. You cannot directly execute CL commands from the Qshell command line. However, Qshell has a system utility you can use to execute CL commands.

The Function-Key Legend

Below the command line is the function-key legend. Table 2.2 describes the function keys that are active in the shell.

Table 2.2: Qshell Function-Key Assignments

Key	Name	Description
F3	Exit	Close the interactive session and end Qshell. Contrast with F12.
F5	Refresh	Refresh the output area.
F6	Print	Copy the contents of the output area to a spooled file.
F7	Page up (roll down)	Page backward through the output area. If a number is on the command line, page back that many lines; otherwise, page back one full screen.
F8	Page down (roll up)	Page forward through the output area. If a number is on the command line, page forward that many lines; otherwise, page forward one full screen.
F9	Retrieve a previous command.	If the cursor is on the command line, retrieve previously executed commands in reverse order. If the cursor is in the output area, retrieve the command on which the cursor rests.

Table 2.2: Qshell Function-Key Assignments, *continued*

Key	Name	Description
F11	Toggle line wrap	Determine whether long lines in the output area are wrapped or truncated.
F12	Disconnect	Close the interactive session, but do not end Qshell. You may resume the Qshell session with the STRQSH command. Contrast with F3.
F13	Clear	Clear the output area. This is more than a clear-screen function. It also clears the session history, so you will not be able to page back through the output area to previously executed commands.
F14	Adjust command line length	The command line is normally four lines long. Pressing F14 with a number adjusts the command area to that number of lines. If no number is on the command line, pressing F14 adjusts the command line to four lines.
F17	Top	Position to beginning of output area.
F18	Bottom	Position to end of output area.
F19	Left	Move the output area window to the left. This is used when the output area is truncated because line wrap is off. (See the description of the F11 key.)
F20	Right	Move the output area window to the right, also used when the output area is truncated.
F21	Command entry	Open a window with an OS/400 command line.

The CMD Parameter

You may specify a Qshell command up to 5,000 characters long in the CMD parameter of the STRQSH command. Here is an example:

```
STRQSH CMD('ls *.csv')
```

In this case, Qshell does not open a terminal session. Instead, it executes the *ls* command and ends.

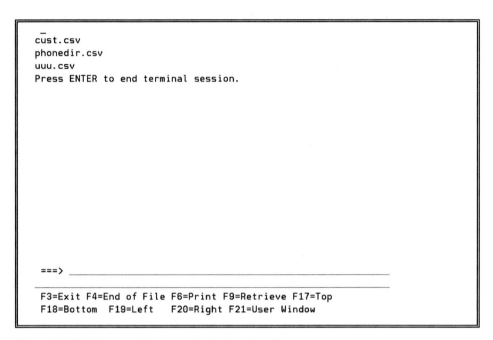

```
 _
cust.csv
phonedir.csv
uuu.csv
Press ENTER to end terminal session.




===>  _____

 F3=Exit F4=End of File F6=Print F9=Retrieve F17=Top
 F18=Bottom  F19=Left   F20=Right F21=User Window
```

Figure 2.3: Qshell opens a temporary terminal session, if necessary.

If the command specified in the CMD parameter produces output, Qshell opens a temporary C runtime terminal session, as shown in Figure 2.3. You can also direct the output elsewhere, as discussed later in this chapter.

Input, however, is a different story. If you are running a script in this manner and Qshell encounters a request for terminal input, it ignores the request.

QSHELL IN BATCH JOBS

You may also run Qshell in a batch job, within certain limits:

- Input requests are ignored.
- If the command produces output, Qshell spools the output.

The following example shows how to submit a Qshell command to run in batch mode:

```
SBMJOB CMD(QSH CMD('rm -f *.csv')) JOB(REMOVEFILE)
```

If the CMD parameter contains the value *NONE, Qshell does nothing and the job ends normally.

REDIRECTING QSHELL OUTPUT

As of V5R2, you may use the QIBM_QSH_CMD_OUTPUT environment variable to control the destination of Qshell output. The allowable values are listed in Table 2.3.

Table 2.3: Allowable Values of Environment Variable QIBM_QSH_CMD_OUTPUT

Value	Description
NONE	The output is discarded.
STDOUT (default)	The output is directed to a C runtime terminal session.
FILE=*name*	The output is directed to the file in *name*. If the file already exists, the output overwrites the previous contents.
FILEAPPEND=*name*	The output is appended to the file in *name*.

In the following example of the QIBM_QSH_CMD_OUTPUT environment variable, the names of comma-delimited files are written to the file lsout.txt in the current directory, replacing any previous contents:

```
ADDENVVAR ENVVAR(QIBM_QSH_CMD_OUTPUT) VALUE('FILE=lsout.txt')
STRQSH CMD('ls *.csv')
```

As another example, the names of files that begin with a lowercase *b* are appended to the end of stream file lsout.txt, which is in the current directory:

```
ADDENVVAR ENVVAR(QIBM_QSH_CMD_OUTPUT)
VALUE('FILEAPPEND=lsout.txt') STRQSH CMD('ls b*')
```

In both of these examples, output is sent to IFS files in the current directory. Writing to a stream file is generally the sensible approach. However, that is not to say that Qshell won't write to a database file. Here, the names of comma-delimited files are written to program-described database file, lsout, in the FILEINFO library:

```
ADDENVVAR ENVVAR(QIBM_QSH_CMD_OUTPUT) +
    VALUE('FILE=/qsys.lib/fileinfo.lib/lsout.file/lsout.mbr')
CRTPF FILE(FILEINFO/LSOUT) RCDLEN(24)
STRQSH CMD('ls *.csv')
```

The output data is written to FILEINFO/lsout, ignoring record length. Each line of output is terminated by a hexadecimal-25 character.

To get a better idea of how output is written to database files, see Figure 2.4, which displays the Qshell output in character format, and Figure 2.5, which displays the output in hexadecimal format.

Processes

On Unix systems, a process is a running program. The Qshell interpreter is a process. Each utility that is not a built-in command runs in its own process. Scripts run in their own processes, unless they are invoked with the source (dot) utility.

Under Qshell, every process runs in its own job, so the terms *process* and *job* are interchangeable.

The Terminal Session

The terminal session appears to be an interactive session, but that is not entirely true. A terminal session is actually a combination of jobs.

When a user starts an interactive Qshell session, OS/400 starts a batch-immediate job running the Qshell interpreter, a program named QZSHSH. At this point, the user is running two jobs: the interactive job and the batch-immediate job.

```
 —
                      Display Physical File Member
File . . . . . . :   LSOUT              Library  . . . . :   QTEMP
Member . . . . . :   LSOUT              Record . . . . . :   1
Control  . . . .                        Column . . . . . :   1
Find . . . . . . .
*...+....1....+....2....
cust.csv3phonedir.csv3uu
u.csv3
                       ****** END OF DATA ******




                                                              Bottom
   F3=Exit    F12=Cancel    F19=Left    F20=Right    F24=More keys
```

Figure 2.4: Qshell ignores the record length of a database file.

```
 —
                      Display Physical File Member
File . . . . . . :   LSOUT              Library  . . . . :   QTEMP
Member . . . . . :   LSOUT              Record . . . . . :   1
Control  . . . .                        Column . . . . . :   1
Find . . . . . . .
*...+....1....+....2....
cust.csv3phonedir.csv3uu
8AAA48AA29899888948AA2AA
3423B325578655499B325544

u.csv3
A48AA2444444444444444444
4B3255000000000000000000

                       ****** END OF DATA ******




                                                              Bottom
   F3=Exit    F12=Cancel    F19=Left    F20=Right    F24=More keys
```

Figure 2.5: Qshell terminates each line of output with a hexadecimal-25 character.

You can use the Work with Active Jobs (WRKACTJOB) and Work with
User Jobs CL command (WRKUSRJOBS) to see which jobs are running. The
information returned by the WRKUSRJOB command is shown in Figure 2.6.

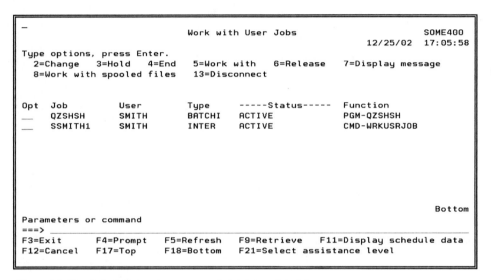

Figure 2.6: The Qshell interpreter runs as a batch immediate job.

If you start a subshell or run a utility, Qshell will start additional jobs as needed.
These have the name QP0ZSPWP, as shown in Figure 2.7.

Under V5R2, you can use Qshell's *ps* (Display Process Status) command to
display information about processes. This command is illustrated in Figure 2.8.

Prestart Jobs

You can speed up processing by using a prestart job, which is a job that begins
running when a subsystem is started. When Qshell starts a new process, it will
use a prestart job if one is available. This improves performance, because the
system does not have to start a new job.

```
   _                         Work with User Jobs                        SOME400
                                                            12/25/02  17:05:58
   Type options, press Enter.
     2=Change    3=Hold    4=End    5=Work with    6=Release    7=Display message
     8=Work with spooled files    13=Disconnect


   Opt  Job        User       Type     -----Status-----  Function
    __   QPOZSPWP   SMITH      BATCHI   ACTIVE            PGM-QZSHSH
    __   QPOZSPWP   SMITH      BATCHI   ACTIVE            PGM-QZSHCHLD
    __   QPOZSPWP   SMITH      BATCHI   ACTIVE            PGM-QZSHCHLD
    __   QZSHSH     SMITH      BATCHI   ACTIVE            PGM-QZSHSH
    __   SSMITH1    SMITH      INTER    ACTIVE            CMD-WRKUSRJOB




                                                                       Bottom
   Parameters or command
   ===>  _____
   F3=Exit      F4=Prompt    F5=Refresh   F9=Retrieve   F11=Display schedule data
   F12=Cancel   F17=Top      F18=Bottom   F21=Select assistance level
```

Figure 2.7: The Qshell interpreter runs as a batch-immediate job.

```
   _                          QSH Command Entry
      5
      6
      7
      8
      9
   /home/smith $
 > ps
        PID DEVICE        TIME FUNCTION       STATUS    JOBID
        595 ssmith1    000:00 cmd-qsh        dspa      042227/smith/ssmith1
        596 -          000:00 pgm-qzshsh     evtw      042228/smith/qzshsh
        602 -          000:00 pgm-find       run       042234/smith/qp0zspwp
        603 -          000:00 pgm-grep       timw      042235/smith/qp0zspwp
        604 -          000:00 pgm-ps         run       042236/smith/qp0zspwp
   /home/smith $


   ===>  _____
         _____


   F3=Exit    F6=Print F9=Retrieve F12=Disconnect
   F13=Clear F17=Top F18=Bottom  F21=CL command entry
```

Figure 2.8: The ps command displays information about Qshell processes.

19

Use the Add Prestart Job Entry (ADDPJE) command to create a prestart job. For example, the following command adds a prestart job to the QINTER subsystem description:

```
ADDPJE SBSD(QSYS/QINTER) PGM(QSYS/QP0ZSPWP)
    INLJOBS(10) THRESHOLD(5) ADLJOBS(10)
    JOBD(QGPL/QDFTJOBD) MAXUSE(1) CLS(QGPL/QINTER)
```

To make Qshell use a prestart job, place a value of *Y* in the environment variable QSH_USE_PRESTART_JOBS. Use the *export* command so that child processes will also use prestart jobs:

```
export -s QSH_USE_PRESTART_JOBS=Y
```

A good place to put this command is in the /etc/profile special script file, which is discussed in chapter 4.

SUMMARY

The Qshell interpreter can run in both interactive and batch environments. In an interactive job, the user can enter commands for immediate execution.

Qshell executes commands in processes, which are implemented as jobs. You can improve the performance of Qshell commands by providing prestart jobs.

Chapter 3
The EDTF Text Editor

EDTF is a simple text editor that is designed for editing stream files. EDTF is a good choice for entering and modifying Qshell programs, known as *scripts*, in the Integrated File System (IFS). EDTF is not the only choice, however; you may instead use text editors on client computers. You can also use EDTF to edit database files, but it is not well suited for this purpose because it knows nothing about database field descriptions.

STARTING EDTF

Use the Edit File CL command (EDTF) to invoke the editor. The EDTF editor has three parameters, which are described in Table 3.1.

Table 3.1: Parameters of the EDTF Command

Parameter	Description
STMF	The name of a stream file in the Integrated File System. If this file does not exist, it will be created. The file name may include a path of directories.
FILE	A database file name, qualified in the format *LIBRARY/NAME*.
MBR	The name of the member in the database file.

You must run EDTF from a CL command line. It will not run from a Qshell command line. To get a CL command line within a Qshell session, press the F21 key.

Qshell scripts may be stored in database files, but they run faster when stored in the root file system of the IFS. All examples in this book assume that scripts are stored in the root, so the FILE and MBR parameters will not be used here.

In Figure 3.1, file case02.qsh is being opened for editing from a CL command line.

```
  MAIN                        OS/400 Main Menu
                                                  System:     SOME400
       Select one of the following:

            1. User tasks
            2. Office tasks
            3. General system tasks
            4. Files, libraries, and folders
            5. Programming
            6. Communications
            7. Define or change the system
            8. Problem handling
            9. Display a menu
           10. Information Assistant options
           11. Client Access/400 tasks

           90. Sign off

       Selection or command
       ===> edtf 'case02.qsh'_____

       F3=Exit F4=Prompt F9=Retrieve F12=Cancel F13=Information Assistant
       F23=Set initial menu
```

Figure 3.1: The EDTF editor is invoked from a CL command line.

Figure 3.2 shows the editing session. Notice that it is similar to the Source Entry Utility (SEU) in several ways:

- There is a command line at the top of the screen for file-level commands.

- Each line in the entry area is preceded by an area in which line commands may be typed.

- Most of the file-level and line commands are almost identical to corresponding SEU commands.

- Most of the display is an entry area, in which you enter the text of the file.

- Most of the EDTF function-key assignments are identical to corresponding assignments in SEU.

However, there are quite a few differences as well. Here are some of the more obvious ones:

- EDTF is a much less robust editor than SEU and does not support nearly as many commands and editing options.

- Lines are not numbered in EDTF sessions.

- EDTF does not present an exit display when the F3 key is pressed.

- EDTF does not include formatted prompting.

```
 Edit File: case02.qsh
 Record :  _1 of     10 by  _8        Column :  _1     59 by _74
 Control : _____

CMD ....+....1....+....2....+....3....+....4....+....5....+....6....+....7....+
        ************Beginning of data**************
 ____ app=$1
 ____ case "$app" in
 ____    GL) echo 'General ledger' ;;
 ____    AP) echo 'Accounts payable' ;;
 ____    AR) echo 'Accounts receivable' ;;
 ____    PR) echo 'Payroll' ;;
 ____    XX | YY) echo 'XX or YY' ;;
 ____    IN) echo 'Inventory' ;;
 ____     *) echo 'Unknown' ;;
 ____ esac
        ************End of Data********************



 F2=Save  F3=Save/Exit  F12=Exit  F15=Services    F16=Repeat find
 F17=Repeat change  F19=Left  F20=Right
```

Figure 3.2: Stream file case02.qsh has been opened for editing.

The top line of Figure 3.2 shows that the name of the open file is case02.qsh. The Record area on the second line indicates that the first record on the display is record 1 of the file. It also shows that there are 10 records in the file, and that the roll keys will page the display eight records at a time. The Column area on the second line in Figure 3.2 indicates that the first column on the display is column 1 of 59 columns in the record. Pressing F19 or F20 windows the display by 74 columns.

You may enter the commands shown in Table 3.2 in the Control area of the editing screen. Notice that most command names have two forms—a short one and a long one. The long forms are unnecessary, because the short names are easier to key.

Table 3.2: Editing Commands for the Control Field

Command	Parameters	Description
F, Find	String	Find a string.
C, Change	old string, new string	Replace a string with another string.
T, Top		Position the view at the top of the file.
B, Bot		Position the view at the bottom of the file.
Print		Print from the current line to the end of the file.

Although the command names are capitalized in the table, they are actually not case-sensitive, so *FIND*, *Find*, and *find* are interchangeable. Parameters, on the other hand, *are* case-sensitive.

The *find* command accepts one parameter: a string for which to search. If the string includes blanks, surround it with single quotation marks or double quotation marks, as in the second of the following two examples:

```
f echo
f "Accounts payable"
```

If the string for which you are searching does not contain either single or double quotation marks, it does not matter which type of quotation marks you use to delimit the search string. However, if the search string contains one type of quotation-mark character, you must surround the string with the other type. To repeat the *find* command, press the F16 key.

The *change* command accepts two parameters: an existing string and the string to replace it. The following lines illustrate this command:

```
c app appl
c 'XX | YY'   'XX | YY | ZZ'
```

To repeat this command, press F17.

The contents of the file are shown in the editing area, between the "Beginning of Data" and "End of Data" markers. Each record of the file begins with a three-character blank area into which editing commands may be entered. Table 3.3 lists these commands and their meanings.

Table 3.3: Editing Commands for the Line-Prefix Field

Command	Description
A	Put moved or copied records after this record.
An	Put n copies of the moved or copied records after this record.
B	Put moved or copied records before this record.
Bn	Put n copies of the moved or copied records before this record.
C	Copy this record.
Cn	Copy n records, beginning with this record.
CC	Copy all records between the two CC commands.
D	Delete this record.

Table 3.3: Editing Commands for the Line-Prefix Field, *continued*

Command	Description
D*n*	Delete *n* records, beginning with this record.
DD	Delete all records between the two DD commands.
I	Insert a blank line after this record.
I*n*	Insert *n* blank lines after this record.
M	Move this record.
M*n*	Move *n* records, beginning with this record.
MM	Move all records between the two MM commands.
R	Repeat this record.
R*n*	Repeat this record *n* times.
RR	Repeat all records between the two RR commands.
RR*n*	Repeat all records between the two RR commands *n* times.
T*n*	Translate *n* records, beginning with this one, to the codepage specified in the Service panel.
TT	Translate all records between the two TT commands to the codepage specified in the Services panel.

Most of the display is reserved for entering the text to be stored in the file. Type the text to the right of the three-byte line-command column. All text must be entered free-format; formatted prompting, such as SEU provides when the F4 key is pressed, is not supported under EDTF.

Below the text-entry area is a function-key legend. Table 3.4 summarizes the function-key assignments for EDTF.

Notice that the F3, F15, F16, F17, F19, and F20 keys behave in much the same way in EDTF as in SEU. Pressing F3 does not present an exit panel to permit you to save or abandon changes. Instead, use the F2 key to save the file at any time. Use F12 to exit without saving changes.

Table 3.4: EDTF Function-Key Assignments

Function key	Name	Description
F2	Save	Save the data and continue editing.
F3	Save/Exit	Save the data and exit the editor. If the file has changed, you will receive a message and will have to press F3 a second time to exit the editor.
F12	Exit	Exit the editor without saving changes. If the file has changed, you will receive a warning message and will have to press F12 a second time to exit the editor.
F15	Services	Specify editing options.
F16	Repeat Find	Find text using the most recent find or change command.
F17	Repeat Change	Change text using the most recent find or change command.
F19	Left	Move left by the width of the window.
F20	Right	Move right by the width of the window.

INTRODUCING THE STREAM-FILE EXERCISES

The following pages provide two simple exercises to help you get started using EDTF. In the first exercise, you will create a stream file and enter text into it. In the second one, you will revise the stream file.

First, you must have a directory in which to store the stream file. If you already have a directory, fine: move along to the next topic. If not, talk to your system administrator and get one. If your system administrator doesn't know what a directory is, or if you *are* the system administrator, then someone, maybe even you, is going to have to create a directory. Here's how to do that:

1. You should have a directory called "/home" on your system. To see whether or not you do, run the Change Current Directory command (CHGCURDIR, CHDIR, or CD) from a CL command line:

```
cd '/home'
```

2. The system will answer with one of two messages, either "Current directory changed" or "Object not found." If you get the second message, there is no home directory. Use the CL Create Directory command (CRTDIR, MKDIR, or MD) to create it:

```
mkdir '/home'
```

3. You should probably create your own directory in which to put your stream files. You may already have a directory and not be aware of it. Use the Display User Profile command (DSPUSRPRF) to find out whether or not you have a home directory:

```
dspusrprf jsmith
```

After you type **dspusrprf** and press Enter, page to the last panel and look for the home-directory prompt.

4. If you need to create a directory of your own, a good convention is to create your directory as a subdirectory of /home and name it with your first initial and last name, as Joe Smith has done in the following command:

```
md '/home/jsmith'
```

This naming convention is not mandatory, of course, but it is a good one to use. Another good convention is /home/*user-profile*, where *user-profile* indicates your user ID. The HOMEDIR (Home Directory) parameter of the Create User Profile command (CRTUSRPRF) defaults to this convention.

CREATING A NEW STREAM FILE

At this point, you should have a directory in which you can place stream files. Use CL's Change Current Directory command (CD) to work from that directory:

```
cd '/home/jsmith'
```

Now you are ready to create the new file. Enter the following command:

```
edtf 'test01.qsh'
```

Unless you already had a file named test01.qsh in your directory, you should see the display in Figure 3.10. If you already have a test01.qsh file, then you will see its contents instead. In that case, use a different file name for this exercise.

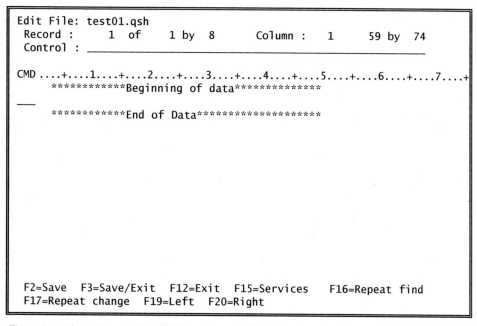

```
Edit File: test01.qsh
  Record :     1  of     1 by  8      Column :   1      59 by  74
  Control : _____

CMD ....+....1....+....2....+....3....+....4....+....5....+....6....+....7....+
        ***********Beginning of data***************
 ___
        ************End of Data********************


















F2=Save   F3=Save/Exit   F12=Exit   F15=Services    F16=Repeat find
F17=Repeat change   F19=Left   F20=Right
```

Figure 3.10: If the file is empty, EDTF provides one blank line.

Since the file is new, EDTF gives one blank line on which to enter data. This is inadequate, because you are going to enter two lines. To add a line, type the letter *I* (in either uppercase or lowercase) in the prefix area of the blank line, as shown in Figure 3.11, and press Enter.

```
Edit File: test01.qsh
  Record :    1  of    1 by  8        Column :    1      59 by  74
  Control : _____

CMD ....+....1....+....2....+....3....+....4....+....5....+....6....+....7....+
          ***********Beginning of data***************
I_
          ***********End of Data********************



F2=Save  F3=Save/Exit  F12=Exit  F15=Services   F16=Repeat find
F17=Repeat change  F19=Left  F20=Right
```

Figure 3.11: Use the Insert command in the prefix area to insert new lines into the editing area.

Now there are two blank lines, so you are ready to write your stream file. Enter the two lines shown in Figure 3.12.

Press the F2 key to save the file to disk, then press the F3 key to exit the editor and return to the CL command line.

REVISING A STREAM FILE

To change the stream file you just created, start by running the EDTF command again to invoke the editor. This time, the system should load the editor with the contents of the test01.qsh file.

```
Edit File: test01.qsh
  Record :      1  of     1 by  8       Column :   1   59 by  74
  Control : _____

CMD ....+....1....+....2....+....3....+....4....+....5....+....6....+....7....+
      ***********Beginning of data***************
___ #!/bin/qsh
___ print "Hello, iSeries world!"
      ************End of Data********************




  F2=Save  F3=Save/Exit  F12=Exit  F15=Services    F16=Repeat find
  F17=Repeat change  F19=Left  F20=Right
```

Figure 3.12: Two lines of text have been entered into the editing area.

Move the cursor to the prefix area of the second record, type *I* (for insert) and press Enter. The editor adds a blank line just before the End of Data marker. Fill in the line as shown in Figure 3.13.

```
Edit File: test01.qsh
  Record :      1  of     1 by  8       Column :   1   59 by  74
  Control : _____

CMD ....+....1....+....2....+....3....+....4....+....5....+....6....+....7....+
      ***********Beginning of data***************
___ #!/bin/qsh
___ print "Hello, iSeries world!"
___ print "Qshell rulz!"
      ************End of Data********************




  F2=Save  F3=Save/Exit  F12=Exit  F15=Services    F16=Repeat find
  F17=Repeat change  F19=Left  F20=Right
```

Figure 3.13: An existing file has been opened and new text has been added.

As before, press F2 and F3 to save the changes and exit the editor.

SUMMARY

The EDTF editor is a general-purpose text editor you can use for creating and modifying Qshell scripts and other text files in the Integrated File System. It is not the only, or even the best, editor for entering Qshell scripts, however—PC-based editors are much more powerful and do not sap system resources. Still, EDTF has the advantage that it is available on all OS/400-based systems.

## Chapter 4

Scripting

As discussed in chapter 3, a Qshell script is a text file that contains commands that Qshell can interpret and execute. Because scripts are not compiled, but interpreted at run time, they might be compared to the OCL and REXX procedures that run on the iSeries.

You are probably accustomed to storing source code in source physical files. Qshell scripts may also be stored in source physical files, but they run faster and demand less system resources if they are stored in stream files in the root file system of the IFS.

In a production environment, Unix programmers and administrators typically store shell scripts in a /bin directory underneath a user's home directory. You can follow that convention while learning to use Qshell and working through this book, but it's not necessary. All that matters is that you have a directory of your own.

A directory is like a source physical file, in that the directory can contain more than one instance of source code. A source physical file has *members*, while a directory has *stream files*. If you don't have your own directory and are not sure how to get one, see "Introducing the Stream-File Exercises" in chapter 3.

NAMING A SCRIPT FILE

Although you can name a script file anything you want, it is probably a good idea to follow the conventions used in the Unix world. Unix script programmers typically begin with a base name. This may be followed by a period and a suffix to indicate the type of script. For example, a suffix of *ksh* indicates a Korn shell script.

The rules for naming files in the root system are very liberal. You may include blanks and punctuation marks in file names, but it is probably best not to do so. A good suffix for Qshell scripts is *qsh,* but that is by no means required.

The example scripts in this book often use the fictitious file name *myscript.qsh.* If you key some of the examples, you will probably want to use other names so you can keep more than one script on disk.

RUNNING A SCRIPT FILE

To run a Qshell script, enter its name on the command line of an interactive shell session and press the Enter key. Qshell may might respond with error 001-0019:

```
Error found searching for command myscript.qsh. No such path or
    directory.
```

If you know that the file exists, the problem is likely that you do not have Execute permission or the PATH environment variable is not set correctly.

The PATH variable contains a list of directories that are to be searched for commands. To view the current setting of PATH, use the following command:

```
echo $PATH
```

Be sure to type the word *PATH* in uppercase letters, because Qshell variable names are case-sensitive.

Look for the name of the directory that contains your script. If your script is in the current directory, look for a leading colon, a trailing colon, two adjacent colons, or the current directory's name. Any of these indicates the presence of the current directory in the search path.

Every file has a set of permissions associated with it that tell who is allowed to read, write, and execute the file. Permissions are defined for the owner of the file, the group to which the owner belongs, and everybody else. Qshell scripts require Read and Execute permissions. (Permissions are discussed in detail in chapter 9.)

When you create an IFS file, you will probably have Read permission, but you may not have Execute permission. If not, you will have to grant yourself Execute permission in order to run the script.

Figure 4.1 shows how to determine and enable Execute permission within an interactive Qshell session. The *-l* option of the *ls* command displays a ten-character string that indicates the permissions. This string is in the first column of the output. The owner permissions are described by the second through fourth characters, which read *rw-* in this example. These characters indicate that the Read and Write attributes are enabled, but the Execute attribute is disabled. Notice the permissions after executing the *chmod* command. The hyphen in the fourth position has been replaced with an *x*. Now you can execute your script.

```
ls  -l  myscript.qsh
-rw-------  1 JSMITH  0              25 Sep  3 09:05 myscript.qsh
/home/JSMITH $
chmod  u+x  myscript.qsh
/home/JSMITH $
ls  -l  myscript.qsh
-rwx------  1 JSMITH  0              25 Sep  3 09:05 myscript.qsh
```

Figure 4.1: Use this code as a pattern for enabling Execute permission for a script.

COMMENTS

At this point, you should know how to create and revise stream files in your directory. You have only one thing left to learn: what to put in those stream files. That is what the rest of this book is all about.

Since every good program requires documentation, one of the first things you should learn is how to include comments in Qshell source code.

Comments begin with the # symbol and span the remainder of the line. The # symbol is referred to by various names, including "pound," "hash," "sharp," and "number." Comments are ignored in Qshell scripts, as are blank lines.

A comment may occupy the entire line or the trailing portion only. Here are examples of both types of comments:

```
# If the -p option was specified, print the output.
shift $OPTIND-1          # shift out the options
```

THE MAGIC NUMBER

If you look at scripts developed for Unix systems, you will frequently see a special comment on the first line. This comment begins with the symbols # and ! (often pronounced "pound bang"), and is called the *magic number*. The purpose of the magic number is to tell Unix which interpreter to load to process the script.

The magic number is discussed in detail in chapter 12. For now, you can ignore it.

EXECUTABLE COMMANDS

You are probably aware that some CL commands are permitted in CL programs only, other CL commands are permitted to run interactively only, and still others may run in either environment. For example, the IF command is only allowed in

CL programs, the GO command runs in interactive jobs only, and SBMJOB works in either environment.

Qshell commands are not restricted in that way. All Qshell commands may run in an interactive session or in a script (although it may not always make sense to enter a certain command in a certain environment).

If you enter a syntactically incomplete command in an interactive session, Qshell responds with the secondary prompt. You can continue to enter line after line of commands, until Qshell determines that execution is possible.

SPECIAL SCRIPTS

When you begin a Qshell session, it automatically executes the following three script files, if they exist:

- The global profile file, /etc/profile—The system administrator uses this file to set system-wide options for all users.

- A file named .profile—After running /etc/profile, Qshell looks in the user's home directory for this profile, which is used for personal customization. (Yes, it begins with a period, and is pronounced "dot profile.") The .profile file is a good place to define environment variables, including the ENV environment variable. Use the DSPUSRPRF command to display your HOME directory. For example, DSPUSRPRF JSMITH.

- The file named in the ENV environment variable—Qshell looks to see if the ENV environment variable has a value. If so, and if that value is the name of an existing file, Qshell executes the file. One of the most common uses of ENV is to define *aliases*, which are short names for a command. (Aliases are discussed in detail in chapter 12.)

Qshell runs these script files in the order given here, and in the current process.

37

YOUR FIRST SCRIPT

Before you proceed, be sure you know how to edit and run Qshell scripts.
Figure 4.2 is a script you can enter and run for practice.

```
# Getting acquainted
print "Please enter your name."
read name
print "Hi, $name. Qshell rulz!"

print "What's your favorite programming language?"
read lang
if [ -z "$lang" ]
    then print "Maybe we can talk at a more convenient time."
         exit 1
fi

lang=$(print $lang | tr '[:lower:]' '[:upper:]')  # convert to caps
case $lang in
    *RPG*) print "Me too!";;
    COBOL*) print "How quaint!";;
    JAVA) print "At least you didn't say \"C\"";;
    C) print "You're a glutton for punishment!";;
    *) print "To each his own."
esac
```

Figure 4.2: Use this script for practice.

To enter and run the script, use the following process:

1. Sign on to an iSeries machine through a terminal or a 5250 emulation
   session.

2. If necessary, change to the directory where you are going to place the
   Qshell script.

3. At a CL command line, type *qsh* and press Enter to begin a Qshell
   session.

4. Since you cannot edit a file directly from Qshell, press the F21 key to get
   a CL command line.

5. Use EDTF to enter the Qshell script. If you are not sure how to use EDTF, see chapter 3.

6. After editing, press Enter from a blank line (or press F12) to close the command-line window and return to Qshell.

7. If necessary, use *chmod* to make the script executable.

8. Type the name of your script on the Qshell command line and press Enter to run it.

If you must edit the script, press F21 to get back to the CL command line. From there, you can use the F9 key to retrieve the previous EDTF command.

Continue running and editing the script in Figure 4.2 as needed, until you have no syntax errors and understand how the script works. Don't worry if you don't understand the syntax of the Qshell commands at this point. That's the purpose of the rest of the book.

SUMMARY

A script is a text file that contains Qshell commands. Typing the file's name and pressing Enter runs all the commands in the script file. To execute a script, you must have Execute permission to the file.

A script may include comments, including the special comment known as the *magic number*, and executable commands. Unlike CL, Qshell does not restrict the execution of Qshell commands to either batch or interactive environments. Therefore, any Qshell command may be used in a script.

Three special scripts run when Qshell starts: /etc/profile, .profile, and the file named in the ENV environment variable.

Chapter 5

Parameters and Variables, Defined

Just as you can pass parameters to RPG programs, CL programs, and OCL procedures, you can pass parameters, or *arguments*, to Qshell scripts. Strictly speaking, an argument is a value that is passed to a script or program, while a parameter is a variable defined in a program to represent the argument. However, it is common in iSeries and AS/400 computing to use the word *parameter* to mean both parameters and arguments. In this book, we try to use the words according to their strict meanings, although even we might occasionally slip up, referring to an argument as a parameter. (There are certainly much worse crimes we could be guilty of.) The important thing to note is that parameters are passed by position, never by keyword.

COMMAND-LINE ARGUMENTS

Command-line arguments follow a command name. They are separated from the command name and from one another by white space, i.e., blanks and/or tabs. (Although you can't type tabs in an interactive Qshell session, a script that was entered from a text editor on another machine might include them.)

The following line of code shows how to run a Qshell script, passing two arguments to it:

```
myscript.qsh    home    jsmith
```

If an argument includes blanks, surround it with single quote (') or double quote
(") marks. For example, either of the following two command lines would work
to pass three arguments, two of which contain embedded blanks:

```
myscript.qsh 'New York' Chicago 'Los Angeles'
myscript.qsh "New York" Chicago "Los Angeles"
```

If an argument includes a single quote or double quote, precede the character
with a backslash (\), like this:

```
myscript.qsh Eat at Joe\'s     # Eat a Joe's
myscript.qsh 48\"              # 48" (48 inches)
```

You may also embed one type of quote within quotes of the other type, as
shown here:

```
myscript.qsh "Eat at Joe's"    # Eat a Joe's
myscript.qsh '48"'             # 48" (48 inches)
```

RETRIEVING PARAMETER VALUES

A script can refer to parameters in one of two ways. The simple form is $n. In
most cases, this form is adequate, but in cases of ambiguity, braces are added, in
the form ${n}. In both forms, *n* represents a number in the range from 1 to 255.

To understand the use of these two forms, consider the following two expressions:

```
$12        # the twelfth positional parameter
${1}2      # the first positional parameter followed by the
             character 2
```

42

The first expression refers to the value of the twelfth positional parameter. The second refers to the first positional parameter, with the digit *2* appended to it. If the first argument has the value *go* and the twelfth argument has the value *mydata.csv*, the expressions yield the values *mydata.csv* and *go2*.

Here is a one-line script that uses two positional parameters:

```
cd   /$1/$2
```

To run the script, you would use a command like this:

```
myscript.qsh    home    jsmith
```

Notice that the arguments are separated by white space. The script would run the following *cd* command:

```
cd   /home/jsmith
```

Qshell replaces the parameter markers with their values before interpreting the command. This means that commands themselves may be stored in positional parameters.

In Figure 5.1, the print command shows that the first positional parameter contains the string *ls*. Qshell replaces the parameter $1 with the value *ls*, no matter where in a command Qshell finds the string.

```
print $1
ls
/home/JSMITH $
$1
arglist.qsh           fix2.qsh            select01.qsh
bin                   fix3.qsh            tema
bu.qsh                ftpmodel.txt        temp.txt
```

Figure 5.1: Execution of commands takes place after substitution, which means a command name may be stored in a positional parameter.

Preventing Parameter Substitution

There are two ways to prevent Qshell from substituting a parameter value for a parameter expression. One is to precede the dollar sign with a backslash. The other is to surround the parameter expression with single quotes.

For instance, consider the short terminal session history shown in Figure 5.2. The first two commands print the fifth positional parameter, which has a value of 24. The last two commands print the string $5.

```
> print $5
  24
> print "$5"
  24
> print \$5
  $5
> print '$5'
  $5
```

Figure 5.2: Single quotes and backslashes prevent interpretation of the dollar sign.

Single quotes are often called *strong quotes*, because they protect the contents of the quoted expression from interpretation. In contrast, double quotes are often called *weak quotes*.

The Set Utility

You can use the *set* utility to assign values to the positional parameters from within a Qshell script. In the following example, the current values of all 255 positional parameters are discarded. The first four parameters are then assigned the values listed in the arguments:

```
set MYLIB MYFILE MYMBR .csv
```

To discard the values of all 255 positional parameters without specifying new values, use two hyphens as the argument to *set*:

```
set --
```

The Shift Utility

The *shift* utility reassigns the positional parameters. By default, Qshell moves each parameter one position to the left. That is, parameter 2 is copied to parameter 1, parameter 3 is copied to parameter 2, parameter 4 is copied to parameter 3, etc. The value of parameter 1 is lost.

This ability makes *shift* particularly well suited for processing all the parameters, one at a time. For example, a script performs a loop to process parameter 1 and then uses the *shift* utility. If parameter 1 is still set, it repeats the loop.

In Figure 5.3, the first parameter is shifted out of the parameter list.

```
set a b c d e f g
/home/JSMITH $
print $1 $2 $3 $4 $5 $6 $7
a b c d e f g
/home/JSMITH $
shift
/home/JSMITH $
print $1 $2 $3 $4 $5 $6 $7
b c d e f g
```

Figure 5.3: No parameter is passed to the shift utility, so one parameter is shifted out of the list.

You may follow *shift* with one argument to tell it how many parameters to shift out of the parameter list. Figure 5.4 shows the parameters shifted four places left. The values of parameters 1 through 4 are discarded.

```
set a b c d e f g
/home/JSMITH $
print $1 $2 $3 $4 $5 $6 $7
a b c d e f g
/home/JSMITH $
shift 4
/home/JSMITH $
print $1 $2 $3 $4 $5 $6 $7
e f g
/home/JSMITH $
```

Figure 5.4: In this example, the shift utility shifts the parameters four positions.

If the argument is zero or negative, the shift utility does not reassign the parameters. If the argument is larger than the number of defined parameters, Qshell responds with message number 001-0058. This message number means "Number of positional parameters to shift must be less than *n*," where *n* is the number of defined parameters.

SPECIAL PARAMETERS

Qshell has eight special parameters, listed in Table 5.1. You do not have to define these parameters or load any values into them.

Table 5.1: Qshell Special Parameters

Parameter	Description
$0 (zero)	Name of shell or shell script
$#	Number of positional parameters
$$	Process ID
$!	Background-process ID
$?	Exit status
$-	Option flags
$*	Positional parameters
$@	Positional parameters

You may surround the second character with braces if you wish. That is, both $0 and ${0} return the shell or script name. Most of these parameters are discussed in detail in this and later chapters. For example, the $? parameter is discussed in chapter 7.

The Difference between $* and $@

Both $* and $@ return the list of positional parameters, but how they return the parameters depends on whether they are unquoted or within double quotes. (Within single quotes, they are not expanded.) Here are the rules:

- When $* and $@ are not quoted, they expand to the list of parameters. Embedded blanks are not preserved.

- When $* is double-quoted, all the parameters are returned as a single argument.

- When $@ is double-quoted, the parameters are returned separately, with embedded blanks preserved. Therefore, "$@" is equivalent to "$1," "$2," "$3," and so on.

Generally, use the following format when referring to all positional parameters:

```
"$@"
```

Use another form only when you specifically need a different behavior.

To illustrate, suppose that three positional parameters have been defined with the values *Joe Smith*, *mydata.txt*, and *12*, respectively. As shown in Figure 5.5, if you ask Qshell how many parameters are defined, you are told that there are three positional parameters with values. Furthermore, the first parameter has the value *Joe Smith*.

```
print $#
3
print $1
Joe Smith
```

Figure 5.5: Three positional parameters have been set. The first has an embedded blank.

Remember that $* and $@ exhibit the same behavior when not quoted. Both return the positional parameters separated by spaces, as shown in Figure 5.6.

```
print $*
Joe Smith mydata.txt 12
print $@
Joe Smith mydata.txt 12
```

Figure 5.6: Without quotation marks, both $ and $@ return the list of parameters separated by spaces.*

Figure 5.7 demonstrates the use of these special parameters in single quotes. As you can see, $* and $@ do not return the same value, because single quotes prohibit parameter substitution.

```
print '$*'
$*
print '$@'
$@
```

Figure 5.7: Strong quotes prevent parameter expansion.

Figure 5.8 shows the difference between $* and $@ when double-quoted. (The *for* loop is covered in chapter 8. At this point, just be aware that *for* executes a *print* command for each positional parameter.) Notice that $* returns all positional parameters as one value, while $@ returns the positional parameters separately.

```
for file in "$*" ; do print $file ; done
Joe Smith mydata.txt 12

for file in "$@" ; do print $file ; done
Joe Smith
mydata.txt
12
```

Figure 5.8: Within double quotes, $* returns all parameters as one argument, but $@ maintains the individual parameter values.

"Unshifting" Parameters

You can use the double-quoted $@ parameter to implement the counterpart of *shift*. That is, you can insert new parameters at the beginning of the parameter list, shifting existing parameters to the right.

Figure 5.9 illustrates this technique. The first *echo* command shows that five positional parameters are set, with values *a*, *b*, *c*, *d*, and *e*. The *set* command replaces the positional parameters with the value *z* and the existing values of the positional parameters. The second *echo* shows the new values of the positional parameters. This is the opposite of *shift*. A new parameter 1 is defined, and all existing parameters are shifted right, instead of left.

```
set a b c d e
/home/JSMITH $
echo $#: "$@"
5: a b c d e
/home/JSMITH $
set z "$@"
/home/JSMITH $
echo $#: "$@"
6: z a b c d e
```

Figure 5.9: You can use "$@" to insert new parameters at the beginning of the list, shifting existing parameters right.

QSHELL VARIABLES

A variable name begins with a letter or underscore (_), which is followed by any combination of letters, digits, and underscores. If you spell the same variable two different ways, Qshell will think you are using two different variables. Variable names are case sensitive, so *DOG*, *Dog*, *dOG*, and *dog* are four different variables.

Variable Declaration

You create a variable by assigning a value to it:

```
variable=value
```

Leave no blanks on either side of the equal sign. If you leave a blank in front of the equal sign, Qshell looks for a command or script with the name of the variable. If you leave a blank after the equal sign, Qshell assigns a null value to the variable. If the value contains blanks, enclose it in either single quotes or double quotes. The quotes are not part of the value.

49

The following lines of code illustrate the creation of a variable:

```
thisvar=/home/jsmith
thisvar="/home/jsmith"
thisvar=
```

The first two assignments are equivalent. In both cases, the value of *thisvar* is /home/jsmith. After the third assignment, *thisvar* has a null value.

Two or more variables may be created in a single statement by separate the assignments with white space, like this:

```
i=0 max=24 name=Jack
```

In this example, variables *i*, *max*, and *name* are defined.

Untyped versus Typed Data

By default, Qshell variables are untyped. That is, the same variable can contain character or numeric data at different times, as Figure 5.10 demonstrates.

```
age="Reason"
/home/JSMITH $
print $age
Reason
/home/JSMITH $
age=49
/home/JSMITH $
print $age
49
```

Figure 5.10: The same variable, age, contains character data and numeric data at different times.

In V5R2, IBM added the *declare* utility, which lets you define the type of data that a variable should contain. This is called *strongly typing* a variable. An alternate name for *declare* is *typeset*. *Declare* utility comes from the bash shell, while *typeset* comes from the Korn shell. Supporting both names helps with porting shell scripts from other systems. Supposedly, *declare* is the preferred form.

The syntax of the *declare* command is as follows:

```
declare [option] name[=value]
```

The supported data types are listed in Table 5.2.

Table 5.2: Data Types Supported by the Declare Utility

Option	Description
E	Floating point
i	Integer
l (ell)	Lowercase character
u	Uppercase character

Figure 5.11 shows one way to declare typed variables. Figure 5.12 is equivalent to Figure 5.11, but uses *typeset* instead of *declare*.

```
name="Joe Smith"
/home/JSMITH $
declare -u uname="$name"
/home/JSMITH $
declare -l lname="$name"
/home/JSMITH $
print $name '|' $uname '|' $lname
Joe Smith | JOE SMITH | joe smith
```

Figure 5.11: The variable name *may contain any type of data. The data in variables* uname *and* lname *will be stored in uppercase and lowercase, respectively.*

```
name="Joe Smith"
/home/JSMITH $
typeset -u uname="$name"
/home/JSMITH $
typeset -l lname="$name"
/home/JSMITH $
print $name '|' $uname '|' $lname
Joe Smith | JOE SMITH | joe smith
```

Figure 5.12: The typeset *utility is an alternate form of* declare.

If you do not list any variables in the command line, *declare* (or *typeset*) lists the variables that have been defined with that type, as shown in Figure 5.13.

```
declare -u
declare -u uname="JOE SMITH"
/home/JSMITH $
declare -l
declare -l lname="joe smith"
```

Figure 5.13: Since no variables are declared, the declare *utility lists the variables of the indicated type.*

You may declare more than one variable at a time. You may also initialize one or more of the variables during declaration, as shown in Figure 5.14.

```
declare -i i=10 j=20 k l=40
/home/JSMITH $
declare -i
declare -i i="10"""
declare -i j="20"
declare -i k=""
declare -i l="40"
/home/JSMITH $
```

Figure 5.14: This example shows how to declare four integer variables and initialize three of those variables with one command.

When using typed variables, however, be careful to initialize them to the proper values for their types. Assigning invalid values to typed variables leads to unpredictable results, as shown in Figure 5.15.

```
typeset -i age=46.5
typeset: 001-0032 Number 46.5 is not valid.
/home/JSMITH $
typeset -i
declare -i age="46.5"
/home/JSMITH $
print $age
46.5
/home/JSMITH $
let age=age*2
let: 001-0032 Number 46.5 is not valid.
/home/JSMITH $
print $age
46.5
```

Figure 5.15: The value 46.5 is not compatible with the integer data type, so Qshell does not recognize the value of age as a number.

Aliases for Data Types

An alias is an alternate name, usually a shortcut, for a command string. Typing an alias name is equivalent to typing the command string the alias represents. In V5R2, Qshell predefines aliases for two data types:

```
alias float='declare -E'
alias integer='declare -i'
```

Figure 5.16 shows variables defined according to these alias definitions.

```
integer age=35
/home/JSMITH $
integer
declare -i age="35"
/home/JSMITH $
float temp=98.6 gun=30.06
/home/JSMITH $
float
declare -E gun="30.06"
declare -E temp="98.6"
```

Figure 5.16: The integer and float aliases have been used instead of declare.

Read-Only Variables

If you precede a variable assignment with *readonly*, the script will not be able to change its value. An example of this is shown in Figure 5.17.

```
readonly filename=JoesData.CSV
/home/JSMITH $
filename=BillsData.CSV
qsh: 001-0065 Variable 1$.*s is read-only and cannot be changed.
/home/JSMITH $
readonly filename=JimsData
readonly: 001-0065 Variable 1$.*s is read-only and cannot be changed.
```

Figure 5.17: The variable filename *is defined as a read-only variable, so its value cannot be changed.*

Under V5R2, you can use the *-r* option of the *declare* and *typeset* utilities to set the read-only attribute of a variable, as shown in Figure 5.18.

```
typeset -r filename=JoesData.CSV
/home/JSMITH $
filename="BillsData.CSV"
qsh: 001-0065 Variable 1$.*s is read-only and cannot be changed.
```

Figure 5.18: The *-r option of* declare *and* typeset *set the read-only attribute.*

Running *readonly* without parameters lists the defined read-only variables.

Retrieving the Value of a Variable

To retrieve the value of a variable, precede its name with a dollar sign. Think of the dollar sign as meaning "the value of." Figure 5.19 shows how to retrieve a variable's value. The first print statement does not return the value of the *name* variable because the dollar-sign prefix has been omitted.

```
name=Jack
/home/JSMITH $
print name
name
/home/JSMITH $
print $name
Jack
```

Figure 5.19: You need the dollar-sign prefix to return a variable's value.

If you prefer, you may enclose the variable name within braces, but the dollar sign is still required as a prefix. Braces are required when another value follows the variable name with no intervening white space. This alternate syntax is illustrated in Figure 5.20.

```
name=Jack
/home/JSMITH $
print $name
Jack
print ${name}
Jack
/home/JSMITH $
print ${name}et
Jacket
```

Figure 5.20: You do not have to surround a variable name with braces except when the variable name abuts another value.

Unset Variables and Null Values

A variable may be unset, or a variable may be set to a null value. There is a difference. A variable with a null value exists, but has no value. Or, if you prefer, it has a zero-length value. An unset variable, on the other hand, is not defined.

Qshell usually ignores the difference between unset and null values, but you can make it distinguish between them, if you wish. To undefine a variable that has previously been defined, use the *unset* utility, as shown in Figure 5.21.

```
print $name
Jack
/home/JSMITH $
unset name
/home/JSMITH $
print $name
/home/JSMITH $
```

Figure 5.21: Use the unset *utility to undefine a previously defined variable.*

By default, Qshell does not mind if you use variables that have not been defined. If you misspell the name of a variable name, Qshell doesn't complain,

55

but returns the null value. If you want Qshell to return an error when it encounters an undefined variable, use the *set* utility, specifying either *-u* or *-o nounset*. Then, when you ask Qshell to retrieve the value of an unset variable, Qshell will send message 001-0021 to the standard error file (stderr), as shown in Figure 5.22.

```
set -u              # or set -o nounset
/home/JSMITH $
name=Jack
/home/JSMITH $
print $neme
qsh: 001-0021 Parameter 1$.*s is not set.
```

Figure 5.22: Qshell can be set to send an error message when an undefined variable is referenced.

PREDEFINED VARIABLES

Qshell predefines several variables, which it uses for two purposes:

- To pass session settings to scripts
- To store session information

Table 5.4 lists some of the predefined variables. They are covered in detail in later chapters.

Table 5.4: Some Predefined Qshell Variables

Variable	Description
JOBNAME	Qualified job name
LINENO	Line number
OLDPWD	Previous working directory
PWD	Working directory
RANDOM	Random number generator

Table 5.4: Some Predefined Qshell Variables, *continued*

Variable	Description
UID	User identifier
CDPATH	Search path for cd
ENV	Environment file
HOME	Home directory
IFS	Internal field separators
PATH	Search path for commands
PS1	Primary prompt string
PS2	Secondary prompt string

Even though you do not declare these variables, you can use them as you would your own. Normally, you retrieve the values of predefined variables, but you do not change them. Figure 5.23 illustrates the use of the $RANDOM predefined variable.

In Figure 5.24, the $HOME predefined variable is used. The user is working from the /home/JSMITH directory. The first *cd* command changes to source physical file SRC in library MYLIB. The *cp* command copies source member MATH to an IFS file in the user's home directory. The second *cd* changes back to the home directory. The *ls* command verifies that the copy was successful.

```
i=0 ; while [ $i -lt 9 ] ; do print $RANDOM ; let "i=i+1" ; done
2656
684
13708
49702
58934
31462
46746
21854
48842
```

Figure 5.23: Use $RANDOM to retrieve a random number.

```
/home/JSMITH $
cd /qsys.lib/mylib.lib/src.file
/qsys.lib/mylib.lib/src.file $
cp MATH.MBR $HOME
/qsys.lib/mylib.lib/src.file $
cd ~
/home/JSMITH $
ls M*
MATH.MBR        MkXYZ.java
/home/JSMITH $
```

Figure 5.24: *Use $HOME to refer to the home directory.*

SUMMARY

You may define parameters and variables to hold data values. There are two types of parameters:

- Positional parameters are accessed by an ordinal number.
- Predefined parameters are those to which the system assigns values.

There are also two types of variables: those whose names are already defined to Qshell, and those whose names you must assign. Before V5R2, variables were not types. As of V5R2, you may assign a data type to a variable if you wish. You may also use the *readonly* utility to specify that a variable's value is unchangeable. You create a variable by assigning a value to it, or by declaring it with the *declare* or *typeset* utility.

Chapter 6

Using Parameters and Variables

You saw in chapter 5 that, when Qshell finds a dollar sign preceding a parameter or variable name, it replaces the reference with the value of the indicated parameter or variable. This is known as *expanding* the parameter or variable.

Both the terms *parameter expansion* and *variable expansion* are used in Unix literature to refer to this process, no matter whether parameters or variables are being discussed. This chapter uses the term *variable expansion* because all facets of expansion are supported with variables, but one type of expansion is not supported with positional parameters.

VARIABLE EXPANSION

In its simplest form, variable expansion returns the value assigned to a parameter or variable. For example, $1 and ${1} expand to the value of the first positional parameter, and $dirname and ${dirname} expand to the value of a variable whose name is dirname. However, Qshell provides operators that permit more powerful methods of variable expansion.

Table 6.1 lists the four expansion operators. Use these operators within the brace form of a variable or parameter. Before the closing brace, include the operator, and follow it with another value, whose function depends on the operator.

Table 6.1: Conditional Expansion Operators

Operator	Description
- (hyphen)	Temporarily substitute for a missing value.
+	Temporarily substitute for an existing value.
=	Assign a new value for missing value. (Not permitted with positional parameters.)
?	Generate an error if a value is missing.

The term *missing value* in Table 6.1 needs some explanation. You might remember from chapter 5 that there is a difference between a variable that is unset and a variable that has a null value. An unset variable is not defined, while a variable with a null value is defined, but empty.

If the operators in Table 6.1 are preceded by a colon, the term *missing value* means "an unset variable or a variable with the null value." Without a preceding colon, the term *missing value* means "an unset variable." As a rule, you will probably want to include the colon, since your consideration when using these parameter operators is more likely to be whether or not a value is missing, not why it is missing. Table 6.2 illustrates this difference more closely. Keep the following in mind to help interpret the table:

- $var indicates that Qshell returns the existing value of the variable.

- *Value* indicates that Qshell returns the value following the operator.

- *Assign value to var* means that the value following the equal sign is assigned to the variable.

- *Null* indicates that Qshell uses a null value in place of the variable reference.

- *Error* means that Qshell displays the message following the question mark, or a default message, and exits a noninteractive shell.

60

Table 6.2: Results of Variable Expansion Operators

Operator	Var Is Defined; Not Null	Var Is Null	Var Is Unset (Undefined)
${var:-value}	$var	value	value
${var-value}	$var	null	value
${var:=value}	$var	assign value to var	assign value to var
${var=value}	$var	null	assign value to var
${var:?[message]}	$var	error	error
${var?[message]}	$var	null	error
${var:+value}	substitute value	null	null
${var+value}	substitute value	substitute value	null

The next several sections of this chapter examine each of the variable expansion operators in detail.

Temporary Substitution for a Missing Value

Use the hyphen operator to temporarily substitute a value when a variable has no value. For example, in Figure 6.1, the variable *name* is undefined (unset), so the first *print* command produces a blank line. The second *print* command prints the value *Joe Smith* because *name* has no value. However, the second *print* does not assign a value to the *name* variable, as the third *print* proves. Once the value *Jack Sprat* is assigned to *name*, the value following the hyphen is not used.

```
print $name

/home/JSMITH $
print ${name:-Joe Smith}
Joe Smith
/home/JSMITH $
```

Figure 6.1: The presence of a colon causes null and unset values to be treated equally (part 1 of 2).

```
print $name
```

/home/JSMITH $
name='Jack Sprat'
/home/JSMITH $
print ${name:-Joe Smith}
Jack Sprat

Figure 6.1: The presence of a colon causes null and unset values to be treated equally (part 2 of 2).

Figure 6.2 provides another example of the hyphen operator. In this case, the first print statement prints the value *Bob* because the variable *name* is undefined (unset). The second *print* does not print *Bob* because no colon precedes the hyphen operator, and *name* is null, but not unset.

```
print ${name-Bob}
```
Bob
/home/JSMITH $
name=
/home/JSMITH $
print ${name-Bob}

/home/JSMITH $

Figure 6.2: This example illustrates the difference between using the hyphen operator with an unset variable and a null variable.

Temporary Substitution of an Existing Value

Qshell also provides a way to temporarily override the existing value of a variable. If the variable has a non-null value, the plus operator substitutes an alternate value. Otherwise, the result of the expansion is a null value.

Consider Figure 6.3. The first two *print* commands print blank lines because *name* is undefined. The third one prints *Bubba* even though *name* has the value *Bill*. The last *print* shows that the plus operator did not change the value of variable *name*.

```
print $name

/home/JSMITH $
print ${name+Bubba}

/home/JSMITH $
name=Bill
/home/JSMITH $
print ${name+Bubba}
Bubba
/home/JSMITH $
print $name
Bill
```

Figure 6.3: These commands illustrate the plus operator.

Assigning a New Value for a Missing Value

Use the equal-sign operator to assign a new value to a variable with no value. That is, the variable continues to have the new value after the expansion. This type of expansion is not allowed for positional parameters.

Figure 6.4 illustrates the equal-sign operator. The variable *name* is unset, so the first *print* command leaves a blank line. The variable expansion in the second *print* assigns the value *Suzy Q* to *name*. The third *print* shows that *name* has kept its new value.

```
print $name

/home/JSMITH $
print ${name:=Suzy Q}
Suzy Q
/home/JSMITH $
print $name
Suzy Q
```

Figure 6.4: The equal-sign operator assigns a new value to a variable with no value.

63

Generating an Error If a Value Is Missing

The question-mark operator causes Qshell to issue an error message if a variable has no value. For example, the first three *print* commands in Figure 6.5 send messages to stderr because *name* is unset. The last *print* command does not send an error message because *name* has a value.

```
print ${name?}
qsh: 001-0021 Parameter 1$.*s is not set.
/home/JSMITH $
print ${name:?}
qsh: 001-0022 Parameter 1$.*s is not set or is null.
/home/JSMITH $
print ${name:?Name is undefined}
Name is undefined
/home/JSMITH $
name='Larry, Curly and Moe'
/home/JSMITH $
print ${name:?Name is undefined}
Larry, Curly and Moe
```

Figure 6.5: These commands illustrate the question-mark operator.

PATTERN MODIFIERS

You can use pattern modifiers to do certain types of string manipulation. Among other uses, pattern modifiers are most frequently used in scripts to manipulate variables containing file name or path name values. The four pattern modifiers are listed in Table 6.3.

Table 6.3: Pattern Modifiers

Operator	Description
#	Remove the shortest match from the beginning.
##	Remove the longest match from the beginning.
%	Remove the shortest match from the end.
%%	Remove the longest match from the end.

These operators do not modify variables. Rather, each one returns a new value you can use in Qshell commands. You can assign the value to another variable, print the value, etc.

Figure 6.6 shows each of the pattern modifiers at work on the variable *var*, which contains a list of consecutive letters interspersed with *x*'s:

- The # operator, working from the beginning of the string, removes the smallest pattern that consists of zero or more characters followed by an *x*, which is *abcdex*.

- The ## operator, working from the beginning of the string, removes the longest pattern that consists of zero or more characters followed by an *x*, which is *abcdexfghxijklmnxopx*.

- The % operator, working from the end of the string, removes the smallest pattern that consists of an *x* followed by zero or more characters, which is *xqrst*.

- The %% operator, working from the end of the string, removes the longest pattern that consists of an *x* followed by zero or more characters, which is *xfghxijklmnxopxqrst*.

```
print $var
abcdexfghxijklmnxopxqrst
/home/JSMITH $
print ${var#*x}
fghxijklmnxopxqrst
/home/JSMITH $
print ${var##*x}
qrst
/home/JSMITH $
print ${var%x*}
abcdexfghxijklmnxop
/home/JSMITH $
print ${var%%x*}
abcde
```

Figure 6.6: Each of the pattern modifiers produces a different result from the same string.

Figure 6.7 shows additional ways to use the pattern modifiers to manipulate strings. Here, the % is used to extract the directory name because it removes as few characters as possible from the end of the string. The ## operator is used to extract the file's base name because it trims all characters as possible through the last slash.

```
filename=/home/jsmith/temp/work1.txt
/home/JSMITH $
dir=${filename%/*}
/home/JSMITH $
print $dir
/home/jsmith/temp
/home/JSMITH $
file=${filename##*/}
/home/JSMITH $
print $file
work1.txt
/home/JSMITH $
```

Figure 6.7: You can use the pattern modifiers with many different Qshell commands.

SUBSTRINGS

With V5R2, Qshell includes a form of variable expansion that allows you to retrieve substrings. It is similar in syntax to substring constructs found in RPG, CL, COBOL, and Java. Here is the substring syntax:

```
${variable:offset[:length]}
```

The offset parameter indicates the position at which to begin extracting the sub-string. The value indicates how far that character is *offset* from the beginning of the string; thus, the first character is at offset zero, not one. Another way to think of the offset is "the number of characters to skip." That is, if you skip zero characters, you begin extraction at the first byte. If the offset is longer than the string, Qshell returns the empty string. The length parameter is optional. If no length is specified, Qshell returns all characters from the offset through the end of the string.

Figure 6.8 demonstrate the use of the substring construction. In Figure 6.8, the first substring operation skips five characters, to begin extracting the remainder of the string at the sixth character. The second substring operation extracts two characters only. The remaining substring operations in Figure 6.8 show that you may use arithmetic expressions as offset and length arguments.

```
somevar=abcdefghij
/home/smith $
print ${somevar:5}
fghij
/home/smith $
print ${somevar:5:2}
fg
integer i=4 len=3
/home/smith $
print ${somevar:i:len}
efg
/home/smith $
print ${somevar:i+1:len}
fgh
print ${somevar:i+1:len+1}
fghi
```

Figure 6.8: The first two print commands show the basic use of the substring syntax. The remaining commands use more complex syntax, involving mathematical expressions.

SUBSTITUTION EXPRESSIONS

V5R2 also introduced two new substitution expansion structures:

```
${variable/pattern/string}
${variable//pattern/string}
```

Notice that there is no trailing slash after the replacement string.

Figure 6.9 provides a simple example of a substitution expression.

```
print $name
Joe Smith
/home/JSMITH $
print ${name/Joe/Fred}
Fred Smith
```

Figure 6.9: The second expression substitutes Fred for Joe.

As Figure 6.10 shows, if the first slash is doubled, all instances of the longest match of the pattern are replaced. If the first slash is not doubled, only the first instance of the longest match of the pattern is replaced.

```
print $title
Director of the Department of Redundancy Department
/home/JSMITH $
print ${title/Department/Bureau}
Director of the Bureau of Redundancy Department
/home/JSMITH $
print ${title//Department/Bureau}
Director of the Bureau of Redundancy Bureau
```

Figure 6.10: In the first substitution, only the first instance of Department *is changed to* Bureau. *In the second, both instances are changed.*

A leading % in the pattern means that the pattern must match at the end of the variable, as shown in Figure 6.11. If no replacement string is given, the pattern is removed, and a leading # in the pattern means that the pattern must match at the beginning of the variable. Figure 6.12 illustrates these points.

```
print $dept
The Department of Redundancy Department
/home/JSMITH $
print ${dept/Department/Bureau}
The Bureau of Redundancy Department
/home/JSMITH $
print ${dept/%Department/Bureau}
The Department of Redundancy Bureau
print ${title/#Director/Supervisor}
Supervisor of the Director of the Department of Redundancy
    Department
/home/JSMITH $
```

Figure 6.11: The percent sign in the third expansion means that the pattern must match at the end of the variable. Therefore, the second occurrence of Department *is changed to* Bureau, *not the first.*

```
print $title
The Director of the Director of the Department of Redundancy
    Department
/home/JSMITH $
print ${title/Director of the /}
The Director of the Department of Redundancy Department
title="Director of the Director of the Department of Redundancy
    Department"
/home/JSMITH $
```

Figure 6.12: Since no replacement string is given in the first expansion, the first instance of Director of the is removed. The second expansion changes Director to Supervisor because Director is found at the beginning of the variable.

Finally, the new substitution expansion structures can be used to strip special characters, as shown in Figure 6.13. The variable *music* contains leading and trailing double quotes. The expansion removes them. Notice that the double-quotes character is prefixed with a backslash in the expansion because of its special meaning to Qshell

```
print $music
"Le Sacre du Printemps"
/home/JSMITH $
print ${music// \"/}
Le Sacre du Printemps
```

Figure 6.13: Substitution expansion structures can be used to remove special characters from a string.

FINDING THE LENGTH OF A VALUE

Qshell includes an expansion operator that returns the length of the value stored in a variable. Here is the syntax:

```
${#variable}
```

Figures 6.14 uses the length expansion operator in a simple expression.

```
print $filename
/home/jsmith/temp/bin/mydata.txt
/home/JSMITH $
print ${#filename}
32
```

Figure 6.14: *The # preceding the variable name indicates that the length of the value of the variable is to be retrieved.*

Here is the operator used in a more complex expression:

```
if [[ ${#1} -lt 5 ]] then
    print "First parameter must be at least five characters
        long." >&2
    exit 2
fi
```

In this example, if the length of the first positional parameter is less than five characters, Qshell sends an error message to the standard error device and exits the script, with an exit status of two.

CONCATENATING STRINGS

While many other languages have concatenation operators, Qshell does not. Qshell does not need a concatenation operator because concatenation is achieved by abutting values. For example, in Figure 6.15, the *filename* variable is assigned the value of the *path* variable followed by a slash and the value of the *file* variable.

```
print $path
/home/JSMITH
/home/JSMITH $
print $file
cust.csv
filename=$path/$file
/home/JSMITH $
print $filename
/home/JSMITH/cust.csv
```

Figure 6.15: *Concatenation is achieved by abutting values (part 1 of 2).*

```
cat $filename
1,10001,"Pye Cherry",25
1,20002,"Moss Pete",25.5
1,30003,"Dover Ben",35
1,40004,"Bellum Sara",45
2,1,"Gunn Tommy",20
2,3,"Unsaturated Polly",35
2,345,"Sox Bobby",-9.75
```

Figure 6.15: Concatenation is achieved by abutting values (part 2 of 2).

To include blanks in a concatenation, enclose the entire assigned string in double quotes, as shown in Figure 6.16. Single quotes would prohibit the variable expansion.

```
firstname=Willie
/home/JSMITH $
lastname=Makit
/home/JSMITH $
fullname="$firstname $lastname"
/home/JSMITH $
print $fullname
Willie Makit
```

Figure 6.16: To include blanks in a concatenation operation, enclose them in double quotes.

NUMERIC CONSTANTS

Qshell supports two types of numeric values: *integer* and *floating-point* (real). Integer values are of the form *base#value*, where *base* is a number between two and 36. If *base#* is omitted, the value is assumed to be base-10. The letters of the alphabet are used as digits in bases greater than 10, where the letter *A* represents 10 and the letter *Z* represents 35. The letters may be in either uppercase or lowercase.

Figure 6.17 contains references to numbers in various bases. The first *printf* command prints the values of *a*, *b*, and *c* in decimal format. The second *printf* prints the values of those variables in hexadecimal format.

```
a=59   b=2#1101   c=16#2F
/home/JSMITH $
printf "%d %d %d\n" $a $b $c
59  13  47
/home/JSMITH $
printf "%X %X %X\n" $a $b $c
3B  D  2F
```

Figure 6.17: *Integer values may be specified in any base from two to 36. The default base is 10.*

Floating-point values may contain fractional portions. They are of the following form:

```
[+|-]number[.number][exponent]
```

The exponent is the letter *E* (or *e*) followed by a number. Figure 6.18 shows examples of floating-point numbers. The first assignment statement assigns values, specified in three different formats, to variables *x*, *y*, and *z*. The second assignment statement assigns values in yet more formats to variables *a* through *f*. The two *printf* commands display the assigned values as floating-point numbers.

```
x=2   y=4.5   z=1.7e10
/home/JSMITH $
printf "%f %f %f\n" $x $y $z
2.000000  4.500000  17000000000.000000
/home/JSMITH $
a=39 b=-55 c=14.246 d=-294.8832 e=1.7e10 f=-2.55e4 g=3.93e-2
  h=-7.4599e-2
/home/JSMITH $
printf "%f\n" $a $b $c $d $e $f
39.000000
-55.000000
14.246000
-294.883200
17000000000.000000
-25500.000000
```

Figure 6.18: *Floating-point numbers may be specified in several ways.*

By default, arithmetic is done with integers. To enable floating-point arithmetic, use the *float* option of the *set* command. This option may be specified in two ways:

```
set   -F
set   -o   float
```

In Figure 6.19, two variables, *x* and *y*, are multiplied, and the product is stored in *z*. When integer arithmetic is active, the multiplication operation fails, and *z* is unchanged. When floating-point arithmetic is active, the multiplication succeeds.

```
print $x $y $z
2 4.5 4
/home/JSMITH $
let z=x*y
let: 001-0032 Number 1.7e10 is not valid.
/home/JSMITH $
print $z
4
/home/JSMITH $
set -F
/home/JSMITH $
let z=x*y
/home/JSMITH $
print $z
9
/home/JSMITH $
```

Figure 6.19: Use the set utility to enable floating-point arithmetic.

ARITHMETIC EXPRESSIONS

An arithmetic expression is a string of tokens that is interpreted as a numeric calculation. The tokens may include variable and parameter names, numeric literals, operators, and parentheses. Variable names used in arithmetic expressions do not have to be preceded by dollar signs, but it is not incorrect to include dollar signs. An unset or null variable is interpreted as zero when used in arithmetic expressions.

The supported arithmetic operators are listed in Table 6.4. They are shown in the table in order of precedence, but you may use parentheses to override their default order.

Table 6.4: Operators Allowed in Arithmetic Expressions

Operator	Description
+, -	Unary plus and minus
!, ~	Logical not, bitwise negation
*, /, %	Multiplication, division, remainder
+, -	Addition, subtraction
<<, >>	Bitwise shifts
>, <, >=, <=	Comparisons
==, !=	Equality, inequality
&	Bitwise AND
^	Bitwise exclusive OR
|	Bitwise OR
&&	Logical AND
||	Logical OR
expr?expr;expr	Conditional evaluation
=, +=, etc.	Assignment operators

You can use arithmetic expressions in the following locations:

- In an arithmetic expansion
- In an argument of the *let* utility
- In the argument of the *shift* utility
- In the arithmetic formats of the *printf* utility
- In arguments of the *test* utility
- In the argument of the *ulimit* utility
- In the *offset* and *length* parameters of the substring variable expansion

The following example demonstrate the use of an arithmetic expression in an argument to the *shift* utility:

```
shift nb+2
```

The *shift* utility adds two to the value in variable *nb* and causes Qshell to shift the positional parameter list by that number of parameters. You could also have added the dollar sign, as follows (although it is not necessary):

```
shift $nb+2
```

The Let Utility

The *let* utility is the usual way to perform arithmetic, especially when you want to assign the result of a calculation to a variable. Here is the syntax of *let*:

```
let arithmetic-expression...
```

You may place more than one expression on a line. The expressions are evaluated from left to right.

Figure 6.20 provides an example so you can better understand the *let* utility. In it, the value assigned to *c* is based on the result of the calculations for *a* and *b*. Before calculating a value for *c*, Qshell assigns values 12 and 60 to *a* and *b* respectively. For that reason, *c* receives a value of 5, not 2.

```
print $a $b $c
10 20 30
/home/JSMITH $
let a=a+2 b=b*3 c=b/a
/home/JSMITH $
print $a $b $c
12 60 5
```

Figure 6.20: The let *utility evaluates the expressions from left to right.*

You can use the *let* utility in several different ways. Here are a few examples, which all add one to the value of variable *j*:

```
let j+=1
let j=j+1
let "j=j+1"
```

Arithmetic Expansion

Arithmetic expansion allows you to embed the result of an arithmetic expression within a command. The syntax is as follows:

```
$(( expression ))
```

Simple arithmetic expansion is demonstrated in the following arithmetic expansion, which examines the remainder after first dividing variable *year* by four, and subsequently dividing by 100 and 400 to determine whether or not *year* is leap year:

```
if [ $(( year % 4 )) -eq 0 ]
then
   if [ $(( year % 100 )) -ne 0 -o $(( year % 400 )) -eq 0 ]
   then
      let count-=1
   fi
fi
```

In Figure 6.21, the values in positional parameters 1 and 5 are added together within the *printf* command.

```
print $1 $5
10 50
/home/JSMITH $
printf "%d\n" $(($1 + $5))
60
```

Figure 6.21: Arithmetic expansion is used to perform arithmetic within Qshell commands.

The positional parameters $1 and $5 in Figure 20 must be preceded by dollar signs in order to distinguish them from the literals 1 and 5. However, variables do not have to be preceded by dollar signs. In Figure 6.22, the arithmetic expansion yields the same result, whether or not the *length* variable is preceded by a dollar sign.

```
size=$((length+1))
/home/JSMITH $
print $size
26
/home/JSMITH $
size=$(($length+1))
/home/JSMITH $
print $size
26
```

Figure 6.22: Prefixing a dollar sign to a variable name usually has no effect in arithmetic expansion.

However, in the case of assignment commands, the presence or absence of a dollar sign *does* matter. In Figure 6.23, for example, the second print command assigns a value to variable *name* because no dollar sign precedes the variable.

```
a=10 b=20 c=30
/home/JSMITH $
print $a $b $c $name
10 20 30
/home/JSMITH $
print $((name=999))
999
/home/JSMITH $
print $a $b $c $name
10 20 30 999
/home/JSMITH $
```

Figure 6.23: Dollar signs should usually be omitted when assignment statements are used in arithmetic expressions.

Compare Figure 6.23 to Figure 6.24, where variable *name* is preceded by a dollar sign in the *echo* command. The arithmetic expansion changes variable *b*, not variable *name*, because Qshell expands *$name* to *b*.

```
a=10 b=20 c=30 name=b
/home/JSMITH $
print $a $b $c $name
10 20 30 b
echo $(($name=999))
999
/home/JSMITH $
print $a $b $c $name
10 999 30 b
/home/JSMITH $
```

Figure 6.24: Prefixing the name *variable with a dollar sign causes a different variable to be modified.*

The Expr Utility

The only thing to remember about using the *expr* utility to carry out arithmetic is this: "Just say no!" Here are some reasons why:

- Qshell starts a new subshell to run *expr*. Starting a subshell degrades performance. Arithmetic expansion runs in the same shell.

- Many of the operators that *expr* uses have special meanings to Qshell, and therefore have to be escaped with the backslash character.

- The *expr* utility handles integer arithmetic only.

- Arguments must be separated from one another by white space.

- The *expr* utility is an old one, from the Bourne shell. Newer arithmetic mechanisms have since been invented.

- The *expr* utility writes the result of an expression to standard output, rather than assigning a value directly to a variable.

The *expr* utility was good for its time, but better ways of doing arithmetic in shells have been invented since then.

Summary

Variable expansion is the process of replacing the token that represents a parameter or variable with a value. Variable expansion allows you to temporarily assign a value to a variable, assign a value to a missing variable, manipulate strings, and extract substrings.

Arithmetic expansion provides a way for you to carry out arithmetic in Qshell scripts. Some Qshell utilities, such as *let*, *shift*, and *test*, also have limited arithmetic abilities.

Chapter 7

The Exit Status and Decision-Making

All Qshell commands update a numeric exit status upon completion. The exit status indicates whether the command behaved normally or not. You can use the exit status for making decisions, for controlling looping, and for testing and recovering from errors. In this chapter, you will learn about the exit status: how to test it, how to set it, how to use it to make decisions, and how to control loops with it.

Exit status is never less than zero, and never more than 255. An exit status of zero usually indicates that the command ended normally, while a positive value usually indicates an error. However, this is not always the case. The file comparison utility (*cmp*), for example, returns a zero if two files are identical, one if they are different, or two or greater if an error occurs. But *cmp* is the exception, not the rule.

You can use the special parameter $? to retrieve the exit status, as shown in Figure 7.1. You won't often need to use the $? special parameter, however. Instead, you'll let the Qshell commands act according to the value of the exit status.

```
cp quack.txt quack.bak
cp: 001-2113 Error found getting information for object/home/JSMITH/quack.txt.
No such path or directory.
/home/JSMITH $
print $?
1
```

Figure 7.1: *The copy fails because there is no file named quack.txt in the current directory. As a result, the exit status is set to a value of one.*

SETTING THE EXIT STATUS

Qshell scripts and subshells also set the exit status before returning to the invoking process. The exit status of the script is the exit status of the last command that ran.

You can use the *exit* command to specify an exit status of your choosing in Qshell scripts and subshells. As mentioned, this command can return a status in the range zero to 255, like this:

```
exit 3
```

This portion of a Qshell script checks to make sure that the caller passed at least one argument:

```
# make sure the first parm was passed
if [ -z $1 ]
    then echo "Usage: ${0#$PWD/} pattern" >&2
         echo [$0] >&2
         exit 1
fi
```

If the first positional parameter in this example has no value, the script sends a message to stderr (the standard error device, usually the terminal) and exits with an exit status of one.

Figure 7.2 shows the *exit* command used with the *print* command. The first *print* command shows the ID of the interactive shell. The *qsh* command starts a subshell (a copy of Qshell running within another copy of Qshell). The second *print* command shows a different ID, which means that the subshell is in control. The *exit* command shuts down the subshell and returns to the first shell, with an exit status of five. The last print command shows that the exit status was returned from the subshell.

```
print $$
9606
/home/JSMITH $
qsh                    # start a subshell
/home/JSMITH $
print $$
9627
/home/JSMITH $
exit 5                 # exit the subshell
/home/JSMITH $
print $?
5
```

Figure 7.2: The exit command can be called to shut down a subshell.

THE TRUE, FALSE, AND NULL UTILITIES

The *true* and *false* utilities perform no action, but return exit-status values zero and one, respectively. These are useful when you need a command to set the exit status, but do not want the command to perform any action.

The *null* utility, which is written as a single colon, always returns a true status. The null utility is illustrated in Figure 7.3.

```
true ; print $?
0
/home/JSMITH $
false ; print $?
1
/home/JSMITH $
: ; print $?
0
```

Figure 7.3 The true and null utilities set the exit status to zero. The false utility sets the exit status to one.

THE IF COMMAND

The *if* command is a decision-making structure that enables a script to take different actions based on the exit status. (Another decision-making structure, *case*, is covered in the next chapter.)

The syntax of the *if* utiity is shown below. Note that the brackets indicate optional elements; they are not part of the syntax and should not be keyed:

```
if list
then list
[elif list
then list]
[else list]
fi
```

A list is a group of commands that are treated as a unit. Qshell executes the first list of commands that follows the *if*. If the exit status of the last command in the list is zero, Qshell executes the list that follows the *then*. Otherwise, Qshell executes the list in the *elif* (else if) or *else* portions of the structure, if they are specified. The end of the *if* structure is marked with *fi*.

Commands must be separated from one another, either with semicolons or end-of-line characters. In the *if* and *elif* parameters, the exit status of the last command is taken as the exit status of the list.

Some shell programmers prefer to place *then* on the same line as *if* or *elif*, as shown in this syntax:

```
if list; then
list
[elif list; then
list]
[else list]
fi
```

Other programmers prefer to place *then* and *else* on lines of their own, like this:

```
if list
then
list
[elif list
then
list]
[else
list]
fi
```

Here is a simple example of the *if* utility, in which Qshell retrieves the value of the variable *todir* and attempts to change to a directory whose name is stored in that variable:

```
if cd $todir
   then echo Now working from $PWD
fi
```

If the change directory (*cd*) command succeeds, the exit status is zero and Qshell runs the *echo* command, which displays a message. If *cd* fails, the exit status is non-zero, *echo* is skipped, and execution of the script continues after the *fi*.

In the following example, *if* is used with the copy (*cp*) command:

```
if cp -t $1 $1.copy
   then echo Copy of $1 to $1.copy is complete.
   else echo Copy of $1 failed.
fi
```

The file named in parameter 1 is copied to a file of the same name with *.copy* appended. That is, file xyz would be copied to xyz.copy. If *cp* succeeds, the exit status is zero and the first *echo* statement runs. If *cp* fails, the exit status is one, so Qshell runs the second *echo* statement instead.

This example illustrates the else-if (*elif*) command:

```
if [ $1 -ge 18 ]
    then categ=A
elif [ $1 -ge 12 ]
    then categ=B
elif [ $1 -ge 8 ]
    then categ=C
else
        categ=D
fi
```

If parameter 1 is less than 18, it's checked against 12. If it's less than 12, it's checked against eight. The *else* clause takes effect only if the *if* and *elif* tests fail. After this code completes, the variable *categ* has a value of A, B, C, or D.

The following example shows that *if* structures can be nested:

```
if [ $pflag = on ]
    then
        if [ $cflag = on ]
            then cp $1 $1.copy
            else cp $default $1.copy
        fi
fi
```

If variable *pflag* does not have a value of *on*, the inner *if* is never executed.

In the next example, *if* is followed by two *cp* commands, separated by end-of-line characters:

```
if cp data01.txt data99.txt
    cp $1 data01.txt
 then mv data99.txt ~/backup
 else exit 1
fi
```

Qshell runs both *cp* commands. If the second command succeeds, Qshell runs the move (*mv*) command. If not, control exits, setting the exit status to one. Whether or not the first *cp* command succeeds doesn't matter.

The following is equivalent to the previous example, except that semicolons separate the commands in the first list:

```
if cp data01.txt data99.txt ; cp $1 data01.txt
then mv data99.txt ~/backup
 else exit 1
fi
```

THE TEST UTILITY

The *test* utility evaluates a condition and sets the exit status. It can do the following:

- Evaluate the type of a file (regular or directory)
- Evaluate file permissions
- Evaluate session status conditions
- Compare strings
- Compare arithmetic expressions

The *test* utility has two formats:

```
test expression
[ expression ]
```

The second form is preferred because it is considered easier to read, and because it makes the coding of compound conditions easier. Whichever form you use, however, be sure to leave white space around everything. Each option, string, and operator must be separated from its neighbor by white space. The brackets in the second form must be set off by blank space as well.

As of V5R2, you can use a new version of the *test* utility, sometimes called the *extended conditional*. The extended conditional utility is the preferred test construct. Its syntax is as follows:

```
[[ expression ]]
```

The main difference between *test* and the extended conditional under Qshell is that the extended conditional is built-in (directly interpreted by the Qshell interpreter), whereas *test* is an external utility, which must run in its own process. For that reason, you should use the extended conditional rather than *test* if your release supports it and compatibility with previous releases of Qshell is not required.

The conditional utilities are usually used with a control flow command like the 'if' command. Although they look unique, there is nothing tricky with conditional utilities formed using brackets. The '[ ]' and '[[ ]]' are another way to specify a test utility. The reason you have so many to choose from is due to the evolution and compatibility requirements of shell interpreters. The test utility evolved into the '[ ]' utility because that utility was syntactically better. The '[ ]' utility evolved into the extended conditional '[[ ]]' because of the benefits awarded a utility built into the command language.

Evaluating File Conditions

The file condition options shown in Table 7.1 test for the existence of a file, and in almost all cases, for some other attribute besides.

Table 7.1: File Condition Options

Option	Description	Release
-b *file*	File is a block special file.	V4R3
-c *file*	File is a character special file.	V4R3
-d *file*	File is a directory.	V4R3
-e *file*	File exists.	V4R3

Table 7.1: File Condition Options, *continued*

Option	Description	Release
File1 -ef *file2*	File1 and file2 are different names for the same file.	V5R2
-f *file*	File is a regular file (not a directory).	V4R3
-g *file*	File's set-group-ID flag is set.	V4R3
-G *file*	File is owned by the effective group ID.	V5R2
-h *file*	File is a symbolic link.	V4R3
-k *file*	File's sticky bit is set.	V4R3
-L *file*	File is a symbolic link; equivalent to the -h option.	V4R3
-N *file*	File is a native object.	V4R3
File1 -nt *file2*	File1 is newer than file2, or file2 does not exist.	V5R2
-O *file*	File is owned by the effective user ID.	V5R2
File1 -ot *file2*	File1 is older than file, or file2 does not exist.	V5R2
-p *file*	File is a pipe.	V4R3
-r *file*	File is readable.	V4R3
-s *file*	File size is greater than zero.	V4R3
-S *file*	File is a socket.	V4R3
-u *file*	File's set-user-ID flag is set.	V4R3
-W *file*	File is writable.	V4R3
-x *file*	File is executable.	V4R3

The following simple example illustrates the use of the *-d* file condition:

```
if [[ -d "$1" ]] ; then cd $1 ; fi
```

If the value in parameter 1 is the name of a directory, Qshell changes to that directory. Notice that the first instance of $1 is in double quotes. Quoting the argument keeps the test from failing if parameter 1 has no value.

The isempty.qsh script in Figure 7.4 uses the -*s* option to determine whether or not the file in parameter 1 has a size greater than zero bytes. If it does, Qshell runs the *null* command, which does nothing but set the exit status to zero. Otherwise, the script sends a message to stdout (the standard output device, by default the terminal) and sets the exit status to two.

```
cat isempty.qsh
if [[ -s "$1" ]]
    then :
    else echo "File $1 is empty"
         exit 2
fi
/home/JSMITH $
ls -l a
-rw-rw-rw-  1 SMITH  0          0 Oct  3 09:50 a
/home/JSMITH $
isempty.qsh a
File a is empty
/home/JSMITH $
print $?
2
/home/JSMITH $
ls -l goodoleboys.txt
-rwxrwx---  1 SMITH  0        746 Sep  6 14:50 goodoleboys.txt
/home/JSMITH $
isempty.qsh goodoleboys.txt
/home/JSMITH $
print $?
0
```

Figure 7.4: Notice that file a is empty, but file goodoleboys.txt is not.

The isempty.qsh script in Figure 7.5 does not return the message "File $1 is empty" if the file does not exist. Instead, the last *else* list is executed if the file in parameter 1 does not exist.

```
cat isempty.qsh
if [[ -f "$1" ]]
    then
        if [[ -s "$1" ]]
            then :
            else
                echo "File $1 is empty"
```

Figure 7.5: This script is a slight improvement on the previous one (part 1 of 2).

```
            exit 2
        fi
    else
        echo "File $1 is not a regular file."
        exit 1
fi
```

Figure 7.5: This script is a slight improvement on the previous one (part 2 of 2).

Evaluating Status Conditions

The *test* utility can evaluate two status conditions, as shown in Table 7.2. To enable and disable options, use the *set* utility to open file descriptors (see the discussion in chapter 10).

Table 7.2: Status Condition Options

Option	Description	Release
-o *opt*	Shell option *opt* is enabled.	V5R2
-t *fd*	File descriptor *fd* is open and associated with a terminal.	V4R3

The following example tests for status conditions:

```
if [[ -o noglob ]]
```

This condition proves true if globbing (path name expansion) has been turned off. That is, this condition is true if the noglobbing option has been turned on.

A more complex example is shown in Figure 7.6. Script read01.qsh is executed twice in this example. The first time, stdin is not redirected; the prompt string is displayed. The second time, stdin is redirected to file phonedir.csv, so the prompt string is not displayed.

```
cat read01.qsh
#! /bin/qsh
if [ -t 0 ]
    then print "Enter name,age,phone."
fi

IFS=','
read name age p
echo $name
echo $age
echo $phone
/home/JSMITH $
read01.qsh
Enter name,age,phone.
Joe,35,456-3456
Joe
35
456-3456
/home/JSMITH $
read01.qsh <phonedir.csv
Larry
22
543-9876
```

Figure 7.6: Script read01.qsh tests file descriptor zero to see if the standard input device (stdin) is assigned to a terminal or not. If stdin is assigned to a terminal, Qshell executes the print *command to display a prompt for the user. If stdin is not assigned to a terminal, the prompt is not displayed.*

Comparing Strings

Table 7.3 lists the operators Qshell uses for string comparisons. The greater-than and less-than string comparison operators do not have to be quoted when used

Table 7.3: String Comparison Options

Operator	Description	Release
-n *string*	String length is not zero. (Variable has a non-null value.)	V4R3
-z *string*	String length is zero. (Variable is null or unset.)	V4R3
string	String is not the null string.	V4R3

Table 7.3: String Comparison Options, *continued*

Operator	Description	Release
string1 = string2	String1 is equal to string2.	V4R3
string1 == string2	String1 is equal to string2. This syntax is newer than the single equal sign, and is preferred in Unix circles.	V5R2
string1 != string2	String1 is not equal to string2.	V4R3
string1 < string2	String1 is before string2, according to the collating sequence. (This applies to the extended conditional only.)	V5R2
string1 > string2	String1 is after string2, according to the collating sequence. (This applies to the extended conditional only.)	V5R2

with the extended conditional. They must be quoted when used with *test*, however. Since these operators are not available on releases prior to V5R2, you should use the extended conditional with the greater-than and less-than string comparison operators.

Here are four brief code fragments that illustrate the string comparison operators:

1. Variable *kflag* is initially set to the value *off*. If the first parameter has the value *-k*, the script sets *kflag* to *on* and shifts out the first parameter:

```
kflag=off
if [ "$1" = "-k" ]
    then kflag=on
        shift
fi
```

2. The condition proves true if the value in the *day* variable has the value *Sat:*

```
if [ "$day" = Sat ]
```

93

It is a good practice to place double quotes around variable names because Qshell will issue an error message if a variable with no value is used in a comparison test.

3. The condition proves true if the *day* variable is unset or null:

```
if [ -z "$day" ]
```

4. The test proves true if variable *answer* has a value of lowercase *y*. Notice that the "equal" test operator is two adjacent equal signs:

```
if [[ $answer == 'y' ]]
```

Comparing Arithmetic Expressions

Arithmetic comparisons are based on numeric values. The arithmetic comparison operators, which are listed in Table 7.4, are different from the string comparison operators. You will get strange errors if you confuse the two.

Table 7.4: Arithmetic Comparison Options

Option	Description	Release
exp1 -eq *exp2*	Expression1 is equal to expression2.	V4R3
exp1 -ne *exp2*	Expression1 is not equal to expression2.	V4R3
exp1 -gt *exp2*	Expression1 is greater than expression2.	V4R3
exp1 -ge *exp2*	Expression1 is greater than or equal to expression2.	V4R3
exp1 -lt *exp2*	Expression1 is less than expression2.	V4R3
exp1 -le *exp2*	Expression1 is less than or equal to expression2.	V4R3

Here is an example of how you might use a numeric comparison:

```
if [ $# -ne 3 ]
   then echo "Usage: ${0#$PWD/} pattern fromfile tofile" >&2
        exit 1
fi
```

The script from which this code is taken expects three positional parameters—no more, and no less. If three parameters are not passed to the script, the *echo* command sends an error message to stderr and exits the script with an exit status of one.

Several more examples of the comparison operators are shown in Figure 7.7. The first two tests use the string comparison operator, =, so *03* does not match *3*. The last two tests use the arithmetic comparison operator, -eq, so *03* does match *3*.

```
eval nbr=3
/home/JSMITH $
if [ $nbr = 3 ] ;      then echo true ; else echo false ; fi
true
/home/JSMITH $
if [ $nbr = 03 ] ;     then echo true ; else echo false ; fi
false
/home/JSMITH $
if [ $nbr -eq 3 ] ;    then echo true ; else echo false ; fi
true
/home/JSMITH $
if [ $nbr -eq 03 ] ; then echo true ; else echo false ; fi
true
```

Figure 7.7: These lines illustrate the difference between the string comparison operators and the arithmetic comparison operators.

Compound Conditions

Qshell permits you to group simple conditional expressions to form compound conditions. The compound conditional operators are listed in Table 7.5.

Table 7.5: Compound Condition Operators

Operator	Description	Release
! *expr*	The expression is false.	V4R3
expr1 -a expr2 *expr1 & expr2*	Both expression1 and expression2 are true.	V4R3
expr1 && *expr2*	Both expression1 and expression2 are true. This form is newer than the -a form, and is preferred.	V5R2
expr1 -o expr2 *expr1 | expr2*	Either expression1 or expression2 is true, or both are true.	V4R3
expr1 || expr2	Either expression1 or expression2 is true, or both are true. This form is newer than the -o form, and is preferred.	V5R2
(expr)	The expression is evaluated regardless of hierarchy of operators.	V4R3

The And operators are evaluated before the Or operators. As usual, you may alter the order of the hierarchy by placing an expression in parentheses. Since the ampersand and pipe characters (& and |) and the open and close parentheses have special meanings to Qshell, precede them with a backslash to "escape" them or use the extended conditional. As part of the command language, the extended conditional lets Qshell know that the ampersand, pipe, and parenthesis operators are being used to form expressions. Qshell will then avoid their other special meanings.

Here is a simple compound condition, which will create a file with the name in the first parameter, if it doesn't already exist:

```
if [ ! -e "$1" ] ; then touch $1 ; fi
```

In the following compound condition, if the value in parameter 1 is not the name of a directory, a backup copy of the file will be made:

```
if [ ! -d "$1" ]          # if parm 1 is not a directory
then cp $1 $1.bak
fi
```

The backup copy of the file will have the same name as the original, with .*bak* appended.

All three tests in the following lines are identical. Each test proves true either if *kflag* is on and *day* is Sat, or if *day* is Sun:

```
if [[ $kflag = on && $day = Sat || $day = Sun ]]
if [ $kflag  = on -a $day = Sat -o $day = Sun ]
if [ $kflag  = on \& $day = Sat \| $day = Sun ]
```

The following three tests are also identical:

```
if [[ $kflag = on && ( $day  = Sat || $day = Sun ) ]]
if [ $kflag  = on -a \( $day = Sat -o $day = Sun \) ]
if [ $kflag  = on \& \( $day = Sat \| $day = Sun \) ]
```

These tests prove true if *kflag* is on and *day* is either Sat or Sun. The parentheses, which must be preceded by backslashes, force Qshell to evaluate the Or operation before evaluating the And operation. The & and | symbols in the third test must also be preceded by backslashes. However, the extended conditional (in the first test) does not require the parentheses to be "escaped" with backslashes.

CONDITIONAL EXECUTION

You can use the && (And) and || (Or) operators between separate tests as a type of conditional execution. The result of one command determines whether or not another command runs. In an And list, the second command runs only if the first one succeeds (i.e., returns an exit status of zero.) In an Or list, the second command runs only if the first command fails. The exit status of the compound expression is the exit status of the last command to run.

Note that && and || look exactly like the && and || that were introduced in the previous section. However, they are not the same. The && and || operators in this section are used to connect separate tests. In the previous section, the && and || were used to form compound conditions within a single test. The && and || of the previous section can only be used with V5R2 and any releases that follow it. The && and || of this section are available with previous releases.

The remainder of this section provides several examples to help you better understand conditional execution. In the first example, if the file named in positional parameter 1 exists and is a regular file, delete it:

```
[ -f $1 ] && rm $1
```

This is equivalent to the following code:

```
if [ -f "$1" ]
    then rm "$1"
fi
```

In the following example, Qshell attempts to make a backup copy of the file named in the first parameter:

```
cp $1 $1.copy || echo File $1 backup failed! >&2
```

If the copy succeeds, control passes to the next statement. If the copy fails, Qshell runs the *echo* command, sending a message to stderr. This is equivalent to the following code:

```
if cp $1 $1.copy
    then :
    else echo File $1 backup failed!
fi
```

The following test proves true if parameter 1 is between 91 and 100, inclusive:

```
if [ "$1" -ge "91" ] && [ "$1" -le "100" ]
```

If the value in the first parameter is greater than or equal to 91, Qshell checks to see if the value of the first parameter is less than or equal to 100. If the value of the first parameter is less than 91, the second test is unnecessary, it is not carried out. Skipping evaluation of unnecessary parts of the expression is commonly referred to as a "short circuit" evaluation.

Qshell performs the tests from left to right, so in the following line, if the value of *day* is *Sat*, Qshell ignores the second test because of the Or condition:

```
if [ $day = Sat ] || [ $day = Sun ] && [ $kflag = on ]
```

If the value of *day* is not *Sat*, Qshell carries out the second test. If either of the first two tests is successful, Qshell evaluates the third test. If both of the first two tests fail, the third test is never carried out. The entire condition proves true if *day* is either *Sat* or *Sun*, and *kflag* has the value *on*.

The following *if* statement has the same tests as the previous example, but the order has been changed:

```
if [ $kflag = on ] && [ $day = Sat ] || [ $day = Sun ]
```

Qshell performs the tests from left to right. If *kflag* has the value *on*, the second test is carried out. If the first two tests are both successful, the third test is not carried out. The third test is carried out only if either of the first two tests fails. Again, the entire condition proves true if *kflag* has the value *on* and *day* is *Sat* or *Sun*.

The example below also has the same tests, but the second and third tests are in parentheses:

```
if [ $kflag = on ] && ([ $day = Sat ] || [ $day = Sun ])
```

In this case, if the first test proves true, Qshell performs the second and third tests in a subshell. The subshell performs the Or and returns a zero or non-zero exit status. Once again, the entire condition proves true if *kflag* has the value *on* and *day* is either *Sat* or *Sun*.

LOOPING STRUCTURES GOVERNED BY THE EXIT STATUS

The *while* and *until* looping structures are both governed by the exit status. The *while* loop is a *top-tested* loop. The body of the loop runs again and again as long as the exit status is true (zero). If the exit status is not zero when *while* is first tested, the body of the loop never runs at all.

The *until* loop is a *bottom-tested* loop. The exit status is examined after each iteration, so the body is executed at least once. It loops until the exit status is zero.

The *while* and *until* constructs are similar in syntax, as you can see here:

```
while list
do list
done
```

```
until list
do list
done
```

Like the *if* command, it is common for some Qshell programmers to combine parts of these commands on the same line, like this:

```
while list; do
    list
done
```

```
until list; do
    list
done
```

The lists referred to in the syntax statements are lists of commands. If a list has more than one command, the exit status of the last command determines the result of the condition. Separate the commands in a list with end-of-line characters (using the Enter key) or semicolons.

It is common in shell script programming to use a *while* loop to process all the input parameters. Here is such a loop:

```
# process the parameters
while [ $1 ]
    do echo $1
        shift
    done
```

The *echo* command displays each parameter's value. In a real application, *echo* would be replaced with the appropriate processing logic.

This *while* loop uses a test utility to determine whether or not the first parameter is defined. If the first parameter has a value, the script displays the value and discards it. Eventually, the last defined parameter will be shifted out, and para meter 1 will become null, stopping the loop. If no parameters are passed to the script, the loop is never entered, and the *echo* and *shift* commands never run.

Here is an example of the *until* loop:

```
until [ -f wakeup ]
    do sleep 60
done
# more commands here
```

101

Qshell continues to loop until a file named *wakeup* exists in the current directory. The *sleep* command suspends execution for 60 seconds before each test.

BREAK AND CONTINUE

The *break* and *continue* utilities provide additional control over *while, until,* and *for* loops. The *break* utility is used to immediately exit a loop; *continue* starts the next iteration of a loop. The syntax of these two commands is shown here:

```
break   [n]
continue  [n]
```

The parameter (*n*) is optional, to indicate how many levels of loops are affected. It defaults to one.

Figures 7.8 through 7.10 provide additional examples of the looping structures. In Figure 7.8, if a line has the value *EOD, the script ignores the remainder of the input.

```
ct=0
while read line
   do
      if [[ $line == "*EOD" ]]
         then
               break
      fi
      let ct+=1
      print $ct: $line
   done
```

Figure 7.8: The break command prematurely ends a loop.

In Figure 7.9, if the first character of an input record is the pound sign indicating a comment, the *continue* command is executed, skipping the *let* and *print* commands.

```
ct=0
while read line
   do
      if [[ ${line:0:1} == "#" ]]
         then
               continue
      fi
      let ct+=1
      print $ct: $line
   done
```

Figure 7.9: The continue command begins the next iteration of a loop.

Figure 7.10 contains two types of commands: those that must be done at least once, and those that may not be done at all. The *true* sets up an infinite loop that must be terminated with *break*. The prompt string will be displayed and the file name will be read at least once. If the user enters a hyphen the first time through the *while*, the other commands in the script will not be executed at all. If the user enters a name that is not the name of a regular file, the *continue* causes Qshell to skip the rest of the commands in the loop.

```
while true
   do
      print "Enter a file name, or - to quit"
      read filename
      if [[ "$filename" = '-' ]]
         then break
      fi
      if [[ ! -f "$filename" ]]
         then print "File $filename is not a regular file."
               continue
      fi
      if cp $filename ${filename}.bak
         then print "File $filename has been backed up."
         else print "File $filename - backup failed."
      fi
   done
```

Figure 7.10: Middle-tested loops contain elements of both top-tested and bottom-tested loops.

SUMMARY

Testing and looping are fundamental parts of every programming language. Qshell has strong testing and looping structures. The *if* utility tests a wide variety of conditions, including file and directory tests, string comparisons, and numeric comparisons.

Two looping structures, *while* and *until*, were introduced in this chapter. The *while* structure implements top-tested loops, which govern commands that might not be executed at all. The *until* structure implements bottom-tested loops, which govern commands that must be executed at least once.

Chapter 8

Additional Control Structures

In addition to the *while* and *until* loops described in the previous chapter, Qshell includes several other control structures: *for*, *select*, and *case*. You will learn how to use these structures in this chapter.

THE FOR LOOP

The *for* looping mechanism executes a body of commands once for each of a list of values. Its syntax is as follows:

```
for variable [in value ...]
do
list
done
```

Here are some things to keep in mind when using *for* loops:

- A *list* is a group of commands treated as a unit. The commands are separated by newline characters or semicolons.

- If *in* and the list of values are omitted, *for* is executed once for each of the positional parameters.

- A semicolon or newline character is required before *done*.

- The exit status of a *for* loop is that of the most recently executed command in the loop.

- You may use *break* to exit a *for* loop and *continue* to start the next iteration of it.

Figures 8.1 and 8.2 provide simple examples of the *for* loop. In Figure 8.1, the loop runs three times. The first time the *suf* variable has the value *txt*, so Qshell lists the names of all text files. The second time *suf* has the value *csv*, so Qshell attempts to list the names of csv files, but there are none. On the third iteration, *suf* has the value *qsh*, a suffix used by convention to denote Qshell scripts.

```
for suf in txt csv qsh; do echo "==$suf files=="; ls *.$suf; done
==txt files==
edity.txt          goodoleboys.txt  temp.txt         test1a.txt
ftpmodel.txt       myfile.txt       test1.txt        upper.txt
==csv files==
ls: 001-2113 Error found getting information for object *.csv.
    No such path or directory.
==qsh files==
arglist.qsh        echoprocess.qsh  theirscript.qsh  yourscript.qsh
bu.qsh             myscript.qsh     tscript.qsh
donde.qsh          read002.qsh      while001.qsh
```

Figure 8.1: *This simple* for *loop runs three times.*

The *for* loop in Figure 8.2 omits the word *in* and the list of values, so the loop processes the positional parameters. Each input file is copied to a file of the same name, with *.bu* appended, in the bu directory that is directly under the current directory.

```
# script name: bu.qsh
# backup files to bu directory
#
# If directory bu does not exist within the current directory, create it.
# If bu exists but is not a directory, error out of the script.
```

Figure 8.2: *The* for *loop in this example processes positional parameters (part 1 of 2).*

```
#
if [[ -e bu ]]
    then
       if [[ ! -d bu ]]
           then
               print -u2 "bu is not a directory -- backup aborted."
               exit 1
       fi
    else
        mkdir bu
fi

# Backup each file named in the positional parameters.
for file
    do
        cp $file bu/$file.bu
    done
```

Figure 8.2: The for *loop in this example processes positional parameters (part 2 of 2).*

THE SELECT CONSTRUCT

The *select* construct was added to Qshell in V5R2. It is almost identical to *for* in its syntax, and like *for*, is a loop. Unlike the *for* construct, however, a *select* doesn't terminate on its own. It is usually ended with a *break* command. The *select* syntax is as follows:

```
select variable in value ...
do
list
done
```

The *select* construct displays a menu of options from which the user may choose. The menu text is written to the standard error device (stderr), not the standard output device (stdout). The choices are numbered sequentially, beginning with one. Qshell places the selected choice number in the variable REPLY. The text of the selected choice is placed in the variable that follows the word *select*.

107

Figure 8.3 shows one way to use a *select* loop.

```
cat myscript.qsh
select typ in Text CSV "Java (source)" "Java (class)" Qshell Quit
    do
        case $REPLY in
            1) print "====Text files==============="
               ls *.txt *.csv;;
            2) print "====CSV files==============="
               ls *.csv;;
            3) print "====Java source code========="
               ls *.java;;
            4) print "====Classes=================="
               ls *.class;;
            5) print "====Qshell scripts==========="
               ls *.qsh;;
            6) break;;
        esac
    done
/home/jsmith $
myscript.qsh
1) Text
2) CSV
3) Java (source)
4) Java (class)
5) Qshell
6) Quit
#?
1
====Text files===============
edity.txt          mydata.csv
ftpmodel.txt       myfile.txt
goodoleboys.txt temp.txt
1) Text
2) CSV
3) Java (source)
4) Java (class)
5) Qshell
6) Quit
#?
4
====Classes==================
ls: 001-2113 Error found getting information for object *.class. No such
    path or directory.
1) Text
2) CSV
```

Figure 8.3: The myscript.qsh script displays a menu of file types and displays certain files depending on the user's choice (part 1 of 2).

```
3) Java (source)
4) Java (class)
5) Qshell
6) Quit
#?
6
/home/jsmith $
```

Figure 8.3: The myscript.qsh script displays a menu of file types and displays certain files depending on the user's choice (part 2 of 2).

In Figure 8.4, the *PS3* variable has been assigned the value "Make a selection," which is more meaningful than the default #? prompt. An asterisk has been added to the loop after option 6 as a "catch-all," to generate an error message when an invalid option is entered.

```
cat myscript.qsh
PS3='Make a selection.'

select typ in Text CSV "Java (source)" "Java (class)" Qshell Quit

    do
        case $REPLY in
            1) print "====Text files==============="
               ls *.txt *.csv;;
            2) print "====CSV files================"
               ls *.csv;;
            3) print "====Java source code========="
               ls *.java;;
            4) print "====Classes=================="
               ls *.class;;
            5) print "====Qshell scripts=========="
               ls *.qsh;;
            6) break;;
            *) print -u2 "Invalid option; try again.";;
        esac
    done
/home/JSMITH $
myscript.qsh
1) Text
2) CSV
3) Java (source)
4) Java (class)
```

Figure 8.4: This version of myscript.qsh adds a more meaningful prompt and basic error-trapping (part 1 of 2).

```
5) Qshell
6) Quit
Make a selection.
4
====Classes=================
Arguable.class                    MakeCSV.class
ExecutiveDecisionMaker.class      Restaurant.class
J1.class                          RestaurantPicker.class
LooselyComparableString.class
1) Text
2) CSV
3) Java (source)
4) Java (class)
5) Qshell
6) Quit
Make a selection.
9
Invalid option; try again.
1) Text
2) CSV
3) Java (source)
4) Java (class)
5) Qshell
6) Quit
Make a selection.
6
/home/JSMITH $
```

Figure 8.4: *This version of myscript.qsh adds a more meaningful prompt and basic error-trapping (part 2 of 2).*

THE CASE CONSTRUCT

The *case* construct is a decision-making structure, like *if*. However, *case* bases decisions on patterns of strings, rather than on exit status. The syntax of *case* is shown here:

```
case value in
   pattern ) list ;; [ pattern ) list ;; ] ...
esac
```

A *pattern* is a string literal. It may include the wildcard characters listed in Table 8.1. Any character that is not a wildcard is to be matched exactly.

To match one of the wildcard characters, precede it with a backslash in the pattern.

Table 8.1: Wildcard Characters for the Case Construct

Character	Description
*	Matches zero or more characters
?	Matches a single character
[ ]	Matches against groups and/or ranges of characters

Each pattern is followed by a close parenthesis. There is no matching open parenthesis. Following the close parenthesis are one or more commands to be performed when the pattern matches the value. The last command for each pattern is followed by two semicolons.

The following pages provide several examples demonstrating how to use *case*. The first example uses a *case* command to convert an English word (stored in the first positional parameter) to a month number:

```
case "$1" in
    [Jj][Aa]*)        month=1;;
    [Ff]*)            month=2;;
    [Mm][Aa][Rr]*)    month=3;;
    [Aa][Pp]*)        month=4;;
    [Mm][Aa][Yy]*)    month=5;;
    [Jj][Uu][Nn]*)    month=6;;
    [Jj][Uu][Ll]*)    month=7;;
    [Aa][Uu]*)        month=8;;
    [Ss]*)            month=9;;
    [Oo]*)            month=10;;
    [Nn]*)            month=11;;
    [Dd]*)            month=12;;
    *)                month=0;;
esac
```

The word that will be converted by this *case* command may be entered in any combination of uppercase and lowercase letters. Only enough of the word to

111

ensure uniqueness is required. Any characters beyond those required for uniqueness are ignored and do not have to be valid. For example, the values *S, s, sept, September, soap,* and *sugar* all cause Qshell to assign a value of nine to the *month* variable. If the word does not match the unique portion of any month name, the final pattern, a single asterisk, sets the *month* variable to zero.

The *case* command below converts a month number to a quarter number:

```
case "$1" in
    [1-3])      quarter=1;;
    [4-6])      quarter=2;;
    [7-9])      quarter=3;;
    1[0-2])     quarter=4;;
    *)          quarter=0;;
esac
```

The first positional parameter in this example is a month number from one to 12. The first pattern matches any one-digit number in the range one through three. The fourth pattern matches a one followed by a number from zero to two. The last case matches anything that doesn't fit the other four cases.

The following is an improvement over the previous example, in that months one through nine may be either one or two digits long:

```
case "$1" in
    0[1-3] | [1-3])     quarter=1;;
    0[4-6] | [4-6])     quarter=2;;
    0[7-9] | [7-9])     quarter=3;;
    1[0-2])             quarter=4;;
    *)                  quarter=0;;
esac
```

The vertical bar is an Or operator. It indicates that either of two patterns is acceptable for a match. Therefore, the first pattern, for example, matches any of these values: 01, 02, 03, 1, 2, 3.

Here is one more example of the *case* structure:

```
allfiles=off
dirfiles=off
regfiles=off
case "$1" in
    \* ) allfiles=on;;
    d  ) dirfiles=on;;
    r  ) regfiles=on;;
    *  ) print -u2 "Parameter 1 is invalid."
         exit 1;;
esac
```

In this example, the asterisk in the first pattern is escaped with a backslash, so the first pattern matches an asterisk. The second and third patterns match lower-case *d* and lowercase *r*, respectively. The last pattern matches anything that did not match the first three parameters, including uppercase *D* and uppercase *R*. The asterisk in the last pattern is a wildcard, which matches any value that did not match the previous patterns. Matching the last pattern causes two actions: an error message is sent to the standard error device, and the script exits with a status of one.

SUMMARY

In this chapter, you have been introduced to the Qshell control structures that are not controlled by the exit status of utilities and scripts. The *for* structure iterates through a list of values. The *case* structure, like *if*, permits decision-making.

The *select* structure gets user input. It is similar to *for* in that it is iterative. It is also similar to *case* in that it executes actions based on a pattern.

113

Chapter 9
The Integrated File System

Business programming on the iSeries usually involves the processing of data stored in relational database tables, either through record-oriented input–output operations or through SQL. But some data doesn't fit well in relational databases, such as files containing pictures or sound. Other data and applications come from systems in which the relational database isn't an integral part of the operating system. For this reason, IBM expanded the OS/400 file system in V3R1 to include a nondatabase method of storing data. The name of this expanded file system is the *Integrated File System*, or *IFS*.

It is important for iSeries professionals to understand the IFS because of the growing importance of nondatabase data and applications in iSeries installations. Since Qshell is an effective interface to the IFS, iSeries professionals would do well to gain an understanding of Qshell.

ORGANIZATION

The IFS includes various file systems. Different releases of OS/400 define different file systems, but some of the most common ones are listed in Table 9.1. All of these file systems can be accessed through common user interfaces, one of which is Qshell. Other user interfaces are CL commands and iSeries Navigator.

Table 9.1: OS/400 File Systems

System	Description
Root	A hierarchical file system with similarities to both DOS and Unix
QOpenSys	A Unix-like file system
QSYS.LIB	The traditional library based file system
QDLS	The folders file system
QOPT	The CD-ROM drive
NFS	A system that provides access to data on servers that use the Network File System
QFileSrv.400	A system that provides access to data on other iSeries systems
QNTC	Windows NT server file system
UDFS	The user-defined file system
QnetWare	A system that provides access to data on NetWare servers

You can use any or all of the file systems depending on the data you are accessing. The Root and the QOpenSys file systems will probably be the file systems you work with the most.

Each file system has distinct functional and performance characteristics. For example, file names in the root system are not case sensitive, but those in QOpenSys are case sensitive. Similarly, file names in the root system may be up to 255 characters long, but a QDLS file name may have only eight characters, plus a zero- to three-character extension.

Directories

A directory is a container for files and other directories. All IFS file systems are organized into directories. The main directory is the root, which contains all the file systems and may also contain other directories and files.

To create a directory, use Qshell's *mkdir* command. For example, the following command creates a directory named *bin*:

```
mkdir bin
```

To delete a directory, it must first be empty. If it is, you can use Qshell's *rmdir* command:

```
rmdir bin
```

To delete a directory that is not empty, use the *rm* command with the *-r* or *-R* option. For example, the following command deletes the bin directory, all its subdirectories, and the files they contain:

```
rm -r bin
```

Be sure you know what you're doing, however, because once a file has been deleted, you can't recover it.

Home and Current Directories

The current directory is the directory where Qshell looks for and stores files when no directory path is specified. That is, if the object reference does not begin with a slash character, Qshell assumes the object is in, or is to be placed in, the current directory.

The following two lines illustrate the use of the home directory in a Qshell *cat* command:

```
cat ftpmodel.txt
cat /home/ftpmodel.txt
```

In the first line, Qshell looks for the ftpmodel.txt file in the current directory. In the second line, Qshell looks for the ftpmodel.txt file in directory/home.

In the following command, member EDITX of source physical file JSMITH/ QRPGLESRC is copied to IFS file editx.txt in the current directory:

```
cp /qsys.lib/jsmith.lib/qrpglesrc.file/editx.mbr editx.txt
```

This command uses the IFS naming conventions for library objects in the QSYS.LIB file system. Naming library objects in the QSYS.LIB file system is discussed later in this chapter.

A user's home directory becomes the current directory at sign-on. The name of the home directory is stored in the user profile. Use the HOMEDIR parameter of the Create User Profile command (CRTUSRPRF) or the Change User Profile command (CHGUSRPRF) to specify a user's home directory. You may also use certain abbreviations to specify the home or current directory, as shown in Table 9.2.

Table 9.2: Directory Abbreviations

Symbol	Description
/ (slash)	The root directory
. (one period)	The current directory
.. (two periods)	The parent directory
~ (tilde)	The home directory
~user	The home directory of user
- (hyphen)	The previous working directory

To change the current directory from within Qshell, use the *cd* command. Issuing this command without arguments, or with the tilde argument by itself, changes to the home directory:

```
cd
cd ~
```

Following the tilde with a user name produces a different result:

```
cd ~jsmith
```

In this case, user jsmith's home directory becomes the current directory.

Issuing the *cd* command with the slash argument causes the root directory to become the current working directory:

```
cd /
```

In the following example, the PS1 variable, Qshell's primary prompt string, has been set to show the current directory followed by a dollar sign:

```
/ $
cd /usr/bin
/usr/bin $
```

The root directory is the current directory before the *cd* command runs. The *cd* command changes to the /usr/bin directory, which is under the root directory.

The *cd* command changes two predefined Qshell variables, PWD and OLDPWD. PWD is set to the name of the new current directory. OLDPWD is set to the name of the current directory before the change. Usage of these two variables is shown in Figure 9.1.

```
print "Current dir=$PWD"
Current dir=/home/JSMITH
$
cd bin
$
print "Current dir=$PWD; previous dir=$OLDPWD"
Current dir=/home/JSMITH/bin; previous dir=/home/JSMITH
```

Figure 9.1: Before the cd command, the current directory is /home/JSMITH. After, the current directory is /home/JSMITH/bin.

By default, the Qshell prompt is a dollar sign. It is a good practice to make Qshell display the name of the current directory in the prompt. As Figure 9.2 shows, you can do this by placing the PWD variable in the primary prompt string, which in this example is variable PS1. Notice that the prompt changes as the current directory is changed.

```
$
PS1='$PWD $'
/home/JSMITH $
cd bin
/home/JSMITH/bin $
cd /qdls
/qdls $
cd
/home/JSMITH $
```

Figure 9.2: Before the assignment operation, the primary prompt is the dollar sign. After the assignment, the prompt is the name of the current working directory followed by a dollar sign.

To display the name of the current working directory in the prompt every time you use Qshell, set the primary prompt string in the .profile file in your home directory and include an *export* command so that the interactive shell will see the assignment:

```
PS1='$PWD $'
export PS1
```

The .profile script is executed every time Qshell is started.

PATHS

The IFS provides for all files to be accessed in a similar manner, regardless of the file systems of which they are a part. Each file system is a directory under the root. The system finds a file by traversing a series of hierarchically organized directories.

The syntax for a path name is similar to path names in DOS/Windows-based and Unix-like systems. Directories are separated from one another and from a file name by the forward slash character. An initial slash indicates the root directory, under which all directories are organized. For example, the following command copies file spc.h in the QOpenSys file system to directory /home/jsmith in the root system:

```
cp /qopensys/usr/include/spc.h /home/jsmith
```

IFS Names for Library Objects

The library system that has been part of OS/400 since the System/38 is known to the IFS as QSYS.LIB. To reference an object in the library system, follow the object name with a period and the object type. Examples of object types and abbreviations are listed in Table 9.3. Note that Qshell sometimes allows these abbreviations to be written in either uppercase or lowercase, but other times accepts only uppercase.

Table 9.3: Object Type Abbreviations

Abbreviation	Description
CMD	Command
DEVD	Device description
FILE	File
JOBD	Job description

121

Table 9.3: Object Type Abbreviations, *continued*

Abbreviation	Description
LIB	Library
MBR	Member
MSGQ	Message queue
PGM	Program
SRVPGM	Service program

Although the library system is not directory-based, objects are referenced with a directory-like syntax. Libraries are treated as if they were subdirectories of the QSYS library. Objects appear to be files or directories within a library. Objects that can be further subdivided, such as database files, appear as directories. The subdivisions, such as physical or logical file members, appear to be files within directories.

Figures 9.3 and 9.4 demonstrate the use of library objects within Qshell *ls* commands.

```
ls /qsys.lib/jsmith.lib
DIVBY0.QRYDFN    MON001.PGM      PROTOS.FILE       SRC.FILE
DIVBYZERO.FILE   MONEVAL4.PGM    PROTOTYPES.FILE   JSMITH.JOBD
EDITX.PGM        MONEVAL5.PGM    QRPGLESRC.FILE
```

Figure 9.3: The ls *(list directory contents) command lists the names of objects in library JSMITH.*

```
ls /qsys.lib/jsmith.lib/qrpglesrc.file
EDITX.MBR        EDITX2.MBR      EDITX3.MBR        MON001.MBR
```

Figure 9.4: The ls *command displays the names of the members in source physical file JSMITH/QRPGLESRC.*

In the following command, member EDITX of source physical file JSMITH/QRPGLESRC is copied to IFS file editx.txt in directory/home/jsmith:

```
cp /qsys.lib/jsmith.lib/qrpglesrc.file/editx.mbr
/home/jsmith/editx.txt
```

The *cat* command in Figure 9.5 shows the source code for RPG program EKOR1, which is stored in file QRPGLESRC in library JSMITH. To call a program within the Qshell environment, type in the name of the program object using the IFS naming convention. This example shows how to call program EKOR1 in library JSMITH.

```
cat /qsys.lib/jsmith.lib/qrpglesrc.file/ekor1.mbr
     H*dftactgrp(*no) actgrp('QILE') bndsrvpgm(qtcp/qtmhcgi)

     D OutputData      s           4096      varying
     D EOL             c                     const(x'0D25')

     D ErrorDS         ds          16

     D   BytesProv                 10i 0 inz(%size(ErrorDS))
     D   BytesAvail                10i 0
     D   ExceptionID               7

     D WriteStdout     pr                    extproc('QtmhWrStout')
     D   Buffer                    4096      varying
     D   BufferLen                 10i 0 const
     D   Error                           like(ErrorDS)
      /free
         OutputData = 'This is a test.' + EOL + EOL;
         WriteStdOut (OutputData: %len(OutputData): ErrorDS);
         WriteStdOut (ExceptionID: 7 : ErrorDS);
         *inlr = *on;
      /end-free
/home/JSMITH $
/qsys.lib/jsmith.lib/ekor1.pgm
This is a test.
```

Figure 9.5: To call a program within Qshell, type its name in IFS format and press Enter.

In most cases, Qshell permits you to use either uppercase or lowercase when specifying object names in the library system. However, in certain cases, such as during parameter expansion, Qshell only matches uppercase characters. For example, Figure 9.6 lists the names of all files in JSMITH/SRC that begin with the letters *md*.

```
ls /qsys.lib/jsmith.lib/src.file/md*.mbr
ls: 001-2113 Error found getting information for object
/qsys.lib/jsmith.lib/src.file/md*.mbr. No such path or directory.
/home/JSMITH $
ls /qsys.lib/jsmith.lib/src.file/md*.MBR
ls: 001-2113 Error found getting information for object
/qsys.lib/jsmith.lib/src.file/md*.MBR. No such path or directory.
/home/JSMITH $
ls /qsys.lib/jsmith.lib/src.file/MD*.mbr
ls: 001-2113 Error found getting information for object
/qsys.lib/jsmith.lib/src.file/MD*.mbr. No such path or directory.
/home/JSMITH $
ls /qsys.lib/jsmith.lib/src.file/MD*.MBR
/qsys.lib/jsmith.lib/src.file/MDATE.MBR
/qsys.lib/jsmith.lib/src.file/MDATET1.MBR
/qsys.lib/jsmith.lib/src.file/MDATEV1.MBR
```

Figure 9.6: Wildcard portions of QSYS.LIB path names must be in uppercase.

The distinction between the situations in which Qshell accepts lowercase and when it requires uppercase can be a little confusing. In general, the processing that Qshell does is case sensitive, while the processing done by QSYS.LIB is case-insensitive.

To understand this, consider the details behind Figure 9.6. To execute the *ls* command, Qshell must first perform parameter expansion on the path name. To expand the parameter, Qshell first uses the file system to retrieve a list of all files in the src.file directory. Among other files, the list of files returned from the QSYS.LIB file system contains MDATE.MBR, MDATET1.MBR and MDATEV1.MBR After retrieving the list, Qshell matches the *md*.mbr* expression to the file names returned. Since Qshell is case sensitive, no files matching the expression are found. When Qshell performs the same parameter expansion again, using MD*.MBR, the file names match the pattern.

Compare this with the example in Figure 9.5. For the commands shown there, Qshell does not need to process the file name or directory strings. Instead, the file names are used to open or run the QSYS.LIB file objects directly. Since the QSYS.LIB file system is case-insensitive, the lowercase names are accepted and Qshell uses the objects.

124

The case-sensitivity of Qshell combined with the case-insensitivity of the file system is similar for any file systems that are case-insensitive. For example, similar behavior occurs in the case-insensitive root file system.

Relative Paths

If a path name does not begin with a slash, it is a *relative* path. That is, the path is assumed to begin from the current directory. Figure 9.7 shows the use of relative paths in *cd bin* commands.

```
/home/JSMITH $
cd bin
/home/JSMITH/bin $
cd /usr
/usr $
cd bin
/usr/bin $
```

Figure 9.7: The first command changes to directory /home/JSMITH/bin, while the second one changes to /usr/bin. The prompt string shows the name of the current directory.

In Figure 9.8, the *ls* and *rm* commands refer to the current directory, since no directory name is given. Note that file names are case sensitive in the QOpenSys file system.

```
cd /QOpenSys
/QOpenSys $
ls
MyData.CSV        QIBM            QSR             usr
/QOpenSys $
rm mydata.csv
rm: 001-2103 Error found getting information for file or
    directory mydata.csv. No such path or directory.
/QOpenSys $
rm MyData.CSV
/QOpenSys $
ls
QIBM      QSR      usr
```

Figure 9.8: The cd command changes the current directory to QopenSys, a POSIX-type file system.

You may use the abbreviations from Table 9.2 in relative path names. For example, the following command moves the ftptemp file from the current directory to the home directory:

```
mv ftptemp ~
```

More examples showing the use of abbreviations in relative path names are given in Figures 9.9 and 9.10.

```
/usr/bin $
cd ..
/usr $
cd ..
/ $
```

Figure 9.9: The prompt string shows the name of the current directory. The two periods are an abbreviation indicating the parent directory.

```
cp ftprun.qsh ../bin
/home/JSMITH/ftp $
```

Figure 9.10: The copy command copies the ftprun.qsh file from the current directory to the bin directory that shares the same parent directory. The current directory is /home/JSMITH/ftp, so the file is copied to /home/JSMITH/bin.

LINKS

Until the IFS was added to OS/400, every object had one name—no more, no less. A library had a name, a job description had a name, a program had a name, and so on. To run a program, you just placed that program's name in the first parameter of a CALL command.

In the real world, however, one person, place, or thing can have many names. Consider the fictitious user featured throughout this book. Suppose that, according to his birth certificate, he is "Joseph Robert Smith," but nobody calls him that. When signing legal documents, he is "Joseph R. Smith." To his mother, he is "Joey." To his wife, he is "Sweetheart." To his children, he is "Dad." To his old college buddies, he is "Joe Bob." All of these are names for the same person, and in a complex world, we might uniquely identify that person with a specific number, much like a United States Social Security number.

Similarly, the IFS allows one object to have more than one name. Under the IFS, each object has a unique *inode number* instead of a name. All internal references to an object contain the inode number. The system stores information about how objects are referenced by directories. Each of these references, or directory entries, is called a *link* to the object. It is the link, not the target object, which has a name. There are two types of links: *hard* links and *symbolic*, or *soft*, links.

Creating Hard Links

A hard link provides direct access to an object. When you create an object, the name you provide becomes the name of the first hard link to the object. You may add other hard links, in effect giving more than one name to a file.

To add a hard link, use the *ln* command. You may use any of the following forms:

```
ln path/existing_file
ln existing_file new_link
ln existing_file target_dir
ln existing_file existing_file...target_dir
```

The term *target_dir* represents a directory into which the new link will be placed.

The *ln* command takes, one, two, or more arguments. If only one argument is given, as in the following example, the argument points to an existing file:

```
ln bin/ftprun.qsh
```

A hard link named ftprun.qsh is created in the current directory. It points to the file ftprun.qsh in the bin directory. The same file appears to be in both directories, but the file is stored in only one location, with links to the file in two directories.

127

If two arguments are given, the first one is the name of an existing file. The second argument may be the name of a new file or a directory in which to create a link of the same name.

The following command creates a link called arglist.qsh in the bin directory that is under the current directory. The link will point to the same file as the showargs.qsh link in /home/jsmith/shellwork:

```
ln /home/jsmith/shellwork/showargs.qsh  bin/arglist.qsh
```

Here is another example:

```
ln /home/jsmith/shellwork/showargs.qsh  bin
```

This command creates a link called showargs.qsh in the bin directory that is under the current directory. The link will point to the same file as the showargs.qsh link in /home/jsmith/shellwork.

If three or more arguments are given, as in Figure 9.11, the last argument is a directory into which the new links are to be placed. The other arguments are the names of existing files for which new links are to be created. The *ln* command in Figure 9.11 creates hard links in the new temp directory. The links are to certain files in the current directory (err.txt, all files whose names begin with out, and upper.txt). The hard links have the same names as the files whose links were copied.

```
mkdir temp
/home/JSMITH $
ln err.txt out* upper.txt temp
/home/JSMITH $
ls temp
err.txt         out.txt         out3         output01.qsh
out.log         out1            output.txt   upper.txt
/home/JSMITH $
```

Figure 9.11: *A new directory called temp is created under the current directory, /home/JSMITH.*

As mentioned earlier, objects have inode numbers instead of names. All hard links to an object reference the same inode number. To see an object's inode number, use the *-i* option of the *ls* command, as shown in Figure 9.12. The number of hard links follows the permissions and precedes the owner's name.

The first *ls* command in Figure 9.12 shows that file phonedir.csv's inode number is 115068, and that there is one hard link. The first *cat* command shows the contents of the phonedir.csv file. There are three records. The *ln* command creates a hard link to the same inode. The new link is called phonenumbers.txt. The second *cat* command shows that the phonenumbers.txt file has the same content as the phonedir.csv file. The last two *ls* commands show that the two files have the inode numbers, and that there are two hard links to the same object

```
ls -il phonedir.csv
115068 -rw-rw----  1 SMITH  0   52 Oct  3 11:26 phonedir.csv
/home/JSMITH $
cat phonedir.csv
Larry,22,543-9876
Moe,24,333-7777
Curly,18,234-7890
/home/JSMITH $
ln phonedir.csv phonenumbers.txt
/home/JSMITH $
cat phonenumbers.txt
Larry,22,543-9876
Moe,24,333-7777
Curly,18,234-7890
/home/JSMITH $
ls -il phonedir.csv
115068 -rw-rw----  2 SMITH  0   52 Oct  3 11:26 phonedir.csv
/home/JSMITH $
ls -il phonenumbers.txt
115068 -rw-rw----  2 SMITH 0    52 Oct  3 11:26 phonenumbers.txt
/home/JSMITH $
```

Figure 9.12: All hard links to an object reference the same inode number.

As you work with hard links, keep in mind some limitations:

- Hard links cannot cross file systems. For example, you cannot create a hard link in the QOpenSys file system to an object in the QSYS.LIB system. If you attempt to create such a link, Qshell responds with error 001-2137 ("Error found creating link xxxxx to object zzzzz. Improper link").

- A hard link cannot be created to an object that does not exist.

- Some file systems, like QSYS.LIB, do not support hard links.

Removing Links

Qshell does not have a delete command. Instead of deleting files and directories, you remove links to the object. When the last hard link is removed, Qshell deletes the object, unless that object is in use at the time. In that case, the object is deleted when it is no longer in use.

The following two examples illustrate the removal of links:

- Remove the link named *err.txt* from the current directory:

```
rm err.txt
```

- Remove the links whose names begin with *out* in directory /home/jsmith/temp:

```
rm /home/jsmith/temp/out*
```

It is important to understand the distinction between removing a link to an in-use file compared to actually deleting an in-use file. When a file is in use, it's reasonable to assume that the file system retains some kind of lock on the file. By deleting an in-use file, you would either have to wait for a lock on the file, or cause some sort of error to the program accessing the file. By removing a link, the file system deletes only the name to the file. The currently running application does not notice this and continues using the file safely. Only the next attempt to open the file will find that the file name no longer exists.

Symbolic Links

Symbolic links address the limitations of hard links. It's easiest to think of a symbolic link as a file that contains a text string representing the path to a target object. You might also think of a symbolic link as a shortcut to an object. Symbolic links have two important advantages over hard links.

- Symbolic links may cross file systems.
- Symbolic links may point to objects that do not exist.

The second point may also be viewed as a disadvantage, since it is possible to clutter the system with symbolic links that are obsolete.

To create a symbolic link, use the *-s* option with the *ln* command, as shown in Figure 9.13. Two symbolic links have been created in the root file system. Both point to program object RAPR in library JS. Notice that the number of hard links (in the second column) is one.

```
ln -s /qsys.lib/js.lib/rapr.pgm
/home/JSMITH $
ln -s /qsys.lib/js.lib/rapr.pgm      rapr
/home/JSMITH $
ls -l rapr*
lrwxrwxrwx 1 SMITH 0 30 Oct 2 4:34 rapr ->       /qsys.lib/js.lib/rapr.pgm
lrwxrwxrwx 1 SMITH 0 03 Oct 2 4:34 rapr.pgm -> /qsys.lib/js.lib/rapr.pgm
```

Figure 9.13: Use the s *option to create symbolic links.*

In general, symbolic links behave like, and are managed identically to, hard links. Table 9.5 provides a brief comparison of hard and symbolic links.

Table 9.5: Hard versus Symbolic Links

Hard Link	Symbolic Link
Referenced object must exist.	Referenced object does not have to exist.
Link always points to an existing object.	Link may point to an object that no longer exists or has never existed.

Table 9.5: Hard versus Symbolic Links, *continued*

Hard Link	Symbolic Link
Referenced object and link must be in the same file system.	Referenced object and link may be in different file systems.
Access to referenced object is fast.	Access to referenced object is slower than with a hard link.
Changing certain attributes becomes slower as more links are added to an object because certain attributes are stored in hard links.	Changing object attributes is unaffected by the number of symbolic links because no attributes are stored in symbolic links.

DISPLAYING THE CONTENTS OF IFS FILES

Because Qshell is tightly coupled to the Integrated File System, it is hardly surprising that Qshell includes commands that retrieve IFS data and display it in various formats. This section presents the utilities that are most commonly used to display the contents of IFS files.

The Cat Utility

The *cat* utility shown in Figure 9.14 concatenates one or more files and sends the output to standard output, which by default is the terminal session in an interactive job. By default, *cat* treats files as text. That is, the file is converted to the job's CCSID before being displayed. This allows you to view any text file in a readable format, regardless of its character set. If you need *cat* to work in binary mode, use the *-c* option.

```
cat ftpmodel.txt
one zxcvb
put INPUTFILE OUTPUTFILE
quit
/home/jsmith $
```

Figure 9.14: The cat utility provides an easy way to display the contents of a file.

The Pr Utility

The *pr* utility copies the contents of one or more files to standard output. It is similar to *cp*, except that *pr* formats and paginates the data. The *pr* utility can do the following:

- Start printing at a certain page of output
- Number lines
- Format a stream of records into multiple columns
- Double-space the output
- Expand tab characters to appropriate numbers of spaces
- Print a heading of your choosing at the top of each page of output
- Print multiple files side by side

However, *pr* cannot write to a printer file from an interactive session. To copy the paginated output to a printer file, you must use the *Rfile* utility, discussed in Chapter 20.

Figure 9.15 shows the *pr* utility paginating the goodoleboys.txt file into 66-line pages with blank lines at the top and bottom of each page. The default page heading shows the date and time, the file name, and the page number.

```
pr   goodoleboys.txt

Oct 22 22:18 2002 goodoleboys.txt Page 1

Name        Born      Phone     Dog       Wife        Shotgun   Paid
=========   ========  ========  ========  =========   ========  =====
Chuck       Dec 25    444-2345  Blue      Mary Sue    12        $2.50
Bubba       Oct 13    444-1111  Buck      Mary Jean   12
Billy Bob   June 11   444-4340  Leotis    Lisa Sue    12
Amos        Jan 4     333-1119  Amos      Abigail     20
Otis        Sept 17   444-8000  Ol' Sal   Sally       12        $5
Claude      May 31    333-4340  Blue      Etheline    12
Roscoe      Feb 2     444-2234  Rover     Alice Jean  410
Arlis       June 19   444-1314  Redeye    Suzy Beth   12        $10.75
Junior      April 30  BR-549    Percival  Lilly Faye  12
Bill        Feb 29    333-4444  Daisy     Daisy       20
Ernest T.   ??        none      none      none        none

( ... more blank lines omitted ...)
```

Figure 9.15: This command paginates the goodoleboys.txt file into 66-line pages.

The *pr* command in Figure 9.16 also paginates the goodoleboys.txt file. This time, however, a colon separates the line number from the data, and instead of the file name, "Membership List" is printed in the title.

```
pr -n:3 -h "Membership List"  goodoleboys.txt

Oct 22 22:18 2002 Membership List Page 1

    1:Name         Born      Phone     Dog        Wife       Shotgun  Paid
    2:==========  ========  ========  ========  ==========  =======  =====
    3:Chuck        Dec 25    444-2345  Blue       Mary Sue    12       $2.50
    4:Bubba        Oct 13    444-1111  Buck       Mary Jean   12
    5:Billy Bob  June 11   444-4340  Leotis     Lisa Sue    12
    6:Amos         Jan 4     333-1119  Amos       Abigail     20
    7:Otis         Sept 17   444-8000  Ol' Sal    Sally       12       $5
    8:Claude       May 31    333-4340  Blue       Etheline    12
    9:Roscoe       Feb 2     444-2234  Rover      Alice Jean  410
   10:Arlis        June 19   444-1314  Redeye     Suzy Beth   12       $10.75
   11:Junior       April 30  BR-549    Percival   Lilly Faye  12
   12:Bill         Feb 29    333-4444  Daisy      Daisy       20
   13:Ernest T.  ??        none      none       none        none


( ... more blank lines omitted ...)
```

Figure 9.16: This version of pr prints the goodoleboys.txt file with different options.

The Od Utility

The *od* utility dumps files in a variety of formats, including character, hexadecimal, octal, signed decimal, unsigned decimal, and floating point, as shown in Figure 9.17. Be aware, however, that the *a* and *c* formats, which dump data in character format, only work for EBCDIC character sets. Also, unprintable data in character format is represented by three-digit octal numbers. In the results from the first command in Figure 9.17, octal 045 represents the linefeed character, with which each record ends.

```
cat personal.data
My name is Joe Smith.
I like cheese.
/home/jsmith $
od -t c personal.data
0000000   M   y       n   a   m   e       i   s       J   o   e       S
0000020   m   i   t   h   .       045 I       l   i   k   e       c   h   e
0000040   e   s   e   .   045
0000051
/home/jsmith $
od -t x personal.data
0000000   d4a84095 81948540 89a240d1 968540e2
0000020   9489a388 4b25c940 93899285 40838885
0000040   85a2854b 25000000
0000051
/home/jsmith $
od -tx1c personal.data
0000000 0d4 0a8 040 095 081 094 085 040 089 0a2 040 0d1 096 085 040 0e2
        M   y       n   a   m   e       i   s       J   o   e       S
0000020   094 089 0a3 088 04b 025 0c9 040 093 089 092 085 040 083 088 085
        m   i   t   h   .       045 I       l   i   k   e       c   h   e
0000040   085 0a2 085 04b 025
        e   s   e   .   045
0000045
/home/jsmith $
```

Figure 9.17: The first od *command displays the file personal.data in character format. The second command displays the same file in hexadecimal format, while the last command displays both formats.*

AUTHORITY

The owner of a file or directory, or a user with *ALLOBJ special authority, can control authority to a file or directory in the IFS. By default, the owner of a file is the user who created the file. The owner can use Qshell's *chown* command or the CL Change Owner command (CHGOWN) to assign ownership to another user profile.

The terms *group* and *group profile* are frequently used interchangeably. A group may be any user profile that has a group identifier. Create a group by adding the group identifier to a new or existing user profile.

To assign a group ID to a user profile, use the GID parameter of the Create User Profile (CRTUSRPRF) or Change User Profile (CHGUSRPRF) CL commands as shown here:

```
CRTUSRPRF USRPRF(ADMINS) PASSWORD(*NONE) +
INLMNU(*SIGNOFF) +TEXT('Administrators group profile')   +
JOBD(somelib/somejobd) GID(*GEN)
```

To assign a user to a group, use the GRPPRF parameter of CRTUSRPRF or CHGUS-RPRF. In the following example, user JSMITH uses group permissions assigned to user ADMINS:

```
CHGUSRPRF USRPRF(JSMITH) GRPPRF(ADMINS)
```

By default, a file is not assigned to a group profile. The file's owner can use the Qshell's *chgrp* command or the CL Change Primary Group command (CHGPGP) to assign a group profile. The following command uses *chgrp* to assign file myfile.txt to group profile ADMINS:

```
chgrp ADMINS myfile.txt
```

This example also uses *chgrp*:

```
chgrp 104 myfile.txt
```

In this case, file myfile.txt is assigned to the group profile whose group ID is 104.

A file's group profile is shown just to the right of the owner's name in the long form of the *ls* command, as Figure 9.18 demonstrates.

```
ls -l *.txt
-rwxrwxrwx  1 JSMITH  0           43 Feb 22   2002 ftpmodel.txt
-rw-rw----  1 JSMITH ADMINS        0 Oct 22 09:14 upper.txt
```

Figure 9.18: File upper.txt is assigned to group ADMINS. File ftpmodel.txt is not assigned to any group.

PERMISSIONS

There are five permissions, but for now, consider only three: read, write, and execute. (The other two are discussed later in this chapter.) Read, write, and execute mean different things for regular files and directories. The differences are shown in Table 9.6.

Table 9.6: Meaning of Permissions

Permission	Files	Directories
Read	View file contents.	Browse directory (read directory information).
Write	Change file contents; append to a file; delete the file.	Add and delete files to and from the directory.
Execute	Run an executable file.	Use as current directory; run executable scripts from the directory; use the directory in a path name.

Sometimes a combination of permissions is required to perform a task. For example, to execute a Qshell script, the user must have both read and execute authority to the script file.

To display file permissions, use the *ls* command with the *-l* (letter "ell") option for files and the *-l* and *-d* options for directories. Permissions are shown in a ten-character file-mode field. The first character of the file mode indicates the type of file. Type symbols are listed in Table 9.7.

Table 9.7: File-Mode Symbols

Symbol	Description	Release
- (hyphen)	Regular file	V4R3
b	Block special file	V4R3
c	Character special file	V4R3
d	Directory	V4R3

Table 9.7: File-Mode Symbols, *continued*

Symbol	Description	Release
l (ell)	Symbolic link	V4R3
p	Pipe	V5R2
s	Socket	V4R3

The other nine characters of the file mode are divided into three groups of three characters. As shown in Table 9.8, the first group of three characters is for owner permissions, the second group is for group permissions, and the last group holds permissions for all other users.

Table 9.8: Classification of Users

User group	Description
Owner	The user with full authority over a file or directory
Group	Members of a group user profile
Others	All other users

Read permission is indicated by an *r* in the first position of a group. Write permission is indicated by a *w* in the second position of a group. Execute permission is indicated by an *x* in the third position of a group. Permissions that are denied are indicated with hyphens.

Consider the ten-character file-mode field *-rwxrw-r--*. Since the first character is a hyphen, the file is a regular file. The three owner characters indicate the owner has read, write, and execute permissions. The group has read and write permissions, and other users have read permission only.

In Figure 9.19, the first *ls* command has just the *-l* option. Permissions are shown in the leftmost column. The second *ls* command, with the *d* option, shows permissions for the directory instead of each file. Without the *d* option, *ls* shows information about the files in the directory.

```
ls -l bin
total: 32 kilobytes
-rwxrw----   1 JSMITH  0              21 Oct 28 18:38 axx
-rwxrw----   1 JSMITH  0              24 Oct 25 10:21 donde.qsh
-rwsrw-rw-   1 JSMITH  0               0 Oct 24 16:32 one
--wxrwx--x   1 JSMITH  0              20 Oct 24 16:34 one.qsh
-rw-rw----   1 JSMITH  0               0 Oct 24 16:31 upper.txt
ls -ld bin
drwxrwsrwx   2 JSMITTH 0           49152 Oct 28 18:35 bin
```

Figure 9.19: To see permissions for a directory, include the d option of the ls command.

Changing Permissions

To change permissions, use the *chmod* (Change Mode) command. You may specify permissions in two ways: *absolute* or *symbolic*. You can accomplish the same task with either mode, but the symbolic mode is probably the easier to work with.

Use symbolic mode when you want to modify some permissions and leave others as they are. Here is its syntax:

```
chmod permissions[,permissions]...file...
```

In symbolic mode, the permissions string consists of three parts. The first part is one or more letters that indicate which users are affected. These are listed in Table 9.9.

Table 9.9: Symbols for Affected Users in Permission String

Symbol	Description
u	Owner
g	Group
o	Other users
a	All users (default)

The second part is a one-character operator that indicates how the permissions are to be applied. These symbols are listed in Table 9.10.

Table 9.10: Chmod Operators

Symbol	Description
+	Permission is granted.
- (hyphen)	Permission is revoked.
=	Permission is assigned according to the user abbreviation that follows. If a space follows the equal sign, all permissions are revoked.

The third part is made up of one or more characters, and indicates which permissions are being altered. These characters are listed in Table 9.11.

Table 9.11: Permission Abbreviations

Symbol	Description
r	Read.
w	Write.
x	Execute.
X	Grant execute permission if any user—owner, group, or others—has execute permission.
u	Permissions are assigned the value of the owner's permissions.
g	Permissions are assigned the value of the group's permissions.
o	Permissions are assigned the value of the other users' permissions.

Figures 9.20 through 9.23 provide several examples illustrating the use of the symbolic mode of the *chmod* command.

```
ls -l myfile.txt
-rw-rw-rw-  1 SMITH  0              0 Oct 24 18:03 myfile.txt
/home/jsmith $
chmod a+x myfile.txt
/home/jsmith $
ls -l myfile.txt
-rwxrwxrwx  1 SMITH  0              0 Oct 24 18:03 myfile.txt
```

Figure 9.20: Grant execute authority for myfile.txt to all users.

```
ls -l myscript.qsh
-rwxrwxrwx  1 SMITH  0              0 Oct 24 21:18 myscript.qsh
/home/smith $
chmod -w,og-x myscript.qsh
/home/smith $
ls -l myscript.qsh
-r-xr--r--  1 SMITH  0              0 Oct 24 21:18 myscript.qsh
```

Figure 9.21: Write permission is revoked for all users. File myscript.qsh is read-only.
Execute permssion is also revoked for everyone except for the owner.

```
ls -l myscript.qsh
-rwxrwxrwx  1 SMITH  0              0 Oct 24 21:18 myscript.qsh
/home/smith $
chmod o= myscript.qsh
/home/smith $
ls -l myscript.qsh
-rwxrwx---  1 SMITH  0              0 Oct 24 21:18 myscript.qsh
```

Figure 9.22: Since no value follows the equal sign, chmod revokes all permissions for
users other than the owner and group.

```
ls -l myscript.qsh
-rwxrwxrwx  1 SMITH  0              0 Oct 24 21:18 myscript.qsh
/home/smith $
chmod o=g-w myscript.qsh
/home/smith $
ls -l myscript.qsh
-rwxrwxr-x  1 SMITH  0              0 Oct 24 21:18 myscript.qsh
```

Figure 9.23: Grant other users (those that are not the owner and not in the group) the
same permissions that the group has, but do not give others write permission, regardless
of whether the group has it or not.

In Figure 9.24, the *ls* command shows that file donde.qsh exists in the current directory, yet when the user tries to run the script, Qshell can't find it. The problem is that donde.qsh was created as a regular file, and by default, Qshell does not grant execute permission to regular files. After using *chmod* to grant execute permission, the user (the file's owner) can run the script.

```
ls donde.qsh
donde.qsh
/home/JSMITH $
donde.qsh
qsh: 001-0019 Error found searching for command donde.qsh.
    No such path or directory.
/home/JSMITH $
chmod u+x donde.qsh
/home/JSMITH $
donde.qsh
Script donde.qsh is running ...
```

Figure 9.24: By default, Qshell does not grant execute authority to regular files.

The absolute mode differs from symbolic mode in that absolute mode overlays all previous permissions. That is, you cannot add or remove just one or two individual permissions. Instead, you must replace all of them. Here is the syntax for the absolute mode of the *chmod* command:

```
chmod permissions file...
```

To use absolute mode, specify a three- or four-digit octal number. The last (or only) three digits indicate owner, group, and others permissions, respectively. The numeric values of the permissions are listed in Table 9.12.

Table 9.12: Numeric Values for Absolute Syntax

Symbol	Description
4	Read
2	Write
1	Execute

To grant more than one type of permission, add the values together. For example, to grant both read and write authority, use a six (the sum of four and two).

Figure 9.25 is a basic example of the absolute mode of the *chmod* command. It gives all users complete access to file myscript.qsh.

```
chmod 777 myscript.qsh
/home/smith $
ls -l myscript.qsh
-rwxrwxrwx  1 SMITH  0              0 Oct 24 21:18 myscript.qsh
```

Figure 9.25: This example uses absolute mode to grant execute permissions.

In Figure 9.26, everyone, including the owner, is granted permission only to read and execute the myscript.qsh file. That is, the file is read-only, even to the owner. To be able to modify the file, the owner must grant himself or herself write permission to it.

```
chmod 555 myscript.qsh
/home/smith $
ls -l myscript.qsh
-r-xr-xr-x  1 SMITH  0              0 Oct 24 21:18 myscript.qsh
/home/smith $
cp arglist.qsh myscript.qsh
cp: 001-0023 Error found opening file myscript.qsh. Permission denied.
/home/smith $
```

Figure 9.26: File myscript.qsh is a read-only Qshell script.

The First Permission Byte

In addition to the read, write, and execute permissions, the s and S permission attributes are included for compatibility with PASEPortable Application Solutions Environment. PASE enables an iSeries machine to run AIX binaries.

Sometimes, users must be permitted temporary access to objects that, for security reasons, they normally are prohibited from using. OS/400 handles such situations by allowing programs to adopt the authority of their owners. Unix systems use a similar method. They permit programs to assume another user ID or group ID while they are running. The *s* symbol is derived from the setuid() and setgid() API calls. These API calls are typically used in the Unix system to implement the behavior similar to iSeries programs that adopt authority.

Use the *s* or *S* symbol in place of *r*, *w*, or *x* to set effective owner and/or group permissions when the file runs. Here is an example of the use of the *s* property:

```
ls -ld b*
drwxrwsrwx   2 JSMITH   0                    45056 Oct 25 17:02 bin
```

The group's execute authority is shown as *s* rather than *x* to indicate that the group permissions for the *bin* directory are assigned at execution time. If the file were not executable, an uppercase *S* would have been shown instead of the lowercase *s*.

The File-Creation Mask

When you create a directory or regular file, OS/400 grants a default set of permissions. For directories, the permissions are 777 minus the file-creation mask. For regular files, the permissions are 666 minus the file-creation mask.

If the file-creation mask has a value of 000, then by default, all users (owner, group, others) have complete access to directories, and read and write access to regular files. This is a security hole that should be filled.

It is common in Unix installations to set the file-creation mask to 022, often by placing the *umask* command in the /etc/profile script. When a directory is created, permissions are set to 777 minus 022, or 755, which means that the owner has complete access to the directory, but everyone else has read and execute authorities only. When a regular file is created, permissions are set to 666 minus 022, or 644, which means that the owner has read and write permissions, but everyone else has read permission only. Another common *umask* value is 077, which grants complete authority to the owner, but no authority to group or others.

Here is the syntax of the *umask* utility:

```
umask [-S] mask
```

To display the setting of the file-creation mask, use umask without a *mask* argument. To view the mask in symbolic form, include the *-S* option. These two options are shown in Figure 9.27.

```
umask
022
/home/smith $
umask -S
u=rwx,g=rx,o=rx
```

Figure 9.27: The file-creation mask is currently set to 022, which means that a file's owner receives all permissions by default, but other users receive only read and execute authorities.

To set the file-creation mask, include the desired mask as the first nonoption argument to *umask*. You may specify the permissions in absolute or symbolic form. For example, the following command sets the file-creation mask to 022:

```
umask 022
```

This prevents all users other than the owner from acquiring write permission when a new file is created.

Figure 9.28 shows the use of the symbolic form to set the file-creation mask to the equivalent of 022 in absolute form.

```
umask -S u=rwx,g=rx,o=rx
/home/smith $
umask
022
```

Figure 9.28· Using symbolic form, the file-creation mask is set to the equivalent of 022 in absolute form.

145

Figure 9.29 also uses the symbolic form. In this case, the owner is given all permissions to new files. Both the group's and others' permissions are set to none.

```
umask -S u=rwx,go=
/home/JSMITH $
umask
077
```

Figure 9.29: The file-creation mask is set such that the owner has all permissions to new files, but group and others have no permissions.

CCSIDs

CCSIDs (pronounced "see-sids") allow data to be stored in character sets that correspond to different collating sequences and national languages. Support for CCSIDs enhances the ability of the iSeries to act as a server and to exchange data with other systems.

The examples in this section illustrate some of the issues you might encounter when working with IFS files.

Displaying a File's CCSID Attribute

There are several ways to determine a file's CCSID attribute. The *ls* command displays CCSIDs if the *-S* option is specified:

```
ls -S [e-h]*
37 echoprocess.qsh      819 ftpmodel.txt          37 helpme
37 edity.txt            819 goodoleboys.txt
```

The file dump command, *od*, displays the CCSID if you specify the *-C* option. As shown, the CCSID is shown before the dumped contents:

```
od -C data.ascii
data.ascii CCSID = 819
0000000   066151 067145 020061 005154 064556 062440 031012
0000016
```

The *attr* command, introduced with V5R2 and shown below, can also display or set a file's CCSID:

```
attr data.ascii CCSID
819
```

Setting the CCSID of an Existing File

You can use the *setccsid* utility to change the CCSID attribute of a file without changing the data in the file. You might need this capability, for example, after having received a file via FTP, as the system might not tag the file with the proper CCSID. As of V5R2, you can also use the *attr* utility to change a file's CCSID.

The *setccsid* and *attr* utilities are illustrated in Figure 9.30 and 9.31.

```
ls -S data.ascii
819 data.ascii
/home/jsmith $
cat data.ascii
line 1
line 2
/home/jsmith $
setccsid 37 data.ascii
/home/jsmith $
cat data.ascii
%Ñ>Á     %Ñ>Á     /home/jsmith $
```

Figure 9.30: The setccsid *utility changes a file's CCSID, but not its contents.*

```
attr data.ascii CCSID
819
/home/jsmith $
cat data.ascii
line 1
line 2
/home/jsmith $
attr data.ascii CCSID=37
/home/jsmith $
cat data.ascii
%Ñ>Á     %Ñ>Á     /home/jsmith $
```

Figure 9.31: You can use the attr *command to change the CCSID attribute. As with* setccsid, *the contents of the file are unaffected.*

File Creation

Many Qshell utilities create files. By default, Qshell tags new files with the current job's default CCSID. This is not always desirable, however. For example, a file that is to be accessed from networked PCs might need to be created in ASCII format.

Use the *touch* utility, shown in Figure 9.32, to create a file with the desired CCSID. In this example, the default CCSID for this job is 37. File "one" was created with CCSID 37 by default. The *C* option causes *touch* to create file "two" with CCSID 819. The *S* option causes the *ls* command to display each file's CCSID attribute

```
touch one
/home/JSMITH $
touch -C 819 two
/home/JSMITH $
ls -Sl one two
  37 one
 819 two
```

Figure 9.32: Use the touch *utility to ensure that a file is created with the proper CCSID.*

Environment Variable QIBM_CCSID

The QIBM_CCSID environment variable was added in V5R2. It specifies the CCSID with which new files are to be tagged. It also indicates the CCSIDs to use for certain translations of data. Table 9.14 lists utilities that use the QIBM_CCSID value.

Table 9.14: Qshell Commands for the IFS

Utility	Change Working Directory	Overridden by -C Option?
nohup	CCSID of the nohup.out file	Yes
rexec	CCSID of data sent to a remote system	Yes
sed	CCSID of created file	No

Table 9.14: Qshell Commands for the IFS, *continued*

Utility	Change Working Directory	Overridden by -C Option?
pax, tar	CCSID of file extracted from archive	No
touch	CCSID of a created file	Yes
tee	CCSID of created files	No

The default value of QIBM_CCSID is zero, which tells Qshell and the utilities to use the job's default CCSID. Another special value is 65535, which means that no data translation is to be done.

Preserving the CCSID Attribute during Copy

By default, the *cp* utility changes the CCSID of an output file to that of the copied file. The effect of this process is demonstrated in Figure 9.32.

```
ls -1S data*
819 data.ascii
 37 data.ebcdic
/home/jsmith $
cat data.ebcdic
line 1
line 2
/home/jsmith $
cp data.ebcdic data.ascii
/home/jsmith $
ls -1S data*
37 data.ascii
37 data.ebcdic
/home/jsmith $
cat data.ascii
line 1
line 2
```

Figure 9.32: By default, cp changes the CCSID of the target file.

To preserve the output file's existing CCSID, use the *-t* (text) option, as shown in Figure 9.33.

149

```
ls -lS data*
819 data.ascii
 37 data.ebcdic
/home/jsmith $
cp -t data.ebcdic data.ascii
/home/jsmith $
ls -lS data*
819 data.ascii
 37 data.ebcdic
/home/jsmith $
cat data.ascii
line 1
line 2
```

Figure 9.33: Include the -t option when copying if you wish to preserve the target file's CCSID attribute.

The Iconv Utility

The *iconv* utility, which was added to Qshell at V5R2, reads one or more input files (or standard input), converts the data from one CCSID to another CCSID, and writes the converted data to standard output. Here is the syntax of *iconv*:

```
iconv -f fromCCSID -t toCCSID [file…]
```

The QIBM_CCSID environment variable and the *C* options discussed earlier in this section will usually be enough support for you when you're dealing with data in different code sets or languages. However, there might be a time when you have a file that is corrupted. Perhaps you want to simply translate some data. By sending the file over a network connection, or because of a bug in your application, you have written data to a file that is tagged with a different CCSID. When you look at a file that shows up as garbage, you might have a data or CCSID problem. The *iconv* utility might be able to help.

Figure 9.34 shows how you might detect and fix such a problem. Using a Qshell utility like *cat*, you see what looks like data corruption in a file named unicode.txt. Looking at the CCSID of the file, you see that it is set to a U.S. English CCSID of 37. Knowing that the file is a Unicode file that came from your Web application, you use *iconv* with a Unicode CCSID of 13488 as the *from* CCSID, and the default CCSID as the *to* CCSID.

The data appears correct, so you know that you've got the CCSID correct. Use the *touch* utility with the *C* option to create a file with the correct CCSID, then use *iconv* again, this time redirecting the output to the newly created file. The *iconv* utility explicitly translates the data being read to the current CCSID of your session. Then, the system implicitly translates that redirected data to match the 13488 CCSID that you've tagged the file with. The result is that unicode2.txt contains the correctly tagged data.

```
cat unicode.txt
 + ? Ï   Ñ Ë   È Ç Á   È Ñ _ Á   Ã ? Ê   / % %   À ? ? À   _ Á >
È ?   Ä ? _ Á   È ?   È Ç Á   / Ñ À   ? Ã   È Ç Á Ñ Ê   Ä ? Í
> È Ê `
/home/jsmith $
ls -S
  819 ascii.txt      37 unicode.txt
/home/jsmith $
iconv -f 13488 -t 0 unicode.txt
Now is the time for all good men
to come to the aid of their country
touch -C 13488 unicode2.txt
/home/jsmith $
iconv -f 13488 -t 0 unicode.txt >> unicode2.txt
/home/jsmith $
ls -S
  819 ascii.txt      37 unicode.txt      13488 unicode2.txt
/home/jsmith $
cat unicode2.txt
  Now is the time for all good men
  to come to the aid of their country
```

Figure 9.34: Use the iconv *utility to do explicit data translations.*

File Comparisons

The file-comparison utility, *cmp*, does not allow for differences in CCSID unless you use the *-t* option. The *-t* option tells *cmp* to translate each input file to the job's CCSID before comparing. Figure 9.35 shows how you might use this option. Files "one" and "two" contain the same data, encoded under different CCSIDs. Without the *-t* option, *cmp* returns an exit status of 1 because it considers the files to be different. When the *-t* option is added to the command, *cmp* returns a status of 0, indicating that the two files contain the same text.

```
ls -S one two
37 one 819 two
/home/jsmith $
cat one
line 1
line 2
/home/jsmith $
cat two
line 1
line 2
/home/jsmith $
cmp one two ; print $?
one two differ: char 1, line 1
1
/home/jsmith $
cmp -t one two ; print $?
0
```

Figure 9.35: Use the t option when comparing files of different CCSIDs.

SUMMARY

The Integrated File System includes all filing systems on the iSeries. It allows the iSeries to store data for which a relational database management system is not suitable. Since Qshell is derived from software that was designed to manage hierarchical file systems, Qshell provides a good interface to nondatabase data. Qshell includes utilities to manage all aspects of files, including creating, deleting, and renaming files and directories; displaying the contents of files; creating hard and symbolic links; controlling authorization to files; and setting the CCSID attribute.

Chapter 10

Input and Output

Not all text data is suitable for storage in a relational database table. For example, letters and memos do not fit the model of rows and columns. A file that is processed as a sequential list of bytes, such as a letter or memo, is known as a *stream file*. Stream files are widely used in business.

Stream files are not organized into rows (records) and columns (fields). A stream-file record is a series of characters that ends with a special code, such as a carriage-return character followed by a line-feed character. Stream-file records may vary in length. One record of a file may be 20 bytes long, the next 150, and a third 12. Stream files may contain binary data (such as sounds or pictures) or text data.

Qshell is well suited to working with stream files. Most Qshell commands read a stream of characters and write a stream of characters.

STANDARD FILES

Qshell defines three standard stream files by default. You do not have to declare, open, or close these files. The default input file is known as standard input and is abbreviated to *stdin*. It is assigned to the keyboard, but you may use redirection to assign it to another file, or a pipeline to read the output of another Qshell script or utility.

There are two predeclared output files: standard output (*stdout*) and standard error (*stderr*). The first is for the normal output of commands, while the second one is for error messages. Both files are directed to the display by default when Qshell runs interactively, but may be redirected to disk files or piped to other Qshell utilities. The fact that there are two output files allows you to separate good output from error output.

The Qshell interpreter is a good example of the use of stream files. In an interactive Qshell session, the input to Qshell is the keyboard, and the output device is the display. The session is a conversation. Each time you press the Enter key, Qshell reads the stream of characters you typed, attempts to carry out your instructions, and gives you a stream of characters as output, even if that output is only a prompt.

A terminal session is shown in Figure 10.1. It shows a user typing the List Directory Contents command (*ls*) to determine what .csv files were in the current directory. Qshell reads the command from stdin and sends the list of file names to stdout. The user then types the Remove Directory Entries command (*rm*) to delete a file. Qshell reads the command from stdin and responds by sending a confirmation message to stderr. Qshell reads the user's response from stdin. And so the dialog continues.

```
/home/JSMITH $
ls *.csv
cust.csv          two.csv           uuu.csv
/home/JSMITH $
rm -i uuu.csv
rm: 001-2145 Do you want to remove the file or directory uuu.csv (Y or N)?
y
/home/JSMITH $
ls *.csv
cust.csv          two.csv
/home/JSMITH $
```

Figure 10.1: By default, Qshell utilities use the keyboard and display devices for input.

REDIRECTION

Stdin, stdout, and stderr may be assigned to devices through a process known as redirection, which is somewhat like an override in OS/400. Qshell supports nine redirection operators, shown in Table 10.1. (The "here" document and noclobber option are explained later in this chapter.)

Table 10.1: Qshell Redirection Operators

Operator	Description
<	Redirect input
<&	Duplicate input
<&-	Close input
<<, <<-	Open a "here" document
>	Replace output
>|	Replace output; ignore the noclobber option
>>	Append output
>&	Duplicate output
>&-	Close output

The most commonly used redirection operators are <, >, and >>. They are illustrated in this section. The others will be explained when file descriptors are discussed.

The redirection operators may be separated from the file names that follow them, but it is not necessary. In other words, the following two commands are equivalent:

```
ls *.qsh >temp.txt
ls *.qsh > temp.txt
```

To illustrate the use of redirection operators, the input data in Figure 10.2 is used as the basis of the examples that follow.

```
cat goodoleboys.txt
Name       Born     Phone    Dog      Wife       Shotgun  Paid
========== ======== ======== ======== ========== ======== =====
Chuck      Dec 25   444-2345 Blue     Mary Sue   12       $2.50
Bubba      Oct 13   444-1111 Buck     Mary Jean  12
Billy BobJune 11    444-4340 Leotis   Lisa Sue   12
Amos       Jan 4    333-1119 Amos     Abigail    20
Otis       Sept 17  444-8000 Ol' Sal  Sally      12       $5
Claude     May 31   333-4340 Blue     Etheline   12
Roscoe     Feb 2    444-2234 Rover    Alice Jean 410
Arlis      June 19  444-1314 Redeye   Suzy Beth  12       $10.75
Junior     April 30 BR-549   Percival Lilly Faye 12
Bill       Feb 29   333-4444 Daisy    Daisy      20
Ernest T.??          none     none     none       none
```

Figure 10.2: The goodoleboys.txt file is used in this chapter's examples.

Figures 10.3 through 10.6 use the Translate Characters utility (*tr*), which can translate characters in one character set to corresponding characters in another character set. *Tr* works well for these examples because it reads from stdin and writes to stdout. In Figure 10.3, the redirection operator causes *tr* to read the goodoleboys.txt file, not the keyboard.

```
tr  [:lower:]  [:upper:]  <goodoleboys.txt
NAME       BORN     PHONE    DOG      WIFE       SHOTGUN  PAID
========== ======== ======== ======== ========== ======== =====
CHUCK      DEC 25   444-2345 BLUE     MARY SUE   12       $2.50
BUBBA      OCT 13   444-1111 BUCK     MARY JEAN  12
BILLY BOB  JUNE 11  444-4340 LEOTIS   LISA SUE   12
AMOS       JAN 4    333-1119 AMOS     ABIGAIL    20
OTIS       SEPT 17  444-8000 OL' SAL  SALLY      12       $5
CLAUDE     MAY 31   333-4340 BLUE     ETHELINE   12
ROSCOE     FEB 2    444-2234 ROVER    ALICE JEAN 410
ARLIS      JUNE 19  444-1314 REDEYE   SUZY BETH  12       $10.75
JUNIOR     APRIL 30 BR-549   PERCIVAL LILLY FAYE 12
BILL       FEB 29   333-4444 DAISY    DAISY      20
ERNEST T.  ??       NONE     NONE     NONE       NONE
```

Figure 10.3: Lowercase letters are translated to their uppercase equivalents. Output goes to the display because stdout is not redirected.

Figure 10.4 also read the goodoleboys.txt file and translates lowercase letters to their uppercase equivalents. In this case, though, output goes to the file upper.txt, erasing any existing data in it. If the file does not exist, it is created.

```
tr   [:lower:]   [:upper:]   <goodoleboys.txt >upper.txt
/home/JSMITH $
cat upper.txt
NAME          BORN       PHONE      DOG       WIFE        SHOTGUN   PAID

=========     ========   ========   =======   ========    =======   =====
CHUCK         DEC 25     444-2345   BLUE      MARY SUE    12        $2.50
BUBBA         OCT 13     444-1111   BUCK      MARY JEAN   12
BILLY BOB     JUNE 11    444-4340   LEOTIS    LISA SUE    12
AMOS          JAN 4      333-1119   AMOS      ABIGAIL     20
OTIS          SEPT 17    444-8000   OL' SAL   SALLY       12        $5
CLAUDE        MAY 31     333-4340   BLUE      ETHELINE    12
ROSCOE        FEB 2      444-2234   ROVER     ALICE JEAN  410
ARLIS         JUNE 19    444-1314   REDEYE    SUZY BETH   12        $10.75
JUNIOR        APRIL 30   BR-549     PERCIVAL  LILLY FAYE  12
BILL          FEB 29     333-4444   DAISY     DAISY       20
ERNEST T.     ??         NONE       NONE      NONE        NONE
/home/JSMITH $
```

Figure 10.4: The > operator replaces data in file upper.txt.

In Figure 10.5, the translated data from the goodoleboys.txt file is appended to
the upper.txt file, so its existing two records are not overwritten. Again, if the
file did not exist, it would be created.

```
cat upper.txt
I LIKE CHEESE!
+ + + + +
/home/JSMITH $
tr   [:lower:]   [:upper:]   <goodoleboys.txt >>upper.txt
/home/JSMITH $
cat upper.txt
I LIKE CHEESE!
+ + + + +
NAME          BORN       PHONE      DOG       WIFE         SHOTGUN   PAID

=========     ========   ========   ========  =========    =======   =====
CHUCK         DEC 25     444-2345   BLUE      MARY SUE     12        $2.50
BUBBA         OCT 13     444-1111   BUCK      MARY JEAN    12
BILLY BOB     JUNE 11    444-4340   LEOTIS    LISA SUE     12
AMOS          JAN 4      333-1119   AMOS      ABIGAIL      20
OTIS          SEPT 17    444-8000   OL' SAL   SALLY        12        $5
CLAUDE        MAY 31     333-4340   BLUE      ETHELINE     12
ROSCOE        FEB 2      444-2234   ROVER     ALICE JEAN   410
ARLIS         JUNE 19    444-1314   REDEYE    SUZY BETH    12        $10.75
JUNIOR        APRIL 30   BR-549     PERCIVAL  LILLY FAYE   12
BILL          FEB 29     333-4444   DAISY     DAISY        20
ERNEST T.     ??         NONE       NONE      NONE         NONE
/home/JSMITH $
```

Figure 10.5: Because of the >> operator, new data is appended to the output file.

157

The *tr* command in Figure 10.6 translates the uppercase letters in source member MYPGM of file MYLIB/QRPGLESRC to their lowercase equivalents. Other characters are unaffected. The output is placed in source member MYPGM2 in the same source physical file.

```
cat /qsys.lib/mylib.lib/qrpglesrc.file/mypgm.mbr
     D CD            S           35    DIM(3) CTDATA PERRCD(1)
     C     *ENTRY         PLIST
     C                    PARM                INDEX           1 0
     C                    PARM                DESCR           35
        *
     C     INDEX          IFLT    1
     C     INDEX          ORGT    35
     C                    MOVE    *ALL'X'   DESCR
     C                    ELSE
     C                    MOVE    CD(INDEX) DESCR
     C                    ENDIF
        *
     C                    RETURN
/home/smith $
tr [:upper:] [:lower:] \
    </qsys.lib/mylib.lib/qrpglesrc.file/mypgm.mbr \
    >/qsys.lib/mylib.lib/qrpglesrc.file/mypgm2.mbr
/home/smith $
cat /qsys.lib/mylib.lib/qrpglesrc.file/mypgm2.mbr
     d cd            s           35    dim(3) ctdata perrcd(1)
     c     *entry         plist
     c                    parm                index           1 0
     c                    parm                descr           35
        *
     c     index          iflt    1
     c     index          orgt    35
     c                    move    *all'x'   descr
     c                    else
     c                    move    cd(index) descr
     c                    endif
        *
     c                    return
```

Figure 10.6: File redirection can be used with database file members.

If the > operator is used alone (that is, it does not follow a command), the effect is to clear the file. Consider this example:

```
>upper.txt
/home/JSMITH $
cat upper.txt
/home/JSMITH $
```

The redirection operator is used without a command, so it clears upper.txt. This is the Qshell version of CL's Clear Physical File Member command (CLRPFM).

A word of warning is in order:

Do not use the same file in both input and redirection operators.

Here is an example of what you should *not* do:

```
# WARNING: Do NOT do the following !!!!
tr [:upper:] [:lower:] < myfile >myfile  # Do NOT do this !!!!
# WARNING: Do NOT do the preceding !!!!
```

The lowercase version of myfile will not replace the uppercase version. Redirection is a function of Qshell, not of *tr*. Therefore, the output redirection operator will clear myfile before *tr* begins to read the data.

THE "NOCLOBBER" OPTION

By default, the > redirection overwrites the contents of an existing file. In Figure 10.7, output.txt is loaded with a list of the Qshell script files (the files with an extension of .qsh). Then, the file is replaced with a list of the names of .csv files.

```
ls *.qsh >output.txt
/home/JSMITH $
ls *.csv >output.txt
/home/JSMITH $
cat output.txt
cust.csv
two.csv
uuu.csv
/home/JSMITH $
```

Figure 10.7: The output of the second ls command replaces, or "clobbers," the output of the first ls command.

159

To prevent the > redirection operator from overwriting an existing file, use the "noclobber" option, which is turned on using the *set -C* command. Figure 10.8 illustrates the use of this command to prevent Qshell from overwriting file output.txt. When the script attempts to replace the contents of output.txt with a list of the names of .csv files, Qshell responds with error message 001-0054. The *cat* command shows that the second list did not change the contents of output.txt.

```
set -C
/home/JSMITH $
ls *.qsh >output.txt
/home/JSMITH $
ls output.txt
output.txt
/home/JSMITH $
ls *.csv >output.txt
qsh: 001-0054 The noclobber option is set and file output.txt already exists.
/home/JSMITH $
cat output.txt
args01.qsh
args02.qsh
args03.qsh
/home/JSMITH $
```

Figure 10.8: Use the noclobber option to prevent accidental erasure of data.

There are two ways to turn on the noclobber option:

```
set -C
set -o noclobber
```

To turn off the noclobber option, use a plus sign instead of a minus sign, like this:

```
set +C
set +o noclobber
```

You can override the noclobber option on a single operation by using the >| redirection operator, as shown in Figure 10.9. The *set* utility turns on the noclobber option. The first *ls* fails because output.txt already exists and the > redirection operator is used. The second *ls* command succeeds because the >| redirection operator overrides the noclobber option. Notice that the > operator (in the first *ls* command) generates an error message, but the >| (in the second *ls* command) does not. The *cat* command shows that the .csv files are listed in file output.txt.

```
set -C
/home/JSMITH $
ls *.csv >output.txt
qsh: 001-0054 The noclobber option is set and file output.txt already exists.
/home/JSMITH $
ls *.csv >|output.txt
/home/JSMITH $
cat output.txt
cust.csv
two.csv
uuu.csv
/home/JSMITH $
```

Figure 10.9: The >| redirection operator overrides the noclobber option.

PIPES AND PIPELINES

A pipeline is a series of commands connected with the pipe symbol, the vertical bar (|). A pipe channels stdout of one command to stdin of another. Figures 10.10 through 10.12 show pipelines in action. Input comes from the goodoleboys.txt file, which was shown in Figure 10.2.

Figure 10.10 shows the use of *grep*, a search utility, to look in the goodoleboys.txt file for records that include the string *444-*. Instead of writing the selected records to stdout, it sends them into the pipe. The sort routine reads from stdin, so it gets the selected data from the pipe, sorts it, and sends it along to stdout. Since stdout is not piped or redirected from sort, the sorted data appears on the display.

```
grep '444-' <goodoleboys.txt | sort
Arlis       June 19    444-1314 Redeye   Suzy Beth    12    $10.75
Billy Bob   June 11    444-4340 Leotis   Lisa Sue     12
Bubba       Oct 13     444-1111 Buck     Mary Jean    12
Chuck       Dec 25     444-2345 Blue     Mary Sue     12    $2.50
Otis        Sept 17    444-8000 Ol' Sal  Sally        12    $5
Roscoe      Feb 2      444-2234 Rover    Alice Jean   410
```

Figure 10.10: Grep is a search utility. It looks for records that match a pattern.

Figure 10.11 uses the *grep* utility with two pipes. *Grep* selects the records that contain *444-* and sends them to *tr*, which converts the lowercase letters to upper-case, leaving all other characters as they are, and passes the data along to the sort utility. After sorting, the data is sent to stdout, which is the display in this case because there is no output-redirection operator or pipe following the sort.

```
grep '444-' <goodoleboys.txt | tr [:lower:] [:upper:] | sort
ARLIS       JUNE 19  444-1314 REDEYE    SUZY BETH   12   $10.75
BILLY BOB  JUNE 11  444-4340 LEOTIS    LISA SUE    12
BUBBA       OCT 13   444-1111 BUCK      MARY JEAN   12
CHUCK       DEC 25   444-2345 BLUE      MARY SUE    12   $2.50
OTIS        SEPT 17  444-8000 OL' SAL   SALLY       12   $5
ROSCOE      FEB 2    444-2234 ROVER     ALICE JEAN  410
```

Figure 10.11: There are two pipes in this pipeline.

Pipes can also be combined with redirection operators, as Figure 10.12 shows. *Grep* selects all goodoleboys.txt records that contain *444-* and sends them to *tr*, which converts lowercase letters to uppercase and passes the data along to *sort*. *Sort* sends the sorted data to the file sorted.txt. In this case, the sorted records containing *444-* are redirected to the file sorted.txt.

```
> grep '444-' <goodoleboys.txt | tr [:lower:] [:upper:] | sort >sorted.txt
  /home/JSMITH $
> cat sorted.txt
  ARLIS       JUNE 19  444-1314 REDEYE    SUZY BETH   12   $10.75
  BILLY BOB  JUNE 11  444-4340 LEOTIS    LISA SUE    12
  BUBBA       OCT 13   444-1111 BUCK      MARY JEAN   12
  CHUCK       DEC 25   444-2345 BLUE      MARY SUE    12   $2.50
  OTIS        SEPT 17  444-8000 OL' SAL   SALLY       12   $5
  ROSCOE      FEB 2    444-2234 ROVER     ALICE JEAN  410
  /home/JSMITH $
```

Figure 10.12: Pipes can be combined with redirection operators.

REDIRECTION OPERATORS AND PIPES

It is common for beginning shell users to confuse redirection operators and pipes. There is, however, a great difference between the two concepts. Consider the following two commands:

```
myscript.qsh > somefile
myscript.qsh | somefile
```

In the first line, the output of myscript.qsh will be stored in *somefile*. In the second command, the output of myscript.qsh is to be read by a program or script called *somefile*. Since files in Unix systems may contain any type of data, including programs, using an output redirection operator instead of a pipe before a program or script destroys or corrupts the program or script.

That warning is worth repeating:

Using an output redirection operator instead of a pipe before a program or script destroys or corrupts the program or script.

It will help you to use these properly if you always look at the filename to which stdout is being redirected. If the file is a program or script, use a pipe. If it is a data file, use a redirection operator. It will also help if you think of a pipe operator as a symbol for a temporary file. Imagine that the command preceding the pipe symbol writes to a temporary file, and the command following the pipe symbol reads the temporary file.

TEE

You might decide that you would like to see the data that travels through a pipe, perhaps for debugging purposes. If so, use the *tee* utility, also known as *duplicate standard input*. As you might guess, the *tee* utility gets its name from the "T" shape a plumber might install in a real pipe to branch its flow between two locations. *Tee* reads stdin and writes the unchanged data to both stdout and one or more other files. The syntax of *tee* utility is shown here:

```
tee [-ai] [file…]
```

By default, *tee* replaces the data in a file that already exists. To append the data instead, use the *a* option. Use of *tee* is shown in Figure 10.13. It passes the output of *grep* along to *tr*, and at the same time makes a copy of the output in the file tee.out. Notice that the data is in mixed case in the tee.out file, because it had not been fed to the *tr* command at that point. Notice also that the data in tee.out is not sorted, because the sort process had not yet run.

```
grep '444-' <goodoleboys.txt | tee tee.out \
>
| tr [:lower:] [:upper:] | sort >sorted.txt
/home/JSMITH $
cat tee.out
Chuck      Dec 25    444-2345 Blue     Mary Sue    12   $2.50
Bubba      Oct 13    444-1111 Buck     Mary Jean   12
Billy Bob  June 11   444-4340 Leotis   Lisa Sue    12
Otis       Sept 17   444-8000 Ol' Sal  Sally       12   $5
Roscoe     Feb 2     444-2234 Rover    Alice Jean  410
Arlis      June 19   444-1314 Redeye   Suzy Beth   12   $10.75
/home/JSMITH $
```

Figure 10.13: After the pipeline finishes, the cat command shows the input that grep was given.

In Figure 10.14, *grep* again selects records that contain the string *444-* from file goodoleboys.txt. Then, *tee* writes the records to two files, tee.out and two.out, and at the same time passes the records to the *sort* utility.

```
grep '444-' <goodoleboys.txt | tee tee.out two.out | sort
Arlis      June 19   444-1314 Redeye   Suzy Beth   12   $10.75
Billy Bob  June 11   444-4340 Leotis   Lisa Sue    12
Bubba      Oct 13    444-1111 Buck     Mary Jean   12
Chuck      Dec 25    444-2345 Blue     Mary Sue    12   $2.50
Otis       Sept 17   444-8000 Ol' Sal  Sally       12   $5
Roscoe     Feb 2     444-2234 Rover    Alice Jean  410
/home/JSMITH $
cat tee.out
Chuck      Dec 25    444-2345 Blue     Mary Sue    12   $2.50
Bubba      Oct 13    444-1111 Buck     Mary Jean   12
Billy Bob  June 11   444-4340 Leotis   Lisa Sue    12
Otis       Sept 17   444-8000 Ol' Sal  Sally       12   $5
Roscoe     Feb 2     444-2234 Rover    Alice Jean  410
Arlis      June 19   444-1314 Redeye   Suzy Beth   12   $10.75
/home/JSMITH $
```

Figure 10.14: The tee utility writes the records from grep to tee.out and two.out, and passes the records to sort (part 1 of 2).

```
cat two.out
Chuck      Dec 25   444-2345 Blue     Mary Sue    12   $2.50
Bubba      Oct 13   444-1111 Buck     Mary Jean   12
Billy Bob  June 11  444-4340 Leotis   Lisa Sue    12
Otis       Sept 17  444-8000 Ol' Sal  Sally       12   $5
Roscoe     Feb 2    444-2234 Rover    Alice Jean  410
Arlis      June 19  444-1314 Redeye   Suzy Beth   12   $10.75
/home/JSMITH $
```

Figure 10.14: The tee utility writes the records from grep to tee.out and two.out, and passes the records to sort (part 2 of 2).

OVERRIDING REDIRECTION

You can temporarily override stdout on a line-by-line basis. That is, even though stdout is assigned to a certain file, you can direct the output of individual commands to other files. Consider this example of redirected output:

```
print "Something"
if [ -z "$1" ]
    then date >>errorlog.txt
         print "Script: $0" >> errorlog.txt
         print "Parm 1 missing, default used." >> errorlog.txt
fi
print "Something else"
```

The first and last *print* commands write to stdout. The output from those commands will go to the display, to a file, or into a pipe, depending on how stdout is directed. Look at the *if* block, however. Three commands—*date*, and two *echo* commands—do not write to stdout, but append to errorlog.txt. Figure 10.15 shows what happens when this code is executed. When the user types the name of the script, error01.qsh, on the command line, Qshell runs the script. Since stdout is not redirected, the first and last *print* commands write the string "Something" and "Something else" to the terminal. The *cat* utility shows what has been written to file errorlog.txt.

165

```
error01.qsh
Something
Something else
/home/JSMITH $
cat errorlog.txt
Wed Dec 25 08:27:35  2002
Script: /home/JSMITH/error01.qsh
Parm 1 missing, default used.
/home/JSMITH $
```

Figure 10.15: The previous script redirected both the stdout and stderr files.

"HERE" DOCUMENTS

A "here" document is a special way of capturing input lines and directing them as a group to another process or file. The "here" document operator, <<, is followed by an end-of-data delimiter string of the programmer's choosing.

Figure 10.16 shows how to create a file from the keyboard using a "here" document. The user chooses the string *EOD* to indicate the end of the input data. The *cat* utility displays the lines to stdout, which is overridden to file mydata.txt.

```
cat <<EOD >mydata.txt
>
Jack,12
>
Bill,20
>
Leroy,15
>
EOD
/home/JSMITH $
cat mydata.txt
Jack,12
Bill,20
Leroy,15
/home/JSMITH $
```

Figure 10.16: This example shows how to use a "here" document to enter data into an IFS file from the keyboard.

You may follow the << operator with a hyphen if you wish. This allows you to enter a tab character before the end-of-data delimiter. Since you can't type a tab character from a 5250 terminal session, you are not likely to use this option unless you edit scripts on an ASCII-based machine.

FILTERS

A filter is a program that reads from stdin and writes to stdout. Filters are designed with a single purpose in mind, and are written to be flexible. The *sort* utility, for example, is a filter that resequences, merges, and sequence-checks text files. Because *sort* is so powerful, it is unlikely that you will need to write another program to sort.

Generally, you should write scripts and programs that embrace the filter philosophy. As a rule, scripts should not converse with the user. For instance, suppose you want the user to enter his or her name when a script begins to run. You could use *print* or *echo* to display a prompt, and use *read* to accept the user's input, like this:

```
echo "Please enter your name:"
read name
```

However, this degree of interactivity would make it difficult or impossible to use the script in a pipeline. It is better to provide a way to specify a command line option. In the following example, the user name is entered through a parameter:

```
myscript.qsh -n 'Joe Smith'
```

As you can see, the use of switches can replace interactive I/O. In this case, the programmer writes the script so that it interprets the parameter following the *n* option as a user's name. This is demonstrated in the following example:

```
if [ "$1" ] && [ "$2" ] && [ $1 = "-n" ]
   then name=$2
   else name=$LOGNAME
fi
```

If the first and second positional parameters are defined and the first parameter is *-n*, the second parameter provides the value for the variable name; otherwise, *name* gets its value from the Qshell predefined variable LOGNAME, which is the ID of the user who is running the shell. There is no need to use *echo* and *read* statements to include the user's name.

I/O UTILITIES

To write effective Qshell scripts, you must learn to make Qshell scripts read data from and write data to files. The Qshell I/O utilities, listed here, are stream-oriented and easy to use:

- Dspmsg
- Echo
- Print
- Printf
- Read

Print

While there is only one input utility, there are several Qshell output utilities. The *print* utility, which writes to output files, is probably the one you'll need most often. Here is its syntax:

```
print [ -nrR ] [ -u [ n ] ] [ argument... ]
```

Print writes zero or more arguments to stdout. Each argument is separated by a space. Unless you include the *-n* option, *print* ends with a newline character, which forces the next output into another record. *Print* lets you embed control sequences (listed in Table 10.2) in output.

Table 10.2: Control-Character Sequences Recognized by Print

Sequence	Description
\a	Sounds the terminal's alarm
\b	Backspaces one character
\c	Ignores subsequent arguments and suppress newline
\f	Formfeed (clears the screen)
\n	Newline (combines carriage return and linefeed)
\r	Return (carriage return, but no linefeed; returns to beginning of the line)
\t	Tab
\v	Vertical tab (linefeed, but no carriage return; moves cursor down)
\\	Prints one backslash character
\0x	EBCDIC character, where x is a one-, two-, or three-digit octal number

If you don't want *print* to interpret the control sequences, use option *-r* or *-R*. Figure 10.17 shows a simple example of the *print* utility.

```
print "Tom\t14\nBobby\t21\nJack\t15"
Tom      14
Bobby    21
Jack     15
```

Figure 10.17: The \t and \n control characters insert tabs and newline characters into the output stream.

To include a backslash in a string, you normally code two backslashes, although one backslash is often sufficient. Single backslashes are acceptable in print commands if they are used before characters that are not control characters. Here, single backslashes are used without problem:

169

```
print "Look in directory \home\mystuff\zipfiles."
Look in directory \home\mystuff\zipfiles.
```

In the commands in Figure 10.18, backslashes must be doubled so control sequences will not be interpreted. With only one backslash after the colon, Qshell interprets the \t sequence as a tab. Doubling the backslash doesn't solve the problem, although it might seem that it should. It is only by coding three backslashes that a single backslash is printed to stdout.

```
print "Look in directory c:\temp\mystuff\zipfiles."
Look in directory c:     emp\mystuff\zipfiles.
/home/JSMITH $
print "Look in directory c:\\temp\mystuff\zipfiles."
Look in directory c:     emp\mystuff\zipfiles.
/home/JSMITH $
print "Look in directory c:\\\temp\mystuff\zipfiles."
Look in directory c:\temp\mystuff\zipfiles.
/home/JSMITH $
```

Figure 10.18: If the character following the backslash is a control character, you will have to code three backslashes to print one.

Printf

The *printf* utility is based on C's *printf* function. It differs from the *print* utility in several ways:

- *Printf* provides a way to format the way variables are printed.

- *Printf* does not automatically generate an end-of-line sequence when it writes. If you want to advance to a new line, you must include a \n control sequence in the format string.

- *Printf* does not support the *print* options. For instance, you cannot use the *-u* option to direct print to a certain file; you have to use a file descriptor with redirection operators.

The syntax of *printf* is as follows:

```
printf format [ argument... ]
```

You must provide at least one argument—a format string—to *printf*. The format string may contain plain text, control characters, and special formatting sequences.

Printf supports the control sequences that *print* supports. That is, you can use \t to tab, \b to backspace, and so on. Again, the *printf* utility does not issue a linefeed after printing unless there is a \n sequence in the format string.

Arguments are matched with formatting sequences from left to right. If there are fewer arguments than formatting sequences, *printf* reuses formatting sequences as often as necessary. In Figure 10.19, for example, there are two conversion characters in the format string, but four arguments following the conversion string. *Printf* uses the format string twice.

```
a=12
/home/JSMITH $
b=28
/home/JSMITH $
c=25
/home/JSMITH $
d=7
/home/JSMITH $
printf "%d %e\n" $a $b $c $d
12 2.800000e+01
25 7.000000e+00
/home/JSMITH $
```

Figure 10.19: Printf reuses the format string as necessary.

The format of a conversion-formatting sequence defines how a value appears in output. Its syntax is as follows:

```
%[flags][width][.precision]conversion
```

Since the percent sign indicates the beginning of a format sequence, you must code two percent signs in order to print one. In addition to the percent sign, you must include a conversion character to tell *printf* how to format an argument. The acceptable conversion characters are listed in Table 10.3. For example, *%d* means that a number is to be printed in decimal format, while *%o* means a number is to be printed in octal format.

Table 10.3: Conversion Characters

Character	Description	Acceptable Data Types
c	Unsigned character	Character
d	Signed decimal number	Integer
e, E	Scientific notation	Real
f	Real number	Real
g, G	Scientific notation with significant digits	Real
i	Signed decimal number	Integer
o	Unsigned octal number	Integer
s	String	Character
u	Unsigned decimal number	Integer
x (lowercase)	Unsigned hexadecimal number with lowercase *a* to *f*	Integer
X (uppercase)	Unsigned hexadecimal number with uppercase *A* to *F*	Integer

You may use the optional portions of the formatting sequence—flags, width, and precision—to further modify the appearance of the output. The five flags are used only with numeric values. You may use more than one of them in a format sequence. The flags and their meanings are listed in Table 10.4.

Table 10.4: Formatting Flag Values

Flag	Description
space	Precede a positive value with a space, a negative value with a minus sign.
+	Precede a positive value with a plus sign, negative values with a minus sign.
- (hyphen)	Left-justify the output.
0 (zero)	Display leading zeros.
#	Precede octal numbers with zero.
	Precede hexadecimal numbers with 0x or 0X.
	For real numbers, display the decimal point.
	For *g* or *G*, display trailing zeros.

The width is the minimum number of characters to be sent to output. If you code an asterisk (*), the width is taken from the next argument. The function of the precision depends on the conversion character, as shown in Table 10.5.

Table 10.5: Precision Characters

Character	Description
d, i, o, u, x, X	Minimum number of digits to be displayed
e, E, f	Number of decimal digits to be displayed
g, G	Maximum number of significant digits
s	Maximum number of characters to be displayed

The next several pages provide examples of the *printf* utility. In the following lines, the variable *price* has the value 19250.2:

```
print $price
19250.2
/home/JSMITH $
printf "$%-.2f\n" $price
$19250.20
```

The *print* utility displays this value with the minimum number of needed digits. The *printf* utility shows two decimal digits because of the precision entry. Both utilities left-adjust the value. *Print* does so by default. *Printf* left-adjusts because of the minus sign.

In the following example, *printf* right-aligns the value of the variable within a field width of 14 digits:

```
print $price
19250.2
printf "$%14.2f\n" $price
$       19250.20
```

Because of the precision, *printf* displays two digits after the decimal point.

In the case of integer values, the precision value specifies the minimum number of digits to be displayed, as shown here:

```
print $count
4
/home/JSMITH $
printf "%.4d\n" $count
0004
```

In this case, the minimum number of digits to display is four.

The asterisk character (*) tells *printf* that the field width is specified in the next argument. In the following example, the field width is four and the value to be printed is seven:

```
printf "%0*d\n" 4 7
0007
```

Here, *printf* right-aligns the value of variable age within a width of 15 characters:

```
print $age
45
/home/JSMITH $
printf "%15i\n" $age
             45
```

When combined with command substitution, *printf* can place edited values into Qshell variables. *Command substitution* is a technique whereby the output of a command is substituted for the command itself. To tell Qshell to use command substitution, enclose the command within parentheses and precede the open parenthesis with a dollar sign:

```
amount=$(printf "$%-12.4f" $price)
/home/JSMITH $
echo "/$amount/"
/$19250.2000   /
```

The *f* in the format string means that the value is to be printed as a floating-point (real) number. The *12* refers to the overall length of the number, including sign and decimal positions. The *4* means that four decimal positions are to be shown. The hyphen means that the number is left-adjusted within the 12 positions. When the dollar sign, which is not part of the formatting sequence, is placed in front of the number, the total length is 13.

Echo

The easiest to use (and least powerful) of the output utilities is *echo*, which sends one or more arguments, followed by an end-of-line sequence, to stdout. The word *echo* can be followed by one or more arguments separated by white space. An argument can be a quoted string, an unquoted string, or a variable. In Figure 10.20, the *lang* variable is interpreted unless surrounded by single quotes.

```
lang=RPG
/home/JSMITH $
echo $lang rulz!
RPG rulz!
/home/JSMITH $
echo "$lang rulz!"
RPG rulz!
/home/JSMITH $
echo '$lang rulz!'
$lang rulz!
/home/JSMITH $
```

Figure 10.20: Echo is easy to use, but not as powerful as print.

Print is superior to *echo* in two ways:

- *Print* allows options.

- *Print* can interpret control commands within the arguments it sends to output files.

Dspmsg

The Display Message (*dspmsg*) utility is a sort of soft-coded *printf* command. This feature was designed to make it easier to use scripts with different national languages. Instead of hard-coding messages in your scripts, you store messages in a message catalog and use *dspmsg* to retrieve them. If you decide to run your scripts in an environment where people use another language, you can translate the messages without having to modify the scripts.

You'll need a message catalog to hold the messages. Creating a message file is not unlike traditional iSeries programming. Enter the source-code directives into a member of a source physical file member and compile it. Table 10.6 explains the directives.

Table 10.6: Message Catalog Directives

Directive	Description
quote *C*	Replace *C* with the character that will be used to delimit message text. By default, there is no message-text delimiter, and therefore no way to include trailing blanks in message text.
set *n comment*	Replace *n* with an integer number to be assigned to a set of messages. You may add a comment.
delset *n comment*	Replace *n* with the number of a message set that is to be removed from the message catalog. You may add a comment.

The source member follows these rules:

- Blank lines are ignored.
- Comments begin with a dollar sign and space.
- Directives begin with a dollar sign that is not followed by a blank.
- Message text begins with a number.

The example source member in Figure 10.21 is shown in a browse session of SEU. The first line is a comment because it begins with a dollar sign and a space. The second line says that the double quote is used as a quotation character to delimit the message text. The third line indicates that the following messages are in set 1. Lines 4.00 through 13.00 define the messages of set 1. The remainder of the source member defines message set 2.

```
Columns  . . . :     1  71            Browse           JSMITHS/SRC
  SEU==>                                                MYMSGCAT
         *************** Beginning of data ***********************
0001.00 $ My message catalog
0002.00 $quote "
0003.00 $set 1
0004.00 1 "File %s not found.\n"
```

Figure 10.21: Use SEU or another editor to enter message text (part 1 of 2).

```
0005.00 2 "Directory %s not found.\n"
0006.00 3 "File %s is a directory.\n"
0007.00 4 "File %s is not a directory.\n"
0008.00 8 "File name was not specified.\n"
0009.00 11 "File name %1$s cannot be created in directory %2$s \
0010.00 because %2$s does not exist.\n"
0011.00 999 "Unexpected error in script %s \n\
0012.00 \t User: %s \n\
0013.00 \t Time: %s \n"
0014.00 $set 2
0015.00 1 "Directory name was not specified. Enter it now."
0016.00 2 "File %s was not found.\n"
0017.00 21 "The number of files cannot be more than %ld.\n"
        ******************* End of data *************************
```

Figure 10.21: Use SEU or another editor to enter message text (part 2 of 2).

You may continue a message by ending all but the last line with a backslash. Messages 11 and 999 of set 1 in Figure 10.21 are continued messages. Message 11 spans two lines of source code; message 999 spans three.

Notice the *%s* and *%ld* sequences. These are placeholders for arguments. Qshell will replace these strings with the arguments you specify when you display a message. If you want a specific argument, follow the percent sign with the ordinal number of the argument and a dollar sign. For instance, *%3$s* on line 9.00 means that the third argument is to be displayed as a string. If you omit the ordinal number and dollar sign, Qshell fills in the arguments in the order you specify them. Table 10.7 provides a quick reference of the placeholders.

Table 10.7: Placeholder Sequences Recognized by Dspmsg

Sequence	Description
%ld	Displays the next argument as an integer
%s	Displays the next argument as a string
%n$ld	Displays the *n*th argument as an integer
%n$s	Displays the *n*th argument as a string

You may also include certain control sequences like those used with *print* and *printf*. The control sequences are listed in Table 10.8. You should end all messages with a \n sequence. If you do not, Qshell will not advance to a new line of output after displaying the message.

Table 10.8: Control-Character Sequences Recognized by Dspmsg

Sequence	Description
\b	Backspaces one character
\f	Formfeed (clears the screen)
\n	Newline (carriage return and linefeed)
\r	Return (carriage return, but no linefeed; returns to beginning of the line)
\t	Tab
\\	Prints one backslash character
\x	EBCDIC character; *x* is a one-, two-, or three-digit octal number

To create or update the message catalog from a source physical file member, use either CL's Generate Message Catalog command (GENCAT) or the Merge Message Catalog command (MRGMSGCLG). The two commands are identical in function. The following command creates a message catalog called mymsgcat in directory /home/jsmith from the source in member MYMSGCAT in MYLIB/MYSRC:

```
GENCAT +
    CLGFILE('/home/jsmith/mymsgcat') +
    SRCFILE('/qsys.lib/mylib.lib/mysrc.file/mymsgcat.mbr')
```

Once the message catalog has been created, you can use Qshell's *dspmsg* utility to write to stdout. Here is the syntax of the *dspmsg* utility:

```
dspmsg [-n] [-s set] catalog msgid [ defaultMsg [ arguments... ] ]
```

The -*n* option prevents Qshell from interpreting the placeholder sequences. The -*s* option tells which message set contains the message to be displayed. The default value is one. Neither option is required. The catalog and msgid parameters, however, *are* required. The catalog name is the one you specified in the CLGFILE parameter of GENCAT or MRGMSGCLG. The message ID comes from the message catalog source code.

The default message is the string to be displayed if the message does not exist. If you do not wish to specify a default message, but do want to specify arguments, use a dummy default message. The arguments to be passed to the message, if there are any, are specified last.

Here is a basic example of *dspmsg*:

```
dspmsg mymsgcat 8
File name was not specified.
```

This command displays message 8 of set 1. Since the -s option is not used, set 1 is assumed.

The following example displays message 8 of set 1, if it exists. If it does not exist, the string *Message not found* is displayed:

```
dspmsg mymsgcat 8 'Message not found'
File name was not specified.
/home/JSMITH $
```

The following example displays message 45 of set 1, if it exists. If it does not exist, it displays *Message not found* and advances to a new line because of the \n option:

```
dspmsg mymsgcat 45 'Message not found\n'
Message not found
/home/JSMITH $
```

The next several examples involve placeholders. This command replaces the *%s* placeholder with the string *mydata.txt*:

```
dspmsg -s 1 mymsgcat 1 'Message not found\n' mydata.txt
File mydata.txt not found.
```

This command replaces the *%s* placeholders with the name of the script, the name of the user, and the current date:

```
dspmsg -s 1 mymsgcat 999 'Message not found\n' $0 $LOGNAME "$(date)"
Unexpected error in script /home/jsmith/myscript.qsh
        User: JSMITH
        Time: Wed Dec 25 11:32:23  2002
```

To substitute a particular value for the placeholder, use a command like this:

```
dspmsg -s 2 mymsgcat 21 'Message not found\n' 12
The number of files cannot be more than 12.
```

Message 21 of set 2 is displayed, with the *%ld* placeholder replaced by the value 12.

Finally, this example displays message 11 of set 1, replacing the *%1$s* placeholder with the value *myfile.text* and both instances of the *%2$s* placeholder with the value *mydir*:

```
dspmsg -s 1 mymsgcat 11 'Message not found\n' myfile.txt mydir
File name myfile.txt cannot be created in directory mydir
    because mydir does not exist.
```

Read

The *read* utility reads a line of data from a file and assigns the data to one or more variables. By default, *read* accepts data from the keyboard.

The *read* utility is Qshell's only input utility. The syntax of *read* is as follows:

---

read [**-r**] [**-p** *prompt*] [**-u** [*n*]] [*name...*]

The three options are listed and briefly explained in Table 10.9.

Table 10.9: "Read" Options

Option	Description
-r	Do not treat the backslash as a continuation character.
-p	Display a prompt string.
-u	Read from a certain file descriptor (unit).

Shell scripts most often read text data, not binary data. That is, Qshell reads everything up to an end-of-line character (usually a linefeed character, but sometimes a carriage return and linefeed sequence) as a record. If a line ends with a backslash (\) followed immediately by the end-of-line sequence, Qshell assumes that the input data is continued on the next record of input. However, if you use the *-r* option, the backslash is not treated as a continuation character.

For example, the following file contains four records, but Qshell will read them as three records if the *-r* option is not specified:

```
This is one record.
This is \
the second record.
This is the third record.
```

The *read* utility places the retrieved data into one or more variables. Do not precede the variable names with a dollar sign! If you do not list at least one variable, *read* places the data into variable REPLY.

The *read* utility separates the contents of the record into fields. By default, fields are separated by white space—one or more blanks, tabs, or newline characters. *Read* fills in the variables with the field values until it runs out of data or variables. If there are more data values than variables, all remaining data values are placed in the last variable.

The script fragment in Figure 10.22 reads text records, breaking the fields on white space.

```
while read name birthmonth birthday phone dog wife rest
  do
    print " Name:    " $name
    print " Dog:     " $dog
    print " Born:    "
    print " Month:   " $birthmonth
    print " Day:     " $birthday
    print " Phone:   " $phone
    print " Wife:    " $wife
    print " Rest:    " $rest
done
```

Figure 10.22: By default, the read utility assumes fields are separated by white space.

Figure 10.23 lists a line of input that could be used for this script, and what the output would look like. Notice that the birth month and day values must be read into two separate values, because they are separated with white space. Notice also that the wife's second name, *Sue*, is placed in the *rest* variable, not included in the *wife* variable as it should be. The *rest* variable serves as a catch-all for the last three values.

```
Input:

Chuck       Dec 25    444-2345 Blue     Mary Sue      12     $2.50

Output:

    Name:     Chuck
    Dog:      Blue
    Born:
```

Figure 10.23: The read utility places remaining fields into the last input variable (part 1 of 2).

```
Month:   Dec
Day:     25
Phone:   444-2345
Wife:    Mary
Rest:    Sue 12 $2.50
```

Figure 10.23: *The* read *utility places remaining fields into the last input variable (part 2 of 2).*

Since values often include spaces, Qshell provides a way to use some other character as a field separator. The field separator is a predefined Qshell variable called *IFS*, for Internal Field Separators. Do not confuse this with the Integrated File System, which is also often called the IFS. When you see the term *IFS* in this book or other Qshell literature, you should be able to tell from context which one the author is referring to. To try to minimize the confusion, this book refers to the Integrated File System as *the IFS* and to the Internal Field Separators variable as *the IFS variable*.

By default, the IFS variable has a value of a single binary zero. This special value tells Qshell that fields are to be separated by white-space characters. To change the value of the IFS variable to another character, such as a comma, use the Qshell assignment operator, as with any other variable:

```
IFS=','
```

Since the input data is now separated by commas rather than white space, the previous script must be modified, as shown in Figure 10.24.

```
while read name birthday phone dog wife rest
  do
     print " Name:    " $name
     print " Dog:     " $dog
     print " Born:    " $birthday
     print " Phone:   " $phone
     print " Wife:    " $wife
     print " Rest:    " $rest
done
```

Figure 10.24: *The revised script is written with the assumption that input is comma-delimited.*

Notice that the birth date is now one field, not two. The revised input and corresponding output are shown in Figure 10.25. Now, the birth date and wife's name are correctly interpreted during the read.

```
Input:

Chuck,Dec 25,444-2345,Blue,Mary Sue,12,$2.50

Output:

    Name:     Chuck
    Dog:      Blue
    Born:     Dec 25
    Phone:    444-2345
    Wife:     Mary Sue
    Rest:     12 $2.50
```

Figure 10.25: Here is the comma-delimited input and the corresponding output.

Finally, the *read* utility's *-p* option allows a prompt string to be displayed on standard error:

```
read -p "Please enter your name:" name
```

You will probably not find much use for this option, because the prompt only displays when the script is run with the source (dot) utility, and the source utility is not the way you will usually want to run Qshell scripts.

FILE DESCRIPTORS

A file descriptor is a single-digit integer that is assigned to an open file. Input and output operations always reference the file descriptor, not the actual file name. Qshell uses file descriptors 0, 1, and 2 for stdin, stdout, and stderr respectively. All three of these file descriptors are assigned to the terminal unless redirected to other files.

Taking explicit control of the file descriptors in a shell script is a rather infrequently used and somewhat complex feature. You might wonder why you would use this feature.

You might need to maintain access to many open files for input and output at the same time. You might be trying to retrofit existing programs or tools that use file or socket descriptors. You might be trying to swap devices so that an application's input and output descriptors match some reasonably complex requirements.

In some cases, the simpler solution of common redirection will serve you well. In other cases, you might need to take direct control of the file descriptors that Qshell maintains and uses for the utilities it invokes.

Redirection Operators

File descriptors 3 through 9 are available for you to use as you wish. To use these file descriptors, you must use the redirection operators listed in Table 10.10. The letters *m* and *n* in the table represent file-descriptor numbers.

Table 10.10: File-Descriptor Redirection Operators

Operator	Description
[n]<	Redirect input.
[n]<&m	Duplicate input. (Merge input streams.)
[n]<&-	Close input.
[n]<<, [n]<<-	Open a "here" document.
[n]>	Replace output.
[n]>|	Replace output; ignore the noclobber option.
[n]>>	Append output.
[n]>&m	Duplicate output (Merge output streams.)
[n]>&-	Close output.

At least some of these should look familiar to you because Table 10.10 is a more complete version of Table 10.1. The file descriptor preceding the redirection operator is optional. If you do not code a file descriptor, Qshell assumes file-descriptor 0 for input operations and file-descriptor 1 for output operations.

Therefore, the following two *tr* commands are equivalent:

```
tr  [:lower:]  [:upper:]  <goodoleboys.txt  >upper.txt
tr  [:lower:]  [:upper:]  0<goodoleboys.txt 1>upper.txt
```

The Ulimit Utility

One of the features added to V5R2 Qshell was the *ulimit* utility, which displays or sets system resources. The *n* option allows you to display or set the maximum number of file descriptors that a process can open, as in the following example:

```
ulimit -n
200
/home/jsmith $
```

Opening and Closing File Descriptors

To open and close files under file descriptors for the current Qshell session or running script, use the *exec* utility with the open and close redirection operators. Here are some examples:

- Open file goodoleboys.txt for input as file descriptor 3:

```
exec 3<goodoleboys.txt
```

- Open a file as input under file descriptor 9 that is named in positional parameter 1:

```
exec 9<$1
```

- Open stdin (file descriptor 0) to file temp.txt:

```
exec < temp.txt
```

- Close stdin (file descriptor 0):

```
exec <&-
```

- Close stdout (file descriptor 1):

```
exec >&-
```

- Close the file opened under file descriptor 3:

```
exec 3<&-
```

- Open file descriptor 7, assigning it to stdout:

```
exec 7>&1
```

Notice that an ampersand, not a dollar sign, precedes the numeral 1. Both file descriptors 1 and 7 point to stdout. The two output streams are merged.

- Assign stderr to wherever stdout is assigned. The two output streams are merged:

```
exec 2>&1
```

You can use the *test* utility to determine whether or not a file descriptor is open and associated with a terminal, as the following example shows:

```
if [ -t 0 ]
then
      print "Enter name,age,phone."
fi
```

If stdin is assigned to the keyboard, Qshell displays the message "Enter name, age, phone." However, if stdin is redirected to another file or if input is coming from a pipe, Qshell does not output the prompting message.

Input through File Descriptors

To read from a file, use the *read* utility with the *-u* option. Follow the *-u* with the number of the file descriptor from which to read. You can separate the option and the file descriptor number, but you don't have to, so the following two commands are equivalent:

```
read -u 5 line
read -u 5 line
```

Output through File Descriptors

There are two ways to write to a file descriptor: an easy way and an easier way. You need to know both methods because the easy way works in all cases, but the easier way only works with the *print* utility.

The easier way is to specify the file descriptor number in the *-u* (unit) option of the *print* utility:

```
print -u 3 $name
```

The easy method is to use a duplication redirection operator (>) with any Qshell command that writes to stdout. Follow the > operator with an ampersand and a file descriptor number. Think of the ampersand as meaning "whatever is assigned to." So, you might read the string *>&3* as "write to whatever is assigned to file descriptor 3." The > operator usually clears the file, but for file descriptors 3 and above, Qshell appends the data instead.

Since both methods work for *print*, the following two statements do the same thing:

```
print -u 7 $name
print $name >&7
```

Each command writes the value in the variable name to the file opened under file descriptor 7.

In Figure 10.26, the first *exec* opens member TEMP in source physical file JSMITHS/QRPGSRC for output with file descriptor 3. The two *echo* commands write to the source member. The second *exec* closes the file. The *cat* command shows that the two lines are in the source physical file member, as they should be.

```
exec 3>/qsys.lib/jsmith.lib/qrpgsrc.file/temp.mbr
echo "line 1" >&3
ecbo "line 2" >&3
exec 3>&-

cat /qsys.lib/jsmith.lib/qrpgsrc.file/temp.mbr
line 1
line 2
/home/JSMITH $
```

Figure 10.26: Qshell output is directed to a source physical file member via a file descriptor.

In the following example, if the first parameter is missing, a message is sent to stderr in order to demonstrate proper usage for the script:

```
if [ -z $1 ]
   then
      print -u2 "Usage: $(basename $0) file ..."
      exit 1
fi
```

Without the redirection operator, the *print* statement would send the output to stdout.

Figure 10.27 builds an FTP script that will be used for logging into an FTP server and exchanging files. First, it reads file tkmjzzypokrtmmoos to get the user ID and file jnnoiiesokjlxrros to get the password. It uses file descriptor 3 for both files, as well as the ftpmodel file, which contains the miscellaneous FTP commands. When it encounters the special commands **get* and **put* in the model file, the script reads the names of files to get and put from two other files, ftpgetlist.txt and ftpputlist.txt. All output is sent to stdout.

```
#!/bin/qsh

# get user id from text file tkmjzzypokrtmmoos
exec 3<tkmjzzypokrtmmoos
read -u 3 id
exec 3<&-

# get password from text file jnnoiiesokjlxrros
exec 3<jnnoiiesokjlxrros
read -u 3 pass
exec 3<&-

# build signon record for remote ftp
print $id $pass

# read ftp commands from model file ftpmodel.txt
exec 3<ftpmodel.txt
while read -u3 modelline
    do
        if [ "$modelline" = '*put' ] ; then
            exec 4<ftpputlist.txt
            while read -u4 dline
                do
                    print put $dline
                done

            exec 4<&-
        elif [ "$modelline" = '*get' ] ; then
            exec 4<ftpgetlist.txt
            while read -u4 dline
                do
                    print get $dline
                done
            exec 4<&-
        else
            print $modelline
        fi
    done
exec 3<&-

# normal end
exit 0
```

Figure 10.27: This script builds an FTP script from five IFS files.

Figure 10.28 shows the input files and the output produced by the script in Figure 10.27.

191

```
Input: tkmjzzypokrtmmoos

myid

Input: jnnoiiesokjlxrros

mypass

Input: ftpmodel.txt

namefmt 1
lcd /home/mydir
cd /home/yourdir
*put
*get
quit

Input: ftpgetlist.txt

inputa
inputb

Input: ftpputlist.txt

data1
data2
data3
data4
data5

Output:

myid mypass
namefmt 1
lcd /home/mydir
cd /home/yourdir
put data1
put data2
put data3
put data4
put data5
get inputa
get inputb
quit
```

Figure 10.28: Here is the input and output of the ftpbuild.qsh script.

Redirection and Compound Statements

Qshell permits redirection with scripts, compound statements, and sub-shells, as well as with individual statements. Using redirection a single time can improve the performance of multiple statement operations by avoiding additional Qshell file operations.

The following two examples of using *while* loops with redirection operators are functionally equivalent.

```
while read line
do echo $line >> temp.txt
done   <goodoleboys.txt
while read line
do echo $line
done   <goodoleboys.txt >> temp.txt
```

The content of file goodoleboys.txt is appended to the output file temp.txt one line at a time. The first example redirects the output of the *echo* command, while the second redirects the output of the entire loop. The example that does the redirection of the entire loop is much faster because it only opens the output file once. The other example causes Qshell to process ten file-open requests.

You may direct input and/or output by placing the redirection after the *done* end-of-loop delimiter or at the end of any other multi-statement block.

Figure 10.29 shows the use of redirection operators with *for* loops. The first loop numbers and lists the positional parameters. The second loop is identical to the first, except that the output of the loop is piped into the *sort* utility.

The example in Figure 10.30 is identical to Figure 10.27, except that file descriptors are not used. Instead, stdin and stdout are redirected with each command, including the loops.

```
pos=0
for i
    do
        let pos=pos+1
        echo $i \($pos\)
    done
mydata.txt   (1)
yourdata.txt  (2)
hisdata.txt  (3)
herdata.txt  (4)
ourdata.txt  (5)
theirdata.txt  (6)

pos=0
for i
    do
        let pos=pos+1
        echo $i \($pos\)
    done | sort
herdata.txt  (4)
hisdata.txt  (3)
mydata.txt   (1)
ourdata.txt  (5)
theirdata.txt  (6)
yourdata.txt  (2)
```

Figure 10.29: Qshell permits redirection of the output produced within any loop.

```
#!/bin/qsh

# get user id from text file tkmjzzypokrtmmoos
read id <tkmjzzypokrtmmoos

# get password from text file jnnoiiesokjlxrros
read pass <jnnoiiesokjlxrros

# build signon record for remote ftp
print $id $pass

# read ftp commands from model file ftpmodel.txt
while read modelline
    do
        if [ "$modelline" = '*put' ] ; then
```

Figure 10.30: Like the script in Figure 10.27, this script produces an FTP script. However, this script uses redirection of loops rather than file descriptors (part 1 of 2).

```
        while read dline
            do
                print put $dline
            done <ftpputlist.txt
    elif [ "$modelline" = '*get' ] ; then
        while read dline
            do
                print get $dline
            done <ftpgetlist.txt
    else
        print $modelline
    fi
done <ftpmodel.txt

# normal end
exit 0
```

Figure 10.30: Like the script in Figure 10.27, this script produces an FTP script. However, this script uses redirection of loops rather than file descriptors (part 2 of 2).

SUMMARY

Qshell is well suited to processing stream files. The primary stream files Qshell uses are standard input, standard output, and standard error. These three files may be redirected to disk files, or they may be piped to other commands. Piping and redirection are the result of programs called *filters*, which make it possible to develop complex applications by joining specialized programs and scripts in sequence.

Qshell includes five utilities that are designed especially for input and output operations. The use of file descriptors enables Qshell to work with more than three files at one time. Qshell also provides an easy way to redirect the output of a loop.

Chapter 11

Command-Line Arguments

As mentioned in chapter 5, the terms *argument* and *parameter* are sometimes used interchangeably in both OS/400 and Unix. However, in this book, we try to be precise in the use of these and related terms:

- An *argument* is a value that is supplied to a called program or script.

- A *parameter* is a value that is received into a program or script.

- An *option*, also called a *switch*, is an argument preceded by a hyphen.

- An *argument of an option* is a non-option value that immediately follows an option.

CONVENTIONAL RULES

Command-line arguments follow a command name. They control the behavior of a script or supply additional information to a script. Arguments are separated from the command name, and from one another, by white space. In the following example, three arguments are supplied to myscript.qsh:

```
myscript.qsh  -n -o mydata.dat
```

Notice the two options that begin with hyphens. Options are typically used to control the behavior of a script, whereas other arguments ("non-options") supply data values to the script.

In script programming, the order in which the options are specified on the command line should not matter. For example, both of the following commands should produce the same results:

```
myscript.qsh   -n -o mydata.dat
myscript.qsh   -o -n mydata.dat
```

Options can also be grouped together behind one hyphen, so the following commands should be equivalent to the previous two:

```
myscript.qsh   -no mydata.dat
myscript.qsh   -on mydata.dat
```

It is up to you, the programmer, to make sure a script can handle any of these forms.

It is also common in Unix shell programming to permit the use of a double hyphen (--) to indicate the end of the options and the beginning of the "non-options." In the following example, the *n* option is specified. The value *mydata.dat* is an argument, but it is not an option argument:

```
myscript.qsh     -n  --  mydata.dat
```

In Figure 11.1, the first *print* command fails because the value of *c*, -3, is interpreted as an option. The second *print* succeeds because the double hyphen tells Qshell that the remaining arguments on the command line are not to be interpreted as options.

```
a=5  b=7
/home/JSMITH $
let c=a-b
/home/JSMITH $
print $c
print: 001-0036 Option 2 is not valid.
/home/JSMITH $
print -- $c
-2
```

Figure 11.1: Qshell might mistake negative numbers for options.

An option may also take an argument of its own. Consider the following example:

```
myscript.qsh  -n  -f  mydata.dat  -p  mydata.prn  -z
```

Four options are passed to the script: *n*, *f*, *p*, and *z*. The *f* option takes the argument *mydata.dat*. The *p* option takes the argument *mydata.prn*. The *n* and *z* options do not take arguments of their own.

EXTRACTING ARGUMENT VALUES

When you write a script, you have to consider two things about arguments:

- Will the script accept option arguments?
- Will the script require a fixed number of arguments?

The following sections present three cases that illustrate these issues.

Case 1: Fixed Number of Non-Option Arguments

The easiest case is when there is a fixed number of arguments and none of them are options. In this case, the meaning of each argument is determined by its position in the list. For example, the following two commands are not equivalent because the order of the arguments determines their meaning:

```
myscript.qsh    mydata.dat      yourdata.dat
myscript.qsh    yourdata.dat    mydata.dat
```

When the script begins, use the special parameter $# to be sure the correct number of arguments was passed. If there were too few or too many, send a message to stderr and exit with a non-zero status code.

The following example verifies that exactly three arguments are passed to the script:

```
# make sure correct number of arguments was passed
if [ "$#" -ne 3 ]
    then echo "Usage: ${0#$PWD/} pattern fromfile tofile" >&2
        exit 1
fi
```

If too many or two few arguments are passed to the script, the script sends an error message to stderr and exits with an exit status of 1.

Case 2: Variable Number of Non-Option Arguments

It is likewise easy to handle the situation in which there is a variable number of arguments and none of them are options. You must test the parameters and take action accordingly. The best way to test for the presence of absence of an argument is with the *n* and *z* options of the extended conditional expression.

In the following example, Qshell writes the value of variable *somevar* to the file named in the second parameter if this parameter has a length that is not zero (i.e., at least two arguments were passed to the script):

```
if [[ -n "$2" ]]
    then echo $somevar >$2
fi
```

If the user passed only one argument, the *echo* would not be carried out.

If your release supports it, use the extended conditional construct with the *n* conditional option. There are two reasons for this. First, the extended conditional is faster than the *test* utility. Second, when used in *test*, the variable expansion must be in double quotes for this code to work correctly. If the double quotes are omitted, the expression will prove true whether or not the second parameter has a value, as in this example:

```
if [ -n $2 ]                    # < ----- ERROR !!!!!!!
    then echo $somevar >$2
fi
```

If parameter 2 is *b*, the expression evaluates to [-n *b*], which proves true. If parameter 2 has no value, the expression evaluates to [-n], which also proves true. To avoid this problem, surround the parameter-substitution expression in double quotes.

Here's another example. Up to 255 arguments may be passed to the following script:

```
while [ $1 ]
    do
        cp $1 $1.bu
        shift
    done
```

Each argument should be a file name. Each file is copied to another file, whose name is the same, but with a suffix of *.bu*. For example, file xyz.txt is copied to file xyz.txt.bu.

Case 3: Options and the Getops Utility

The last case to consider is that of using options. Options must precede the non-option arguments. The usual method for handling options is to process the option arguments first, shift them out, then process the remaining arguments, as in the previous two cases.

This is a task you should not attempt to do by hand. There are two possibilities to consider, which makes for messy programming:

1. The options may have been entered singly, or one or more options may have been grouped behind a single hyphen. For example, the following are all equivalent:

```
myscript.qsh –dx
myscript.qsh -d –x
myscript.qsh -xd
```

2. An argument to an option may be joined to the option letter or separated by white space:

```
myscript.qsh -f somefile.txt
myscript.qsh -fsomefile.txt
```

The *getopts* utility makes easy work of processing the options. Here is its syntax:

```
getopts   option-string   variable
```

The option string lists the expected options, with no preceding hyphen. Follow an option that takes an argument of its own with a colon (:). For example, the following script is written to expect five options: *b*, *c*, *d*, *k*, and *t*. The *d* and *t* options are expected to be followed by arguments of their own:

```
while getopts bcd:kt: argname
```

Each time *getopts* is executed, Qshell returns another option from the command line. The name of the option is stored in the variable without a preceding hyphen. For example, the short script arglist.qsh in Figure 11.2 does nothing but list the options that are passed to it.

```
cat arglist.qsh
while getopts vf:l option
    do
        echo $option
    done
/home/JSMITH $
arglist.qsh -vl
v
l
/home/JSMITH $
arglist.qsh -v -l
v
l
/home/JSMITH $
arglist.qsh -l -f mydata.csv
l
f
```

Figure 11.2: The getopts *utility makes easy work of extracting options and their arguments.*

If the option is expected to have an argument, that argument's value is stored in the special variable OPTARG. If an option is not expected to have an argument following it, the value of OPTARG is undefined. Figure 11.3 shows the use of the OPTARG variable. The arglist.qsh script has been modified to list the OPTARG variable. The value of OPTARG is not defined for option *l* ("ell").

```
cat arglist.qsh
while getopts vf:l option
    do
        echo $option $OPTARG
    done
/home/JSMITH $
arglist.qsh -l -f mydata.csv
l
f mydata.csv
/home/JSMITH $
arglist.qsh -f mydata.csv -l
f mydata.csv
l mydata.csv
```

Figure 11.3: The getops *utility places an option's argument into variable OPTARG .*

You do not have to leave white space between an option and its argument, but doing so can promote readability. In Figure 11.4, the *f* option is separated from its argument in the first invocation of arglist.qsh, but not separated from its argument in the second invocation.

```
cat arglist.qsh
while getopts vf:1 option
    do
        echo $option
    done
/home/JSMITH $
arglist.qsh -f mydata.csv
f mydata.csv
/home/JSMITH $
arglist.qsh -fmydata.csv
f mydata.csv
```

Figure 11.4: Qshell allows you to leave white space between an option and its argument, but does not require you to do so.

OPTIND is another option-related special variable that you will need. Qshell uses OPTIND to keep up with its place while working through the list of options. After Qshell has finished processing all the options, OPTIND will have a value one greater than the number of arguments in the option list. For that reason, shifting OPTIND minus one argument removes all the options.

The script in Figure 11.5 permits three options: *v, f,* and *p*. The *f* option is to be followed by a file name. One or more non-option arguments may follow the options.

Two variables, *vflag* and *pflag*, are initialized to the value *off*. The *while* loop extracts the options. As each argument is processed, the *case* structure modifies at most one variable. The *vflag* and *pflag* variables are changed to *on* if the *v* and *p* options are specified. If the *f* option is found, Qshell copies the following argument, which is in variable OPTARG, into the variable *filename*. The *shift* utility drops the options, so that the first positional parameter contains the first non-option argument.

If an invalid option is entered, the last case, the wildcard character (the asterisk), is matched. The script sends a message to stderr reminding the user of the proper usage and exits with a status of 1.

```
# process the options
vflag=off
pflag=off

while getopts vf:p argname
do
   case $argname in
   v) vflag=on;;
   p) pflag=on;;
   f) filename=$OPTARG;;
   *) print -u2 "Usage: $(basename $0): [-vp] [-f file] [-] file ..."
                                    exit 1;;
   esac
done

# get rid of options
shift $OPTIND-1

# At this point, the settings of the v and p options
# are in variables vflag and pflag, the argument to the f option
# (if it was specified) is in variable filename, and the first
# non-option argument is in positional parameter 1.
```

Figure 11.5: It is customary to shift out the options after having processed them.

If *getopts* encounters an option that is not listed in the option list, or does not find an argument to an option that is followed by a colon in the option list, it sends an error to stderr. This is illustrated in Figure 11.6.

```
cat arglist.qsh
while getopts vf:1 option
   do
      echo [$option] $OPTARG
   done
/home/JSMITH $
arglist.qsh -v -w -f
[v]
getopts: 001-0036 Option w is not valid.
[?]
getopts: 001-0038 Required argument for option f is not specified.
[?]
```

Figure 11.6: The getopts *utility replaces invalid options with a question mark and sends error messages to stderr.*

Be aware that errors were originally sent to standard output. In V5R2, this was changed by a PTF so that errors would be sent to the standard error file, as occurs in Unix shells.

SUMMARY

Qshell programming relies on the presence of option and non-option arguments to control the behavior of scripts and supply scripts with necessary data values. Qshell programmers should write scripts that conform to the customary standards for passing arguments. The *getopts* utility provides an easy way to extract arguments from a command invocation.

Chapter 12

Commands

Some commands are built into the Qshell interpreter. These are called *built-in utilities*. Other commands are separate executable files, or *external commands*. Qshell must locate these files in order to execute them. The external commands supplied with Qshell are stored in directory /usr/bin. If you have installed PASE, the Portable Application Solutions Environment, which permits you to execute AIX binaries, you may also run the PASE utilities, which are stored in /QOpenSys/usr/bin.

The *type* command, which was added to Qshell in V5R2, tells you how a command is implemented. As you can see in Figure 12.1, *echo* is a built-in utility, *break* is a special built-in utility, *for* is a reserved word, and *rexec* is a file.

```
type echo
echo is a shell built-in.
/home/jsmith $
type break
break is a special shell built-in.
/home/jsmith $
type for
for is a reserved word.
/home/jsmith $
type rexec
rexec is /usr/bin/rexec.
```

Figure 12.1: Use the type command to determine how a utility is implemented.

An alternative that works in V4R4 and later releases is the *whence* utility with the *-v* option, shown in Figure 12.2.

```
whence -v echo
echo is a shell built-in.
/home/JSMITH $
whence -v continue
continue is a special shell built-in.
/home/JSMITH $
whence -v if
if is a reserved word.
/home/JSMITH $
whence -v grep
grep is /usr/bin/grep.
```

Figure 12.2: The -v option of whence tells how a utility is implemented.

Yet another alternative is *command -V*, shown in Figure 12.3. Note that the *V* must be capitalized.

```
command -V read
read is a shell built-in.
/home/jsmith $
command -V exec
exec is a special shell built-in.
/home/jsmith $
command -V do
do is a reserved word.
/home/jsmith $
command -V find
find is /usr/bin/find.
```

Figure 12.3: Command -V is equivalent to whence -v.

REGULAR AND SPECIAL BUILT-IN UTILITIES

Built-in utilities are divided into two groups: special and regular. Special built-in utilities must conform to certain POSIX standards:

- A syntax error in a special built-in utility may cause the shell to abort. A syntax error in a regular built-in may not cause the shell to abort.

■ Variable assignments must remain in effect after the utility completes. Variable assignments made during the execution of regular built-in or other utilities do not remain in effect after the utility completes.

The special built-ins for V5R2 are listed in Table 12.1. To make a special built-in utility run as if it were a regular built-in utility, run it under the *command* utility.

Table 12.1: Special Built-in Utilities

Name	Description
break	Exit the loop.
: (colon)	Interpret as a null command.
continue	Begin the next iteration of a loop.
. (dot)	Execute commands in the current environment.
eval	Construct a command from arguments.
exec	Execute commands; open, close, or copy file descriptors.
exit	Exit the shell.
export	Set the export attribute for variables.
readonly	Set the read-only attribute for variables.
return	Exit a function.
set	Set or unset positional parameters and options.
shift	Discard positional parameters.
trap	Monitor signals.
unset	Unset variables and functions.

DUAL IMPLEMENTATIONS

Some utilities are implemented as both built-in and external utilities. Qshell normally runs the built-in version. The executable file version is included for reasons of backward-compatibility with systems that did not implement the utility as a built-in.

Figure 12.4 shows that the echo utility is implemented both as a built-in and external file in Qshell. The *a* option of the *type* and *whence* utilities tell Qshell to list all implementations of a command.

```
type -a echo
echo is a shell built-in.
echo is /usr/bin/echo.
/home/jsmith $
whence -a echo
echo is a shell built-in.
echo is /usr/bin/echo.
```

Figure 12.4: *Some utilities are implemented both as built-in and external utilities. Normally Qshell will run the built-in version.*

In Figure 12.5, Qshell uses the *echo* built-in to run the first *echo* command and an external file to run the second. Both commands produce identical results, but the first one runs much faster than the second.

```
echo $QSH_VERSION
V5R2M0
/home/jsmith $
/usr/bin/echo $QSH_VERSION
V5R2M0
```

Figure 12.5: *Built-in utilities are faster than their external counterparts.*

SCRIPT INTERPRETERS

As you know, a script is a text file that contains commands. When you run a Qshell script, Qshell reads commands from the text file in the same way that it reads commands from the keyboard. That is, Qshell reads a command, interprets it, executes it, and proceeds to the next command. Scripts run in a new process, unless invoked with the source (dot) operator. For more information about scripts, see chapter 4.

However, Qshell is not the only program that can interpret scripts. When Qshell runs a script, it begins by checking the first line for a *magic number*, the

#! sequence. If the script file contains a magic number, Qshell loads the specified utility and passes the name of the script file to the utility as an argument. Figure 12.6 shows this behavior in action. The script file sayit has one record, a magic-number record that points to the external version of the *echo* utility. When Qshell executes sayit, it loads the *echo* utility and passes to it the name of the script. Thus, Qshell runs the command *sayit /home/jsmith/sayit*, which writes the name of the script to standard output.

It might be interesting to note that it is hard to write any interesting scripts using *echo*, because *echo* doesn't actually read a file passed to it and execute the commands in the file. Instead, it simply echoes the parameters—in this case, the filename.

```
cat sayit
#! /bin/echo
/home/jsmith $
sayit
/home/jsmith/sayit
/home/jsmith $
```

Figure 12.6: The echo *utility is used here as a script interpreter.*

You can use this feature to run other programs, such as your own programs and PASE utilities. Running your own programs is discussed in chapter 19. Figure 12.7 gives an example that runs a PASE utility. Notice the magic number pointing to the directory of PASE binaries. Since the C shell is a PASE utility, the script must be stored in an ASCII file and lines must end with a linefeed character, not with the carriage-return linefeed combination that is commonly in use.

If there is no magic-number record, a shell attempts to run a script file directly. For this reason, you do not need the magic number if you are using Qshell and want Qshell to run the script.

```
cat demo4.csh
#! /QOpenSys/usr/bin/csh

set file = $1

if  ( $file == "" ) then
    echo "Usage: $0 file"
    exit 1
endif

if  ( ! -f $file ) then
    echo "File $file does not exist."
    exit 2
endif
cp $file $file.ba
```

Figure 12.7: The magic number is necessary to make this C shell script run under PASE.

EXTERNAL UTILITIES AND THE MAGIC NUMBER

The external versions of built-in utilities are not worthless. You can use them to run scripts. This is not a terribly useful technique, but it does come in handy on occasion.

The traditional iSeries user interface has one control language, CL, and one shell, the CL command interpreter. Within a Qshell environment or on a Unix system, however, any program that reads the standard input file and writes to the standard output file can be used as a script interpreter, as shown in Figure 12.8.

```
ls re*
read002.qsh        removeme
/home/jsmith $
cat removeme
#! /bin/rm
/home/jsmith $
removeme
/home/jsmith $
ls re*
read002.qsh
/home/jsmith $
```

Figure 12.8: The removeme file deletes itself.

The file removeme in Figure 12.8 has one line, a magic number that executes the external version of the *rm* utility. When the removeme file is executed as a command, Qshell executes the external version of *rm* with *removeme* as its argument. The result is that Qshell deletes the removeme file. A self-deleting file is not uncommon in Unix shell scripts. The presence or absence of such files is tested to control processing within a script.

A common task in many introductory computer science classes is to write a program that can completely print its own source code. To impress your friends, you could write that program trivially using a shell script of the following form:

```
#! /bin/cat
```

No, that's not a typo. The entire shell script that prints itself is this single line, with the subtle behaviors of shell scripting behind it. Figure 12.9 provides a larger example of this concept. It does basically the same thing, but is a bit more useful and realistic in day-to-day use.

```
cat crib
#! /bin/cat
Subdirectory for EDI:                      /home/EDI
Subdirectory for our scripts:              /home/scripts
---
To reset files to re-receive EDI:          qsh runedi -r
---
To delete a directory & everything under it:  rm -r
To get date as YYYYMMDD :                  date '+%Y%m%d'
/home/jsmith $
chmod +x crib
/home/jsmith $
crib
#! /bin/cat
Subdirectory for EDI:                      /home/EDI
Subdirectory for our scripts:              /home/scripts
---
To reset files to re-receive EDI:          qsh runedi -r
---
To delete a directory & everything under it:  rm -r
To get date as YYYYMMDD :                  date '+%Y%m%d'
/home/jsmith $
```

Figure 12.9: Thanks to the magic number, the crib file lists itself to standard output.

In Figure 12.9, the user has placed reminders into an online "crib" sheet. The first command shows the contents of file "crib." Notice that the magic number runs the external version of the *cat* utility. The *chmod* command makes crib executable. The last command shows crib at work. When the user types *crib* and presses Enter, Qshell reads the magic-number line to see which program is to interpret the file. Qshell loads the external version of *cat*, passing the name of the file, *crib*, as an argument.

Even though the external utilities are in directory/usr/bin, the magic numbers in the previous examples specify /bin. The reason for specifying /bin is to be compatible with Unix systems, which store external utilities in /bin. On the iSeries, /bin is a symbolic link to /usr/bin. (Symbolic links are discussed in chapter 9.)

ALIASES

An alias is an alternate name for a command. Usually, the alias is an abbreviation of a command and one or more arguments. An alias overrides built-in and regular utilities of the same name.

To define an alias, use the *alias* utility. To remove an alias, use the *unalias* utility. These utilities are illustrated in Figure 12.10. In this example, *ll* ("long listing") is an alias for the *ls* utility with the *l* ("ell") option.

```
alias ll='ls -l'
/home/jsmith $
ll *.txt
-rwx---rwx  1 JSMITH  0            800 Oct 19 15:59 edity.txt
-rwxrwxrwx  1 JSMITH  0             43 Feb 22  2002 ftpmodel.txt
-rwxrwxrwx  1 JSMITH  0            746 Oct 22 22:18 goodoleboys.txt
-rwxrwxrwx  1 JSMITH  JSMITHGP      0 Oct 24 18:03 myfile.txt
-rw-rw-rw-  1 JSMITH  JSMITHGP     51 Oct 23 17:34 temp.txt
-rw-rw-rw-  2 JSMITH  0             7 Feb  4  2002 test1.txt
-rw-rw-rw-  2 JSMITH  0             7 Feb  4  2002 test1a.txt
/home/jsmith $
unalias ll
/home/jsmith $
ll *.txt
qsh: 001-0019 Error found searching for command ll. No such path or directory.
```

Figure 12.10: Use the alias and unalias utilities to define and undefine aliases.

V5R2 Qshell predefines three aliases, all having to do with data types:

- float='declare -E'
- functions='declare -f'
- integer='declare -i'

To display the defined aliases, use the *alias* command with no non-option arguments, as shown in Figure 12.11. The first three in this example are predefined in Qshell V5R2. The last two have been defined within the Qshell session.

```
alias
float='declare -E'
functions='declare -f'
integer='declare -i'
ll='ls -l'
path='echo $PATH'
/home/jsmith $
```

Figure 12.11: The alias *command without arguments lists the defined aliases.*

To remove all aliases, use the *unalias* command with the *a* option, as shown in Figure 12.12.

```
alias
float='declare -E'
functions='declare -f'
integer='declare -i'
ll='ls -l'
path='echo $PATH'
/home/jsmith $
unalias -a
/home/jsmith $
alias
/home/jsmith $
```

Figure 12.12: Use the unalias *utility to remove aliases.*

RESERVED WORDS

Certain tokens that are used for flow control in shell scripts are known as
reserved words. Qshell will not stop you from using them as names for your
own commands, but you should not do so. Compared to other Unix and Unix-
like shells, however, Qshell is more lenient. Many shells forbid you from naming variables with reserved-word names.

The Qshell reserved words are listed by related-command group in Table 12.2.

Table 12.2: Qshell Reserved Words

if	then	elif	else	fi
case	esac			
for	in			
While				
Until				
do	done			
{	}			
function				
[[	]]			

FUNCTIONS

A function is a set of commands grouped under a command name. Functions
correspond to subroutines, procedures, functions, and so forth in other
programming languages.

Functions are discussed in detail in chapter 13. For now, you need to know that
a function is invoked in the same way as any other command: by typing its
name.

SIMPLE AND COMPOUND COMMANDS

Unix literature differs on the definition of simple and compound commands. Some Unix sources propose a third type of command—the complex command.

For purposes of this book, a simple command is one that you can run from a Qshell prompt. A simple command may or may not include arguments, variable assignments, and redirections. Qshell reserved words are not considered to be simple commands.

Compound commands are structures made of simple commands. Compound commands allow you to do complex things without writing a script. Qshell treats a compound command as a unit. There are several types of compound commands:

- Lists of simple commands separated by semicolons
- Pipelines
- Looping structures (*while*, *until*, and *for*)
- Conditional structures (*if*, *case*, &&, and ||)
- Functions
- Scripts

For example, the following compound command renames all .txt files of a directory, changing the extension to .text:

```
for i in *.txt; do j=$(echo $i | sed -e 's/.txt/.text/');
echo $i $j; mv $i $j; done
```

THE CMD PARAMETER

To start the Qshell, use the Start Qshell command (STRQSH or QSH), as discussed in chapter 2. This command accepts one parameter: the name of a Qshell command to execute. The command may be up to 5,000 characters long. The default value of the CMD parameter is *NONE, which tells Qshell to begin an interactive session.

You may specify a Qshell command in the CMD parameter of STRQSH. For example, the following command runs Qshell in batch mode:

```
STRQSH CMD('ls *.csv')
```

When the CMD parameter contains a Qshell command, Qshell does not open a terminal session. Instead, Qshell executes the command and ends. If the command produces output, Qshell opens a temporary C runtime terminal session. This is shown in Figure 12.13.

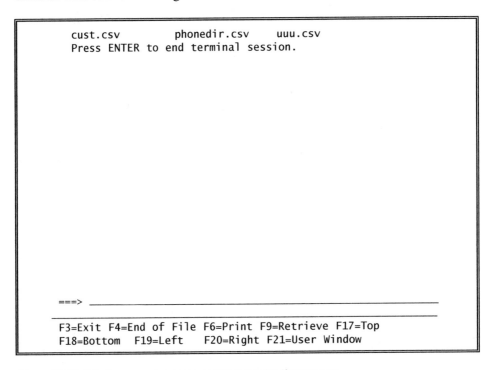

Figure 12.13: Qshell opens a temporary terminal session if necessary.

Use the QIBM_QSH_CMD_OUTPUT environment variable if you wish to direct the output elsewhere. Table 12.3 shows the possible values you can use.

Table 12.3: Acceptable Values for QIBM_QSH_CMD_OUTPUT

Value	Definition
STDOUT	Send the output to a temporary C runtime terminal session. This is the default.
NONE	Discard the output.
FILE=*pathname*	Replace the contents of the file in *pathname* with the output.
FILEAPPEND= *pathname*	Append the output to the file.

Input is another matter. When you specify a command in the CMD parameter, Qshell ignores requests for terminal input. If you want the command to read input, you must use redirection.

PROCESSES

A *process* in Unix parlance roughly corresponds to a *job* in iSeries architecture. In the case of Qshell, the two are the same for all practical purposes. A process is implemented as a job.

A process is a running program. When you start a Qshell terminal session, you start a process. A process has attributes that define it. Among these attributes are the following:

- Environment variables
- The file-creation mask
- Open files
- File redirection
- Permissions
- The current directory
- Signals

Built-in utilities, reserved word commands, functions, and "dotted" scripts run in the process from which they are invoked. To execute other commands, such as scripts and executable files, Qshell has to create other processes. The process that creates other processes is called the *parent* process. A created process is called a *child* process.

A child process inherits attributes from the parent shell. Some, such as the current directory, are inherited automatically. Others, such as variables, are not inherited unless you specify that they should be inherited. In V5R2, you can use the Display Process Status utility (*ps*) to list active processes, as shown in Figure 12.14.

```
ps
    PID DEVICE       TIME FUNCTION      STATUS    JOBID
    2398 sjsmith5   000:00 cmd-qsh       dspa      003675/jsmith/sjsmith5
    2411 -          000:00 pgm-qzshsh    evtw      003693/jsmith/qzshsh
    2414 -          000:00 pgm-qzshsh    evtw      003696/jsmith/qp0zspwp
    2415 -          000:00 pgm-ps        run       003697/jsmith/qp0zspwp
```

Figure 12.14: The ps *utility displays current processes.*

Subshells

A subshell is one type of child process. A subshell is a copy of Qshell running under another copy of Qshell. You can start a subshell by running the *qsh* command or the *sh* command from a Qshell process, or by surrounding the command name with parentheses. Use the *exit* command to end a subshell and return control to the parent.

For example, the parent process in Figure 12.15 is numbered 1981. Executing the *qsh* command appears to change nothing, as the Qshell prompt remains the dollar sign. However, the fact that another copy of Qshell is now communicating with the terminal is shown by the second *print* command, which shows that process 1982 is active. The *exit* command ends process 1982, putting process 1981 back in control of the terminal session.

```
print $$
1981
/home/jsmith $
qsh
$
print $$
1982
$
exit
/home/jsmith $
print $$
1981
/home/jsmith $
```

Figure 12.15: Use the exit command to end a subshell and return control to the parent.

In Figure 12.16, variable *name* is defined in the parent process, but its definition is not passed along to the subshell.

```
name=Joe
/home/jsmith $
print $$ $name
1981 Joe
/home/jsmith $
qsh
$
print $$ $name
1983
$
exit
/home/jsmith $
print $$ $name
1981 Joe
```

Figure 12.16: A child process cannot access the variables of the parent process.

You may use the *qsh* command with the *c* option to execute a command in a subshell. In this case, the subshell does not communicate with the terminal, but executes the command and ends. For example, in this example, Qshell creates a new shell instance to run script file myscript.qsh:

```
qsh -c myscript.qsh
```

Qshell and Child Processes

Qshell automatically starts child processes to run scripts and external commands, to process redirection and pipelines, to handle groups of commands, and to implement background processes. Surrounding a command, whether simple or compound, with parentheses forces Qshell to run the command in a child process.

In Figure 12.17, there are two compound commands that change the current directory and list directory contents. The first one runs in the current shell, but the second one, the one in parentheses, runs in a subshell. You can determine this fact by looking at the Qshell prompt that follows the output of each command, because the prompt has been set to show the name of the current directory. In the first instance, the current directory is the /bin directory. This means that the *cd* command ran in the current shell. In the second instance, the current directory is the /home/jsmith directory, which means that the *cd* command executed in a different shell.

```
/home/jsmith $
cd bin ; ls
donde.qsh          one.qsh            two
one                ten                upper.txt
/home/jsmith/bin $
cd ..
/home/jsmith $
(cd bin ; ls)
donde.qsh          one.qsh            two
one                ten                upper.txt
/home/jsmith $
```

Figure 12.17: Surrounding a command with parentheses forces execution in a separate process.

Exporting Variables to Child Processes

A child process does not automatically inherit the values of variables from the parent process. If you want child processes to inherit the value of a variable, you must set the variable's export property. For example, in Figure 12.18, the *export* keyword ensures that child processes will use the values of these variables, rather than default values.

```
cat .profile
export PATH="$PATH/home/jsmith/bin:"
export PS1='$PWD $'
export ENV=tscript.qsh
/home/jsmith $
```

Figure 12.18: It is common for the .profile file to export global variables to child processes.

If you prefer, you can assign a value to a variable and export the variable in two steps:

```
cat .profile
PATH="$PATH/home/jsmith/bin:"
export PATH
/home/jsmith $
```

You may use *set*'s allexport option to cause Qshell to set the export attribute of all variables. It has two forms:

```
set -a
set -o allexport
```

To turn off the *allexport* option, use a plus sign instead of a hyphen:

```
set -a
name='Joe Smith'
dept=Accounting
set +a
license='A2102'
```

The *name* and *dept* variables will be exported to subshells. The variable *license* will not be exported.

223

Exporting Aliases to Child Processes

Child processes do not inherit aliases defined in the parent process. If you want child processes to inherit an alias, do the following:

- Create a Qshell script file and place the alias in it.

- In the .profile file, assign the name of the file you created to the ENV environment variable and export its value.

When a new instance of Qshell begins to run, the commands in the file named by the ENV variable will be executed, as shown in Figure 12.19. The .profile file assigns a value of tscript.qsh to the ENV variable. Since this variable is exported, the tscript.qsh script will be executed each time a child process begins. Since the alias *path* is defined in tscript.qsh, this alias will be defined in all child processes.

```
cat .profile
export PATH="$PATH/home/jsmith/bin:"
export PS1='$PWD $'
export ENV=tscript.qsh
/home/jsmith $
cat tscript.qsh
alias path='echo $PATH'
```

Figure 12.19: To export an alias to a child process, define the export in the file named in the ENV environment variable.

LOCATING COMMANDS

As discussed earlier in this chapter, two or more commands may have the same name, but be implemented differently. In such a case, Qshell uses the following order of precedence to decide which implementation to run:

1. Reserved word
2. Alias
3. Special built-in
4. Function
5. Regular built-in
6. Executable file

You can override this search order to a point because of the following rules:

- The command utility ignores aliases and functions.
- The *builtin* utility will only run a built-in.
- An initial backslash ignores aliases and functions.

For example, in Figure 12.20, an *echo* function has been created. It displays all arguments, preceding them with an arrow made of two equal signs and a greater-than sign. Qshell gives precedence to this function unless *echo* is run under the built-in utility.

```
function echo ()
>
{
>
   print "==> $@"
>
}
/home/jsmith $
type -a echo
echo is a shell built-in.
echo is a function.
echo is /usr/bin/echo.
/home/jsmith $
echo $QSH_VERSION
==> V5R2M0
/home/jsmith $
builtin echo $QSH_VERSION
V5R2M0
```

Figure 12.20: Echo is a regular built-in utility, so it normally has precedence.

In Figure 12.21, an alias is created with the same name as the *ls* utility, which is an executable file in the /usr/bin directory. The alias takes precedence over the file unless the alias is preceded by a backslash.

The Path Variable

When you run an application or script, Qshell does not search all directories in the IFS. It searches only the directories listed in the PATH variable. If Qshell does not find an executable file of the proper name, it writes an error message to stderr.

```
ls *.txt
edity.txt          goodoleboys.txt   temp.txt            test1a.txt
ftpmodel.txt       myfile.txt        test1.txt
/home/jsmith $
alias ls='ls -l'
/home/jsmith $
type -a ls
ls is an alias for ls -l.
ls is /usr/bin/ls.
/home/jsmith $
ls *.txt
-rwx---rwx   1 JSMITH   0              800 Oct 19 15:59 edity.txt
-rwxrwxrwx   1 JSMITH   0               43 Feb 22  2002 ftpmodel.txt
-rwxrwxrwx   1 JSMITH   0              746 Oct 22 22:18 goodoleboys.txt
-rwxrwxrwx   1 JSMITH   JSMITHGP         0 Oct 24 18:03 myfile.txt
-rw-rw-rw-   1 JSMITH   JSMITHGP        51 Oct 23 17:34 temp.txt
-rw-rw-rw-   2 JSMITH   0                7 Feb  4  2002 test1.txt
-rw-rw-rw-   2 JSMITH   0                7 Feb  4  2002 test1a.txt
/home/jsmith $
\ls *.txt
edity.txt          goodoleboys.txt   temp.txt            test1a.txt
ftpmodel.txt       myfile.txt        test1.txt
```

Figure 12.21: Preceding the command name ls *with a backslash tells Qshell to ignore the alias.*

The PATH variable contains a list of directories that are to be searched for external files. The directories must be separated by colons. The default value for PATH is */usr/bin:*. If you want Qshell to search the current directory, you must include the current directory in the path name.

There are four ways to indicate the current directory. You can use:

1. An initial colon in the path value
2. Two adjacent colons within the path value
3. A trailing colon on the path
4. A period in the path variable

The following example uses the *print* utility to display the current path:

```
print $PATH
/usr/bin:/home/jsmith/bin:
```

In this example, there are two directories in the path. Because the path name ends with a colon, Qshell will also search the current directory after searching the directories in the path.

To define the path, assign a value to the PATH variable:

```
PATH=/:/home/jsmith:/usr/bin:/home/jsmith/bin
```

To add more directories to a path, include the $PATH expansion in an assignment to the PATH variable. Surround the assigned value with double quotes, not single quotes, so that Qshell can substitute the current path into the assignment:

```
print $PATH
/usr/bin:/home/jsmith/bin:
/home/jsmith $
PATH="$PATH/QOpenSys/usr/bin"
/home/jsmith $
print $PATH
/usr/bin:/home/jsmith/bin:/QOpenSys/usr/bin
```

The Hash Utility

The *hash* utility, shown in Figure 12.22, maintains a list of the locations of utilities. When a utility is executed for the first time in a Qshell session, *hash* searches for the utility and stores its location in a list. When the utility is later executed in the same process, Qshell does not have to look through directories for the utility, but retrieves the utility from the location named in the list.

```
hash
ls=/usr/bin/ls
donde.qsh=/home/jsmith/bin/donde.qsh
mv=/usr/bin/mv
function echo
```

Figure 12.22: The hash utility stores the locations of utilities in a list.

You may use the *-r* option of *hash* to clear the list of utility locations, as shown in Figure 12.23.

227

```
hash
rm=/usr/bin/rm
ls=/usr/bin/ls
/home/jsmith $
hash -r
/home/jsmith $
hash
/home/jsmith $
```

Figure 12.23: The -r option clears the hash table.

With V5R2, IBM added the *p* option to the *hash* utility, which allows you to store a utility's location in the list. The utility name may be different from the base file name. The syntax of *hash*'s *p* option is shown here:

```
hash -p filename utility
```

For example, in the following command, Qshell is to look for the donde.qsh script in directory /home/jsmith:

```
hash -p /home/jsmith/donde.qsh donde.qsh
```

In the following example, whenever Qshell is told to run the *wer* command, it will run script donde.qsh in directory /home/jsmith:

```
hash -p /home/jsmith/donde.qsh wer
```

RUNNING COMMANDS IN THE BACKGROUND

Unix systems allow shell commands to run in either *foreground* or *background*. When a command runs in foreground, it is in direct communication with a terminal. A background process, on the other hand, runs asynchronously. It cannot communicate directly with the terminal, and halts if it encounters an I/O request.

However, Qshell does not have the same concept of foreground and background jobs. A command that is sent to background runs asynchronously, but it continues to interact with the terminal session. This means that multiple processes may communicate with a terminal simultaneously. Therefore, it might be a good idea to redirect the input and output of background processes.

```
find /myd -exec grep -il 'print' {} \; > prt-f.txt 2>errors.txt &
[1]  1744
/myd $
ls *.txt
edity.txt        goodoleboys.txt temp.txt
errors.txt       myfile.txt       test1.txt
ftpmodel.txt     print-files.txt test1a.txt
/myd $
cat temp.txt
Junior      April 30 BR-549   Jcival Lilly Faye     12
/myd $
rm temp.txt
/myd $[1] Done find /myd -exec grep -il 'print' {} ; >prt-f.txt 2>err.txt &
/myd $
cat prt-f.txt
/myd/bin/donde.qsh
/myd/temp1/casewild.qsh
/myd/bu.qsh
/myd/casewild.qsh
/myd/demo.csh
/myd/donde.qsh
/myd/listargs.qsh
/myd/read002.qsh
/myd/select01.qsh
/myd/while001.qsh
/myd/fix2.qsh
/myd $
cat err.txt
grep: 001-0023 Error found opening file /myd/bin/one.qsh. Permission denied.
grep: 001-2113 Error found getting information for object /myd/temp.txt.
   No such path or directory.
```

Figure 12.24: It is a good practice to run long-running processes in background and direct their output to disk files.

To run a command in a background process, end the command with an ampersand (&). Qshell responds with the number and ID of the background process. When the background process is finished, Qshell sends another notification message. Since the *find* command in Figure 12.24 is expected to run a long time, it is submitted to a background process, which the system numbers as

1744. While the *find* is running, the user runs the *ls*, *cat*, and *rm* utilities. Qshell sends a message when the background job completes. At this point, the user views the output of the *find* command, which was directed to disk files.

To cancel a background process, use the *kill* command, like this:

```
find /home/smith -exec grep -il 'print' {} \;> prt-f.txt 2>errors.txt &
[1]  1893
/home/jsmith $
kill 1893
/home/jsmith $
```

When you end a Qshell session, background processes are also terminated. Use the *nohup* (No Hangup) utility to enable a process to continue to run after Qshell ends. For example, with this command, process 1979 will continue to run when the Qshell session is ended:

```
nohup find /myd -exec grep -il 'print' {} \;> prt-f.txt 2>errors.txt &
 [1]  1979
/home/jsmith $
```

The *nohup* utility was added to Qshell in V5R2.

COMMAND SUBSTITUTION

In command substitution, the output of a command replaces the command itself. It is as if the output of the command had been keyed, rather than the command itself.

There are two ways to specify command substitution. The old, and now discouraged, method is to surround the command with backquotes. The new, preferred, way is to precede the command with the *$(* string (a dollar sign followed by an open parenthesis) and close it with a close parenthesis.

Any command, utility, alias, script, or program can be used in a command-substitution expression. And, a command-substitution expression can be used anywhere—as an option, filename, string, etc.—in any part of a Qshell script. Figure 12.25 gives an example of command substitution. Qshell runs the *date* command, which prints a formatted date to standard output. The output of *date* replaces the substitution expression. The result is that the current date is inserted into the name of the incoming EDI backup file.

```
cp edi-in  edi-in-$(date '+%Y-%m-%d').bak
/home/jsmith $
ls edi*
edi-in                    edi-in-2003-01-03.bak
```

Figure 12.25: Command substitution replaces a command with its output.

THE SOURCE (DOT) UTILITY

The *source* (or dot) utility executes a script or function within the current process, not in a child process. Running a script or function under the *source* utility is equivalent to keying the commands within the current process.

The *source* utility has the following two forms:

```
. scriptname
source scriptname
```

In releases prior to V5R2, you must use the "dot" form of the *source* utility. As of V5R2, you may use either form.

A common use of the *source* utility is to initialize variables that will be used throughout the remainder of the Qshell session. Qshell uses the *source* utility to execute the .profile, etc/profile, and $ENV startup files.

The closest counterparts in traditional iSeries programming are RPG's /COPY and COBOL's COPY directives or C/C++ #include directives, which include source code at compilation, as if the contents of the copybooks or header files had been keyed directly into the source member.

An example of the *source* utility is shown in Figure 12.26. Whoami.qsh is a single-line script that prints the ID of the process in which the script is running. The interactive Qshell session is process 2399, as the *print* command shows. Running whoami.qsh without the dot operator causes Qshell to start another process, 2405. Running whoami.qsh with the dot operator causes Qshell to run the script in the current process, as if the *print* command in the script had been typed in the current process.

```
cat whoami.qsh
print "I am process $$."
/home/jsmith $
print $$
2399
/home/jsmith $
whoami.qsh
I am process 2405.
/home/jsmith $
. whoami.qsh
I am process 2399.
```

Figure 12.26: Failing to run the whoami.qsh script under the source utility produces erroneous results in this example.

In Figure 12.27, SetMyEnv.qsh is a script file that assigns values to certain variables. The first *print* command shows that the *name* and *dept* variables have no values in the current process. Running the script without the dot operator does not affect the current process. However, after running the script with the dot operator, the variables are defined.

```
cat SetMyEnv.qsh
name='Joe Smith'
firstname=Joe
lastname=Smith
dept=Accounting
/home/jsmith $
print $name $dept

/home/jsmith $
SetMyEnv.qsh
/home/jsmith $
```

Figure 12.27: Sourcing a script is a good way to assign values to frequently used variables (part 1 of 2).

```
print $name $dept
```

```
/home/jsmith $
. SetMyEnv.qsh
/home/jsmith $
print $name $dept
Joe Smith Accounting
```

Figure 12.27: Sourcing a script is a good way to assign values to frequently used variables (part 2 of 2).

THE XARGS UTILITY

The *xargs* utility (Execute Arguments) reads arguments from standard input and passes them to a command. If no command is given, *xargs* uses the *echo* command.

To understand how *xargs* works, suppose that an input stream contains four records with the values *AB*, *CD*, *EF*, and *GH*. When *xargs* reads these values, it combines them into one record of values separated by white spaces. This single record is passed as arguments to the command that is listed as *xargs'* first non-option argument. If that command were *rm*, for example, Qshell would execute the following:

```
rm AB CD EF GH
```

If no command is given, *echo* is used by default.

Figures 12.28 and 12.29 give examples of *xargs*. In Figure 12.28, *xargs* effectively combines four records into one, passing the records as arguments to *echo* (the default command).

```
cat names.txt
Joe
Bill
Bob
Arlis
/home/jsmith $
xargs <names.txt
Joe Bill Bob Arlis
/home/jsmith $
```

Figure 12.28: Xargs combines multiple records into one and passes them to a utility.

In Figure 12.29, the first *grep* command looks for the word *print* in all files of the current directory. However, it does not search subdirectories. The second *grep* does search subdirectories; however, it does not tell which file contains which lines, and it runs slowly. The reason for these problems is that the *find* command launches a new instance of *grep* for each file name it finds. The third command solves both of these problems. The names of the files found are sent to *xargs*, which passes them *en masse* to one instance of the *grep* command, as if the user had typed one *grep* and listed all of the file names as arguments.

```
grep print *
bu.qsh:      print -u2 "bu is not a directory - backup aborted."
casewild.qsh:    *  ) print -u2 "Parameter 1 is invalid."
demo.csh:print "Number of arguments: $#"
demo.csh:      printf "%3d (%s)\n" $argnbr "$1"
donde.qsh:print "I am script $0."
/home/jsmith $
find $PWD -exec grep print {} \;
print "I am script $0."
print "here i'm is"
       *  ) print -u2 "Parameter 1 is invalid."
           print -u2 "bu is not a directory - backup aborted."
       *  ) print -u2 " Parameter 1 is invalid."
print "Number of arguments: $#"
     printf "%3d (%s)\n" $argnbr "$1"
print "I am script $0."
/home/jsmith $
find . -type f -print | xargs grep print
./bin/donde.qsh:print "I am script $0."
./bin/one.qsh:print "here i'm is"
./temp1/casewild.qsh:    *  ) print -u2 "Parameter 1 is
invalid."
./bu.qsh:    print -u2 "bu is not a directory - backup aborted."
./casewild.qsh:    *  ) print -u2 "Parameter 1 is invalid."
./demo.csh:print "Number of arguments: $#"
./demo.csh:      printf "%3d (%s)\n" $argnbr "$1"
./donde.qsh:print "I am script $0."
```

Figure 12.29: The third command uses xargs to solve the problems with the previous two commands.

There's an interesting side effect of the *xargs* utility as it relates to *grep*. As shown above, when *grep* is searching more than one file, it shows the name of the file containing the match. However, when using *xargs*, there's no guarantee that the last call to *grep* will have more than one file. For example, the *find* utility might find 29 file names, and *xargs* determines that 28 of them can fit on the first *grep* command line. The second *grep* command line generated by *xargs* will contain only one file. If a match occurs in that single file, *grep* will not show the file name.

A common solution to this is to use the null file /dev/null in the *grep*. The following *xargs* command guarantees there are always two or more files in the generated *grep* command:

```
find . -type f -print | xargs grep print /dev/null
```

THE EXEC UTILITY

The *exec* utility is used primarily for controlling file descriptors, but it has another function: You may use it to replace an executing program with another program. No new process is created. This is similar to CL's Transfer Control command (TFRCTL) or the Unix-type C API that is also named exec().

When you run a command via *exec*, Qshell replaces the current copy of the Qshell interpreter with the command. When that program ends, control does not return to the Qshell interpreter. Instead, the process ends.

This matches the series of steps that Qshell goes through when creating a new process. The new process begins by running the shell, then uses *exec* to run the command passed to it, since there is no need to return to the shell.

COMMAND INTERPRETATION

Before Qshell can execute a command, it must make substitutions for certain tokens in the command. For example, all occurrences of the string *$1* must be replaced by the value of the first position's parameter. This process, known as *word expansion*, consists of four steps:

1. Tilde expansion, parameter expansion, command substitution, and arithmetic expansion

2. Field splitting

3. Path-name expansion (globbing)

4. Quote removal

Tilde expansion, parameter expansion, command substitution, and arithmetic expansion all have the same precedence. They are done as follows:

- *Tilde expansion*—Qshell replaces ~ and *~user* with the name of the user's home directory. Qshell replaces ~+ with the value of the PWD variable.

- *Parameter expansion*—Qshell replaces $*n* and ${*n*}with the value of the *n*th positional parameter. Qshell replaces $*var* and ${*var*} with the value of a variable. (Parameter expansion is discussed in chapter 6.)

- *Command substitution*—As mentioned earlier in this chapter, Qshell executes a command that is surrounded by $(and) or backquotes and replaces the command with its output.

- *Arithmetic expansion*—Qshell replaces arithmetic expressions surrounded by $((and)) with their calculated values. (Arithmetic expansion is also discussed in chapter 6.)

If the IFS variable is not null, Qshell uses the value of the IFS variable to divide the command into tokens. This process is called *field splitting*. There will not necessarily be a one-to-one correspondence between the number of delimited tokens in the original command and the number of fields resulting from field expansion, as an original token may be divided into more than one field.

Path-name expansion is more commonly known as *globbing*. This step is omitted if the noglob option has been set. (Globbing is discussed in more detail in chapter 14.)

The final step is to remove the single quote, double quote, and backslash quotation characters.

At this point, the command is passed to the Qshell interpreter for execution.

THE EVAL UTILITY

Qshell's normal method of operation is to retrieve a command, make appropriate substitutions, and execute the result. The *eval* utility causes Qshell to make two passes through the command before execution.

The *eval* utility constructs a command string, which it then passes to Qshell for execution. It is similar in concept to the QCMDEXC or the C system() API, which executes a CL command stored in a string.

For example, consider Figure 12.30. To understand how this example works, execute the *date* command by itself. If the date is January 2, 2003, *date* sends the string *sysYear=03 sysMonth=01 sysDay=02* to standard output. Notice that the string contains three perfectly good variable assignments. To get the system to execute those variable assignments, use command substitution and *eval*. Command substitution replaces the *date* command with its output, three assignment commands. The *eval* utility then passes the three assignments to Qshell for execution. The result is that the current year, month, and day are written to variables *sysYear*, *sysMonth*, and *sysDay*, respectively.

```
date '+sysYear=%y sysMonth=%m sysDay=%d'
sysYear=03 sysMonth=09 sysDay=09
/home/jsmith $
eval $(date '+sysYear=%y sysMonth=%m sysDay=%d')
/home/jsmith $
print $sysMonth
01
/home/jsmith $
print $sysDay
02
/home/jsmith $
print $sysYear
03
```

Figure 12.30: This example combines command substitution and eval to assign and define three current date variables.

To view what steps *eval* is taking, set the *xtrace* option, as shown in Figure 12.31. This option causes Qshell to write each command to stdout before executing it.

```
set -x
/home/jsmith $
eval $(date '+sysYear=%y sysMonth=%m sysDay=%d')
+   date +sysYear=%y sysMonth=%m sysDay=%d
+   date +sysYear=%y sysMonth=%m sysDay=%d
+   eval sysYear=03 sysMonth=01 sysDay=02
+   sysYear=03 sysMonth=01 sysDay=02
/home/jsmith $
```

Figure 12.31: Use the xtrace *option to view the steps* eval *takes.*

SUMMARY

Qshell executes commands of several types: regular and special built-in utilities, reserved words, aliases, functions, and external files. These commands may be used alone or combined into compound commands.

Each command runs in a process, which is similar to an iSeries job. Some commands run in the current process, while others run in child processes under the shell that spawned them. Child processes do not automatically receive the values of the variables of their calling processes. The *export* utility causes Qshell to define variables in child processes.

To find a command, Qshell searches the directories listed in the PATH environment variable. The current directory is not searched unless it is listed in the path.

There are several ways to run a command: in background mode, through command substitution, in the current process under the source utility, through the *xargs* utility, and through the *exec* utility.

Before executing a command, Qshell substitutes values for certain tokens through the process of word expansion. The *eval* utility causes Qshell to make two substitution passes before executing the command.

Chapter 13
Functions

A Qshell function, like a Qshell script, is a group of commands that is given a name. Functions differ from scripts in that functions become part of the invoking environment, whereas scripts are stored in files. Qshell can execute a function from memory, whereas it must load a script from an external stream file.

Qshell functions are similar to subroutines, functions, and procedures in other languages, and therefore can be used to implement modularity in Qshell scripts. While functions are usually defined in scripts or profile files, at times it is useful to type a function into an interactive session to help automate ad hoc repetitive tasks.

One of the most important things to understand about functions is that they execute in the caller's process. Qshell begins a new process when it runs a script or external utility, but it does not start a new process when it executes a function. This means that functions are more efficient than scripts, and that a function can change its caller's variables directly.

FUNCTION SYNTAX

There are two acceptable ways to define a function. The older way, taken from the Bourne shell, works on all releases of Qshell. Here is the syntax:

```
function-name() {
... commands
}
```

The function name is followed by empty parentheses, which serve no purpose except to tell Qshell that a function is being defined. Next is an open brace, which may be on the same line or on the following line. The commands follow. They may follow the brace on the same line or the next line. The function is terminated with a closing brace on a line by itself.

The newer way to define a shell, introduced with V5R2, is like the function definition structure of the Korn shell. Its syntax is shown here:

```
function function-name {
... commands
}
```

This syntax differs from the older syntax in two ways: The function begins with the reserved word *function*, and the empty parentheses are not coded.

A function must be defined before it can be invoked. For this reason, it is customary to place function definitions at the beginning of scripts.

In Figure 13.1, the user has typed the definition of the *lcname* (Lowercase Name) function into an interactive session. Since the function was defined in this session, it may be invoked from the command line. Note that the entire function has been coded on one input line. Since the closing brace is required to be on a line by itself, a semicolon is necessary to separate it from the rest of the function definition.

```
function lcname { echo $1 | tr '[:upper:]' '[:lower:]' ; }
/home/jsmith $
filename=/QSYS.LIB/MYLIB.LIB/MYFILE.FILE/MYMBR.MBR
/home/jsmith $
lcname $filename
/qsys.lib/mylib.lib/myfile.file/mymbr.mbr
```

Figure 13.1: The lcname function has one compound command, which uses the tr (translate) utility to convert uppercase letters to the corresponding lowercase ones.

Here is the same function defined with the older syntax:

```
lcname() { echo $1 | tr '[:upper:]' '[:lower:]' ; }
```

DISPLAYING FUNCTION DEFINITIONS

Use the *declare* (or *typeset*) utility to display the names and definitions of defined functions. Use the *F* option to display the names of defined functions, and the *f* option to display the definitions of defined functions, as shown in Figure 13.2. If you follow the option with the name of a function, *declare* shows information about that function only. If you do not include a function name, *declare* shows information about all defined functions.

```
declare -F
ucname
lcname
/home/jsmith $
declare -f
function ucname()
{
   echo ${1} | tr '[:lower:]' '[:upper:]'
}
function lcname()
{
   echo ${1} | tr '[:upper:]' '[:lower:]'
}
/home/jsmith $
declare -f ucname
function ucname()
{
   echo ${1} | tr '[:lower:]' '[:upper:]'
}
/home/jsmith $
```

Figure 13.2: Use the declare utility to display the names and definitions of functions.

In V5R2, Qshell defines the alias *functions* as the equivalent of *declare -f*. Figure 13.3 illustrates this concept.

When you use the *declare* utility to display the definition of a function, do not expect to see the same syntax that was used when the function was defined. For example, in Figure 13.4, the *rev* (reverse) function is defined with the old, Bourne-shell syntax, but the *declare* utility (executed through the *functions* alias) displays the function definition in the new function definition syntax. Notice, too, that the $n notation for positional parameters is used when defining the function, but the displayed definition uses the ${n} notation.

```
functions
function lcname()
{
   echo ${1} | tr '[:upper:]' '[:lower:]'
}
/home/jsmith $
```

Figure 13.3: The functions *alias lists all defined functions.*

```
rev() {
>
echo $2 $1
>
}
/home/jsmith $
rev a b
b a
/home/jsmith $
functions rev
function rev()
{
   echo ${2} ${1}
}
/home/jsmith $
```

Figure 13.4: The internal definition of a function might not match the original definition.

DELETING FUNCTION DEFINITIONS

To "undefine" a function, use the *unset* utility with the *-f* option. Figure 13.5 illustrates the *unset* command.

```
lcname $filename
/qsys.lib/mylib.lib/myfile.file/mymbr.mbr
/home/jsmith $
```

Figure 13.5: After the unset *utility runs, Qshell no longer finds the lcname function (part 1 of 2).*

242

```
unset -f lcname
/home/jsmith $
lcname $filename
qsh: 001-0019 Error found searching for command lcname.
    No such path or directory.
```

Figure 13.5: After the unset utility runs, Qshell no longer finds the lcname function (part 2 of 2).

PARAMETERS

You may pass arguments to a function, just as you pass them to a script. The function can reference the passed values as positional parameters, using the same *$n* or *${n}* notation that scripts use.

Special parameters also have appropriate values within a function. For example, the special parameter $# used in the nonfunction portion of a script returns the number of arguments passed to the script. When $# is used within a function, it returns the number of arguments passed to the function. The special parameter $0 is an exception. It does not have a special value within a function. Whether it's used in a function or in the nonfunction section of a script, $0 always returns the script name. (For a full list of special parameters, see chapter 5.)

The script in Figure 13.6 illustrates the use of positional parameters in a function. In it, the stripcmt.qsh script removes comments from stdin and writes to stdout. The script contains function *delcmt*, which deletes the first pound sign and everything following it from the first positional parameter. Notice that function *delcmt* refers to the first positional parameter twice. Also notice that the stripcmt.qsh script is not foolproof; it assumes that the first pound sign in a line indicates a comment. That might not be true.

```
cat stripcmt.qsh
function delcmt
{

    if [[ -z "$1" ]]
        then
```

Figure 13.6: Stripcmt.qsh uses a function to remove comments from input lines (part 1 of 3).

243

```
                echo " "
                return 0
        fi

        echo "$1" | cut -d'#'-f1
        return 0
}
# end function delcmt

while read line
    do
        delcmt "$line"
    done
/home/jsmith $
cat bu.qsh
# Backup script.
#
# Copy the files listed in the positional parameters to
# the bu directory

if [[ -e bu ]]              # bu exists; be sure it's a directory
    then
        if [[ ! -d bu ]]
            then
                print -u2 "bu is not a directory – backup
aborted."

                exit 1
        fi
    else
        mkdir bu
fi

for file
    do
        cp $file bu/$file.bu
    done
/home/jsmith $
stripcmt.qsh <bu.qsh



if [[ -e bu ]]
then
if [[ ! -d bu ]]
```

Figure 13.6: Stripcmt.qsh uses a function to remove comments from input lines (part 2 of 3).

```
then
print -u2 "bu is not a directory - backup aborted."
exit 1
fi
else
mkdir bu
fi

for file
do
cp $file bu/$file.bu
done
/home/jsmith $
```

Figure 13.6: Stripcmt.qsh uses a function to remove comments from input lines (part 3 of 3).

VARIABLES

A function may reference the variables that are defined in the script in which the function is defined. Such variables are called *global* variables. For example, in the following fragment of a Qshell script, the *init* function establishes initial values of two global variables. After *init* has executed, the print statement writes the string *Joe Smith* to stdout:

```
function init {
 firstname=Joe
 lastname=Smith
}

init
print $firstname $lastname
```

A function may also define local variables that are known only within the function. To define a local variable, use the local utility. In V5R2, you may use the *declare* and *typeset* utilities to define local variables within functions. No special options are needed. Any variable that is declared with *typeset* or *declare* within a function is local to the function.

The following function illustrates the use of global and local variables:

```
function lastchar {
   local length=${#1}
   if [ $length -gt 0 ]
       then clast=$(echo $1 | cut -c $length)
   else
       clast=''
   fi
}
```

Variable *length* is local to the *lastchar* function. Variable *clast* is global and may be referenced anywhere in the script, including within the *lastchar* function.

The script in Figure 13.7 was written for a V5R1 system, which does not have the substring parameter-expansion operators that were introduced in V5R2. It copies the characters in the first parameter to standard output, one character per output line. It includes two functions, *firstchar* and *chopfirst*. Function *firstchar* modifies global variable *c1*. Function *chopfirst* uses both local and global variables.

In Figure 13.8, there are two variables named *length*. One is a global variable, while the other is local to function *a*. When *length* is referenced in function *a*, the local *length* variable is used. Outside of function *a*, the global *length* is used.

```
cat func04.qsh
###### list each character of an argument

# function firstchar --
# place the first character of a string
# into global variable c1

firstchar() {
  c1=$(echo "$1" | cut -c 1)
}

# function chopfirst --
# place all but the first character of
```

Figure 13.7: In function chopfirst, both local and global variables are used (part 1 of 2).

```
# a string into global variable afterfirst

chopfirst() {
    local length=${#1}
    if [ $length -gt 1 ]
        then afterfirst=$(echo "$1" | cut -c 2-$length)
    else
        afterfirst= ' '
    fi
}

# Begin main routine

valu=$1
until [ -z "$valu" ] ; do
    firstchar "$valu"
    echo $c1
    chopfirst "$valu"
    valu= "$afterfirst"
    done
/home/JSMITH $
func04.qsh "RPG IV"
R
P
G

I
V
/home/JSMITH $
```

Figure 13.7: In function chopfirst, both local and global variables are used (part 2 of 2).

```
cat myscript.qsh
function a {
    local length
    length=2
    print "a             " $length
}

length=1
print "Value of the length variable"
print "============================="
print "Routine       Value"
print "============================="
print "main             " $length
```

Figure 13.8: This example uses a local variable named length and a global variable named length (part 1 of 2).

```
a
print "main                    " $length
print "=============================="
/home/jsmith $
myscript.qsh
Value of the length variable
==============================
Routine        Value
==============================
main            1
a               2
main            1
==============================
/home/jsmith $
```

Figure 13.8: This example uses a local variable named length and a global variable named length (part 2 of 2).

Figure 13.9 also has both a global variable named *length* and, in function *b*, a local variable named *length*. Function *a* refers to *length*, but since it does not have a local variable of that name, it uses the value of the most recently activated *length* variable. So, if function *a* is called directly from the main procedure, it uses the global *length* variable. If it is called from function *b*, *a* uses *b*'s *length* variable.

```
cat myscript.qsh
function a {
    print "a              " $length
}

function b {
    local length
    length=3
    print "b              " $length
    a
    print "b              " $length
}

length=1
print "Value of the length variable"
print "=============================="
print "Routine        Value"
```

Figure 13.9: A function uses the definition of the most recently created instance of a variable defined outside of itself (part 1 of 2).

```
print "============================"
a
print "main              " $length
b
print "main              " $length
a
print "main              " $length
print "============================"
/home/jsmith $
myscript.qsh
Value of the length variable
============================
Routine      Value
============================
a            1
main         1
b            3
a            3
b            3
main         1
a            1
main         1
============================
/home/jsmith $
```

Figure 13.9: A function uses the definition of the most recently created instance of a variable defined outside of itself (part 2 of 2).

Starting with V5R2, you can use the *declare* and *typeset* utilities to define local variables in functions, as shown in Figure 13.10. Function *init* changes the value of global variable *lastname*, but not global variable *firstname*.

```
cat myscript.qsh
function init {
 declare firstname
 firstname=Joe
 lastname=Smith
 print $firstname $lastname
}

firstname=Sue
init
print $firstname $lastname
/home/jsmith $
```

Figure 13.10: This script was written for a V5R2 system, where you can use the declare and typeset utilities to define local variables (part 1 of 2).

249

```
myscript.qsh
Joe Smith
Sue Smith
/home/jsmith $
```

Figure 13.10: This script was written for a V5R2 system, where you can use the declare and typeset utilities to define local variables (part 2 of 2).

Normally, any options that are changed with the *set* utility within a function affect the calling environment in which the function is defined. You may make the - (hyphen) special variable local to a function. However, doing so restricts the changes that can be made to options of the function itself. Figures 13.11 and 13.12 illustrate the difference. Notice the *ls* command in each figure. In Figure 13.11, the *x* option has been affected globally, causing the *ls* command to be echoed to stdout. In Figure 13.12, the *x* option is changed locally, so the *ls* command is not echoed.

```
function ucname {
>
    set -x
>
    echo $1 | tr '[:lower:]' '[:upper:]'
>
}
/home/jsmith $
ucname "Joe Smith"
+   echo Joe Smith
+   tr [:lower:] [:upper:]
JOE SMITH
/home/jsmith $
ls t*.qsh
+   ls tfunctions.qsh theirscript.qsh tscriot.qsh tscript.qsh
tfunctions.qsh   theirscript.qsh tscriot.qsh      tscript.qsh
/home/jsmith $
```

Figure 13.11: The set command, which is executed within the function, affects the entire session.

250

```
function ucname {
>
   local -
>
   set -x
>
   echo $1 | tr '[:lower:]' '[:upper:]'
>
}
/home/jsmith $
ucname "Joe Smith"
+   echo Joe Smith
+   tr [:lower:] [:upper:]
JOE SMITH
/home/jsmith $
ls t*.qsh
tfunctions.qsh   theirscript.qsh tscriot.qsh       tscript.qsh
/home/jsmith $
```

Figure 13.12: Defining the - special variable to be local restricts the effect of the set command.

INVOKING FUNCTIONS

Invoke functions by name, just as you would invoke built-ins, external utilities, and aliases. In Figure 13.13, a function is invoked from more than one line of the sendfile.qsh script, which sends a file to a destination. If there is an error in the way the command is invoked, the script runs the *usage* function, which displays a synopsis of how the command is to be used, and aborts the script. In a true production script, the *usage* function would probably be called from several places, not just two.

```
cat sendfile.qsh
# Send a file via ...

function usage {
   local scriptname=$(basename $0)
   print "$scriptname usage:"
   print "    $scriptname [-r] [-d destination] file ..."
```

Figure 13.13: The usage function is called from two places in the script (part 1 of 2).

```
    exit 1
}

# process the options
resend=off

while getopts rd: argname
do
    case $argname in
      r) resend=on;;
      d) dest=$OPTARG;;
      ?) usage;;
    esac
done

# get rid of options
shift $OPTIND-1

# make sure at least one filename
# was entered

if [[ -z $1 ]]
    then
        usage
    fi

filename=$1
print "Sending $filename..."

# ... more commands omitted ...

exit 0
/home/jsmith $
sendfile.qsh
sendfile.qsh usage:
    sendfile.qsh [-r] [-d destination] file ...
/home/jsmith $
sendfile.qsh -x
getopts: 001-0036 Option x is not valid.
sendfile.qsh usage:
    sendfile.qsh [-r] [-d destination] file ...
/home/jsmith $
sendfile.qsh -r
sendfile.qsh usage:
    sendfile.qsh [-r] [-d destination] file ...
```

Figure 13.13: The usage function is called from two places in the script (part 2 of 2).

252

RETURN AND THE EXIT STATUS

A function returns an exit status between zero and 255, inclusive. By convention, an exit status of zero indicates that a function completed normally. The caller is not required to do anything with the exit status.

Use the *return* utility if you want to assign the exit status. If you do not assign the exit status, the function returns the exit status of the last-executed command. Assignment of the exit status is illustrated here:

```
backup_file() {
   if [ -z $1 ]
      then return 41
   elif [ ! -e $1 ]
      then return 42
   elif [ ! -f $1 ]
      then return 43
   else
      cp $1 $1.copy
   fi
}
```

In this example, the exit status may be any of several values:

- Status 41—No argument was passed to the function.
- Status 42—The argument is not the name of an existing file.
- Status 43—The argument is not the name of a regular file.
- Status 0—The *cp* command completed successfully.
- Other non-zero status—The *cp* command failed.

The *exit* and *return* utilities both set the exit status, but do not confuse the two. If you invoke the *exit* utility in a function, Qshell will shut down the entire script.

Because the function returns an exit status, you can code a function call wherever a condition is allowed. If you need to check the status code for a certain value, use the $? parameter in the caller. The following example illustrates both of these concepts:

```
if backup_file $1
  then :
  else echo "Backup of file $1 failed; exit status was $?." >&2
fi
```

The backup_file function is invoked from an *if* command. If the function fails to make a copy of the file, the *else* clause is executed, sending a message to the standard error device.

RETRIEVING OUTPUT FROM FUNCTIONS

Functions cannot modify the arguments that are passed to them. There are two ways to return output from a function. One way is to modify global variables, like this:

```
lastchar() {
  local length=${#1}
  if [ $length -gt 0 ]
      then clast=$(echo $1 | cut -c $length)
  else
      clast=''
  fi
}
```

The *lastchar* function in this example copies the last character of the first argument into global variable *clast*. Since clast is not defined within the function, it is global and may be referenced outside of the function.

The other common way to retrieve data from a function is to write to stdout. You can use the command-substitution technique to direct the output to a variable. This is shown in Figure 13.14. The *lcname* function writes the lowercase equivalent of an argument to standard output. The command substitution forces the output into variable *varx*.

```
function lcname { echo $1 | tr '[:upper:]' '[:lower:]' ; }
/home/jsmith $
varx= "Joe Smith"
/home/jsmith $
echo $varx
Joe Smith
/home/jsmith $
varx=$(lcname "Joe Smith")
/home/jsmith $
echo $varx
joe smith
/home/jsmith $
```

Figure 13.14: Functions can return data to calling routines by writing to stdout.

SUMMARY

A Qshell function is like a subroutine, function, or procedure in other languages. Functions are defined within a process, so they execute more quickly than external files. Like functions and subroutines in other languages, functions promote modularity in Qshell scripts. Functions may contain local variables and receive parameters. Functions may be defined using the Bourne-shell syntax or the newer Korn-shell syntax. Like scripts, built-in utilities, and internal commands, functions are invoked by typing their names.

Chapter 14

Path-Name Expansion

Before Qshell interprets a command or passes arguments to a utility, it examines the command string for special characters called *wildcards* and replaces expressions with lists of file names. This process is formally known as *path-name expansion* but is commonly called *globbing*. Globbing gives you an easy way to work with groups of files while writing only a little bit of code.

It is important to understand that globbing is something Qshell does, not something that Qshell *commands* do. Qshell commands, whether scripts or utilities, just see the results of globbing. (Contrast this behavior to that of MS-DOS, which requires that the individual commands process wildcards for themselves.)

GLOBBING

Qshell could not glob were it not for metacharacters, also known as wildcards. Metacharacters are characters that represent other characters. For example, the letter a and the digit 5 are not metacharacters. They cannot represent other characters. The question mark, however, is a metacharacter because it can match any character. The globbing metacharacters are listed in Table 14.1.

Table 14.1: Metacharacters Used in Globbing

Character	Description
*	Matches zero or more characters
?	Matches exactly one character
[ ]	Matches ranges or groups of characters
!	Negates a group or range of characters
\	Escapes (disables) the metacharacter that follows it

The following example shows the use of the asterisk metacharacter:

```
print *

arglist.qsh bin bu.qsh casemon.qsh caseqtr.qsh casewild.qsh data.ascii
data.ebcdic donde.qsh echoprocess.qsh edity.txt ftpmodel.txt
goodoleboys.txt helpme mydata.csv myfile.txt myscript.qsh protos.jar
protos.savf qsh_trace read002.qsh select01.qsh temp.txt test1.txt
test1a.txt theirscript.qsh tscript.qsh upper.txt
```

Before executing the *print* utility, Qshell replaces the asterisk with a list of the files in the current directory.

An example of the question-mark metacharacter is shown here:

```
ls -dF ???
x.2*    x.y      bin/
```

The *ls* command displays the names of files with three-character names. The *d* option prevents the display of the contents of subdirectories. The *F* option appends a slash (/) to the end of directory names, an asterisk (*) to the end of executable file names, and an at sign (@) to the end of the names of symbolic links.

Globbing is case-sensitive. The following command uses the asterisk to copy all files whose names begin with a lowercase *c* to directory temp1:

```
cp c* temp1
```

Using Metacharacters with a Script

You can get a better feel for globbing by writing a shell script that prints the positional parameters. Such a script is listed in Figure 14.1, where it is named listargs.qsh.

```
# script name: listargs.qsh
#
declare -i argnbr=0
print "Number of arguments: $#"
while [ "$1" ]
    do
      let argnbr=argnbr+1
      printf "%3d (%s)\n" $argnbr "$1"
      shift
    done
```

Figure 14.1: The listargs.qsh script shows the effects of globbing.

The following example shows how the listargs.qsh script works without any globbing. Notice that Qshell has preserved the blanks in quoted strings.

```
listargs.qsh Qshell rulz "Qshell rulz" 'Qshell rulz' "Qshell  rulz"
Number of arguments: 5
   1 (Qshell)
   2 (rulz)
   3 (Qshell rulz)
   4 (Qshell rulz)
   5 (Qshell  rulz)
```

Running listargs.qsh with various globbing expressions shows you what Qshell does to the metacharacters before passing control to a script. In the first use of globbing with listargs.qsh, Qshell expands the *.txt* expression into a list of all files that end with a period followed by *txt*:

```
listargs.qsh *.txt
Number of arguments: 8
    1 (edity.txt)
    2 (ftpmodel.txt)
    3 (goodoleboys.txt)
    4 (myfile.txt)
    5 (temp.txt)
    6 (test1.txt)
    7 (test1a.txt)
    8 (upper.txt)
```

Since there are eight *.txt* files in the current directory, the listargs.qsh script runs as if the user had entered the eight file names as arguments.

The next example expands the globbing expression into a list of all file names that have an *e* as the second character:

```
listargs.qsh ?e*
Number of arguments: 7
    1 (helpme)
    2 (read002.qsh)
    3 (select01.qsh)
    4 (temp.txt)
    5 (temp1)
    6 (test1.txt)
    7 (test1a.txt)
```

In a slightly more complex example, you can use globbing to expand the expression into a list of files whose names begin with either an *h* or an *r*:

```
listargs.qsh [hr]*
Number of arguments: 2
    1 (helpme)
    2 (read002.qsh)
```

The following globbing expression illustrates a range of file names:

```
listargs.qsh [d-g]*
Number of arguments: 7
    1 (data.ascii)
    2 (data.ebcdic)
    3 (donde.qsh)
    4 (echoprocess.qsh)
    5 (edity.txt)
    6 (ftpmodel.txt)
    7 (goodoleboys.txt)
```

All files whose names begin with any letter from *d* to *g* are listed. Globbing can also have the opposite effect, for example, listing files whose names do *not* begin with a letter in the range *d* to *t*:

```
listargs.qsh [!d-t]*
Number of arguments: 11
    1 (arglist.qsh)
    2 (bin)
    3 (bu.qsh)
    4 (casemon.qsh)
    5 (caseqtr.qsh)
    6 (casewild.qsh)
    7 (upper.txt)
    8 (while001.qsh)
    9 (x.2)
   10 (x.y)
   11 (yourscript.qsh)
```

Finally, here is a fairly complex use of metacharacters:

```
listargs.qsh [d-t][eiy][i-m]*
Number of arguments: 6
    1 (demo.csh)
    2 (helpme)
    3 (select01.qsh)
    4 (tema)
    5 (temp.txt)
    6 (temp1)
```

Qshell includes filenames that begin with any letter between *d* and *t*, followed by an *e*, *i*, or *y*, followed by any letter from *i* to *m*, followed by zero or more characters.

Unmatched Expansion Expressions

If no filenames match the expansion pattern, Qshell passes the unmodified expression to the utility or script, as shown here:

```
echo x*x*
x*x*
/home/jsmith $
echo e*e*
echoprocess.qsh
```

There are no files in the current directory whose names begin with an *x* and have another *x* in the file name, so the first *echo* displays the argument as it was keyed. However, the second *echo* is expanded because there is one file whose name begins with an *e* and has an embedded *e*.

Globbing and Case-insensitive File Systems

In some case-insensitive file systems, letters used in patterns must be in uppercase. This is especially applicable to the qsys.lib (library) file system. (Although the qsys.lib file system is case insensitive, it stores object names in uppercase.) When using globbing for the library file system, be sure to use uppercase letters in the pattern, as shown in Figure 14.2. The first time listargs.qsh runs, the expression in parameter 1 is passed unmodified to the script. However, the second time listargs.qsh runs, the expression is globbed into four file names.

```
listargs.qsh /qsys.lib/smith.lib/*.pgm
Number of arguments: 1
  1 (/qsys.lib/smith.lib/*.pgm)
/home/jsmith $
```

Figure 14.2: When globbing is used with the library system, wildcard expressions must be in uppercase letters (part 1of 2).

```
listargs.qsh /qsys.lib/smith.lib/*.PGM
Number of arguments: 4
    1 (/qsys.lib/smith.lib/EDITX.PGM)
    2 (/qsys.lib/smith.lib/MON001.PGM)
    3 (/qsys.lib/smith.lib/MONEVAL4.PGM)
    4 (/qsys.lib/smith.lib/MONEVAL5.PGM)
```

Figure 14.2: When globbing is used with the library system, wildcard expressions must be in uppercase letters (part 2 of 2).

PREVENTING GLOBBING

You may tell Qshell not to expand path names. One simple way is to precede a metacharacter with a backslash character, like this:

```
echo *
donde.qsh one one.qsh ten two upper.txt
/home/jsmith/bin $
echo \*
*
```

Qshell expands the asterisk in the first *echo* command to a list of files in the current directory. However, the backslash in the second *echo* command prevents globbing, which makes the second *echo* print the asterisk literally.

In the following example, the first *echo* command displays the names of files that begin with the letter *t*, while the second command prints the string *t*:

```
echo t*
tema temp.txt temp1 test1.txt test1a.txt theirscript.qsh tscript.qsh
/home/jsmith $
echo t\*
t*
```

Notice that the second *echo* does not print the backslash, since the backslash serves as an escape character.

A second way to prevent globbing is to place single quotes or double quotes around metacharacters, like this:

```
echo ?e*m*
demo.csh helpme tema
/home/jsmith $
echo '?e*m*'
?e*m*
/home/jsmith $
echo "?e*m*"
?e*m*
```

You can also disable Qshell's automatic globbing feature. To do so, use the *set* command with the *noglob* option, as shown here:

```
# to disable globbing
set -o noglob
set -F
```

```
# to enable globbing
set +o noglob
set +F
```

Notice that *set* has two forms. In the short form, shown in Figure 14.3, you use a lowercase *f*. In the longer form, you use a lowercase *o* followed by *noglob*, as shown in Figure 14.4.

```
echo ?e*m*
demo.csh helpme tema temp.txt temp1
/home/jsmith $
set -f
/home/jsmith $
echo ?e*m*
?e*m*
/home/jsmith $
set +f
/home/jsmith $
echo ?e*m*
demo.csh helpme tema temp.txt temp1
```

Figure 14.3: This example illustrates the shorter form of the set command for disabling and enabling globbing.

```
echo d*
data.ascii data.ebcdic demo.csh donde.qsh
/home/jsmith $
set -o noglob
/home/jsmith $
echo d*
d*
/home/jsmith $
set +o noglob
/home/jsmith $
echo d*
data.ascii data.ebcdic demo.csh donde.qsh
```

Figure 14.4: This example illustrates the longer form of the set command for disabling and enabling globbing.

WHEN GLOBBING FAILS

Depending on the utility, globbing might fail if the expansion produces more than 255 arguments. In that case, you might be able to achieve your objective by using the *xargs* utility to process a portion of the expanded arguments at a time. The *xargs* utility, which was discussed in chapter 12, reads data from standard input and passes it along to a command as arguments.

For example, the source physical file JSMITH/SRC in Figure 14.5 has 459 members. The *print* command is able to list the names of the members, but the *ls* command is not, due to a limitation in the number of parameters allowed for

```
print /qsys.lib/jsmith.lib/src.file/*.MBR
/qsys.lib/jsmith.lib/src.file/ADDREC2R.MBR /qsys.lib/jsmith.lib/src.file/ADDREC
D.MBR /qsys.lib/jsmith.lib/src.file/ADDRECPF.MBR/qsys.lib/jsmith.lib/src.file/A
DRECR.MBR /qsys.lib/jsmith.lib/src.file/AFPM01.MBR /qsys.lib/jsmith.lib/src.fil
... (many lines omitted) ...
.lib/src.file/YPGM01CL.MBR /qsys.lib/jsmith.lib/src.file/YPGM01RG#2.MBR /qsys.l
ib/jsmith.lib/src.file/YPGM01RG.MBR /qsys.lib/jsmith.lib/src.file/YPGM02RG#2.MBR
/qsys.lib/jsmith.lib/src.file/YPGM02RG.MBR
/home/JSMITH $
ls -l /qsys.lib/jsmith.lib/src.file/*.MBR > dirlist.txt
qsh: 001-0085 Too many arguments specified on command.
/home/JSMITH $
print /qsys.lib/jsmith.lib/src.file/*.MBR | xargs -n 255 ls -ld > dirlist.txt
```

Figure 14.5: You can sometimes use the xargs utility to get around the globbing restriction of 255 arguments in the expansion.

a program object. Recall that *print* is a built-in utility and not an external utility implemented by a program object. The *xargs* utility receives groups of 255 member names and sends them to the *ls* command.

SUMMARY

All users of Qshell should master globbing because it is inherent in all Qshell commands. Globbing, also called path-name expansion, occurs when Qshell substitutes file names for strings containing wildcard characters.

Chapter 15

Scripts—Debugging, Signals, and Traps

Normally, a Qshell script begins execution with the first line and continues until control reaches the end of the script, or until an *exit* command is found. However, things don't always happen the way they should.

Occasionally, bad things happen to good scripts. This chapter discusses strategies that you can use to both debug and bulletproof your shell scripts.

DEBUGGING USING OPTION SETTINGS

The first and most widely used script debugging strategy involves tracing the script. Tracing a shell script outputs information about the variable and parameter substitution that occurs. Tracing also lists the commands that Qshell executes while the script is running.

Figure 15.1 shows a shell script that has a rather trivial problem: It produces extra spaces in the output messages.

Use the *-x* option (*xtrace*) of the qsh interpreter to turn on tracing for the entire shell script. The shell script will show trace output of its progress. Qshell uses a prefix of the PS4 variable to indicate trace output. The PS4 variable holds a plus sign if it hasn't been changed.

```
cat trace.qsh
#!/usr/bin/qsh
1="Now is the time\nfor all good men\n"
1="$1 to come to the aid\nof their country"
num=$(echo $1 | wc -w)
/usr/bin/echo "There are $num words in the quote"
num=$(echo $1 | wc -l)
/usr/bin/echo "There are $num lines in the quote"
trace.qsh
There are          16 words in the quote
There are           4 lines in the quote
```

Figure 15.1: This script is used to demonstrate Qshell tracing.

Figure 15.2 demonstrates the problem script from Figure 15.1 with the *-x* option added to the interpreter. This example shows that the *num* variable is set to the value 16, with leading spaces coming from the output of the *wc -w* command.

```
cat trace1.qsh
#!/usr/bin/qsh -x
1="Now is the time\nfor all good men\n"
1="$1 to come to the aid\nof their country"
num=$(echo $1 | wc -w)
/usr/bin/echo "There are $num words in the quote"
num=$(echo $1 | wc -l)
/usr/bin/echo "There are $num lines in the quote"
trace1.qsh
+  1=Now is the time\nfor all good men\n
+  1=Now is the time\nfor all good men\n to come to the aid\nof their
   country
+  echo Now is the time\nfor all good men\n to come to the aid\nof
   their country
+  wc -w
+  num=        16
+  /usr/bin/echo There are        16 words in the quote
There are          16 words in the quote
+  echo Now is the time\nfor all good men\n to come to the aid\nof
   their country
+  wc -l
+  num=        4
+  /usr/bin/echo There are        4 lines in the quote
There are          4 lines in the quote
```

Figure 15.2: Use the -x option to the qsh interpreter to trace the entire shell script.

Sometimes, tracing the entire script produces too much output. Use the *set* utility to trace a portion of a script or to turn on tracing in an interactive session. Use *set -x* to turn on the *x (xtrace)* option, as shown in Figure 15.3 To turn off the *xtrace* option, use *set +x*.

```
cat trace2.qsh
#!/usr/bin/qsh
1="Now is the time\nfor all good men\n"
1="$1 to come to the aid\nof their country"
set -x
num=$(echo $1 | wc -w)
set +x
/usr/bin/echo "There are $num words in the quote"
num=$(echo $1 | wc -1)
/usr/bin/echo "There are $num lines in the quote"
trace2.qsh
+  echo Now is the time\nfor all good men\n to come to the aid\nof
   their country
+  wc -w
+  num=        16
+  set +x
There are        16 words in the quote
There are        4 lines in the quote
```

Figure 15.3: Turn on the tracing option (set -x) for part of the script, then turn it off again.

Although *xtrace* is by far the most frequently used tracing option, the *set* utility supports other trace-related settings that can aid in script debugging. Use these options, shown in Table 15.1, to enhance the debugging of script problems.

Table 15.1: Options Related to Debugging Scripts

Option	Description
-e	The "error exit" option causes the script to exit if a command fails and the exit status of the command has not been tested. The If, Elif, While, or Until statements, or the || or && operators, test the exit status of a command.
-j	The "job trace" option causes Qshell to print a status message with the iSeries' fully qualified job name and the pid (process ID) of each job that is started.

Table 15.1: Options Related to Debugging Scripts, *continued*

Option	Description
-l (letter "ell")	The "log commands" option causes Qshell to write each command to a message in the iSeries job log before running the command. The -l option is provided in v5r2.
-m	The "monitor" option causes Qshell to print a status message when a job completes.
-t	The "trace" option causes Qshell to write internal trace information to the qsh_trace file in the user's home directory.
-u	The "unset" option causes Qshell to write an error message to stderr and exit immediately when it expands a shell variable that is not set.
-v	The "verbose" option causes Qshell to echo all input from stdin back to stderr during processing.
-x	The "xtrace" option causes Qshell to trace commands (after expansion and substitution). Trace output is preceded by the value of the PS4 variable.

SIGNALS

When an unexpected error happens in a process or script, the system sometimes generates a signal. Your script can use signals to handle error conditions. Handling error conditions using signals is transparent to most of the script and helps prevents undetected errors from propagating and causing more serious ones.

The *trap* and *kill* utilities allow your scripts or interactive Qshell sessions to deal with signals. The two utilities are related; *trap* allows a script to receive signals, while *kill* allows the script to send signals.

To see a list of the signals, use the *kill* or *trap* command with the *-l* option, as shown in Figure 15.4. The *-l* option was added to *trap* in V5R2; earlier releases require the *kill* command.

```
kill -l
 1) ABRT       2) FPE        3) ILL        4) INT        5) SEGV
 6) TERM       7) USR1       8) USR2       9) IO        10) bad trap
11) bad trap  12) KILL      13) PIPE      14) ALRM      15) HUP
16) QUIT      17) STOP      18) TSTP      19) CONT      20) CHLD
21) TTIN      22) TTOU      23) URG       24) POLL      25) bad trap
26) bad trap  27) WINCH     28) bad trap  29) bad trap  30) bad trap
31) bad trap  32) BUS       33) DANGER    34) PRE       35) SYS
36) TRAP      37) PROF      38) VTALRM    39) XCPU      40) XFSZ
41) bad trap  42) bad trap  43) bad trap  44) bad trap  45) bad trap
46) bad trap  47) bad trap  48) bad trap  49) bad trap  50) bad trap
51) bad trap  52) bad trap  53) bad trap  54) bad trap  55) bad trap
56) bad trap  57) bad trap  58) bad trap  59) bad trap  60) bad trap
61) bad trap  62) bad trap  63) bad trap
/home/jsmith $
```

Figure 15.4: Use the kill command with the -l option to view the list of defined signals.

There are 63 possible signals, numbered 1 through 63, but not all are defined or used by the system. The undefined signals are indicated by the text *bad trap*.

The defined signals have names. You can reference a signal by its name or by its number. It is better to reference signals by name, because they are not assigned the same numbers on all systems. For example, the interrupt signal, INT, is signal 4 in Qshell, but signal 2 in many Unix shells. Scripts that use the signal names are more easily ported to other systems than those that use signal numbers.

You may follow the -l option of the *kill* utility with a signal name or number. A signal number causes *kill* to display the signal's name. A signal name causes *kill* to display the signal's number. This is not true of *trap*, however. The *trap* command can include the -l option, but the option cannot be followed by a signal name or number. Figure 15.5 illustrates this use of the *kill* utility. Following the -l option with a three gives signal 3's name: ILL. Following the -l option with CONT gives the number of the CONT signal: 19.

```
kill -l 3
ILL
kill -l CONT
19
```

Figure 15.5: The kill utility interprets signal names and numbers.

You will not have to deal with most of these signals, because OS/400 and Qshell typically do not generate them. The ones you will probably use most are the INT signal, which is sent when you select option 2 from the System Request menu, and the TERM signal, which is sent when you use *kill* to terminate a process.

In addition to these signals, there are three "pseudo-signals," listed in Table 15.2. They are called pseudo-signals because they are not caused by interrupts from the operating system. Instead, they are regularly generated events that you can treat as if they were unexpected events. Two of them, DEBUG and ERR, are provided as aids for debugging. The EXIT signal is provided as a way to force final processing, no matter how a script ends.

Table 15.2: Pseudo-Signals

Name	Number	Description
DEBUG	None	Occurs after execution of a command
ERR	None	Occurs when a utility returns a non-zero exit status
EXIT	0	Occurs when a script or shell ends

Keep the following technical notes in mind when using signals:

- OS/400 provides a rich and robust set of services (both proprietary and portable) that allows an application program to tolerate and recover from any number of error conditions. Usually, error conditions are sent to the application using OS/400 exceptions, not signals.

- OS/400 exceptions are quite similar to Java or C++ exceptions.

- Because of historical details of OS/400's implementation, signals and the Unix-type *kill* utility are used only with those iSeries jobs that use relatively new operating-system services.

- The *kill* utility sends signals based on a process ID. In general, OS/400 identifies jobs by the three-part fully qualified job name.

There are good reasons for not allowing every OS/400 job to receive signals. Many system services, processing systems, and other applications were written long before the implementation of signals, Qshell, or Unix-type APIs. Those traditional applications are not written for and cannot tolerate receiving signals; they do not know how to clean up after being interrupted or ended due to a signal.

Forcing release-to-release compatibility problems for source code or applications is an anathema for the iSeries, so older, traditional applications are simply not exposed to the iSeries signals infrastructure. Only by using signals, Qshell or other Unix-type related system services directly are those applications exposed to signals. You can be sure that anything that explicitly uses signals, or anything that displays, prints, or retrieves a job-process ID (like the getpid() API or the Qshell special variable $$) will perform the appropriate system initialization so that the job is enabled for signals.

THE TRAP UTILITY

Use the *trap* utility to control a script's reaction to a signal (or a pseudo-signal). You can ignore a signal or execute one or more commands of your choosing. Here is the syntax of *trap*:

```
trap action signal...
```

Replace *signal...* with the names and/or numbers of one or more signals that are to be trapped. Replace *action* with one of the options listed in Table 15.3. For the *action* parameter, list one or more commands to be executed when one of the signals is received.

If there are embedded blanks, surround the command with single quotes or double quotes. If there are two or more commands, separate them with semicolons—or, better yet, put them into a subroutine. When the signal is received, Qshell executes the action, then continues with the statement after the one that caused the interrupt, unless the action terminates the script.

Table 15.3: Signal Actions

Action	Description
commands or 'commands' or "commands"	Execute a list of commands.
- (hyphen) or omitted	Reset to default behavior.
two apostrophes or two quotes	Ignore the signal.

Here are a few more things to keep in mind when using the *trap* utility:

- If the action is a single hyphen, each signal in the list is reset to its default behavior. For most signals, the default behavior is to terminate the script immediately without raising the EXIT pseudo-signal.

- If you redefine the behavior of a signal, the script might no longer terminate automatically, so you might need to include an *exit* command.

- If the action consists of two adjacent quotes, or if the action is omitted, the signal is ignored.

- Only one *trap* can be active for a signal. If two *trap* commands are executed for the same signal, the second *trap* replaces the first.

On a Unix-based system with the correct type of terminal (for example, a TTY or Telnet session), the operating system sends the INT signal when the user presses the Control-C key combination. On a 5250 terminal emulator, on the other hand, Control-C is mapped differently. There, option 2 (End Previous Request) of the System Request menu is the closest match. The Qshell terminal generates an INT signal when the "End Previous Request" option is used so that you can interrupt running applications.

In Figure 15.6, the INT signal is trapped. Option 2 of the System Request menu is used when the script is waiting for user input, but it is not visible because it generates no output. The generated INT signal causes the script to run function HandleInt, which sends a message to stderr and ends the script with an exit status of 3. The first two *trap* commands are identical. Since there are no embedded blanks in the command, the single quotes are optional.

```
cat handleint.qsh
#!/usr/bin/qsh
# the following two lines are identical
trap 'HandleInt' INT
trap HandleInt INT

function HandleInt {
    print -u2 "Script was aborted."
    exit 3
}

echo "Do you want to continue?"
read response

echo "You said: $response"
./HandleInt.qsh
Do you want to continue?
Script was aborted.
```

Figure 15.6: The INT signal is raised from option 2 of the System Request menu, interrupting the script.

The script in Figure 15.7 begins by creating two work files whose names include the process ID. When the script ends, the EXIT signal is sent, causing the script to delete the work files. Note that there are three places where the script can end, but the *rm* utility will run, no matter how the script ends.

```
cat handleexit.qsh
#!/usr/bin/qsh
trap Cleanup EXIT

function Cleanup {
    echo "Cleaning up files"
    rm temp.*.$$
}

echo "Starting work file 1" > temp.1.$$
echo "Starting work file 2" > temp.2.$$
cat temp.*.$$
# All done, script ends normally with a call
# to the exit utility or at the end of the file
./handleexit.qsh
Starting work file 1
Starting work file 2
Cleaning up files
```

Figure 15.7: The EXIT signal is raised when the script ends normally.

If any command in the script in Figure 15.8 returns a non-zero exit status, Qshell aborts the script immediately, setting the exit status to 5. The first *print* command executes, but the second one does not because no command *br549* exists.

```
cat handleerr.qsh
#!/usr/bin/qsh
trap 'echo "Whoa!"; exit 5' ERR
print 'do something.'
br549
print 'do something else'
./handleerr.qsh
do something.
./handleerr.qsh: 001-0019 Error found searching for command
    br549. No such path or directory.
Whoa!
print $?
5
```

Figure 15.8: Use the ERR pseudo-signal to detect errors as they occur.

The *-e* (error exit) option setting provides the same basic support as setting up a trap for the ERR signal. The *-e* option setting provides less flexibility, however, because your script exits immediately with a predefined exit status. Figure 15.9 demonstrates using *-e* instead of the *trap ERR* statement.

```
cat handleerr2.qsh
#!/usr/bin/qsh
set -e
print 'do something.'
br549
print 'do something else'
./handleerr2.qsh
do something.
./handleerr2.qsh: 001-0019 Error found searching for command
    br549. No such path or directory.
print $?
127
```

Figure 15.9: Use the -e (error exit) option to detect errors as they occur.

The script in Figure 15.10 does not include any error-trapping logic. Qshell sends an error message, but still assigns the invalid value to the *TradingPartner* variable.

```
cat trading.qsh
#!/usr/bin/qsh
declare -i TradingPartner
print 'Enter the trading partner ID'
read TradingPartner
print $TradingPartner
exit 0
./trading.qsh
Enter the trading partner ID
35.8
read: 001-0032 Number 35.8 is not valid.
35.8
```

Figure 15.10: Failure to trap an error can result in subsequent errors.

Contrast the script in Figure 15.10 with the one in Figure 15.11. The new script uses additional error-trapping logic to detect the errors that occur in a block of code. The first *trap* command tells Qshell to print an error message when any command returns a non-zero status code. The second *trap* resets the ERR signal to its default action. If the *read* command encounters a value that is not of the integer type, the usual error message is written to the special file /dev/null, so that the user never sees it. The ERR condition is raised, causing the user to see the message in the *trap* command.

Figure 15.12 demonstrates a script that confirms and optionally ignores the INT signal. In the example output for this script, the user chooses option 2 from the System Request menu while the script is attempting to read the user's name.

The first portion of the script defines a trap for the ENDRQS command, so that if the user chooses option 2 from the System Request menu, Qshell runs function *ConfirmCancel*. The *ConfirmCancel* function issues a warning message and requires the user to enter the word *YES* in capital letters to cancel execution. If the user enters *YES*, the script sends a cancellation message to stdout and exits with status 33. Otherwise, the script continues execution from the point at which the user chose option 2.

Figure 15.12 also demonstrates a rather subtle but important concept: the distinction between the shell script and the utilities used. Recall that each utility

```
cat trading2.qsh
#!/usr/bin/qsh
declare -i TradingPartner

trap 'print "Trading partner ID is a whole number; try again."' ERR
while true
do
    print 'Enter the trading partner ID'
    read TradingPartner 2> /dev/null
    if [[ $? -eq 0 ]] then
        break
    fi
done
# Reset the trap
trap ERR

print $TradingPartner
exit 0
./trading2.qsh
Enter the trading partner ID
49024G
Trading partner ID is a whole number; try again.
Enter the trading partner ID
49024.5
Trading partner ID is a whole number; try again.
Enter the trading partner ID
49024
49024
```

Figure 15.11: Use the ERR pseudo-signal to detect specific error conditions.

run by a shell script is either a built-in utility processed by Qshell directly, or a regular utility started in a separate job. Notice in Figure 15.12 that there is both a trap handler registered (the *ConfirmCancel* function) and error-checking logic with a loop for processing the *read* utility. At the point shown in the figure, the script is processing the "read name" command line.

When the user chooses option 2 from the System Request menu, the interrupt occurs. It first interrupts the *read* utility, and then causes Qshell to run the trap handler (the *ConfirmCancel* function). Regardless of the action of the *ConfirmCancel* function, *read* has already been interrupted. The script detects the error (the return from *read* being interrupted), and retries the operation.

278

```
cat confirmint.qsh
#!/usr/bin/qsh
trap ConfirmCancel INT

function ConfirmCancel {
    print "You have asked to cancel script $0."
    print "Cancelling this script may result in corrupted data."
    print "If you wish to cancel, type YES."
    read confirmation
    if [[ "$confirmation" == YES ]]
        then
            print "Script $0 was cancelled."
            exit 33
    else
            print "Script $0 is continuing."
    fi
}

# CAREFUL. Writing infinite loops like this can
# cause apparent hangs if a recurring error is detected.
while true
do
    print 'What is your name?'
    read name
    if [[ $? -eq 0 ]] then
        break
    fi
done

echo "Hello $name"
./confirmint.qsh
What is your name?
You have asked to cancel script ./confirmint.qsh.
Cancelling this script may result in corrupted data.
If you wish to cancel, type YES.
no
Script ./confirmint.qsh is continuing.
What is your name?
Fred
Hello Fred
```

Figure 15.12: Use care with using or automating the INT signal.

The example in Figure 15.13 shows how to disable the ENDRQS (End Request) command. If the user selects the option 2 from the System Request menu, nothing happens. After the "read name" command line, the second *trap* restores the default action of the ENDRQS command, which is to immediately terminate the script.

```
cat ./ignoreint.qsh
#!/usr/bin/qsh
# CAREFUL. Writing infinite loops like this can
# cause apparent hangs if a recurring error is detected.
while true
do
    print 'What is your name?'
    trap "" INT
    read name
    trap - INT
    if [[ $? -eq 0 ]] then
        break
    fi
done
echo "Hello $name"
./ignoreint.qsh
What is your name?
Fred
Hello Fred
```

Figure 15.13: Use trap to disable an interrupt.

THE KILL UTILITY

You have seen the way that scripts can handle signals and pseudo-signals through the *trap* utility. Those same scripts might need to send signals.

Somewhat misnamed for its most frequently used action, *kill* explicitly sends any signal to a job. In its simplest form or using the correct parameters, the *kill* utility can be loosely equated to the CL command ENDJOB (End Job), in that it can terminate a process. In this form, it requires only one parameter: the process ID of the job to be terminated. In the absence of other parameters, *kill* sends the TERM signal (assigned the number 6 in OS/400) to the process, terminating it.

In its other forms, *kill* sends arbitrary signals to a job or jobs. These signals are used by scripts or programs for various indicators and for more general actions. Other than terminating a job, the second most common use of *kill* is to tell a job to "refresh" in some fashion. For example, use *kill* to send a signal that, when received, causes the target job to reread its configuration files and restart with the new configuration.

The syntax of the *kill* command is as follows:

```
kill [-signal] process-id...
kill [-s signal-name] process-id...
kill [-n signal-number] process-id...
kill -l [signal-name ...]
```

Details about the options for *kill* are given in Table 15.4.

Table 15.4: Options for the Kill Utility

Option	Description
-l *name/number*	List the signals given by the signal-name parameters, or list all signals if no parameters are specified.
-n *number*	Send signal number *number* to the list of process IDs specified.
-s *name*	Send signal name *name* to the list of process IDs specified.
-*signal*	A shortcut for the -n or -s option, the signal name or number can be immediately prefixed by a dash to send the signal.

You may use the *-s* and *-n* options to send signals other than TERM. Follow the *-n* option with the signal, or follow *-s* with a signal name. The *-l* option was demonstrated in Figures 15.4 and 15.5.

Use special care if you're familiar with the *kill* utility on other platforms. Signal numbers are assigned different values on various platforms. For example, a command like *kill -9* won't act as expected. Instead, use the *kill* utility with the name of the signal, such as *kill -KILL*.

For each form of the *kill* utility, the process-id parameter can be given in one of three forms to indicate a particular job:

- Use the integer process ID assigned to the job by the system.
- Use a percent sign (%) plus the Qshell job number.
- Use a percent sign plus the beginning characters of a Qshell job name.

Figure 15.14 demonstrates a simple script, receiver.qsh, which provides a generic signal-handling tool. Use this script to experiment with the *kill* utility. The example shown submits the receiver.qsh script in the background and sends the TERM signal (the default signal) using the process ID that Qshell displays when starting jobs in the background.

```
cat receiver.qsh
#!/usr/bin/qsh
# This script is a generic signal receiver script.
# It is used to demonstrate handling signals.
if [ "$1" = "" ]; then
    echo "Usage: receiver.qsh [signal-name]..."
    exit 1
fi

trap HandleSignal $*

function HandleSignal {
    echo "Script receiver.qsh received a signal. Ending."
    exit 0
}

while true; do
    echo "Script receiver.qsh is trapping signals: $*"
    sleep 10;
done
receiver.qsh TERM &
[1]  194
Script receiver.qsh is trapping signals: TERM
kill 194
Script receiver.qsh received a signal. Ending.
```

Figure 15.14: Send the TERM signal to a running script using the process ID.

The example shown in Figure 15.15 builds slightly on Figure 15.14. In this example, the command lines for the *kill* utility also use the *%number* Qshell shortcut to target the running script using the Qshell job number. The Qshell job number and the job name of submitted Qshell jobs can be listed using the *jobs* utility. Be aware that the Qshell job number and job name differ from the iSeries job number and job name.

Using the same receiver.qsh script as Figure 15.14, the TERM signal in Figure 15.15 is first sent to the running script. The script terminates immediately because it does not trap the TERM signal. The second attempt sends the USR1 signal to the running script. Since the script is trapping the USR1 signal, the handler runs and prints out the message.

```
receiver.qsh USR1 USR2 &
[1]   197
Script receiver.qsh is trapping signals: USR1 USR2
kill %1
jobs
[1]   Terminated                      receiver.qsh USR1 USR2 &
receiver.qsh USR1 USR2 &
[1]   198
Script receiver.qsh is trapping signals: USR1 USR2
kill -USR1 %1
Script receiver.qsh received a signal. Ending.
```

Figure 15.15: Send the TERM signal and the USR1 signal using the Qshell job-number shortcut.

The example in Figure 15.16 again uses the receiver.qsh script. In this case, the Qshell *jobs* utility displays the running Qshell jobs. The INT signal is sent to the running script using the *%jobname* shortcut. Since the receiver.qsh script is trapping the INT signal, it runs the Handler subroutine and exits.

```
receiver.qsh INT &
[1]   202
Script receiver.qsh is trapping signals: INT
jobs
[1]   Running                         receiver.qsh INT &
kill -INT %receiver
Script receiver.qsh received a signal. Ending.
```

Figure 15.16: Send the INT signal using the Qshell job name shortcut.

SUMMARY

In this chapter, you've learned about some advanced Qshell programming features:

- Use Qshell option settings with the *set* utility to trace and debug your shell scripts.

- Use traps and signals to handle complex and unexpected error conditions. Detecting simple errors early can prevent more serious errors later.

- Use the *kill* utility to manage running scripts or provide simple event-notification between scripts.

Chapter 16

Archives and Compression

Working with a large number of related files can sometimes be cumbersome and time-consuming. Archive files help reduce the complexity of file manipulation. By grouping related files together into a single archive file, moving and transferring that one file has the effect of moving or transferring all of the individual files. The individual files are extracted when desired.

Users familiar with iSeries save files will find similarities in the way other archive files are used to back up, move, or transfer groups of files. The iSeries save file is an archive file.

The most common types of archive files are zip files, jar files, and tar files. The archive file type refers to the utility used to create the archive file. For example, a *zip* utility creates zip archive files.

A compressed archive file uses less space than the sum of all of the individual files that it contains. Some archive utilities, such as *jar*, use data compression when creating the archive file, while others, such as *tar*, do not. You can, however, use compression utilities to compress data in archive files that do not use data compression themselves. For example, archive files created by the *tar* utility are commonly compressed using the compress utility.

Archive files are binary files that have defined data formats. When transferring archive files (perhaps using FTP), always transfer in binary mode. The Qshell *archive* utility converts the data as required by the utility during insertion or extraction of files from the archive files.

EXAMPLE DATA

The examples in this chapter use an assortment of files, links, and directories as the source of the data. For demonstration purposes, the examples all use the *v* option to verbosely display the *tar* processing that occurs. The example data is listed in Figure 16.1

```
ls -l
total: 36 kilobytes
-rwxr-xr-x  1 JSMITH  0        107 Jul 13 15:45 HelloC.c
-rwxr-xr-x  1 JSMITH  0        118 Jul 13 15:45 HelloCpp.C
drwxrwsrwx  2 JSMITH  0       8192 Jul 13 15:46 data
lrwxrwxrwx  1 JSMITH  0         37 Jul 13 15:44 goodoleboys.sql ->
    /home/jsmith/src/data/goodoleboys.sql
lrwxrwxrwx  1 JSMITH  0         37 Jul 13 15:44 goodoleboys.txt ->
    /home/jsmith/src/data/goodoleboys.txt
lrwxrwxrwx  1 JSMITH  0         31 Jul 13 15:43 qcsrc ->
    /qsys.lib/jsmith.lib/qcsrc.file

ls -lL data qcsrc
data:
total: 40 kilobytes
-rw-rw----  1 JSMITH  0       3341 Jul 13 15:46 customers.txt
-rw-rw----  1 JSMITH  0      13400 Jul 13 15:46 notes.txt

qcsrc:
total: 228 kilobytes
-rwx---rwx  1 JSMITH  0      73431 Jul 13 15:42 GOODBYE.MBR
-rwx---rwx  1 JSMITH  0      19434 Jul 13 15:42 HELLO.MBR
-rwx---rwx  1 JSMITH  0      73431 Jul 13 15:43 TEST.MBR
```

Figure16.1: These files and directories are used by the archive examples in this chapter.

TAR

Tar, the *tape archive* utility, is named for its ability to read, write, and list files on a tape drive. A tar file is a binary file; the tar file format specifies an ASCII file format. The *tar* utility converts files inserted into the archive to ASCII. When extracting files, the *tar* utility converts files extracted from the archive to EBCDIC (the default CCSID of the job). Setting the QIBM_CCSID environment variable to a value other than zero causes *tar* to convert the ASCII data in the archived file to that CCSID.

Like tape media, a tar file contains a sequential list of file or directory entries. The same source file may be present in the tar file more than once. If you add or update file entries in a tar file, the entries are added to the end.

When the *tar* utility encounters a directory, it processes the directories recursively unless the directory is a symbolic link. Symbolic-link processing is controlled by the *H*, *L*, and *P* options.

The syntax of *tar* is shown here:

```
tar operation option [...] [tar-file] [block-size] [files...]
```

Tar Options

The first option character passed to *tar* is the operation that *tar* should perform. Exactly one option for the operation is required from the list shown in Table 16.1. Specify the tar-file parameter if the *f* option is used; otherwise, the tar-file parameter defaults to the file *archive.tar*. *Tar* assumes that the first argument consists of one or more options. For this reason, the options do not have to be preceded by a hyphen.

If no files are specified for an extract or list operation, all files in the archive are targeted. If no files are specified for a create, update, or append operation, the filenames are read from standard input.

All other options for *tar* are optional. They are shown in Table 16.2, and affect the way that the tar operation is carried out.

Table 16.1: Operations for Tar

Operation	Description
c	Create a new archive file.
x	Extract files from an archive file.
t	List files in an archive file.
r	Append files to an existing archive file.
u	Update files in the archive file. The *u* option is rather misleading, because updated files are actually added to the end of the archive, similar to what you might expect the *r* option to do.

Table 16.2: Options for Tar

Option	Description
b	This option indicates that the next argument is the blocksize argument. The blocksize argument is used to define the size of the block when creating an archive file.
e	Exit immediately if an error is encountered.
f	This option indicates that the next argument is the archive file argument. Use an archive file name of – (dash) to read or write the archive to standard input or standard output. If unspecified, tar uses a default archive filename of archive.tar.
m	Modification times of extracted files are not restored when extracting files from the archive file.
O	Extracted files are assigned the owner and group of the current user. Saved owner and group settings are not restored from the archive file.
p	Preserve the file mode, access, and modification times, as well as owner and group settings, of files when extracting files from the archive file.
v	Use verbose mode. Write additional information about files processed during any operation.
w	Wait for a confirmation from the user before taking any action.

Table 16.2: Options for Tar, *continued*

Option	Description
H	Remove references to symbolic links for files specified on the command line. Archive the files referred to by the links instead of the symbolic links themselves.
L	Remove references to all symbolic links encountered. Archive the files referred to by the links instead of the symbolic links themselves.
P	Do not remove references to symbolic links. Archive the symbolic links themselves instead of the files referred to by the symbolic links. This is the default symbolic-link behavior.
X	While processing directories recursively, do not process directories that have a different device ID (for example, symbolic links to directories in a different file system).

Tar Examples

This section contains several examples that demonstrate some basic *tar* operations. Figure 16.2 demonstrates how to create an archive file. The default symbolic-link behavior is as if the *P* option were used. Therefore, the qcsrc and goodoleboys symbolic links are copied directly to the archives. The *l* (list) operation shows that the symbolic links are present in the archive file, not the files to which the links point.

```
tar vc *
HelloC.c
HelloCpp.C
archive.tar
data
data/customers.txt
data/notes.txt
goodoleboys.sql
goodoleboys.txt
qcsrc
tar: 001-2298 For archive file tar and volume 1, 9 files were
     processed with 0 bytes read and 0 bytes written.
```

Figure 16.2: The default archive file contains all files and directories in the current directory (part 1 of 2).

```
ls -l archive.tar
-rw-rw-rw-   1 JSMITH    0          30720 Jul 13 16:02 archive.tar
tar tv
-rwxr-xr-x   1 JSMITH    0              0 Jul 13 15:45 HelloC.c
-rwxr-xr-x   1 JSMITH    0              0 Jul 13 15:45 HelloCpp.C
-rw-rw-rw-   1 JSMITH    0              0 Jul 13 16:02 archive.tar
drwxrwsrwx   2 JSMITH    0              0 Jul 13 15:46 data
-rw-rw----   1 JSMITH    0              0 Jul 13 15:46 data/customers.txt
-rw-rw----   1 JSMITH    0              0 Jul 13 15:46 data/notes.txt
lrwxrwxrwx   1 JSMITH    0              0 Jul 13 15:44 goodoleboys.sql =>
     /home/jsmith/src/data/goodoleboys.sql
lrwxrwxrwx   1 JSMITH    0              0 Jul 13 15:44 goodoleboys.txt =>
     /home/jsmith/src/data/goodoleboys.txt
lrwxrwxrwx   1 JSMITH    0              0 Jul 13 15:43 qcsrc =>
     /qsys.lib/jsmith.lib/qcsrc.file
```

Figure 16.2: The default archive file contains all files and directories in the current directory (part 2 of 2).

Figure 16.3 demonstrates the *w* (Wait for Confirmation) option that prompts the user for individual file actions. Only the HelloC.c file is added to the archive file. A subsequent *tar* update operation (the *u* option) adds HelloC.c to the archive file again, but this time the user renames the file "HelloC-version2.c." Used this way, the *tar* utility provides a rudimentary historical view of a changing data file.

```
tar cw H*
tar: Starting interactive file rename operation.
tar: The current file is HelloC.c with mode -rwxr-xr-x  and a
     modification time of Jul 13 17:01.
tar: Enter a new name, or a period (".") to quit, or press
     Enter to skip this file:
.
tar: The file name is not changed.
tar: Starting interactive file rename operation.
tar: The current file is HelloCpp.C with mode -rwxr-xr-x  and
     a modification time of Jul 13 17:01.
tar: Enter a new name, or a period (".") to quit, or press
     Enter to skip this file:
tar: The file is skipped.
tar tvf archive.tar
-rwxr-xr-x  1 JSMITH    0              0 Jul 13 17:01 HelloC.c
tar: 001-2298 For archive file tar and volume 1, 1 files were
     processed with 0 bytes read and 102400 bytes written.
```

Figure 16.3: Options can be used to confirm file operations (part 1 of 2).

```
tar wuf archive.tar HelloC.c
tar: Starting interactive file rename operation.
tar: The current file is HelloC.c with mode -rwxr-xr-x  and a
    modification time of Jul 13 17:01.
tar: Enter a new name, or a period (".") to quit, or press
    Enter to skip this file:
HelloC-version2.c
tar: The file name is changed to HelloC-version2.c.
tar tvf archive.tar
-rwxr-xr-x  1 JSMITH    0          0 Jul 13 17:01 HelloC.c
-rwxr-xr-x  1 JSMITH    0          0 Jul 13 17:01 HelloC-version2.c
tar: 001-2298 For archive file tar and volume 1, 2 files were
    processed with 0 bytes read and 199168 bytes written.
```

Figure 16.3: Options can be used to confirm file operations (part 2 of 2).

Use the *L* option to create an archive file containing the current directory (the dot). With this option, the files or directories referred to by symbolic links (in Figure 16.4, qcsrc, goodoleboys.sql, and goodoleboys.txt) are copied directly into the archive instead of the links. When extracting those objects, only the files remain.

```
tar cLf archive-file.tar .
tar: 001-2298 For archive file tar and volume 1, 14 files were
    processed with 0 bytes read and 0 bytes written.
tar tvf archive-file.tar
drwxrwsrwx  2 JSMITH    0          0 Jul 13 16:26 .
-rw-rw-rw-  1 JSMITH    0          0 Jul 12 16:39 ./goodoleboys.sql
-rw-rw-rw-  1 JSMITH    0          0 Jun 29 13:03 ./goodoleboys.txt
drwx---rwx  2 JSMITH    0          0 Jul 13 15:43 ./qcsrc
-rwx---rwx  1 JSMITH    0          0 Jul 13 15:42 ./qcsrc/GOODBYE.MBR
-rwx---rwx  1 JSMITH    0          0 Jul 13 15:42 ./qcsrc/HELLO.MBR
-rwx---rwx  1 JSMITH    0          0 Jul 13 15:43 ./qcsrc/TEST.MBR
-rwxr-xr-x  1 JSMITH    0          0 Jul 13 15:45 ./HelloCpp.C
-rwxr-xr-x  1 JSMITH    0          0 Jul 13 15:45 ./HelloC.c
drwxrwsrwx  2 JSMITH    0          0 Jul 13 15:46 ./data
-rw-rw----  1 JSMITH    0          0 Jul 13 15:46 ./data/customers.txt
-rw-rw----  1 JSMITH    0          0 Jul 13 15:46 ./data/notes.txt
-rw-rw-rw-  1 JSMITH    0          0 Jul 13 16:28 ./archive.tar
-rw-rw-rw-  1 JSMITH    0          0 Jul 13 16:26 ./test.tar
tar: 001-2298 For archive file tar and volume 1, 14 files were
    processed with 0 bytes read and 266240 bytes written.
```

Figure 16.4: The L option follows symbolic links.

Figure 16.5 demonstrates a combination of the *X* and *L* options. While the *L* option causes tar to follow all symbolic links, the *X* option prevents *tar* from writing the contents of directory qcsrc, because *qcsrc* refers to a different file system.

```
tar cvXL .
.
./goodoleboys.sql
./goodoleboys.txt
./qcsrc
./HelloCpp.C
./HelloC.c
./data
./data/customers.txt
./data/notes.txt
./archive.tar
./test.tar
tar: 001-2298 For archive file tar and volume 1, 11 files were
     processed with 0 bytes read and 0 bytes written.
tar tvf archive.tar
drwxrwsrwx   2 JSMITH   0        0 Jul 13 16:26 .
-rw-rw-rw-   1 JSMITH   0        0 Jul 12 16:39 ./goodoleboys.sql
-rw-rw-rw-   1 JSMITH   0        0 Jun 29 13:03 ./goodoleboys.txt
drwx---rwx   2 JSMITH   0        0 Jul 13 15:43 ./qcsrc
-rwxr-xr-x   1 JSMITH   0        0 Jul 13 15:45 ./HelloCpp.C
-rwxr-xr-x   1 JSMITH   0        0 Jul 13 15:45 ./HelloC.c
drwxrwsrwx   2 JSMITH   0        0 Jul 13 15:46 ./data
-rw-rw----   1 JSMITH   0        0 Jul 13 15:46 ./data/customers.txt
-rw-rw----   1 JSMITH   0        0 Jul 13 15:46 ./data/notes.txt
-rw-rw-rw-   1 JSMITH   0        0 Jul 13 16:32 ./archive.tar
-rw-rw-rw-   1 JSMITH   0        0 Jul 13 16:26 ./test.tar
tar: 001-2298 For archive file tar and volume 1, 11 files were
     processed with 0 bytes read and 92160 bytes written.
```

Figure 16.5: Use the X option to avoid files in other file systems.

If no file names are passed to *tar* on the command line, *tar* reads the file names from standard input. In Figure 16.6, the *ls* utility is used to enter all files in the current directory. As each filename is read by *tar*, that file is added to the archive.

```
ls -1 | tar cvf test.tar
HelloC.c
HelloCpp.C
archive.tar
```

Figure 16.6: By default, tar reads file names from standard input (part 1 of 2).

```
data
data/customers.txt
data/notes.txt
goodoleboys.sql
goodoleboys.txt
qcsrc
tar: 001-2298 For archive file tar and volume 1, 9 files were
    processed with 0 bytes read and 0 bytes written.
tar tvf test.tar
-rwxr-xr-x  1 JSMITH     0          0 Jul 13 15:45 HelloC.c
-rwxr-xr-x  1 JSMITH     0          0 Jul 13 15:45 HelloCpp.C
-rw-rw-rw-  1 JSMITH     0          0 Jul 13 16:24 archive.tar
drwxrwsrwx  2 JSMITH     0          0 Jul 13 15:46 data
-rw-rw----  1 JSMITH     0          0 Jul 13 15:46 data/customers.txt
-rw-rw----  1 JSMITH     0          0 Jul 13 15:46 data/notes.txt
lrwxrwxrwx  1 JSMITH     0          0 Jul 13 15:44 goodoleboys.sql =>
    /home/jsmith/src/data/goodoleboys.sql
lrwxrwxrwx  1 JSMITH     0          0 Jul 13 15:44 goodoleboys.txt =>
    /home/jsmith/src/data/goodoleboys.txt
lrwxrwxrwx  1 JSMITH     0          0 Jul 13 15:43 qcsrc =>
    /qsys.lib/jsmith.lib/qcsrc.file
tar: 001-2298 For archive file tar and volume 1, 9 files were
    processed with 0 bytes read and 61440 bytes written.
```

Figure 16.6: By default, tar reads file names from standard input (part 2 of 2).

Figure 16.7 demonstrates restoring individual files from an archive. The archive contents are first shown using the *t* (List) option. The *x* (Extract) option extracts files that match the patterns passed on the command line. In this example, a wildcard is used. The pattern with the wildcard must be quoted on the Qshell command line to prevent Qshell from expanding it and allow the *tar* utility to expand the wildcard. Restore all files by specifying no filename parameters on the command line.

```
tar tvf archive.tar
drwxrwsrwx  2 JSMITH     0          0 Jul 13 16:45 .
lrwxrwxrwx  1 JSMITH     0          0 Jul 13 15:44 ./goodoleboys.sql =>
    /home/jsmith/src/data/goodoleboys.sql
lrwxrwxrwx  1 JSMITH     0          0 Jul 13 15:44 ./goodoleboys.txt =>
    /home/jsmith/src/data/goodoleboys.txt
lrwxrwxrwx  1 JSMITH     0          0 Jul 13 15:43 ./qcsrc =>
    /qsys.lib/jsmith.lib/qcsrc.file
-rwxr-xr-x  1 JSMITH     0          0 Jul 13 15:45 ./HelloCpp.C
```

Figure 16.7: The tar utility also restores files from an archive (part 1 of 2).

```
-rwxr-xr-x  1 JSMITH   0     0 Jul 13 15:45 ./HelloC.c
drwxrwsrwx  2 JSMITH   0     0 Jul 13 15:46 ./data
-rw-rw----  1 JSMITH   0     0 Jul 13 15:46 ./data/customers.txt
-rw-rw----  1 JSMITH   0     0 Jul 13 15:46 ./data/notes.txt
-rw-rw-rw-  1 JSMITH   0     0 Jul 13 16:45 ./archive.tar
-rw-rw-rw-  1 JSMITH   0     0 Jul 13 16:26 ./test.tar
tar: 001-2298 For archive file tar and volume 1, 11 files were
    processed with 0 bytes read and 92160 bytes written.
tar xvf archive.tar './Hello*' ./data
./HelloCpp.C
./HelloC.c
./data
./data/customers.txt
./data/notes.txt
tar: 001-2298 For archive file tar and volume 1, 11 files were
    processed with 0 bytes read and 92160 bytes written.
tar xvf archive.tar
.
./goodoleboys.sql
./goodoleboys.txt
./qcsrc
./HelloCpp.C
./HelloC.c
./data
./data/customers.txt
./data/notes.txt
./archive.tar
./test.tar
tar: 001-2298 For archive file tar and volume 1, 11 files were
    processed with 0 bytes read and 92160 bytes written.
```

Figure 16.7: The tar utility also restores files from an archive (part 2 of 2).

The *u* (Update) option updates files in an archive. Updated files are inserted into the archive again. The listings in Figure 16.8 (*tar tvf*) show the contents of the tar file before and after the update. After the update, note that the files HelloC.c and HelloCpp.C are present in the archive twice with different file timestamps. When the HelloC.c file is extracted, the *tar* utility processes the archive sequentially (like a tape drive). The HelloC.c file is encountered twice and extracted each time. The result is that the latest version of the HelloC.c file with timestamp "Jul 13 16:58" is extracted.

```
tar tvf archive.tar
-rwxr-xr-x  1 JSMITH     0        0 Jul 13 15:45 HelloC.c
-rwxr-xr-x  1 JSMITH     0        0 Jul 13 15:45 HelloCpp.C
drwxrwsrwx  2 JSMITH     0        0 Jul 13 15:46 data
-rw-rw----  1 JSMITH     0        0 Jul 13 15:46 data/customers.txt
 rw-rw----  1 JSMITH     0        0 Jul 13 15:46 data/notes.txt
lrwxrwxrwx  1 JSMITH     0        0 Jul 13 16:54 goodoleboys.sql =>
    /home/jsmith/src/data/goodoleboys.sql
lrwxrwxrwx  1 JSMITH     0        0 Jul 13 16:54 goodoleboys.txt =>
    /home/jsmith/src/data/goodoleboys.txt
lrwxrwxrwx  1 JSMITH     0        0 Jul 13 16:54 qcsrc =>
    /qsys.lib/jsmith.lib/qcsrc.file
tar: 001-2298 For archive file tar and volume 1, 10 files were
    processed with 0 bytes read and 215040 bytes written.
ls -l Hello*
-rwxr-xr-x  1 JSMITH     0    92160 Jul 13 16:58 HelloC.c
-rwxr-xr-x  1 JSMITH     0      118 Jul 13 16:58 HelloCpp.C
tar uvf archive.tar Hello*
tar: 001-2315 The archive is being read to position to the end
    of the archive.
done.
HelloC.c
HelloCpp.C
tar: 001-2298 For archive file tar and volume 1, 10 files were
    processed with 0 bytes read and 114176 bytes written.
tar tvf archive.tar
-rwxr-xr-x  1 JSMITH     0        0 Jul 13 15:45 HelloC.c
-rwxr-xr-x  1 JSMITH     0        0 Jul 13 15:45 HelloCpp.C
drwxrwsrwx  2 JSMITH     0        0 Jul 13 15:46 data
-rw-rw----  1 JSMITH     0        0 Jul 13 15:46 data/customers.txt
-rw-rw----  1 JSMITH     0        0 Jul 13 15:46 data/notes.txt
lrwxrwxrwx  1 JSMITH     0        0 Jul 13 16:54 goodoleboys.sql =>
    /home/jsmith/src/data/goodoleboys.sql
lrwxrwxrwx  1 JSMITH     0        0 Jul 13 16:54 goodoleboys.txt =>
    /home/jsmith/src/data/goodoleboys.txt
lrwxrwxrwx  1 JSMITH     0        0 Jul 13 16:54 qcsrc =>
    /qsys.lib/jsmith.lib/qcsrc.file
-rwxr-xr-x  1 JSMITH     0        0 Jul 13 16:58 HelloC.c
-rwxr-xr-x  1 JSMITH     0        0 Jul 13 16:58 HelloCpp.C
tar: 001-2298 For archive file tar and volume 1, 10 files were
    processed with 0 bytes read and 215040 bytes written.
tar xvf archive.tar HelloC.c
HelloC.c
HelloC.c
tar: 001-2298 For archive file tar and volume 1, 12 files were
    processed with 0 bytes read and 307200 bytes written.
```

Figure 16.8: The u *option updates files in an archive.*

THE JAR UTILITY

The *jar* (*Java archive*) utility includes data compression in the file format. Most convenient because of the widespread use of zip files, *jar* creates and extracts zip file archives. *Jar's* zip files are compatible with the PkZip and WinZip applications that are typically used on Windows workstations.

The *jar* utility has syntax similar to *tar*. See chapter 23 for a detailed description of the *jar* utility.

THE PAX UTILITY

The *pax* (*portable archive exchange*) utility enables access to less commonly used archive file formats, so you can use it to exchange data with older systems. The *pax* utility supports six different file formats, listed in Table 16.3.

Table 16.3: File Formats Supported by Pax

Format	Description
cpio	A data format defined by the Posix 1003.2 standard
bcpio	An older version of the cpio format; seldom used and not very portable
sv4cpio	The UNIX System V release 4 version of the cpio file format
sv4crc	The UNIX System V release 4 version of the cpio file format that uses file CRC checksums
tar	An old tar file format used by BSD UNIX 4.3
ustar	The data format defined for tar by the Posix 1003.2 standard

There are four main forms of *pax*: list, read, write, and copy. Each uses different arguments. Here is their basic syntax:

```
pax [list-options] [-f archive-file] [file-pattern]
pax -r [read-options] [-f archive-file] [file-pattern]
pax -w [write-options] [-f archive-file] [files…]
pax -r -w [copy-options] [-f archive-file] [files…] directory
```

Although *pax* might come in handy in some instances, it is infrequently used. Other than the tar format, the file formats that *pax* supports are not common ones.

Pax Options

The presence or absence of the option characters *r* and *w* control the operation that *pax* should perform. Other options control behavior of the list, read, write or copy operations. The options for *pax* are listed in Table 16.4.

Table 16.4: Options for the Pax Utility

Option	Description
a	Append files to an existing *archive file*. This is used with the write operation.
A	Use the pax utility as if it's the old tar utility.
b *<blocksize>*	Specify a block size for writing to the archive file. The block size is a multiple of 512, and the maximum size is 32,256. End the blocksize parameter with a *b* or *k* to specify the parameter as the number of blocks or number of kilobytes. Permissible blocksize values depend on the file format.
B *<size>*	The maximum size of the archive file written is set to the size parameter. End the size parameter with a *b*, *k*, or *m* to specify it as the number of 512-byte blocks, kilobytes, or megabytes.
c	Complement (invert) the *file-pattern* or *files* parameters. All individual files except those matching the *file-pattern* or *files* parameters are targeted for the operation.
C *<ccsid>*	Convert data from CCSID 819 (ASCII) to the CCSID specified when files are extracted.
d	Do not recurse into directories.
D	This is similar to the -u option, but the file inode change time is used instead of the file modification time.
E *<errors>*	This holds the number of errors tolerated while trying to read a corrupted archive. Valid values are none, zero, or another integer value. Don't use a value of none, however, because the pax utility could loop forever on a corrupted archive.

297

Table 16.4: Options for the Pax Utility, *continued*

Option	Description
f *archive-file*	Specify the archive file used. If not specified, the pax utility uses standard input or standard output for the archive data. The pax utility prompts for subsequent archive-volume file names if required.
G *<groupname>*	Match files using the group name after the *file-pattern* or *files* parameters. If the groupname string starts with a pound sign (#), it is the group number instead of the name.
i	Interactively prompt the user to rename files. Respond with a blank line to skip a file, a period (dot) to use the current name of the file, or the new file name that pax should use.
H	Remove references to symbolic links for files specified on the command line. Archive the files referred to by the links instead of the symbolic links themselves.
k	Keep (do not replace) existing files.
l	Link files when doing a copy operation. If possible, hard links are used between the source files and the target files. The data is only present in the file system once.
L	Remove references to all symbolic links encountered. Archive the files referred to by the links instead of the symbolic links themselves.
n	Stop selecting files that match the *file-pattern* parameter after the first file matches.
o*<name=value>*	This is optional information to modify the behavior of the algorithm used to extract or write the particular archive file format.
p*<privileges>*	Indicate file privileges and settings. Use multiple privileges or multiple instance of the –p option to specify more than one privilege. *a*—Do not preserve file access times. *e*—Preserve all file privileges and settings of the files. *m*—Do not preserve modification times. *o*—Preserve the owner information (user ID and group ID). *p*—Preserve file mode (authority).
P	Do not remove references to symbolic links; the default symbolic link behavior. Archive the symbolic links themselves instead of the files referred to by the symbolic links.

Table 16.4: Options for the Pax Utility, *continued*

Option	Description
s *<subst>*	Substitute file-name text for files matched by the *file-pattern* or *files* parameter. The value of the subst string is specified as */match/replace/[gp]*, where *match* is a regular expression. (See chapter 18 for more information about regular expressions.)
t	Retain the file-access times of any file that the pax utility accesses. File-access times are reset to the values that they had prior to pax accessing them.
T [*<from>*][,*<to>*]	Match files using the time and date range after the *files-pattern* or *files* parameter. Either the from parameter or the to parameter may be omitted. Files older than the to parameter and newer than the from parameter are selected.
u	Update files based on the file-modification time. Files extracted that are older than an existing file are skipped. Files written to an archive are skipped if they are older than existing files in the archive.
U *<username>*	Match files using the user name after the *file-pattern* or *files* parameters. If the user name starts with a pound sign (#), it is the user number instead of the name.
v	Process the operation verbosely.
x *<format>*	Specify the archive file format. The file format is detected automatically for existing archive files.
-X	While processing directories recursively, do not process directories that have a different device ID (for example, symbolic links to directories in a different file system).
Y	Similar to the *−D* option, but the file-inode change time is used instead of the file-modification time after any file rename operations have finished.
Z	Similar to the *−u* option, but the file-inode change time is used instead of the file-modification time after any file-rename operations have finished.

Pax examples

Figure 16.9 shows how to create a tar archive with *pax*.

```
pax -wvx ustar -f archive.tar *
HelloC.c
HelloCpp.C
archive.tar
data
data/customers.txt
data/notes.txt
goodoleboys.sql
goodoleboys.txt
qcsrc.file
pax: 001-2298 For archive file ustar and volume 1, 9 files were
    processed with 0 bytes read and 0 bytes written.
ls -l archive.tar
rw-rw-rw-  1 JSMITH  0            122880 Jul 25 20:47 archive.tar
```

Figure 16.9: You can create a tar-format file archive using the pax utility.

You can also use *pax* to list the contents of a tar file archive, as shown in Figure 16.10. The *x* option is not required because *pax* automatically detects the file format of an existing archive.

```
pax -vf archive.tar
-rwxr-xr-x  1 JSMITH   0        0 Jul 13 17:01 HelloC.c
-rwxr-xr-x  1 JSMITH   0        0 Jul 13 17:01 HelloCpp.C
drwxrwsrwx  2 JSMITH   0        0 Jul 13 15:46 data
-rw-rw----  1 JSMITH   0        0 Jul 13 15:46 data/customers.txt
-rw-rw----  1 JSMITH   0        0 Jul 13 15:46 data/notes.txt
lrwxrwxrwx  1 JSMITH   0        0 Jul 13 16:54 goodoleboys.sql =>
    /home/jsmith/src/data/goodoleboys.sql
lrwxrwxrwx  1 JSMITH   0        0 Jul 13 16:54 goodoleboys.txt =>
    /home/jsmith/src/data/goodoleboys.txt
lrwxrwxrwx  1 JSMITH   0        0 Jul 25 20:44 qcsrc.file =>
    /qsys.lib/jsmith.lib/qcsrc.file
pax: 001-2298 For archive file ustar and volume 1, 8 files were
    processed with 0 bytes read and 122880 bytes written.
```

Figure 16.10: The pax utility can also be used to list the contents of a tar archive.

COMPRESS AND UNCOMPRESS

Data compression is typically used in conjunction with archive files to reduce the size of archive files. The *compress* and *uncompress* utilities replace a file with a compressed or uncompressed version of the file. Any IFS file can be compressed, but the best compression with the *compress* utility is achieved for text files. The *compress* and *uncompress* utilities are virtually identical in syntax, and they operate as a pair:

```
compress [options] [files...]
uncompress [options] [files...]
```

Compressed files have a file extension of .Z. For example, the result of compressing a file named "readme.txt" is a smaller file named "readme.txt.Z." The *uncompress* utility is used on the .Z file to expand it to its original content.

You might be better off compressing data with the *jar* utility instead of these compression utilities. The *jar* utility creates and extracts zip files and may give you better data compression and better cross platform portability.

The Compress and Uncompress Options

The options for *compress* and *uncompress* are listed in Table 16.5.

Table 16.5: Options for Compress and Uncompress

Option	Description
c	Write the output to standard output. The files given are not modified.
f	Used only for the compress utility, to force compression even if no reduction in size occurs.
v	Print compression information for each file.
b *<bits>*	The compress and uncompress tools use a modified Lempel-Ziv compression algorithm. Use this to specify the maximum number of bits used for the replacement codes in the algorithm. The *bits* parameter must be from nine to 16. In all but the most advanced cases, you won't need to specify the number of bits to use because compress and uncompress choose appropriately.

The *compress* and *uncompress* utilities are very simple. Enter *compress* or *uncompress* with the file names you want to compress listed as arguments. In

Figure 16.11, for example, the archive.tar file contains only text data. The *compress* utility reduces the size of the archive.tar file significantly.

```
ls -l archive*
-rw-rw-rw-  1 JSMITH  0        10240 Jul 25 22:32 archive.tar
compress -v archive.tar
archive.tar.Z: 93.03% compression
ls -l archive*
-rw-rw-rw-  1 JSMITH  0          714 Jul 25 22:32 archive.tar.Z
uncompress -v archive.tar.Z
ls -l archive*
-rw-rw-rw-  1 JSMITH  0        10240 Jul 25 22:32 archive.tar
```

Figure 16.11: Compression has a significant effect on text files.

Use the *zcat* utility to copy the contents of a compressed file to stdout. The first *ls* command in Figure 16.12 shows that the file fone.txt is the only file whose name begins with the string *fone*. After compression, fone.txt has been replaced with fone.txt.Z. The *zcat* utility writes the uncompressed contents of the archive to stdout.

```
ls -l fone*
-rw-rw----  1 JSMITH  0          251 Dec 25 13:41 fone.txt
/home/JSMITH $
cat fone.txt
Name       Phone     Fax       Cell
========= ========= ========= =========
Larry      234-5678  234-6789  234-1111
Moe        345-6789  345-7890  345-2022
Abbott     456-7890  456-8901  none
Costello  987-6543  none      987-3323
Curly      876-5432  876-4321  876-4441
/home/JSMITH $
compress -v fone.txt
fone.txt.Z: 29.48% compression
/home/JSMITH $
ls -l fone*
-rw-rw----  1 JSMITH  0          177 Dec 25 13:41 fone.txt.Z
/home/JSMITH $
zcat fone.txt.Z
```

Figure 16.12: Use zcat to view the contents of a compressed file (part 1 of 2).

```
Name      Phone     Fax       Cell
========  ========  ========  ========
Larry     234-5678  234-6789  234-1111
Moe       345-6789  345-7890  345-2022
Abbott    456-7890  456-8901  none
Costello  987-6543  none      987-3323
Curly     876-5432  876-4321  876-4441
```

Figure 16.12: Use zcat to view the contents of a compressed file (part 2 of 2).

SUMMARY

Archive files are good mechanisms to reduce the complexity of manipulating large numbers of files in Qshell. Data-compression utilities available in Qshell can also help with network performance and size requirements when dealing with large archives. The Java *jar* utility can be used as a very portable data compression tool. The *pax* utility is dated, and no longer often used.

Chapter 17

Grep

Grep is a scan utility that originated with Unix systems, but is now implemented in many environments, including Qshell. The *grep* utility looks for files that contain character strings. Although *grep* is typically used with text files, it may also be used with binary files.

Anyone who deals with the Integrated File System should learn to use *grep*, because the Find String Using PDM command (FNDSTRPDM) won't work with IFS files. Even if you don't deal with IFS, you still might want use *grep* because it works with source physical files and has more powerful search capabilities than FNDSTRPDM.

Different sources give different versions of the origin of the term *grep*, but it's likely that it comes from a search command in the ed and ex text editors. The command is g/re/p, where *g* indicates that the search is global (that is, over the entire file), *re* indicates that a regular expression describes the search string, and *p* indicates that the results are to be printed (i.e., displayed on the screen).

Here is the syntax of *grep*:

```
grep [options] regular-expression [input-files]
```

REGULAR EXPRESSIONS

The regular-expression parameter is the string for which you are searching. The simplest form of a regular expression is an exact sequence of characters for which the system is to search. In the following example, *grep* searches all files whose names end with *.java* (i.e., all Java source files) in the current directory for the string *print*:

```
grep print *.java
```

By default, the search is case-sensitive, so this *grep* command will not find *Print*, *PRINT*, *pRINT*, or any other combination of cases.

Grep would be useful even if this were the only kind of search it could perform, but *grep* can do much more, because it knows how to interpret metacharacters (sophisticated versions of wildcards). Table 17.1 describes these special symbols and their meanings.

Table 17.1: Metacharacters for Use with Grep

Metacharacter	Description
. (period)	Match any character except end-of-line.
*	Match zero or more occurrences of the preceding pattern.
^	Match from the beginning of the line.
$	Match from the end of the line.
[ ]	Match any character within the brackets. Ranges may be specified with a hyphen.
[^]	Negates the groups or ranges of characters in the brackets. The caret must be the first character within the brackets.
\{m\}	Match exactly *m* occurrences of the preceding pattern.
\{m,\}	Match *m* or more occurrences of the preceding pattern.

Table 17.1: Metacharacters for Use with Grep, *continued*

Metacharacter	Description
\{m,n\}	Match *m* to n occurrences of the preceding pattern.
\	Turn off the special meaning of the following pattern.
\(\)	Define a back reference to save matched characters as a pattern. The matched pattern can be referred to with a backslash followed by a number later in the expression.

You may also use certain symbolic names in place of characters. These are shown in Table 17.2.

Table 17.2: Symbolic Names

Symbol	Description
[[:alpha:]]	Any letter in either case
[[:upper:]]	Any uppercase letter
[[:lower:]]	Any lowercase letter
[[:digit:]]	Any decimal digit
[[:xdigit:]]	Any hexadecimal digit, where A-F may be upper or lowercase
[[:alnum:]]	Any letter or decimal digit
[[:space:]]	Any space, tab, carriage-return, or formfeed character
[[:blank:]]	Any space or tab character
[[:punct:]]	Any punctuation mark
[[:cntrl:]]	Any control character
[[:print:]]	Any printable character
[[:graph:]]	Any character that is not a letter, digit, or punctuation mark

Grep Examples

To illustrate how regular expressions work, several *grep* examples follow, along with explanations of what each one accomplishes. The data file being searched is goodoleboys.txt, shown in Figure 17.1.

```
cat goodoleboys.txt
Name        Born     Phone     Dog       Wife       Shotgun  Paid
=========== ======== ========= ========= ========== ======== =====
Chuck       Dec 25   444-2345  Blue      Mary Sue   12       $2.50
Bubba       Oct 13   444-1111  Buck      Mary Jean  12
Billy Bob   June 11  444-4340  Leotis    Lisa Sue   12
Amos        Jan 4    333-1119  Amos      Abigail    20
Otis        Sept 17  444-8000  Ol' Sal   Sally      12       $5
Claude      May 31   333-4340  Blue      Etheline   12
Roscoe      Feb 2    444-2234  Rover     Alice Jean 410
Arlis       June 19  444-1314  Redeye    Suzy Beth  12       $10.75
Junior      April 30 BR-549    Percival  Lilly Faye 12
Bill        Feb 29   333-4444  Daisy     Daisy      20
Ernest T.   ??       none      none      none       none
```

Figure 17.1: The goodoleboys.txt file is used for the search examples that follow.

The first example simply finds all lines that begin with uppercase C:

```
grep ^C  goodoleboys.txt
Chuck       Dec 25   444-2345  Blue      Mary Sue   12       $2.50
Claude      May 31   333-4340  Blue      Etheline   12
```

Figure 17.2 is a slightly more complex example. It finds all lines that end with a zero. The first form of *grep* shown in the figure is used with files that are delimited with a single linefeed character, as is typical of Unix files. The second form is for files that are delimited with a combination of carriage-return and linefeed characters. The [[:cntrl:]] expression allows for the carriage return.

```
grep '0$' goodoleboys.txt

grep '0[[:cntrl:]]$' goodoleboys.txt

Chuck       Dec 25   444-2345  Blue      Mary Sue   12       $2.50
Amos        Jan 4    333-1119  Amos      Abigail    20
Roscoe      Feb 2    444-2234  Rover     Alice Jean 410
Bill        Feb 29   333-4444  Daisy     Daisy      20
```

Figure 17.2: Find lines that end with a zero.

The following *grep* command looks for lines that contain a dollar sign followed by any two characters and a period:

```
grep '\$..\.' goodoleboys.txt
Arlis       June 19   444-1314 Redeye   Suzy Beth    12      $10.75
```

The first two periods function as metacharacters. The dollar sign and last period do not because they are preceded with backslashes.

These two *grep* commands find lines that contain a single quote:

```
grep " ' "    goodoleboys.txt
grep \' goodoleboys.txt
Otis        Sept 17   444-8000 Ol' Sal  Sally        12      $5
```

The first line shows that double quotes can "escape" single quotes.

This command finds lines with three zeros together:

```
grep '0\{3\}' goodoleboys.txt
Otis        Sept 17   444-8000 Ol' Sal  Sally        12      $5
```

Figure 17.3 expands on the previous examples to find lines where the same uppercase letter followed by a lowercase letter is repeated. The \(and \) pair indicates that the match is to be saved as a pattern, which can be referred to as \1. If other patterns were saved, they would be referred to as \2, \3, etc. These expressions are known as *back references*.

In the first line returned, the pattern *Bu* is found twice. In the second line, *Ro* is repeated. In the third line, *Sa* is repeated.

```
grep '\([A-Z][a-z]\).*\1' goodoleboys.txt
Bubba       Oct 13    444-1111 Buck     Mary Jean    12
Amos        Jan 4     333-1119 Amos     Abigail      20
Otis        Sept 17   444-8000 Ol' Sal  Sally        12      $5
Roscoe      Feb 2     444-2234 Rover    Alice Jean   410
Bill        Feb 29    333-4444 Daisy    Daisy        20
```

Figure 17.3: Find lines where a particular pair of uppercase and lowercase letters are repeated.

Figure 17.4 illustrates the use of *grep* metacharacters that have to do with including and excluding characters in a search.

```
grep '^[CR]' goodoleboys.txt
Chuck      Dec 25    444-2345 Blue     Mary Sue      12    $2.50
Claude     May 31    333-4340 Blue     Etheline      12
Roscoe     Feb 2     444-2234 Rover    Alice Jean    410

grep '^[C-R]' goodoleboys.txt
Name       Born      Phone    Dog      Wife       Shotgun  Paid
Chuck      Dec 25    444-2345 Blue     Mary Sue      12     $2.50
Otis       Sept 17   444-8000 Ol' Sal  Sally         12     $5
Claude     May 31    333-4340 Blue     Etheline      12
Roscoe     Feb 2     444-2234 Rover    Alice Jean    410
Junior     April 30  BR-549   Percival Lilly Faye    12
Ernest T.  ??        none     none     none          none

grep '^[^p-r]' goodoleboys.txt
Amos       Jan 4     333-1119 Amos     Abigail       20
Roscoe     Feb 2     444-2234 Rover    Alice Jean    410
```

Figure 17.4: *Find lines that begin with* C *or* R, *then find lines that begin with any letter between* C *and* R *(inclusive). Finally, find lines that contain an* A *that is not followed by a letter from* p *to* r, *inclusive.*

The three *grep* commands in Figure 17.5 use symbolic names. The first command finds lines with an alphabetic character, in either case, followed by a hyphen. The second command finds lines with white space followed by exactly three digits and more white space. The last command finds lines where a letter is followed by a punctuation mark.

```
grep '[[:alpha:]]-' goodoleboys.txt
Junior     April 30  BR-549   Percival Lilly Faye    12

grep '[[:space:]][[:digit:]]\{3\}[[:space:]]' goodoleboys.txt
Roscoe     Feb 2     444-2234 Rover    Alice Jean    410

grep '[[:alpha:]][[:punct:]]' goodoleboys.txt
Otis       Sept 17   444-8000 Ol' Sal Sally          12     $5
Junior     April 30  BR-549   Percival Lilly Faye    12
Ernest T.  ??        none     none     none          none
```

Figure 17.5: *These commands illustrate the use of symbolic names.*

Figures 17.6 and 17.7 combine metacharacters and symbolic names to perform complex searches. Figure 17.6 finds lines whose first non-blank token is a group of five to seven letters in any case. Figure 17.7 finds lines that contain a zero followed by a printable character, and then finds lines where the zero is followed by a control character.

```
grep '^[[:space:]]*[[:alpha:]]\{5,7\}[[:space:]]' goodoleboys.txt
Chuck      Dec 25    444-2345 Blue    Mary Sue   12   $2.50
Bubba      Oct 13    444-1111 Buck    Mary Jean  12
Billy Bob  June 11   444-4340 Leotis  Lisa Sue   12
Claude     May 31    333-4340 Blue    Etheline   12
Roscoe     Feb 2     444-2234 Rover   Alice Jean 410
Arlis      June 19   444-1314 Redeye  Suzy Beth  12   $10.75
Junior     April 30  BR-549   Percival Lilly Faye 12
Ernest T.  ??        none     none    none       none
```

Figure 17.6: Find lines whose first non-blank token is a group of five to seven letters in any case.

```
grep '0[[:print:]]' goodoleboys.txt
Billy Bob June 11   444-4340 Leotis  Lisa Sue   12
Otis      Sept 17   444-8000 Ol' Sal Sally      12   $5
Claude    May 31    333-4340 Blue    Etheline   12
Arlis     June 19   444-1314 Redeye  Suzy Beth  12   $10.75
Junior    April 30  BR-549   Percival Lilly Faye 12

grep '0[[:cntrl:]]' goodoleboys.txt
Chuck     Dec 25    444-2345 Blue    Mary Sue   12   $2.50
Amos      Jan 4     333-1119 Amos    Abigail    20
Roscoe    Feb 2     444-2234 Rover   Alice Jean 410
Bill      Feb 29    333-4444 Daisy   Daisy      20
```

Figure 17.7: Find lines where the character 0 (zero) is followed by a printable character, then find lines where zero is followed by a control character.

Quotes

A search pattern does not have to be enclosed in quotes if it does not contain any white space or special characters. In the following example, *grep* searches for the string *an*:

```
grep an goodoleboys.txt
```

However, there's nothing wrong with placing single or double quotes around a search string that has no blanks. Therefore, the following two *grep* commands are equivalent to the previous one:

```
grep 'an' goodoleboys.txt
grep "an" goodoleboys.txt
```

When the search argument includes a parameter or variable, you need to use quotes, unless you are sure that the parameter or variable will never contain blanks. Even so, it is good to use quotes just to be on the safe side.

The *grep* command in Figure 17.8 fails when $searchname is not quoted because Qshell sees *Billy* as the search string, *Bob* as the first file name, and *goodoleboys.txt* as the second file name. *Grep* succeeds only when the search argument is quoted.

```
/home/JSMITH $
searchname= 'Billy Bob'
/home/JSMITH $
grep $searchname goodoleboys.txt
grep: 001-0023 Error found opening file Bob. No such path or directory.
/home/JSMITH $
grep "$searchname" goodoleboys.txt
```

Figure 17.8: The grep search fails if the search pattern is not quoted because of an embedded space.

Single quotes and double quotes function differently in Qshell. Single quotes, also called *strong quotes*, protect from parameter substitution. Double quotes, also called *weak quotes*, permit parameter substitution.

Figure 17.9 illustrates this point. The *echo* command shows that the fifth positional parameter has the value *444*. Parameter substitution occurs in the first *grep* command, in which the search pattern is not quoted, and the second *grep* command, in which the search pattern is delimited by weak quotes. In the third *grep* command, parameter substitution does not take place; *grep* looks for the string *$5* (five dollars).

Did you notice the strange thing that *grep* does in this example? It matches a literal dollar-sign character ($) instead of treating it as an end-of-line metacharacter. Why? If the dollar sign is interpreted as end-of-line, then *$5* is an illegal regular expression. Although taking advantage of this behavior will show that you are a real *grep* guru, you shouldn't rely on it. It's tricky and unclear to whoever might be changing the script later—even if that person is you. Instead, to search for a literal dollar sign, use *\$*.

```
echo $5
444
/home/JSMITH $
grep $5 goodoleboys.txt
Chuck      Dec 25    444-2345 Blue     Mary Sue     12    $2.50
Bubba      Oct 13    444-1111 Buck     Mary Jean    12
Billy Bob June 11    444-4340 Leotis   Lisa Sue     12
Otis       Sept 17   444-8000 Ol' Sal  Sally        12    $5
Roscoe     Feb 2     444-2234 Rover    Alice Jean   410
Arlis      June 19   444-1314 Redeye   Suzy Beth    12    $10.75
Bill       Feb 29    333-4444 Daisy    Daisy        20
/home/JSMITH $

grep "$5" goodoleboys.txt
Chuck      Dec 25    444-2345 Blue     Mary Sue     12    $2.50
Bubba      Oct 13    444-1111 Buck     Mary Jean    12
Billy Bob June 11    444-4340 Leotis   Lisa Sue     12
Otis       Sept 17   444-8000 Ol' Sal  Sally        12    $5
Roscoe     Feb 2     444-2234 Rover    Alice Jean   410
Arlis      June 19   444-1314 Redeye   Suzy Beth    12    $10.75
Bill       Feb 29    333-4444 Daisy    Daisy        20
/home/JSMITH $

grep '$5' goodoleboys.txt
Otis       Sept 17   444-8000 Ol' Sal  Sally        12    $5
```

Figure 17.9: Strong quotes forbid parameter substitution; weak quotes allow it.

Here is the rule of thumb you should keep in mind:

Use double quotes if the search string includes the name of a variable whose value is to be substituted. Otherwise, use single quotes.

Files

You may list one or more file names at the end of the *grep* command. Each name can be an individual file, or it may contain wildcard characters for filename expansion (globbing, discussed in chapter 14). If you omit the input-files parameter, *grep* reads from stdin. The only time you are likely to omit the input-files parameter, however, is when *grep* is reading the output of another command through a pipeline.

In the following example, output of the List Directory Contents command (*ls*) is the input to *grep*:

```
ls   |   grep   -i   '[A-Z][12]'
```

This example lists files in the current directory whose names contain a letter of the alphabet, followed by either a one or a two.

There are several different ways to fill in the input-files parameter. One way is to list a file name, like this:

```
grep '22.34'  mydata.csv
```

In this case, only one file (mydata.csv) is searched for in the current directory. You can specify a full path on the file name, of course:

```
grep '22.34'  /home/jsmith/mydata.csv
```

You may want to use globbing to search more than one file at a time. The following example shows how to search all the CSV files in the current directory:

```
grep   '22.34'  *.csv
```

In the preceding two examples, the input-files parameter has only one argument. You can list more than one file, if you wish, separating them with white space. The command shown here searches three files:

```
grep '22.34' fileone.csv filetwo.csv filethree.csv
```

All of these commands search IFS files, but you can search source physical file members, too. For example, the next command searches all members of MYLIB/MYSRC for the string *pgm*:

```
grep    'pgm'    /qsys.lib/mylib.lib/src.file/*
```

You can mix and match IFS files and source physical files, too. In this command, grep searches all members of a source physical file, as well as all HTML and text files in the current IFS directory:

```
grep 'pgm' /qsys.lib/js.lib/src.file/*   *.htm*   *.txt
```

OPTIONS

Options can be added to affect the behavior of *grep*. Table 17.3 contains a list of the permitted options.

The following examples illustrate how you can use options to run more powerful searches. This command searches for the string *bi*, regardless of case:

```
grep -i bi goodoleboys.txt
Billy Bob June 11    444-4340 Leotis   Lisa Sue     12
Amos       Jan 4     333-1119 Amos     Abigail      20
Bill       Feb 29    333-4444 Daisy    Daisy        20
```

Table 17.3: Grep Options

Option	Description	Release
-E	Use extended regular expressions (egrep, discussed later in this chapter).	V4R3
-F	Treat metacharacters literally. (See the discussion of fgrep, later in this chapter).	V4R3
-H	If the -R option is specified, symbolic links on the command line are followed. Symbolic links encountered in the tree traversal are not followed.	V5R2
-L	If the -R option is specified, both symbolic links on the command line and symbolic links encountered in the tree traversal are followed.	V5R2
-P	If the -R option is specified, no symbolic links are followed.	V5R2
-R	If the file designates a directory, grep searches each file in the entire subtree connected at that point.	V5R2
-c	Output consists of file names and the number of matched lines.	V4R3
-e	Multiple search patterns follow, separated by newline characters.	V4R3
-f	The argument following -f is the name of a file that contains search patterns. Each pattern must be separated by a newline character.	V4R3
-h	Do not print the filename.	V4R3
-i, -y	Ignore the case of letters in making comparisons.	V4R3
-l (ell)	Output consists of filenames, not matching lines.	V4R3
-n	Print a line number. This option is ignored if the -c, -l, or -s options are specified.	V4R3
-q	Quiet mode; no messages are printed.	V4R3
-s	Suppress the error messages ordinarily written for nonexistent or unreadable files. Other messages are not suppressed.	V4R3
-v	Invert the search—print the lines that do not match the search patterns.	V4R3
-w	Search for the expression as a whole word.	V4R3
-x	Match only if the search pattern is the only thing on the line. The -w option is ignored if specified.	V4R3

316

This example searches for *Bill* as a whole word, not as part of a word:

```
grep -w Bill goodoleboys.txt
Bill       Feb 29   333-4444 Daisy    Daisy        20
```

The example in Figure 17.10 returns lines that meet any of three criteria, as if the conditions were concatenated with ORs. *Grep* finds lines that include an uppercase *C*, followed by any character, followed by a lowercase *u*. *Grep* also includes lines that contain the string *BR*, as well as those that end with the character *5* followed by any other character.

```
/home/JSMITH $
> grep -e 'C.u
>
> BR
>
> 5.$' goodoleboys.txt
Chuck      Dec 25   444-2345 Blue     Mary Sue     12  $2.50
Otis       Sept 17  444-8000 Ol' Sal  Sally        12  $5
Arlis      June 19  444-1314 Redeye   Suzy Beth    12  $10.75
Junior     April 30 BR-549   Percival Lilly Faye   12
```

Figure 17.10: Grep returns lines that meet any of three criteria.

Figure 17.11 carries out the same search as in Figure 17.10, but reads the search patterns from file greppats.txt instead of from the command line.

```
/home/JSMITH $
cat greppats.txt
C.u
BR
5.$
/home/JSMITH $
grep -f greppats.txt goodoleboys.txt
Chuck      Dec 25   444-2345 Blue     Mary Sue     12  $2.50
Otis       Sept 17  444-8000 Ol' Sal  Sally        12  $5
Arlis      June 19  444-1314 Redeye   Suzy Beth    12  $10.75
Junior     April 30 BR-549   Percival Lilly Faye   12
```

Figure 17.11: Grep reads the search patterns from file greppats.txt to carry out the search.

EXTENDED REGULAR EXPRESSIONS (EGREP)

Extended regular expressions are an alternative to the basic regular expressions discussed so far in this chapter. When you use an extended regular expression, grep recognizes a different set of metacharacters, which are listed in Table 17.4.

Table 17.4: Egrep Metacharacters

Metacharacter	Description
. (period)	Match any character except end of line.
| (vertical bar)	Perform an OR.
?	The preceding pattern is optional and is to be matched at most once.
*	The preceding pattern is optional and is to be matched zero or more times.
+	The preceding pattern is not optional and is to be matched one or more times.
^	Match from the beginning of the line.
$	Match from the end of the line.
[]	Match any character within the brackets. Ranges may be specified with a hyphen.
\	Turn off the special meaning of the following character.
()	Group characters or patterns into a larger pattern for more complex matches. For example, *(abc)+ matches abc, abcabc, abcabcabc,* etc.

There are two ways to use the alternate metacharacter set. One way is with the *egrep* utility; the other is to use *grep* with the *-E* option. The following examples illustrate the *egrep* features that differ from basic regular expressions. In the first example, *egrep* finds lines that contain either *Oct* or *Feb*:

```
egrep 'Oct|Feb' goodoleboys.txt
Bubba       Oct 13    444-1111 Buck    Mary Jean   12
Roscoe      Feb 2     444-2234 Rover   Alice Jean  410
Bill        Feb 29    333-4444 Daisy   Daisy       20
```

The following command finds lines with an uppercase *B*, zero or one *i*, and a lowercase *l*:

```
egrep 'Bi?l'         goodoleboys.txt
Chuck       Dec 25    444-2345 Blue    Mary Sue    12    $2.50
Billy Bob June 11     444-4340 Leotis  Lisa Sue    12
Claude      May 31    333-4340 Blue    Etheline    12
Bill        Feb 29    333-4444 Daisy   Daisy       20
```

Finally, this example finds lines where an uppercase *E* is preceded by zero or more spaces:

```
egrep ' *E'          goodoleboys.txt
Claude      May 31    333-4340 Blue    Etheline    12
Ernest T. ??          none     none    none        none
```

FGREP

You can tell *grep* to interpret metacharacters literally when you are looking for a character that would otherwise be interpreted as a metacharacter. For example, you might wish to search for a period, which *grep* interprets as a wildcard that stands for any character. You have already learned one method to have the period metacharacter interpreted literally, which is to precede it with a back-slash, as shown here:

```
grep '\.' goodoleboys.txt
```

A second method is to use the -F option, which tells *grep* to treat metacharacters literally:

```
grep -F '.' goodoleboys.txt
```

A third method is to use the *fgrep* utility. Fgrep, which stands for *fast grep* or *fixed grep* (depending on whom you ask), does not interpret metacharacters. The following example illustrates the use of *fgrep*:

```
fgrep '.' goodoleboys.txt
```

The *fgrep* method is probably the easiest of the three. However, it cannot be used when you want to interpret some metacharacters literally, but make others use their wildcard abilities, as in this example:

```
grep '\$[0-9]*\.[0-9]*.$' goodoleboys.txt
```

This command searches for records that have a dollar sign, then zero or more digits, then a period, then zero or more digits again, and finally one other character, anchored at the end of the line. Table 17.5 shows the parts of this search string.

Table 17.5: A Search String, Explained

Symbols	Description
\$	Search for a dollar sign.
[0-9]*	Search for zero or more digits.
\.	Search for a period.
[0-9]*	Search for zero or more digits, again.
.	Search for any character.
$	Search for the end-of-line anchor.

EXIT STATUS

Many Unix utilities only return a non-zero error status in case of an error. *Grep* is a bit more useful. As Table 17.6 shows, *grep* distinguishes between an error and a case of not finding the search string. For example, if the file does not exist, the exit status is 2.

Table 17.6: Exit Status Codes Set by Grep

Status	Description
0	The search string was found.
1	The search string was not found in the specified files.
>1	An error occurred.

Sometimes, *grep* both succeeds and fails. In Figure 17.12, for example, *grep* finds the first file, but not the second one. *Grep* reports failure even though the search was partially successful.

```
grep 'B[lu]'  goodoleboys.txt    nosuchfile.data
goodoleboys.txt:Chuck  Dec 25  444-2345 Blue  Mary Sue  12 $2.50
goodoleboys.txt:Bubba  Oct 13  444-1111 Buck  Mary Jean 12
goodoleboys.txt:Claude May 31  333-4340 Blue  Etheline  12
grep: 001-0023 Error found opening file nosuchfile.data.
   No such path or directory.
/home/JSMITH $
echo $?
2
/home/JSMITH $
```

Figure 17.12: Grep reports failure if any part of the search process fails.

In Figure 17.13, the order of the files is reversed. *Grep* never searches the second file, since the first file does not exist.

```
grep 'B[lu]'  nosuchfile.data  goodoleboys.txt
grep: 001-0023 Error found opening file nosuchfile.data.
   No such path or directory.
/home/JSMITH $
echo $?
2
/home/JSMITH $
```

Figure 17.13: Grep reports failure as soon as possible.

321

Figure 17.14 contains a similar example, using source physical file members rather than IFS files. Notice the exit status of each command.

```
grep -i 'goto' /qsys.lib/jsmith.lib/qrpglesrc.file/M*.MBR
/home/JSMITH $
echo $?
1
grep -i 'goto' /qsys.lib/jsmith.lib/qrpglesrc.file/B*.MBR
grep: 001-0023 Error found opening file
/qsys.lib/jsmith.lib/qrpglesrc.file/B*.MBR. No such path or
    directory.
/home/JSMITH $
echo $?
2
/home/JSMITH $
```

Figure 17.14: Grep distinguishes between an unsuccessful search and nonexistent source physical file members.

The first *grep* returns an exit status of one because there are members that start with *M*, but none have *goto* in them. The second *grep* returns an exit status of two because there are no members that start with *B* in file QRPGLESRC in library JSMITH.

SUMMARY

The *grep* utility searches files for strings that match a pattern coded as a regular expression. *Grep* is very powerful because it allows regular expressions to include metacharacters. The *egrep* and *fgrep* utilities are variations on *grep* that are useful when *grep's* normal behavior does not achieve the desired results.

Chapter 18

Sed

Programmers are accustomed to source editors. The iSeries has Source Entry Utility (SEU), the Edit File command (EDTF), and Code/400. In addition to many free and commercial text editors, all Windows-based PCs have the Notepad editor.

The commands and methods vary, but all of these editors are interactive programs. *Sed*, on the other hand, is a noninteractive editor. It applies one or more commands to a stream of text and produces a stream file in the process. Since *sed* does not directly change the input text, it is a nondestructive editor. Otherwise, *sed* does the same sorts of things that interactive editors do. You can replace text strings with other strings, insert new lines, delete lines, and so forth. The difference is that you can do it in a batch-type mode.

There are some good reasons to use *sed*:

- "You don't have to be present to win." If you need to modify an FTP script at 1 A.M. daily to include *put* commands for all the files in a certain subdirectory, *sed* will do the job for you while you sleep.

- *Sed* is a filter. It can be used when editing data in any Qshell command pipeline or command-substitution statement. No scripts or data files are needed.

- *Sed* doesn't mind modifying extremely large files that interactive editors complain about. Only the current input record and holding buffer are in memory at any time.

- *Sed* will happily apply a long sequence of edits that you might not want to type on a recurring basis.

- *Sed* can be the basis for source-code generation utilities.

- *Sed's* pattern-matching ability is more powerful than the search functions of the iSeries' interactive editors.

- After you get comfortable with the *sed* utility, you can make changes more quickly than with interactive editors.

Sed uses two sources of input. Data to be edited is read from the standard input stream or one or more stream files. A list of commands is read from the command line or disk files. A list of *sed* commands stored in a disk file is called a *sed script*.

Sed reads a line of input into a buffer and applies all appropriate editing commands. Once all edits have been made, it writes the modified line to stdout and reads the next line of input. Figure 18.1 shows a pseudocode summary of this logic.

```
while not end of input
  copy the next input record into the pattern space
  for each editing command
          if the editing command applies to this input record
                  apply the editing command to the pattern space
          end if
  end for
  if write to stdout is not prohibited by command or option
          write the pattern space to stdout
  end if
end while
```

Figure 18.1: This is the basic sed processing logic.

Sed uses two buffers: the *pattern space* and the *holding buffer*. The pattern space is the buffer into which an input record is read. Normally, the pattern space contains one record, but you can use the N function to add additional records to the pattern space. All edits take place on the contents of the pattern space.

The holding buffer is an additional buffer into which the pattern space may be placed for later retrieval.

FORMS OF THE SED COMMAND

The syntax of the *sed* command comes in two forms, as follows:

```
sed [-an] command [file…]
sed [-an] [-e command] [-f command_file] [file…]
```

You will use one form or the other, but not both, in one command. The first form is the simpler one: one *sed* command is used to edit the input file(s). If no input files are used, *sed* edits data read from stdin. Here is a command of this type:

```
sed '/A/d' goodoleboys.txt
```

The *sed* command is /A/d. The input file is goodoleboys.txt, and the modified data is written to stdout.

You need to use the second form when you want to apply more than one editing command to the input. This type of command is shown in the following example:

```
sed -e 's/Daisy/Ethel/' -f seddata1.txt goodoleboys.txt
```

The *e* option allows you to include editing commands within the command string itself, while the *f* option tells *sed* to read editing commands from a file. In this example, *sed* reads commands from two places. First, it applies the command following the *e* option. Then, it applies the commands in the seddata1.txt file. If the *e* option followed the *f* option, *sed* would apply the commands in seddata1.txt file first.

You can use the filter form of *sed* when you're doing interactive or scripted Qshell work. Sometimes, a *sed* solution is easier to write correctly than other forms of Qshell variable expansion and substitution.

Here is an example of *sed* as a filter:

```
for i in *.txt ; do j=$(echo $i | sed -e 's/\.txt$/.new/');
echo mv $i $j; done
```

This example sends all text-file names in the current directory to *sed* in a command substitution. *Sed* changes each name so that it has an extension of *.new*, and assigns the result to the *j* variable. The loop then generates a command using the *mv* utility to rename the original text file to the new file. The *mv* command isn't executed directly; instead, *echo* is used to display the *mv* command to standard output. Displaying generated Qshell commands is always a prudent debugging step before executing them.

SED OPTIONS

The four options for *sed* are listed in Table 18.1.

Table 18.1: Sed Options

Option	Description
a	Delay opening of files to which output is directed with the w command.
e	Read a sed command from the following argument.
f	Read sed commands from the file named in the following argument.
n	Do not automatically write to stdout.

The *a* option delays the opening of files that are to be overwritten until the last possible moment. Normally, Qshell clears files that are to be overwritten before *sed* begins to run. This means that files will be cleared that might not be written to. The *a* option ensures that a file is not cleared unless it is written to.

The *e* option, which is repeatable, precedes a *sed* command. The *f* option, which is also repeatable, precedes the name of a file in which *sed* commands are stored. The *e* and *f* options are not mutually exclusive. As you saw in the previous example, you may use both of them in the same command.

The *n* option tells sed not to automatically write the contents of the pattern space to stdout after applying all editing commands.

SED COMMANDS

A *sed* command consists of three parts: the address, a function, and arguments. You may precede the address and function parts of the command with white space. As the following syntax shows, the only required part is the function:

```
[address[,address]]function[arguments]
```

Let's look at each of the three parts in more detail.

Address

The address identifies the lines to be selected. Depending on the function, you may specify no address, a single address, or two addresses separated from one another by a comma.

If you do not specify an address, all lines of the input file are selected for editing. If you specify one address, only the lines matching the address are edited. If you specify two addresses, *sed* edits one or more ranges of lines.

Each address can be

- A line number, from all input files numbered consecutively

- A dollar sign, to indicate the last line of the last input file

- A regular expression delimited by the forward-slash character, /

The regular expressions are similar to the basic regular expressions that grep and other utilities recognize, but *sed* adds two features of its own:

- The escape sequence \n matches the newline character.

- Any character other than a backslash or newline may be used as a delimiter in regular expressions. Any delimiter may be escaped with a backslash.

Table 18.2 lists the regular-expression metacharacters for *sed*.

Table 18.2: Metacharacters for Use with Sed

Metacharacter	Description
. (period)	Match any character except end-of-line.
*	Match zero or more occurrences of the preceding character.
^	Match from the beginning of the line.
$	Match from the end of the line.
[ ]	Match any character within the brackets. Ranges may be specified with a hyphen.
[^]	Negate the groups or ranges of characters in the brackets. The caret must be the first character within the brackets.
\\{m\\}	Match exactly *m* occurrences of the preceding character.
\\{m,\\}	Match *m* or more occurrences of the preceding character.
\\{m,n\\}	Match *m* to n occurrences of the preceding character.
\\	Turn off the special meaning of the following character.
\\(\\)	Define a back reference to save matched characters as a pattern. The saved pattern can be referenced with a backslash followed by a number.
//	Match the last-used regular expression.

Function and Arguments

The function is the command itself. It tells *sed* what to do with the input record. All functions are one character long. They are listed in Table 18.3.

Table 18.3: Sed Functions

Function	Arguments	Description	Maximum Addresses
a	text	Write text to stdout after writing the pattern space.	1
b	label (optional)	Branch to a label. If a label is not specified, branch to the end of the list of functions.	2
c	text	Replace line(s) with new text.	2
d		Do not write the pattern space to stdout.	2
D		Delete the pattern space up to and including the first newline character	2
g		Copy the holding buffer to the pattern space.	2
G		Append the holding buffer to the pattern space.	2
h		Copy the pattern space to the holding buffer.	2
H		Append the pattern space to the holding buffer.	2
i	text	Write text to stdout before writing the pattern space.	1
l(ell)		Replace nonprintable characters with visual representations.	2
n		Write the pattern space to stdout (unless the-n option was specified), and read the next line of input into the pattern space.	2
N		Append the next input line to the pattern space	2

Table 18.3: Sed Functions, *continued*

Function	Arguments	Description	Maximum Addresses
p		Print the pattern space to stdout immediately.	2
P		Print the pattern space, up to and including the first newline character, immediately.	2
q		Terminate the editing session after processing the current input record.	1
r	file name	Read a file into stdout.	1
s	search string, replacement string, flags	Substitute one string for another.	2
t		Branch if substitutions have been made.	2
w	file name	Write the pattern space to a file.	2
x		Exchange the contents of the holding buffer and the pattern space.	2
y		Replace each character in a set with the corresponding character of another set.	2
=		Write the line number to stdout.	1
: (colon)	label	Define a label as a target for a branch.	0

You may negate a function by preceding it with an exclamation point. The following example deletes all lines except line 2:

```
sed '2!d' goodoleboys.txt
```

You may also include more than one function for an address. Enclose the group of functions in braces, and follow each function with a semicolon and at least one space, as shown here:

```
sed '2{h; d; }' goodoleboys.txt
```

When *sed* reads line 2, it executes two functions, *h* and *d*.

Instead of a semicolon and space, you may also separate functions with newline characters, like this:

```
sed '2{
> h
> d
> }' goodoleboys.txt
```

As you can see, *sed* allows each function to be listed on its own line. When *sed* reads line 2, it executes two functions, *h* and *d*. Notice that the commands are separated by newline characters rather than by semicolons. The greater-than signs are the Qshell secondary prompt character.

EXAMPLES

The examples on the following pages are provided to illustrate how *sed* works. The input data is taken from file goodoleboys.txt, shown in Figure 18.2.

```
cat goodoleboys.txt
Name        Born      Phone     Dog      Wife       Shotgun  Paid
==========  ========  ========  ========  ==========  =======  =====
Chuck       Dec 25    444-2345  Blue      Mary Sue    12       $2.50
Bubba       Oct 13    444-1111  Buck      Mary Jean   12
Billy Bob   June 11   444-4340  Leotis    Lisa Sue    12
Amos        Jan 4     333-1119  Amos      Abigail     20
Otis        Sept 17   444-8000  Ol' Sal   Sally       12       $5
Claude      May 31    333-4340  Blue      Etheline    12
Roscoe      Feb 2     444-2234  Rover     Alice Jean  410
Arlis       June 19   444-1314  Redeye    Suzy Beth   12       $10.75
Junior      April 30  BR-549    Percival  Lilly Faye  12
Bill        Feb 29    333-4444  Daisy     Daisy       20
Ernest T.   ??        none      none      none        none
```

Figure 18.2: The goodoleboys.txt file is the basis for the examples in this chapter.

Delete

The Delete command, *d*, does not actually delete records from the input files. Instead, it omits them from the output stream. When *sed* encounters a *d* command, it ignores the remainder of the editing commands and continues immediately with the next input record. For example, the command in Figure 18.3 deletes the first two lines. Since *sed* prints lines by default, all other lines are written to stdout.

```
sed '1,2d' goodoleboys.txt
Chuck       Dec 25    444-2345 Blue     Mary Sue     12    $2.50
Bubba       Oct 13    444-1111 Buck     Mary Jean    12
Billy Bob   June 11   444-4340 Leotis   Lisa Sue     12
Amos        Jan 4     333-1119 Amos     Abigail      20
Otis        Sept 17   444-8000 Ol' Sal  Sally        12    $5
Claude      May 31    333-4340 Blue     Etheline     12
Roscoe      Feb 2     444-2234 Rover    Alice Jean   410
Arlis       June 19   444-1314 Redeye   Suzy Beth    12    $10.75
Junior      April 30  BR-549   Percival Lilly Faye   12
Bill        Feb 29    333-4444 Daisy    Daisy        20
Ernest T.   ??        none     none     none         none
```

Figure 18.3: Delete the first two lines.

In Figure 18.4, the exclamation point is used for negation, so all lines that do *not* contain the string *444-* are deleted.

```
sed '/444-/!d' goodoleboys.txt
Chuck       Dec 25    444-2345 Blue     Mary Sue     12    $2.50
Bubba       Oct 13    444-1111 Buck     Mary Jean    12
Billy Bob   June 11   444-4340 Leotis   Lisa Sue     12
Otis        Sept 17   444-8000 Ol' Sal  Sally        12    $5
Roscoe      Feb 2     444-2234 Rover    Alice Jean   410
Arlis       June 19   444-1314 Redeye   Suzy Beth    12    $10.75
```

Figure 18.4: Delete all lines that do not contain the string 444-.

The dollar sign by itself, specified as an address as shown in Figure 18.5, symbolizes the last record of the file. The dollar sign preceded by a backslash, as shown in Figure 18.6, is interpreted literally instead of as the symbol for end-of-line.

```
sed '$d'  goodoleboys.txt
Name       Born     Phone    Dog       Wife       Shotgun  Paid
=========  =======  =======  ========  =========  =======  =====
Chuck      Dec 25   444-2345 Blue      Mary Sue   12       $2.50
Bubba      Oct 13   444-1111 Buck      Mary Jean  12
Billy Bob  June 11  444-4340 Leotis    Lisa Sue   12
Amos       Jan 4    333-1119 Amos      Abigail    20
Otis       Sept 17  444-8000 Ol' Sal   Sally      12       $5
Claude     May 31   333-4340 Blue      Etheline   12
Roscoe     Feb 2    444-2234 Rover     Alice Jean 410
Arlis      June 19  444-1314 Redeye    Suzy Beth  12       $10.75
Junior     April 30 BR-549   Percival  Lilly Faye 12
Bill       Feb 29   333-4444 Daisy     Daisy      20
```

Figure 18.5: Delete the last record of the file.

```
sed '/ \$/d'  goodoleboys.txt
Name       Born     Phone    Dog       Wife       Shotgun  Paid
=========  =======  =======  ========  =========  =======  =====
Bubba      Oct 13   444-1111 Buck      Mary Jean  12
Billy Bob  June 11  444-4340 Leotis    Lisa Sue   12
Amos       Jan 4    333-1119 Amos      Abigail    20
Claude     May 31   333-4340 Blue      Etheline   12
Roscoe     Feb 2    444-2234 Rover     Alice Jean 410
Junior     April 30 BR-549   Percival  Lilly Faye 12
Bill       Feb 29   333-4444 Daisy     Daisy      20
Ernest T.  ??       none     none      none       none
```

Figure 18.6: Delete the lines that contain a dollar sign.

In Figure 18.7, *sed* deletes the range between a record containing *Jun* and one containing *Sal*. *Sed* finds *Jun* in Billy Bob's record and *Sal* in Otis's record. It resumes the search and finds *Jun* in Arlis' record. Since no following records contain *Sal*, *sed* deletes everything through the end of the file.

```
sed '/Jun/,/Sal/d'  goodoleboys.txt
Name       Born     Phone    Dog     Wife       Shotgun  Paid
=========  =======  =======  ======  =========  =======  =====
Chuck      Dec 25   444-2345 Blue    Mary Sue   12       $2.50
Bubba      Oct 13   444-1111 Buck    Mary Jean  12
Claude     May 31   333-4340 Blue    Etheline   12
Roscoe     Feb 2    444-2234 Rover   Alice Jean 410
```

Figure 18.7: Delete each range between a record containing Jun and one containing Sal.

The command in Figure 18.8 starts deleting at the third record, and continues through the first record containing the string *BR*.

```
sed '3,/BR/d' goodoleboys.txt
Name        Born      Phone      Dog       Wife        Shotgun   Paid
=========   ========  ========   ========  =========   =======   =====
Bill        Feb 29    333-4444   Daisy     Daisy         20
Ernest T.   ??        none       none      none          none
```

Figure 18.8: Delete from the third record through the first record containing the string BR (Junior's record).

In the final example of deletion, the command in Figure 18.9 simply deletes all records that begin with *B*.

```
sed '/^B/d' goodoleboys.txt
Name        Born      Phone      Dog       Wife        Shotgun   Paid
=========   ========  ========   ========  =========   =======   =====
Chuck       Dec 25    444-2345   Blue      Mary Sue      12      $2.50
Amos        Jan 4     333-1119   Amos      Abigail       20
Otis        Sept 17   444-8000   Ol' Sal   Sally         12      $5
Claude      May 31    333-4340   Blue      Etheline      12
Roscoe      Feb 2     444-2234   Rover     Alice Jean    410
Arlis       June 19   444-1314   Redeye    Suzy Beth     12      $10.75
Junior      April 30  BR-549     Percival  Lilly Faye    12
Ernest T.   ??        none       none      none          none
```

Figure 18.9: Delete each record that begins with a B.

Substitute

The Substitute command, *s*, replaces data in the pattern space. Here is the syntax of this command:

```
s/regular-expression/replacement/flags
```

The *s* command is followed by a delimiter of the programmer's choosing, which is often the forward slash. (The backslash and newline characters are not allowed to serve as delimiters.) The value to be replaced follows the first delimiter. This is a regular expression, similar to the regular expressions many Unix utilities use.

The replacement string follows another delimiter. The replacement string can include two special substitution values:

- An ampersand (&) stands for the matched characters.

- A backslash followed by a single digit indicates a back reference to a matching pattern that was saved with the \(\) metacharacter pair.

The permitted flags are listed in Table 18.4.

Table 18.4: Substitution Flags

Flag	Description
g	Global substitution; make all possible substitutions on each line.
p	Write the pattern space to stdout.
w file	Write the pattern space to a file.
0 to 9	Substitute the nth occurrence of the search string only.

If *sed* replaces one string with another, the substitution flags take effect. If the matched pattern and replacement string are equivalent, a replacement is still considered to have been made.

The comand in Figure 18.10 changes the first *B* in each record to an asterisk. It is not necessary to escape the asterisk, since it is in the replacement area and therefore not interpreted as a metacharacter. Notice that only the first *B* in the records for Bubba and Billy Bob was changed to an asterisk.

Figures 18.11 and 18.12 produce the same results of changing all *B*s in each record to asterisks. However, Figure 18.12 uses a pound sign as a delimiter, instead of a forward slash.

```
sed 's/B/*/' goodoleboys.txt
```

Name	*orn	Phone	Dog	Wife	Shotgun	Paid
Chuck	Dec 25	444-2345	*lue	Mary Sue	12	$2.50
*ubba	Oct 13	444-1111	Buck	Mary Jean	12	
*illy Bob	June 11	444-4340	Leotis	Lisa Sue	12	
Amos	Jan 4	333-1119	Amos	Abigail	20	
Otis	Sept 17	444-8000	Ol' Sal	Sally	12	$5
Claude	May 31	333-4340	*lue	Etheline	12	
Roscoe	Feb 2	444-2234	Rover	Alice Jean	410	
Arlis	June 19	444-1314	Redeye	Suzy *eth	12	$10.75
Junior	April 30	*R-549	Percival	Lilly Faye	12	
*ill	Feb 29	333-4444	Daisy	Daisy	20	
Ernest T.	??	none	none	none	none	

Figure 18.10: Change the first B in each record to an asterisk.

```
sed 's/B/*/' goodoleboys.txt
```

Name	*orn	Phone	Dog	Wife	Shotgun	Paid
Chuck	Dec 25	444-2345	*lue	Mary Sue	12	$2.50
*ubba	Oct 13	444-1111	*uck	Mary Jean	12	
*illy *ob	June 11	444-4340	Leotis	Lisa Sue	12	
Amos	Jan 4	333-1119	Amos	Abigail	20	
Otis	Sept 17	444-8000	Ol' Sal	Sally	12	$5
Claude	May 31	333-4340	*lue	Etheline	12	
Roscoe	Feb 2	444-2234	Rover	Alice Jean	410	
Arlis	June 19	444-1314	Redeye	Suzy *eth	12	$10.75
Junior	April 30	*R-549	Percival	Lilly Faye	12	
*ill	Feb 29	333-4444	Daisy	Daisy	20	
Ernest T.	??	none	none	none	none	

Figure 18.11: The g option tells sed to globally substitute in the pattern buffer.

```
sed 's#B#*#g' goodoleboys.txt
```

Name	*orn	Phone	Dog	Wife	Shotgun	Paid
Chuck	Dec 25	444-2345	*lue	Mary Sue	12	$2.50
*ubba	Oct 13	444-1111	*uck	Mary Jean	12	
*illy *ob	June 11	444-4340	Leotis	Lisa Sue	12	
Amos	Jan 4	333-1119	Amos	Abigail	20	
Otis	Sept 17	444-8000	Ol' Sal	Sally	12	$5
Claude	May 31	333-4340	*lue	Etheline	12	
Roscoe	Feb 2	444-2234	Rover	Alice Jean	410	
Arlis	June 19	444-1314	Redeye	Suzy *eth	12	$10.75
Junior	April 30	*R-549	Percival	Lilly Faye	12	
*ill	Feb 29	333-4444	Daisy	Daisy	20	
Ernest T.	??	none	none	none	none	

Figure 18.12: Use the pound sign (#) as a delimiter.

The command in Figure 18.13 changes Chuck's dog's name from *Blue* to *Petey*. The string *Chuck* is the address, *s* is the command, and *Blue* and *Petey* are the arguments to the command.

```
sed '/Chuck/s/Blue /Petey/' goodoleboys.txt
```

Name	Born	Phone	Dog	Wife	Shotgun	Paid
Chuck	Dec 25	444-2345	Petey	Mary Sue	12	$2.50
Bubba	Oct 13	444-1111	Buck	Mary Jean	12	
Billy Bob	June 11	444-4340	Leotis	Lisa Sue	12	
Amos	Jan 4	333-1119	Amos	Abigail	20	
Otis	Sept 17	444-8000	Ol' Sal	Sally	12	$5
Claude	May 31	333-4340	Blue	Etheline	12	
Roscoe	Feb 2	444-2234	Rover	Alice Jean	410	
Arlis	June 19	444-1314	Redeye	Suzy Beth	12	$10.75
Junior	April 30	BR-549	Percival	Lilly Faye	12	
Bill	Feb 29	333-4444	Daisy	Daisy	20	
Ernest T.	??	none	none	none	none	

Figure 18.13: Change Chuck's dog's name from Blue to Petey.

In Figure 18.14, the string *(12/02)* is appended to every record that ends with a period followed by two digits. The period character is escaped with a backslash in the substitution expression because it is a metacharacter. If the forward slash had been used as the substitution delimiter, as in the previous example, it would also have to be escaped. However, the pound sign (#) is used here as the substitution delimiter, so it is not necessary to escape the slash.

```
sed 's#\.[0-9][0-9]$#& (12/02)#' goodoleboys.txt
```

Name	Born	Phone	Dog	Wife	Shotgun	Paid
Chuck	Dec 25	444-2345	Blue	Mary Sue	12	$2.50 (12/02)
Bubba	Oct 13	444-1111	Buck	Mary Jean	12	
Billy Bob	June 11	444-4340	Leotis	Lisa Sue	12	
Amos	Jan 4	333-1119	Amos	Abigail	20	
Otis	Sept 17	444-8000	Ol' Sal	Sally	12	$5
Claude	May 31	333-4340	Blue	Etheline	12	
Roscoe	Feb 2	444-2234	Rover	Alice Jean	410	
Arlis	June 19	444-1314	Redeye	Suzy Beth	12	$10.75 (12/02)
Junior	April 30	BR-549	Percival	Lilly Faye	12	
Bill	Feb 29	333-4444	Daisy	Daisy	20	
Ernest T.	??	none	none	none	none	

Figure 18.14: Add the string (12/02) to every record that ends with a period followed by two digits.

The command in Figure 18.15 appends the string ** *Committee* ** to the end of each line, starting with the first record containing *Blue* and ending with the last record containing *Blue*.

```
sed '/Blue/,/Blue/s/$/ ** Committee **/' goodoleboys.txt
Name        Born      Phone    Dog      Wife      Shotgun  Paid
=========   ========  =======  =======  ========  =======  =====
Chuck       Dec 25    444-2345 Blue     Mary Sue  12        $2.50 ** Committee **
Bubba       Oct 13    444-1111 Buck     Mary Jean 12       ** Committee **
Billy Bob   June 11   444-4340 Leotis   Lisa Sue  12       ** Committee **
Amos        Jan 4     333-1119 Amos     Abigail   20       ** Committee **
Otis        Sept 17   444-8000 Ol' Sal  Sally     12        $5 ** Committee **
Claude      May 31    333-4340 Blue     Etheline  12       **Committee **
Roscoe      Feb 2     444-2234 Rover    Alice Jean 410
Arlis       June 19   444-1314 Redeye   Suzy Beth 12        $10.75
Junior      April 30  BR-549   PercivalLilly Faye 12
Bill        Feb 29    333-4444 Daisy    Daisy     20
Ernest T.   ??        none     none     none      none
```

Figure 18.15: From the first record containing Blue to the last record containing Blue, add the string ** Committee ** to the end of the line.

The command in Figure 18.16 has been entered on two lines. Qshell displays the secondary prompt, >, to show that the command is not complete. Because the Enter key was pressed between the two lines, there is a newline character in the replacement pattern. The backslash character that ends the first command line is necessary to "escape" the Enter key.

In Figure 18.17, *sed* looks for capital letters preceded by spaces. When it finds such a combination, it replaces the space with a newline character.

```
sed 's/ \([A-Z]\) /\
    >
\1/' goodoleboys.txt
Name
Born        Phone    Dog      Wife      Shotgun   Paid
=========   ======== ======== ======== ========= =======  =====
Chuck
Dec 25      444-2345 Blue     Mary Sue  12        $2.50
```

Figure 18.16: For each input record, sed looks for the first blank that is followed by an uppercase letter. The \(\) combination tells sed to save the uppercase letter as pattern 1. Sed substitutes a new line followed by the letter saved in pattern (part 1 of 2).

Bubba					
Oct 13	444-1111	Buck	Mary Jean	12	
Billy					
Bob June	11 444-4340	Leotis	Lisa Sue	12	
Amos					
Jan 4	333-1119	Amos	Abigail	20	
Otis					
Sept 17	444-8000	Ol' Sal	Sally	12	$5
Claude					
May 31	333-4340	Blue	Etheline	12	
Roscoe					
Feb 2	444-2234	Rover	Alice Jean	410	
Arlis					
June 19	444-1314	Redeye	Suzy Beth	12	$10.75
Junior					
April 30	BR-549	Percival	Lilly Faye	12	
Bill					
Feb 29	333-4444	Daisy	Daisy	20	
Ernest					
T. ??	none	none	none	none	

Figure 18.16: For each input record, sed looks for the first blank that is followed by an uppercase letter. The \(\) combination tells sed to save the uppercase letter as pattern 1. Sed substitutes a new line followed by the letter saved in pattern (part 2 of 2).

```
sed 's/ \([A-Z]\) / \
>
\1/g' goodoleboys.txt
Name
Born
Phone
Dog
Wife
Shotgun
Paid
========= ======== ======== ======== ========= ======= =====
Chuck
Dec 25   444-2345
Blue
Mary
Sue      12    $2.50
Bubba
Oct 13   444-1111
Buck
```

Figure 18.17: Replace the space before an uppercase letter with a newline character (part 1 of 2).

```
Billy
Mary
Jean     12
Bob
June  11    444-4340
Leotis
Lisa
Sue      12
Amos
Jan  4      333-1119
Amos
Abigail 20
Otis
Sept  17    444-8000
Ol'
Sal
Sally    12      $5
Claude
May  31     333-4340
Blue
Etheline 12
Roscoe
Feb  2      444-2234
Rover
Alice
Jean     410
Arlis
June  19    444-1314
Redeye
Suzy
Beth     12      $10.75
Junior
April 30
BR-549
Percival
Lilly
Faye     12
Bill
Feb  29     333-4444
Daisy
Daisy    20
Ernest
T.  ??       none     none     none      none
```

Figure 18.17: Replace the space before an uppercase letter with a newline character (part 2 of 2).

Print

By default, *sed* prints the pattern space to stdout after processing all applicable edit commands. You can disable the automatic write to stdout by specifying the -n option in the *sed* command.

Sed provides the Print command, *p*, to let you control printing if you prefer. When *sed* encounters the print command, it prints the line to stdout immediately. The pattern space remains as-is, and further edits may be made if desired.

There are two primary reasons to use the *p* command:

- You wish to write additional output to stdout.
- You wish to control when output is sent to stdout.

For example, in Figure 18.18, when *sed* finds a line that contains *Bi*, it forces the line to print. The result is that matched lines are printed twice.

```
sed '/Bi/p' goodoleboys.txt
Name        Born       Phone     Dog       Wife        Shotgun   Paid
=========   ========   ========  ========  ==========  =======   =====
Chuck       Dec 25     444-2345  Blue      Mary Sue    12        $2.50
Bubba       Oct 13     444-1111  Buck      Mary Jean   12
Billy Bob   June 11    444-4340  Leotis    Lisa Sue    12
Billy Bob   June 11    444-4340  Leotis    Lisa Sue    12
Amos        Jan 4      333-1119  Amos      Abigail     20
Otis        Sept 17    444-8000  Ol' Sal   Sally       12        $5
Claude      May 31     333-4340  Blue      Etheline    12
Roscoe      Feb 2      444-2234  Rover     Alice Jean  410
Arlis       June 19    444-1314  Redeye    Suzy Beth   12        $10.75
Junior      April 30   BR-549    Percival  Lilly Faye  12
Bill        Feb 29     333-4444  Daisy     Daisy       20
Bill        Feb 29     333-4444  Daisy     Daisy       20
Ernest T.   ??         none      none      none        none
```

Figure 18.18: Print lines containing Bi *twice*.

The following command, on the other hand, prints just lines containing the string *Bi*:

```
sed -n '/Bi/p' goodoleboys.txt
Billy Bob   June 11    444-4340  Leotis    Lisa Sue    12
Bill        Feb  29    333-4444  Daisy     Daisy       20
```

Sed does not print lines to stdout automatically because of the n option. Another example of this option is shown in Figure 18.19.

In Figure 18.20, when *sed* finds a record that contains either two or three adjacent fours, it prints the record as it was read, then substitutes an "at" sign (@) for the fours.

```
sed -n '3,5{p; s/4/*/gp; }' goodoleboys.txt
Chuck      Dec 25    444-2345  Blue    Mary Sue    12    $2.50
Chuck      Dec 25    ***-23*5  Blue    Mary Sue    12    $2.50
Bubba      Oct 13    444-1111  Buck    Mary Jean   12
Bubba      Oct 13    ***-1111  Buck    Mary Jean   12
Billy Bob  June 11   444-4340  Leotis  Lisa Sue    12
Billy Bob  June 11   ***-*3*0  Leotis  Lisa Sue    12
```

Figure 18.19: Print lines 3 through 5 twice—before and after substituting asterisks for fours.

```
sed '/4\{2,3\}/{p; s/4\{2,3\}/@/; }' goodoleboys.txt
Name       Born      Phone     Dog       Wife        Shotgun  Paid
=========  ========  ========  ========  =========   =======  =====
Chuck      Dec 25    444-2345  Blue      Mary Sue    12       $2.50
Chuck      Dec 25    @-2345    Blue      Mary Sue    12       $2.50
Bubba      Oct 13    444-1111  Buck      Mary Jean   12
Bubba      Oct 13    @-1111    Buck      Mary Jean   12
Billy Bob  June 11   444-4340  Leotis    Lisa Sue    12
Billy Bob  June 11   @-434     0 Leotis  Lisa Sue    12
Amos       Jan 4     333-1119  Amos      Abigail     20
Otis       Sept 17   444-8000  Ol' Sal   Sally       12       $5
Otis       Sept 17   @-8000    Ol' Sal   Sally       12       $5
Claude     May 31    333-4340  Blue      Etheline    12
Roscoe     Feb 2     444-2234  Rover     Alice Jean  410
Roscoe     Feb 2     @-2234    Rover     Alice Jean  410
Arlis      June 19   444-1314  Redeye    Suzy Beth   12       $10.75
Arlis      June 19   @-1314    Redeye    Suzy Beth   12       $10.75
Junior     April 30  BR-549    Percival  Lilly Faye  12
Bill       Feb 29    333-4444  Daisy     Daisy       20
Bill       Feb 29    333-@4    Daisy     Daisy       20
Ernest T.  ??        none      none      none        none
```

Figure 18.20: Substitute an "at" sign for double or triple fours.

Append and Insert

You can have *sed* add lines to the output stream, either before or after lines that match the address. Use the *a* command to append (write after the selected line) and the *i* command to insert (write before the selected line). Follow the command with a backslash and continue on the following line. End each line of the added text, except the last one, with a backslash, as shown in Figure 18.21.

```
sed '/ 410/a\
>
===> Needs a bigger gun
>
'    goodoleboys.txt
Name        Born      Phone     Dog       Wife        Shotgun   Paid
=========   ========  ========  ========  ==========  ========  =====
Chuck       Dec 25    444-2345  Blue      Mary Sue    12        $2.50
Bubba       Oct 13    444-1111  Buck      Mary Jean   12
Billy Bob   June 11   444-4340  Leotis    Lisa Sue    12
Amos        Jan 4     333-1119  Amos      Abigail     20
Otis        Sept 17   444-8000  Ol' Sal   Sally       12        $5
Claude      May 31    333-4340  Blue      Etheline    12
Roscoe      Feb 2     444-2234  Rover     Alice Jean  410
===> Needs a bigger gun
Arlis       June 19   444-1314  Redeye    Suzy Beth   12        $10.75
Junior      April 30  BR-549    Percival  Lilly Faye  12
Bill        Feb 29    333-4444  Daisy     Daisy       20
Ernest T.   ??        none      none      none        none
```

Figure 18.21: Append a line after every record containing a blank followed by 410. Notice the backslash after the a command.

In Figure 18.22, two lines of text are inserted before each line containing the string *June*, to indicate that dues should be paid. Again, there is a backslash after the *i* command, as well as after the first of two lines of the added text.

```
sed '/ June/i\
>
| | | Needs to pay Dues | | |\
>
V V V                   V V V
>
'    goodoleboys.txt
```

Figure 18.22: Before each line containing the string June, insert two lines of text that indicate that dues should be paid (part 1 of 2).

Name	Born	Phone	Dog	Wife	Shotgun	Paid
==========	========	========	========	=========	========	=====
Chuck	Dec 25	444-2345	Blue	Mary Sue	12	$2.50
Bubba	Oct 13	444-1111	Buck	Mary Jean	12	

```
| | | Needs to pay Dues | | |
V V V                     V V V
```

Billy Bob	June 11	444-4340	Leotis	Lisa Sue	12	
Amos	Jan 4	333-1119	Amos	Abigail	20	
Otis	Sept 17	444-8000	Ol' Sal	Sally	12	$5
Claude	May 31	333-4340	Blue	Etheline	12	
Roscoe	Feb 2	444-2234	Rover	Alice Jean	410	

```
| | | Needs to pay Dues | | |
V V V                     V V V
```

Arlis	June 19	444-1314	Redeye	Suzy Beth	12	$10.75
Junior	April 30	BR-549	Percival	Lilly Faye	12	
Bill	Feb 29	333-4444	Daisy	Daisy	20	
Ernest T.	??	none	none	none	none	

Figure 18.22: Before each line containing the string June, insert two lines of text that indicate that dues should be paid (part 2 of 2).

Quit

The Quit command, *q*, terminates *sed* after the current record is processed. No more input lines are read. In Figure 18.23, *sed* quits the edit when it finds a record containing the string *410*. Notice that the record that matched the address pattern is the last one written to stdout.

Figure 18.24 shows two editing commands. The second one replaces all fours with asterisks in records that contain the string *Feb*. Note that Roscoe's record is changed, but Bill's is not because the *q* command precedes the *s* command.

In Figure 18.25, *sed* also applies two editing commands to each line of the goodoleboys.txt file. The first command looks for two adjacent one characters. If it finds a record with two ones, it quits the edit. The second command

```
sed '/410/q' goodoleboys.txt
```

Name	Born	Phone	Dog	Wife	Shotgun	Paid
==========	========	========	========	=========	========	=====
Chuck	Dec 25	444-2345	Blue	Mary Sue	12	$2.50
Bubba	Oct 13	444-1111	Buck	Mary Jean	12	

Figure 18.23: Quit the edit when the string 410 is found (part 1 of 2).

```
Billy Bob  June 11    444-4340  Leotis    Lisa Sue     12
Amos       Jan 4      333-1118  Amos      Abigail      20
Otis       Sept 17    444-8000  Ol' Sal   Sally        12      $5
Claude     May 31     333-4340  Blue      Etheline     12
Roscoe     Feb 2      444-2234  Rover     Alice Jean   410
```

Figure 18.23: Quit the edit when the string 410 is found (part 2 of 2).

substitutes *J* for *Per*. If it makes such a substitution, *sed* writes the record to file temp.txt. Since the *a* switch is not present, file temp.txt is cleared before editing begins. If *sed* finds a record with two ones before finding a record with the value *Per* in it, nothing is written to temp.txt.

```
sed -e '/Dai/q' -e '/Feb/s/4/*/g' goodoleboys.txt
Name        Born      Phone     Dog       Wife         Shotgun  Paid
=========   ========  ========  ========  =========    =======  =====
Chuck       Dec 25    444-2345  Blue      Mary Sue     12       $2.50
Bubba       Oct 13    444-1111  Buck      Mary Jean    12
Billy Bob   June 11   444-4340  Leotis    Lisa Sue     12
Amos        Jan 4     333-1119  Amos      Abigail      20
Otis        Sept 17   444-8000  Ol' Sal   Sally        12       $5
Claude      May 31    333-4340  Blue      Etheline     12
Roscoe      Feb 2     ***-223*  Rover     Alice Jean   *10
Arlis       June 19   444-1314  Redeye    Suzy Beth    12       $10.75
Junior      April 30  BR-549    Percival  Lilly Faye   12
Bill        Feb 29    333-4444  Daisy     Daisy        20
```

Figure 18.24: Replace all fours with asterisks in records that contain the string Feb.

```
sed -e '/ll/q' -e 's/Per/J/w temp.txt' goodoleboys.txt
Name        Born      Phone     Dog       Wife         Shotgun  Paid
=========   ========  ========  ========  =========    =======  =====
Chuck       Dec 25    444-2345  Blue      Mary Sue     12       $2.50
Bubba       Oct 13    444-1111  Buck      Mary Jean    12
/home/smith $
cat temp.txt
/home/smith $
```

Figure 18.25: Apply two editing commands to each line of goodoleboys.txt.

Transform

The Transform command, *y*, replaces each character in a set with a correspon-ding character in another set. For example, in Figure 18.26, when *sed* finds a line that contains the string *June*, it replaces all lowercase letters with their uppercase equivalents.

```
sed \
>
'/June/y/abcdefghijklmnopqrstuvwxyz/ABCDEFGHIJKLMNOPQRSTUVWXYZ/' \
>
goodoleboys.txt
Name       Born       Phone      Dog        Wife       Shotgun  Paid
=========  ========   ========   ========   =========  =======  =====
Chuck      Dec 25     444-2345   Blue       Mary Sue   12       $2.50
Bubba      Oct 13     444-1111   Buck       Mary Jean  12
BILLY BOB  JUNE 11    444-4340   LEOTIS     LISA SUE   12
Amos       Jan 4      333-1119   Amos       Abigail    20
Otis       Sept 17    444-8000   Ol' Sal    Sally      12       $5
Claude     May 31     333-4340   Blue       Etheline   12
Roscoe     Feb 2      444-2234   Rover      Alice Jean 410
ARLIS      JUNE 19    444-1314   REDEYE     SUZY BETH  12       $10.75
Junior     April 30   BR-549     Percival   Lilly Faye 12
Bill       Feb 29     333-4444   Daisy      Daisy      20
Ernest T.  ??         none       none       none       none
```

Figure 18.26: Replace lowercase letters with uppercase ones for records containing the string June.

Change

The Change command, *c*, replaces the pattern space with a different string of characters, as shown in Figure 18.27. When *sed* finds a line containing the string *Amos*, it replaces the contents of the pattern space with the text following the *c* command. The effect is that the entire record is replaced.

```
sed '/Amos/c\
>
Bilford    Nov 22    333-2244 Phideaux Polly Ann    20
>
' goodoleboys.txt
```

Figure 18.27: Replace each record that contains the string Amos (part 1 of 2).

Name	Born	Phone	Dog	Wife	Shotgun	Paid
=========	========	========	========	=========	=======	=====
Chuck	Dec 25	444-2345	Blue	Mary Sue	12	$2.50
Bubba	Oct 13	444-1111	Buck	Mary Jean	12	
Billy Bob	June 11	444-4340	Leotis	Lisa Sue	12	
Bilford	Nov 22	333-2244	Phideaux	Polly Ann	20	
Otis	Sept 17	444-8000	Ol' Sal	Sally	12	$5
Claude	May 31	333-4340	Blue	Etheline	12	
Roscoe	Feb 2	444-2234	Rover	Alice Jean	410	
Arlis	June 19	444-1314	Redeye	Suzy Beth	12	$10.75
Junior	April 30	BR-549	Percival	Lilly Faye	12	
Bill	Feb 29	333-4444	Daisy	Daisy	20	
Ernest T.	??	none	none	none	none	

Figure 18.27: Replace each record that contains the string Amos (part 2 of 2).

List Nonprinting Characters

The List Nonprinting Characters command is *l*, a lowercase letter "ell." You can use it when you need to see the control characters that are embedded in a file, as shown in Figure 18.28.

```
sed -n 'l' goodoleboys.txt
```

Name	Born	Phone	Dog	Wife	Shotgun	Paid$
=========	========	========	========	=========	=======	=====$
Chuck	Dec 25	444-2345	Blue	Mary Sue	12	2.50
Bubba	Oct 13	444-1111	Buck	Mary Jean	12$	
Billy Bob	June 11	444-4340	Leotis	Lisa Sue	12$	
Amos	Jan 4	333-1119	Amos	Abigail	20$	
Otis	Sept 17	444-8000	Ol' Sal	Sally	12	5
Claude	May 31	333-4340	Blue	Etheline	12$	
Roscoe	Feb 2	444-2234	Rover	Alice Jean	410$	
Arlis	June 19	444-1314	Redeye	Suzy Beth	12	10.75
Junior	April 30	BR-549	Percival	Lilly Faye	12$	
Bill	Feb 29	333-4444	Daisy	Daisy	20$	
Ernest T.	??	none	none	none	none$	

Figure 18.28: The only nonprintable characters in this file are the end-of-line characters, which sed represents with a dollar sign.

Read

The Read command, *r*, reads in an entire file after processing the current input record, as shown in Figure 18.29.

```
cat notice.txt
===========================================================
=         suspended for non-payment of dues              =
===========================================================
sed '/Bubba/r notice.txt' goodoleboys.txt
Name       Born     Phone    Dog       Wife      Shotgun  Paid
=========  =======  =======  =======   =========  =======  =====
Chuck      Dec 25   444-2345 Blue      Mary Sue     12     $2.50
Bubba      Oct 13   444-1111 Buck      Mary Jean    12
===========================================================
=         suspended for non-payment of dues              =
===========================================================
Billy Bob June 11  444-4340 Leotis    Lisa Sue     12
Amos       Jan 4   333-1119 Amos      Abigail      20
Otis       Sept 17 444-8000 Ol' Sal   Sally        12      $5
Claude     May 31  333-4340 Blue      Etheline     12
Roscoe     Feb 2   444-2234 Rover     Alice Jean  410
Arlis      June 19 444-1314 Redeye    Suzy Beth    12     $10.75
Junior     April 30 BR-549  Percival  Lilly Faye   12
Bill       Feb 29  333-4444 Daisy     Daisy        20
Ernest T.  ??      none     none      none       none
```

Figure 18.29: When sed finds a record containing Bubba, it reads file notice.txt file into the output stream.

In Figure 18.30, when *sed* finds a record that contains the string *444-*, it reads the file 444.txt into the output stream.

```
cat 444.txt
** long distance phone call **
/home/JSMITH $
sed '/444-/r 444.txt' goodoleboys.txt
Name       Born     Phone    Dog       Wife      Shotgun  Paid
=========  =======  =======  =======   =========  =======  =====
Chuck      Dec 25   444-2345 Blue      Mary Sue     12     $2.50
** long distance phone call **
Bubba      Oct 13   444-1111 Buck      Mary Jean    12
** long distance phone call **
Billy Bob June 11  444-4340 Leotis    Lisa Sue     12
** long distance phone call **
Amos       Jan 4   333-1119 Amos      Abigail      20
Otis       Sept 17 444-8000 Ol' Sal   Sally        12      $5
** long distance phone call **
Claude     May 31  333-4340 Blue      Etheline     12
```

Figure 18.30: Read 444.txt into the output stream when the string 444- is found (part 1 of 2).

```
Roscoe      Feb 2     444-2234  Rover     Alice Jean  410
** long distance phone call **
Arlis       June 19   444-1314  Redeye    Suzy Beth   12       $10.75
** long distance phone call **
Junior      April 30  BR-549    Percival  Lilly Faye  12
Bill        Feb 29    333-4444  Daisy     Daisy       20
Ernest T.   ??        none      none      none        none
```

Figure 18.30: Read 444.txt into the output stream when the string 444- is found (part 2 of 2).

Figure 18.31 illustrates the use of the read command in an FTP application. The ftpshell file contains the commands needed to send files using FTP. The *reqs record is a placeholder that tells *sed* where to insert *put* commands.

The *puts* subdirectory has the files that are to be sent to the remote system. The *ls* command loads the file names into ftptemp. *Sed* places the word *put* and a space at the beginning of each record to generate FTP *put* commands.

Sed runs a second time to replace the *reqs record in ftpshell with the generated *put* statements. When *sed* finds a record that contains an asterisk followed by an *r*, it reads the ftprequests and deletes the *r record from the output stream. The result is the FTP script in the ftpscript file, which can be used with the FTP CL command to send all the files in the *puts* subdirectory.

```
cat ftpshell
myid
mypass
namefmt 1
*reqs
quit

/home/JSMITH/ftp $
ls puts
pfile1.txt        pfile2.txt        pfile3.txt
/home/JSMITH/ftp $
cat ftprun.qsh
#! /bin/qsh
# nightly ftp run

# get list of files to put
ls puts >ftptemp
```

Figure 18.31: Two sed commands are used to generate an FTP script (part 1 of 2).

349

```
# insert put in front of each file name
sed 's/^/put /' ftptemp >ftprequests

# put requests are now in ftprequests

# merge ftp instructions and ftprequests
sed '/\*r/{
r ftprequests
d
} ' ftpshell >ftpscript

/home/JSMITH/ftp $
ftprun.qsh
/home/JSMITH/ftp $
cat ftpscript
myid
mypass
namefmt 1
put pfile1.txt
put pfile2.txt
put pfile3.txt
quit

/home/JSMITH/ftp $
```

Figure 18.31: Two sed commands are used to generate an FTP script (part 2 of 2).

Write

The Write command, *w*, writes the pattern space to a file. As shown in Figure 18.32, the file is cleared before the first input record is processed, unless the *a* option is used. If the *a* option is used, the file is cleared just before the first record is written to it.

```
sed '/444-/w fours.txt' goodoleboys.txt
```

Name	Born	Phone	Dog	Wife	Shotgun	Paid
=========	========	========	========	=========	=======	=====
Chuck	Dec 25	444-2345	Blue	Mary Sue	12	$2.50
Bubba	Oct 13	444-1111	Buck	Mary Jean	12	
Billy Bob	June 11	444-4340	Leotis	Lisa Sue	12	
Amos	Jan 4	333-1119	Amos	Abigail	20	

Figure 18.32: Sed writes all records that contain the string 444- to file fours.txt. If fours.txt already contains data, the data is replaced (part 1 of 2).

Otis	Sept 17	444-8000	Ol' Sal	Sally	12	$5
Claude	May 31	333-4340	Blue	Etheline	12	
Roscoe	Feb 2	444-2234	Rover	Alice Jean	410	
Arlis	June 19	444-1314	Redeye	Suzy Beth	12	$10.75
Junior	April 30	BR-549	Percival	Lilly Faye	12	
Bill	Feb 29	333-4444	Daisy	Daisy	20	
Ernest T.	??	none	none	none	none	none

cat fours.txt

Chuck	Dec 25	444-2345	Blue	Mary Sue	12	$2.50
Bubba	Oct 13	444-1111	Buck	Mary Jean	12	
Billy Bob	June 11	444-4340	Leotis	Lisa Sue	12	
Otis	Sept 17	444-8000	Ol' Sal	Sally	12	$5
Roscoe	Feb 2	444-2234	Rover	Alice Jean	410	
Arlis	June 19	444-1314	Redeye	Suzy Beth	12	$10.75

Figure 18.32: Sed writes all records that contain the string 444- to file fours.txt. If fours.txt already contains data, the data is replaced (part 2 of 2).

The Line-number Function

The Line-number function, =, writes the number of a matching line to stdout. If there is no address before the function, all input lines match, as shown in Figure 18.33.

Figure 18.34 shows the command with an address. In this case, *sed* prints the numbers of lines that contain *Feb*.

```
sed = goodoleboys.txt
1
```

Name	Born	Phone	Dog	Wife	Shotgun	Paid

```
2
```

=========	========	========	========	==========	=======	=====

```
3
```

Chuck	Dec 25	444-2345	Blue	Mary Sue	12	$2.50

```
4
```

Bubba	Oct 13	444-1111	Buck	Mary Jean	12	

```
5
```

Billy Bob	June 11	444-4340	Leotis	Lisa Sue	12	

```
6
```

Amos	Jan 4	333-1119	Amos	Abigail	20	

```
7
```

Figure 18.33: Since there is no address before the function, each line number is written to stdout (part 1 of 2).

Otis	Sept 17	444-8000	Ol' Sal	Sally	12	$5
8						
Claude	May 31	333-4340	Blue	Etheline	12	
9						
Roscoe	Feb 2	444-2234	Rover	Alice Jean	410	
10						
Arlis	June 19	444-1314	Redeye	Suzy Beth	12	$10.75
11						
Junior	April 30	BR-549	Percival	Lilly Faye	12	
12						
Bill	Feb 29	333-4444	Daisy	Daisy	20	
13						
Ernest T.	??	none	none	none	none	

Figure 18.33: Since there is no address before the function, each line number is written to stdout (part 2 of 2).

```
sed '/Feb/=' goodoleboys.txt
```

Name	Born	Phone	Dog	Wife	Shotgun	Paid
=========	========	========	========	=========	=======	=====
Chuck	Dec 25	444-2345	Blue	Mary Sue	12	$2.50
Bubba	Oct 13	444-1111	Buck	Mary Jean	12	
Billy Bob	June 11	444-4340	Leotis	Lisa Sue	12	
Amos	Jan 4	333-1119	Amos	Abigail	20	
Otis	Sept 17	444-8000	Ol' Sal	Sally	12	$5
Claude	May 31	333-4340	Blue	Etheline	12	
9						
Roscoe	Feb 2	444-2234	Rover	Alice Jean	410	
Arlis	June 19	444-1314	Redeye	Suzy Beth	12	$10.75
Junior	April 30	BR-549	Percival	Lilly Faye	12	
12						
Bill	Feb 29	333-4444	Daisy	Daisy	20	
Ernest T.	??	none	none	none	none	

Figure 18.34: Print the numbers of lines that contain Feb.

Next

The Next commands, *n* and *N*, force *sed* to read the next input record.

The *n* command tells *sed* to cease processing commands against the pattern space, write the pattern space to stdout (unless otherwise prohibited), and read the next input record into the pattern space. The effect is that any further editing commands are skipped.

In Figure 18.35, when *sed* finds a line containing *Feb*, it executes the *n* command, which causes it to skip the substitute command. The line is written to stdout, and the next line is brought into the pattern space. The effect is that *sed* replaces all zeros and fours on every line that does not contain the string *Feb*.

```
sed -e '/Feb/n' -e 's/[04]/*/g' goodoleboys.txt
Name        Born      Phone     Dog      Wife       Shotgun  Paid
==========  ========  ========  =======  =========  =======  =====
Chuck       Dec 25    ***-23*5  Blue     Mary Sue   12       $2.5*
Bubba       Oct 13    ***-1111  Buck     Mary Jean  12
Billy Bob   June 11   ***-*3**  Leotis   Lisa Sue   12
Amos        Jan *     333-1119  Amos     Abigail    2*
Otis        Sept 17   ***-8***  Ol' Sal  Sally      12       $5
Claude      May 31    333-*3**  Blue     Etheline   12
Roscoe      Feb 2     444-2234  Rover    Alice Jean 410
Arlis       June 19   ***-131*  Redeye   Suzy Beth  12       $1*.75
Junior      April 3*  BR-5*9    Percival Lilly Faye 12
Bill        Feb 29    333-4444  Daisy    Daisy      20
Ernest T.   ??        none      none     none       none
```

Figure 18.35: Replace all zeros and fours on every line that does not contain Feb.

In Figure 18.36, *sed* reads the file, replacing all fours with asterisks and all threes with *X*s until it gets to Claude's record. At that point, it replaces the fours in Claude's record with asterisks, writes to stdout, brings Roscoe's record into the pattern space, replaces the threes with *X*s, and continues as usual. The result is that all fours and threes are replaced in all records except Claude's and Roscoe's. In Claude's records, only the fours are replaced; in Roscoe's record, only the threes.

```
sed -e 's/4/*/g' -e '/Claude/n' -e 's/3/X/g' goodoleboys.txt
Name        Born      Phone     Dog      Wife       Shotgun  Paid
==========  ========  ========  =======  =========  =======  =====
Chuck       Dec 25    ***-2X*5  Blue     Mary Sue   12       $2.50
Bubba       Oct 1X    ***-1111  Buck     Mary Jean  12
Billy Bob   June 11   ***-*X*0  Leotis   Lisa Sue   12
Amos        Jan *     XXX-1119  Amos     Abigail    20
```

Figure 18.36: Replace fours and threes in all records except Claude's and Roscoe's (part 1 of 2).

Otis	Sept 17	***-8000	Ol' Sal	Sally	12	$5
Claude	May 31	333-*3*0	Blue	Etheline	12	
Roscoe	Feb 2	444-22X4	Rover	Alice Jean	410	
Arlis	June 19	***-1X1*	Redeye	Suzy Beth	12	$10.75
Junior	April X0	BR-5*9	Percival	Lilly Faye	12	
Bill	Feb 29	XXX-****	Daisy	Daisy	20	
Ernest T.	??	none	none	none	none	

Figure 18.36: Replace fours and threes in all records except Claude's and Roscoe's (part 2 of 2).

The *N* command tells *sed* to append the next record to the pattern space and separate the two records with a newline character, before continuing with the next *sed* command.

The first *sed* command in Figure 18.37 numbers the lines. Output consists of alternating records of line numbers and data. This is piped into another *sed* command, which combines every pair of records into one record. The second *sed* reads a record that contains a line number, then begins to process the functions. The *N* function reads the next input record and appends it to the pattern space. At this point, the pattern space contains a line number, a newline character, and a data record. The *s* command replaces the newline character that separates the two records with a blank. The records are numbered on the left. This is similar to using the *cat* utility with the *n* option.

```
sed = goodoleboys.txt | sed 'N; s$\n$  $'
```

	Name	Born	Phone	Dog	Wife	Shotgun	Paid
1	Name	Born	Phone	Dog	Wife	Shotgun	Paid
2	=========	========	========	========	==========	=======	=====
3	Chuck	Dec 25	444-2345	Blue	Mary Sue	12	$2.50
4	Bubba	Oct 13	444-1111	Buck	Mary Jean	12	
5	Billy Bob	June 11	444-4340	Leotis	Lisa Sue	12	
6	Amos	Jan 4	333-1119	Amos	Abigail	20	
7	Otis	Sept 17	444-8000	Ol' Sal	Sally	12	$5
8	Claude	May 31	333-4340	Blue	Etheline	12	
9	Roscoe	Feb 2	444-2234	Rover	Alice Jean	410	
10	Arlis	June 19	444-1314	Redeye	Suzy Beth	12	$10.75
11	Junior	April 30	BR-549	Percival	Lilly Faye	12	
12	Bill	Feb 29	333-4444	Daisy	Daisy	20	
13	Ernest T.	??	none	none	none	none	

Figure 18.37: The effect of these two commands is similar to using the cat utility with the -n option.

Using the Holding Buffer

The *h* and *H* commands copy the pattern space to the holding buffer. The *h* command tells *sed* to replace the contents of the holding buffer, while the *H* tells *sed* to append to the contents of the holding buffer.

The holding buffer can be retrieved later with the *g* and *G* functions. To replace the contents of the pattern space, use *g*. To append the holding buffer to the pattern space, use *G*. You can swap the contents of the two buffers with either the *x* function or the substitute function's *x* flag.

In Figure 18.38. Otis's record is stored in the holding buffer and deleted from the output stream. When the last input record is read, the holding buffer is appended to the pattern space. The effect is that *sed* moves Otis's record to the end of the file.

As each record in Figure 18.39 is read, the pattern buffer is swapped with the current contents of the holding space, and the holding space is appended to the

```
sed -e '/Otis/{h; d; }' -e '$G' goodoleboys.txt
```

Name	Born	Phone	Dog	Wife	Shotgun	Paid
=========	========	========	========	=========	=======	=====
Chuck	Dec 25	444-2345	Blue	Mary Sue	12	$2.50
Bubba	Oct 13	444-1111	Buck	Mary Jean	12	
Billy Bob	June 11	444-4340	Leotis	Lisa Sue	12	
Amos	Jan 4	333-1119	Amos	Abigail	20	
Claude	May 31	333-4340	Blue	Etheline	12	
Roscoe	Feb 2	444-2234	Rover	Alice Jean	410	
Arlis	June 19	444-1314	Redeye	Suzy Beth	12	$10.75
Junior	April 30	BR-549	Percival	Lilly Faye	12	
Bill	Feb 29	333-4444	Daisy	Daisy	20	
Ernest T.	??	none	none	none	none	
Otis	Sept 17	444-8000	Ol' Sal	Sally	12	$5

Figure 18.38: Move the record containing Otis to the end of the file.

```
sed -n -e '{x; H; }' -e '${x; p; }' goodoleboys.txt
```

Ernest T.	??	none	none	none	none
Bill	Feb 29	333-4444	Daisy	Daisy	20
Junior	April 30	BR-549	Percival	Lilly Faye	12

Figure 18.39: List the file in reverse order (part 1 of 2).

Name	Born	Phone	Dog	Wife	Shotgun	Paid
Arlis	June 19	444-1314	Redeye	Suzy Beth	12	$10.75
Roscoe	Feb 2	444-2234	Rover	Alice Jean	410	
Claude	May 31	333-4340	Blue	Etheline	12	
Otis	Sept 17	444-8000	Ol' Sal	Sally	12	$5
Amos	Jan 4	333-1119	Amos	Abigail	20	
Billy Bob	June 11	444-4340	Leotis	Lisa Sue	12	
Bubba	Oct 13	444-1111	Buck	Mary Jean	12	
Chuck	Dec 25	444-2345	Blue	Mary Sue	12	$2.50
=========	========	========	========	=========	=======	=====
Name	Born	Phone	Dog	Wife	Shotgun	Paid

Figure 18.39: List the file in reverse order (part 2 of 2).

pattern buffer. This places the new record at the end of the holding space, with a newline character separating the new record from the previous contents of the holding space. When the last input record is processed, the first command will have placed all records in the holding buffer in reverse order. The second command, which is executed only when the last record is processed, places the holding space into the pattern space and prints out the pattern space. The result is that the file is listed in reverse order.

SED SCRIPTS

A *sed script* is a file containing *sed* commands. Instead of keying all the commands on the Qshell command line, you can tell *sed* to read the commands from the file. Use the *f* option followed by the file name to start a script file. In the file, place one editing command on each line.

To place comments in a *sed* script, begin them with a pound sign (#). Do not place comments on lines with other executable code. You can also leave blank lines for readability. A special comment of #n on the first record of the *sed* script is equivalent to the n option. That is, it suppresses the automatic write to stdout.

The sedcmd1.txt file in Figure 18.40 is a *sed* script containing five records: one comment and four editing commands. The first three editing commands in this example delete undesired records. The last replaces the blank in Billy Bob's name with a hyphen. *Sed* reads the goodoleboys.txt file, applying the commands,

356

and sends the output to a While loop. The loop sends the formatted birth month and name to Sort, which prints the data in alphabetical order by month of birth.

```
cat sedcmd1.txt
# Sort members by birthmonth name
/=/d
/??/d
/Born/d
s/Billy /Billy-/
/home/JSMITH $
sed -f sedcmd1.txt goodoleboys.txt | \
>
while read name born rest ; \
>
do printf '%-10s %-10s\n' $born $name ; done | sort
April      Junior
Dec        Chuck
Feb        Bill
Feb        Roscoe
Jan        Amos
June       Arlis
June       Billy-Bob
May        Claude
Oct        Bubba
Sept       Otis
```

Figure 18.40: The sed script in sedcmd1.txt prints the lines in goodoleboys.txt in alphabetical order by month of birth.

You can use the *t* and *b* functions to branch within lists of *sed* commands. While you can use branching when entering *sed* commands on the command line, it is more likely that you'll use them in *sed* scripts. The *b* command causes an unconditional branch to a *label*, which is a line that begins with a colon and a label name. The *t* command causes a branch only if a substitution is made. If a label is not specified, *sed* branches past the remaining commands.

The sedcmd2.txt *sed* script in Figure 18.41 involves branching. The first branch, *1,2b*, tells *sed* to exit the script if it is processing either of the first two lines. None of the remaining script applies to the goodoleboys.txt data. The two other branches depend on whether or not the string *444-* is found in a record.

```
cat sedcmd2.txt
# remove Paid column from headings
1s/  Paid//
2s/  =====$//
1,2s/^/    /
1,2b

# data lines
# remove Paid figures
s/\$[0-9]*\.*[0-9]*$//

# if 444 prefix
/444-/!b not444
# show "local number"
s/444-[0-9]\{4\}/local   /
s/^/    /
b

# if not 444 prefix
:not444
y/abcdefghijklmnopqrstuvwxyz/ABCDEFGHIJKLMNOPQRSTUVWXYZ/
s/^/===> /
/home/JSMITH $
sed -f sedcmd2.txt goodoleboys.txt
```

	Name	Born	Phone	Dog	Wife	Shotgun
	=========	========	========	========	=========	=======
	Chuck	Dec 25	local	Blue	Mary Sue	12
	Bubba	Oct 13	local	Buck	Mary Jean	12
	Billy Bob	June 11	local	Leotis	Lisa Sue	12
===>	AMOS	JAN 4	333-1119	AMOS	ABIGAIL	20
	Otis	Sept 17	local	Ol' Sal	Sally	12
===>	CLAUDE	MAY 31	333-4340	BLUE	ETHELINE	12
	Roscoe	Feb 2	local	Rover	Alice Jean	410
	Arlis	June 19	local	Redeye	Suzy Beth	12
===>	JUNIOR	APRIL 30	BR-549	PERCIVAL	LILLY FAYE	12
===>	BILL	FEB 29	333-4444	DAISY	DAISY	20
===>	ERNEST T.	??	NONE	NONE	NONE	NONE

Figure 18.41: Sed scripts may include branching operations.

SUMMARY

Sed is a batch editor that applies editing commands to a stream file or standard input, and produces modified output. It is useful for editing such files when human interaction is not needed. *Sed* is often used to build scripts for other utilities, such as FTP.

Chapter 19

Writing Programs for Qshell

If you have a specific goal you want to accomplish within Qshell, the first thing you should do is look for a utility or sequence of utilities that will serve your purpose. If no utility is available, you should write a Qshell script. If the Qshell language cannot do what you need, you'll have to write a program.

Although any program can run under Qshell, a program must do the following four tasks to be useful from within shell scripts and consistent with other Qshell utilities:

1. Read from the standard input device *(stdin)*.
2. Write to the standard output device *(stdout)*.
3. Write to the standard error device *(stderr)*.
4. Return an exit status to Qshell.

Writing programs that can operate under Qshell is not difficult at all. It is especially easy in C, C++, and Java, because those languages have functions to handle standard input and output. However, it is not difficult in RPG or COBOL, either.

This chapter explains how to write programs that can run under Qshell.

RUNNING PROGRAMS WITHIN QSHELL

Qshell doesn't use the call command to start a program. Instead, you must type the program's name, in IFS style. The following example illustrates how a program can run within Qshell:

```
/qsys.lib/mylib.lib/myshellpgm.pgm
```

Program MYSHELLPGM is stored in library MYLIB. To run the program within Qshell, enter the program's name in IFS format.

A second example is given in Figure 19.1. Note that the name of the program is given in IFS notation.

```
ls -l t[h-k]* | /qsys.lib/jsmith.lib/reversestr.pgm
tacgsmtloht        2002  92 rpA 806      0  HTIMSJ 1   ---xwrxwr-
fig.pu-bmuht       2002  81 tcO 773      0  HTIMSJ 1   ---xwrxwr-
niedlit            2002  02 peS 54       0  HTIMSJ 1   ----wr-wr-
tuoedlit           2002  02 peS 54       0  HTIMSJ 1   ----wr-wr-
ttaywedlit         2002  72 peS 824      0  HTIMSJ 1   ----wr-wr-
soommtrkopyzzjmkt  2002  31 peS 6        0  HTIMSJ 1   -wr-wr-wr-
/home/JSMITH $
```

Figure 19.1: Program REVERSESTR in library JSMITH reads the output of the ls command, reverses each line, and writes to stdout.

Perhaps a better method for running programs is by means of symbolic links. You can create a symbolic link either by using CL's Add Link command (ADDLNK) or by using Qshell's *ln* command.

The following example shows how to create a symbolic link from CL:

```
ADDLNK OBJ('/qsys.lib/jsmith.lib/reversestr.pgm') +
    NEWLNK('/home/jsmith/revstr') +
    LNKTYPE(*SYMBOLIC)
```

The ADDLNK command creates a symbolic link called *revstr*, which points to program REVERSESTR in library JSMITH.

To create a symbolic link within Qshell, use the *ln* utility with the *-s* option, as shown here:

```
ln -s /qsys.lib/jsmith.lib/reversestr.pgm revstr
```

Regardless of which method you use, the symbolic link is created in the IFS and points to a program in the library file system.

Qshell's *ls* (List Directory Contents) command can indicate symbolic links in several ways. The *l* (letter "ell") option indicates symbolic links in two ways:

- By placing the letter *l* ("ell") in the first position of the permissions
- By listing the name of the link, following by the character sequence ->
  and the name of the program in IFS format

In the following example, the fact that *mylnk* is a symbolic link is indicated by the letter *l* in the first position of the permissions, and also by the name of the link followed by an arrow and the name of the program:

```
ls -l revs*
lrwxrwxrwx 1 SMITH 0 35 May 4 12:52
blnk -> /qsys.lib/s.lib/bpgm.pgm
/home/jsmith $
```

The *blnk* in the example is an alternate name for program BPGM, in library S.

The *F* option of the *ls* command indicates a symbolic link by affixing an "at" symbol (@) to the end of the name of a symbolic link. This option also appends an asterisk (*) to the names of executable files and a slash (/) to the names of directories. Figure 19.2 provides an example of this option. The file revstr is the only symbolic link in this directory. The *ls* utility indicates this fact by adding the "at" sign to the end of the file name. The file isempty.qsh is the only executable file, and temp is the only directory.

Once the symbolic link has been created, you can use it to run the program within Qshell, as Figure 19.3 illustrates. Program REVERSESTR in library JSMITH

```
ls -F
isempty.qsh*     temp/              zebra
revstr@          upper.txt          zugzwang
/home/jsmith/temp $
```

Figure 19.2: Use the F option to distinguish regular files from directories and executables.

```
ls -l t[h-k]* | revstr
tacgsmtloht           2002  92 rpA 806    0  HTIMSJ 1   ---xwrxwr-
fig.pu-bmuht          2002  81 tc0 773    0  HTIMSJ 1   ---xwrxwr-
niedlit               2002  02 peS 54     0  HTIMSJ 1   ----wr-wr-
tuoedlit              2002  02 peS 54     0  HTIMSJ 1   ----wr-wr-
ttaywedlit            2002  72 peS 824    0  HTIMSJ 1   ----wr-wr-
soommtrkopyzzjmkt 2002  31 peS 6      0  HTIMSJ 1   -wr-wr-wr-
/home/jsmith $
```

Figure 19.3: An alias executes a program within a pipeline.

reads the output of the *ls* command and writes to stdout. The name of the program is specified in the symbolic link *revstr*.

WRITING RPG PROGRAMS FOR QSHELL

RPG is not as well-suited as Java and C for writing Qshell programs, since it does not have direct support for the standard devices, nor can it directly return an exit status. This only makes sense, since RPG was designed to access databases, not stream files. However, RPG programs *can* run in Qshell, and the fact that RPG programs can access the database, data areas, data queues, and other objects is a good reason to consider it as an appropriate language for Qshell programs.

Binding to C Functions

There are several ways to make RPG use the standard device files. One method is to bind RPG programs to C functions. Figure 19.4 lists the source code of RPG program, REVERSESTR, which reverses the characters in each line read from standard input. Notice that this program binds to C's *gets*, *puts*, and *exit* functions.

Figure 19.5 shows REVERSESTR at work.

```
// read from stdin and write a reversed string to stdout

H dftactgrp(*no) actgrp(*new) bnddir('QC2LE')

D GetString       pr                    *   extproc('gets')
D                                    4096a
D PutString       pr                  10i 0 extproc('puts')
D                                    4096a
D Exit            pr                        extproc('exit')
D                                    10i 0 value
D ReverseString   pr                 4096a
D    String                          4096a

D PStatus         s                     *
D pssrStatus      s                     n
D Info            s                  4096a
D Outfo           s                  4096a

/free
       PStatus = GetString (Info);
       dow PStatus <> *null;
          Outfo = ReverseString (Info);
          PutString (Outfo);
          PStatus = GetString (Info);
       enddo;
       *inlr = *on;
       exit (0);

       // ********************************** //

       begsr *pssr;

       *inlr = *on;
       if pssrStatus = *off;
          pssrStatus = *on;
       else;
          return;
       endif;
       exit (1);
       return;

       endsr;

/end-free
```

Figure 19.4: You can write RPG programs that run in Qshell by binding to C input-output functions (part 1 of 2).

```
      //  *********************************  //

P ReverseString     b
D                   pi            4096a
D String                         4096a

D ndx               s             10i 0
D Workfo            s            4096a     varying

  /free
     for ndx = 1 to %len(String);
         if %subst(String: ndx: 1) = x'00';
             leave;
         endif;
         Workfo = %subst(String: ndx: 1) + Workfo;
     endfor;
     Workfo = Workfo + x'00';
     return (Workfo);

  /end-free
P                   e
```

Figure 19.4: You can write RPG programs that run in Qshell by binding to C input-output functions (part 2 of 2).

```
ls -l ba*
-rwxrwxrwx   1 JSMITH   0             313 Jun   3   2002 backup.qsh
-rwxrwx---   1 JSMITH   0             156 Aug  28   2002 batch01.qsh
/home/JSMITH $
ls -l ba* | /qsys.lib/jsmith.lib/reversestr.pgm
hsq.pukcab  2002    3 nuJ 313         0  HTIMSJ 1  xwrxwrxwr-
hsq.10hctab 2002   82 guA 651         0  HTIMSJ 1  ---xwrxwr-
/home/JSMITH $
```

Figure 19.5: RPG program REVERSESTR reads the output of the ls command, reversing each line and writing to standard output.

The Unix-type APIs

Perhaps a better way than binding to C functions is to use the Unix-type APIs, because they handle stream-file lines of any length. The Unix-type APIs that you will need are Read, Write, and Exit. You can access these APIs via the QC2LE binding directory.

The Read API gets a specified number of characters from an input file. If fewer than the specified number of characters remain in the file, Read gets the remainder of the file. Read gets any characters it finds, including control characters such as carriage-return and linefeed. That is, RPG does not read the input line by line, but character by character. It is up to you, the programmer, to decide what to do with the retrieved data.

RPG program NBRLINES, shown in Figure 19.6, reads from standard input and numbers the lines as they are written to standard output. This is similar in function to the *cat* utility with the n option. Take note of the following:

- The H spec refers to binding directory QC2LE so the compiler can find the APIs.

- The Read, Write, and Exit APIs are prototyped as ReadStream, WriteStream, and exit, respectively.

- Each ReadStream operation is to file descriptor 0, stdin.

- The WriteStream operations are to file descriptors 1 (stdout) and 2 (stderr).

- The ReadStream and WriteStream operations must refer to the addresses of (pointers to) the input and output variables.

- The program checks the input data for linefeed characters to determine when a new line begins.

The ReadStream procedure attempts to retrieve 4,096 bytes of input from stdin (file descriptor 0). The number of bytes read is returned into variable *datalen*. On all reads except the last, the system returns 4,096 bytes of data. On the last successful read, *datalen* may return fewer bytes. When ReadStream tries to read past the end of file, the system returns a value of zero.

After each execution of ReadStream, the program enters a loop that examines each character of data and decides what action to take. If the character is not a linefeed character, it is added to the end of an output string. If the character is a linefeed, the output string is written to stdout, and the program prepares to build a new line of output.

```
     * To compile:
     * CRTBNDRPG PGM(xxx/NBRLINES) +
     *            SRCFILE(xxx/QRPGLESRC) SRCMBR(NBRLINES)

H option(*srcstmt) bnddir('QC2LE') dftactgrp(*no) actgrp(*new)

D ReadStream      pr            10i 0 extproc('read')
D   fd                          10i 0 value
D   info                          * value
D   length                      10u 0 value

D WriteStream     pr            10i 0 extproc('write')
D   fd                          10i 0 value
D   outfo                         * value
D   length                      10u 0 value

D exit            pr                  extproc('exit')
D                               3u 0 value

D                 sds
D   PgmName           *proc
D   PgmStatus          11     15
D   PgmStmtNbr         21     28
D   PgmException       40     46
D   PgmErrorMsg        91    170

D LF              c                   const('x25')
D ix              s             10i 0
D ox              s             10i 0
D datalen         s             10i 0
D lineno          s             10i 0
D NewLine         s               n   inz(*on)
D pssrStatus      s               n
D info            s            4096a
D outfo           s            4096a

    /free
        datalen = ReadStream (0: %addr(info): %size(info));
        dow datalen > *zero;
          for ix = 1 to datalen;
            if NewLine;
              lineno += 1;
              outfo = %editc(lineno:'4') + ': ;'
              WriteStream (1: %addr(outfo): %len(%trimr(outfo))+1);
              NewLine = *off;
```

Figure 19.6: The NBRLINES program uses the Unix-type APIs to process std input and output
(part 1 of 2).

```
                endif;
                ox += 1;
                %subst(outfo:ox:1) =  %subst(info:ix:1);
                if %subst(info:ix:1) = LF;
                    WriteStream (1: %addr(outfo): ox);
                    ox = *zero;
                    NewLine = *on;
                endif;
            endfor;
            datalen = ReadStream (0: %addr(info): %size(info));
        enddo;
        if ox > *zero;
            WriteStream (1: %addr(outfo): %len(%trimr(outfo)));
        endif;
        *inlr = *on;
        exit (0);

      // ====================================================

    begsr *pssr;

        *inlr = *on;
        if pssrStatus = *off;
            pssrStatus = *on;
        else;
            return;
        endif;

        outfo = 'Unexpected error.' + LF;
        WriteStream (2: %addr(outfo): %len(%trimr(outfo)));
        outfo = 'Program....: '  + PgmName + LF;
        WriteStream (2: %addr(outfo): %len(%trimr(outfo)));
        outfo = 'Statement..: ' + PgmStmtNbr + LF;
        WriteStream (2: %addr(outfo): %len(%trimr(outfo)));
        outfo = 'Status.....: ' + PgmStatus + LF;
        WriteStream (2: %addr(outfo): %len(%trimr(outfo)));
        outfo = 'Exception..: ' + PgmException + LF;
        WriteStream (2: %addr(outfo): %len(%trimr(outfo)));
        outfo = PgmErrorMsg + LF;
        WriteStream (2: %addr(outfo): %len(%trimr(outfo)));
        exit (1);

    endsr;

/end-free
```

Figure 19.6: The NBRLINES program uses the Unix-type APIs to process std input and output (part 2 of 2).

Figure 19.7 shows the output from a normal run of program NBRLINES.

```
ls test* | /qsys.lib/jsmith.lib/nbrlines.pgm
          1: test01.qsh
          2: test02.qsh
          3: test03.qsh
          4: test04.qsh
          5: test04a.qsh
          6: test05.qsh
          7: test06.qsh
          8: test07.qsh
          9: test08.qsh
         10: test1.pl
/home/JSMITH $
```

Figure 19.7: The RPG program NBRLINES reads the output of the ls command and writes to stdout, numbering lines in the process.

If something goes wrong, the *pssr subroutine writes an error message to stderr. Figure 19.8 shows the output of an abnormal run of NBRLINES.

```
ls test* | /qsys.lib/jsmith.lib/nbrlines.pgm
          1: test01.qsh
Unexpected error.
Program....: NBRLINES
Statement..: 00005100
Status.....: 00000
Exception..: MCH1211
Attempt made to divide by zero for fixed point operation.
/home/JSMITH $
echo $?
1
/home/JSMITH $
```

Figure 19.8: If NBRLINES encounters an error, it writes descriptive information to the stderr file and sets the exit status to one.

The previous example shows one way that NBRLINES indicates success or failure—by writing to either stdout or stderr. In addition, the exit procedure sets the return code to zero to indicate that the program ran successfully, or to one to indicate that the program ended abnormally.

A Better Solution

You can make these APIs easier to use by wrapping them in subprocedures that assume file descriptors, allow constant values, and do not use pointers. This section presents a service program that implements these improvements.

Figure 19.9 contains the source code from which the subprocedure is built. The source member, STDIO, is first compiled to create a module. Then, the module is used to create a service program, also named STDIO.

```
* Service program to handle stdio

* to create:
* CRTRPGMOD MODULE(xxx/STDIO) +
*    SRCFILE(xxx/QRPGLESRC) SRCMBR(STDIO)
* CRTSRVPGM SRVPGM(xxx/STDIO) MODULE(STDIO)

H nomain bnddir('QC2LE')

/define stdio_srvpgm
/copy prototypes,stdio

// **************** stdin *************** //

P stdin           b                       export
D                 pi              10i 0
D   info                        4096a     varying

D length          s               10i 0
D buffer          s             4096a

/free
monitor;
length = ReadStream (0: %addr(buffer): %size(buffer));
if length > *zero;
   info = %subst(buffer: 1: length);
else;
   %len(info) = *zero;
endif;
return length;
```

Figure 19.9: Wrapping the Unix-type APIs in a subprocedure makes them easier to use (part 1 of 3).

```
on-error;
   stderr ('Unexpected error in stdin routine.' + CRLF);
   cexit (1);
   return -1;
endmon;
/end-free
P                       e


// **************** stdout *************** //

P stdout            b                       export
D                   pi
D   outfo                         4096      const varying

D buffer            s             4096

/free
monitor;
   buffer = outfo;
   WriteStream (1: %addr(buffer): %len(outfo));
on-error;
   stderr ('Unexpected error in stdout routine.' + CRLF);
   cexit (1);
   return;
endmon;
/end-free
P                       e


// **************** stderr *************** //

P stderr            b                       export
D                   pi
D   outfo                         4096      const varying

D buffer            s             4096

/free
monitor;
   buffer = outfo;
   WriteStream (2: %addr(buffer): %len(outfo));
on-error;
   cexit (1);
   return;
endmon;
/end-free
P                       e
```

Figure 19.9: Wrapping the Unix-type APIs in a subprocedure makes them easier to use (part 2 of 3).

```
// **************** exit *************** //

P exit             b                        export
D                  pi
D   status                        3u 0 value

/free
   cexit (status);
/end-free
P                  e
```

Figure 19.9: Wrapping the Unix-type APIs in a subprocedure makes them easier to use (part 3 of 3).

Both the service program and any programs that reference it require procedure prototypes for the I/O subprocedures. The prototype member in Figure 19.10 not only defines procedure prototypes, but frequently used constants, as well. The last part of the member is conditioned by compiler condition stdio_srvpgm, which should be defined when creating the subprocedure module and undefined when creating calling modules.

```
* read stdin, write stdout and stderr
* update exit status
* define constants needed by programs that use this service pgm

* define condition stdio_srvpgm when compiling the service pgm
* but not when compiling programs that use the service pgm

D TAB            c                     const(x'05')
D CR             c                     const(x'0d')
D LF             c                     const(x'25')
D CRLF           c                     const(x'0d25')

D stdin          pr          10i 0
D   info                     4096a    varying

D stdout         pr
D   outfo                    4096     const varying

D stderr         pr
D   outfo                    4096     const varying

D stdwrite       pr
```

Figure 19.10: Programs that use the standard I/O subprocedures should include this copybook member (part 1 of 2).

```
D   fd                              10i 0 value
    D   outfo                         4096      const varying

D exit             pr
D                                   3u 0 value

/if defined(stdio_srvpgm)

D ReadStream       pr              10i 0 extproc('read')
D   fd                              10i 0 value
D   info                              *   value
D   length                         10u 0 value

D WriteStream      pr              10i 0 extproc('write')
D   fd                              10i 0 value
D   outfo                             *   value
D   length                         10u 0 value

D cexit            pr                     extproc('exit')
D                                   3u 0 value

/endif
```

Figure 19.10: Programs that use the standard I/O subprocedures should include this copybook member (part 2 of 2).

Figure 19.11 is the source code for another version of the NBRLINES program. It differs from the previous version in that it uses the routines in the STDIO service program.

```
* Copy from standard input to standard output, numbering lines

* To compile:
* CRTRPGMOD MODULE(xxx/NBRLINES) +
*           SRCFILE(xxx/QRPGLESRC) +
*           SRCMBR(NBRLINES)
* CRTPGM    PGM(NBRLINES) +
*           MODULE(NBRLINES) +
*           BNDSRVPGM(STDIO)
H option(*srcstmt)

    /copy prototypes,stdio

D                   sds
D   PgmName         *proc
```

Figure 19.11: This RPG program binds to the standard I/O subprocedures (part 1 of 3).

```
D   PgmStatus              11      15
D   PgmStmtNbr             21      28
D   PgmException           40      46
D   PgmErrorMsg            91     170

D ix               s              10i 0
D datalen          s              10i 0
D lineno           s              10i 0
D NewLine          s                 n    inz(*on)
D pssrStatus       s                 n
D info             s              4096a    varying
D outfo            s              4096a    varying

    /free
        datalen = stdin (info);
        dow datalen > *zero;
           for ix = 1 to datalen;
              if NewLine;
                 lineno += 1;
                 outfo = %editc(lineno:'4') + ': ';
                 NewLine = *off;
              endif;
              outfo =   outfo + %subst(info:ix:1);
              if %subst(info:ix:1) = LF;
                 stdout (outfo);
                 %len(outfo) = *zero;
                 NewLine = *on;
              endif;
              endfor;
              datalen = stdin (info);
           enddo;
           if %len(outfo) > *zero;
              stdout (outfo);
           endif;
           *inlr = *on;
           exit (0);

     //  ====================================================

begsr *pssr;

        *inlr = *on;
        if pssrStatus = *off;
           pssrStatus = *on;
        else;
           return;
        endif;
```

Figure 19.11: This RPG program binds to the standard I/O subprocedures (part 2 of 3).

```
          stdout ('Unexpected error.' + LF);
          stdout ('Program....: ' + PgmName + LF);
          stdout ('Statement..: ' + PgmStmtNbr + LF);
          stdout ('Status.....: ' + PgmStatus + LF);
          stdout ('Exception..: ' + PgmException + LF);
          stdout (PgmErrorMsg + LF);
          exit (1);

        endsr;

/end-free
```

Figure 19.11: This RPG program binds to the standard I/O subprocedures (part 3 of 3).

WRITING COBOL PROGRAMS FOR QSHELL

Writing COBOL programs that will operate within Qshell is similar in concept to writing RPG programs for Qshell. Figure 19.12 contains the source code for a COBOL version of NBRLINES. Like the RPG module in Figure 19.11, this COBOL module binds to the Unix-type APIs.

```
     process nomonoprc nostdtrunc

     Identification division.
     Program-ID.    NbrLines.

   * Copy from standard input to standard output, numbering lines

   * To compile:
   *     CRTCBLMOD MODULE(xxx/NBRLINES)
   *               SRCFILE(xxx/SRC)
   *               SRCMBR(NBRLINES)
   *     CRTPGM PGM(NBRLINES)
   *            MODULE(NBRLINES)
   *            BNDDIR(QC2LE)

     Environment division.

     Data division.
     Working-storage section.
     01  LineFeed        pic x             value x"25".
     01  ix              pic s9(9) binary  value zero.
```

Figure 19.12: This COBOL module binds to the Unix-type APIs (part 1 of 3).

```
01  ox              pic s9(9) binary  value zero.
01  LineNbr         pic s9(9) binary  value zero.
01  LineNbrOut      pic z(9).
01  Info            pic x(4096).
01  InfoAddress     pointer.
01  Outfo           pic x(4096).
01  OutfoAddress    pointer.
01  DataLen         pic s9(9) binary  value zero.
01  ReturnCode      pic s9(9) binary  value zero.
01  NewLine         pic x             value "Y".

Procedure division.
Main-Paragraph.

    Set InfoAddress to address of Info.
    Set OutfoAddress to address of Outfo.

    Perform Read-Data.
    Perform Process-data
        until DataLen <= zero.
    Stop run.

Process-data.
    Perform varying ix from 1 by 1
        until ix > DataLen
        if NewLine = "Y"
            perform StartNewLine
        end-if
        Compute ox = ox + 1
        Move Info(ix:1) to Outfo(ox:1)
        If Info(ix:1) = LineFeed
            perform Write-routine
            move "Y" to NewLine
        end-if
    end-perform.
    Perform Read-Data.

StartNewLine.
    Compute LineNbr = LineNbr + 1.
    Move LineNbr to LineNbrOut.
    Move LineNbrOut to Outfo(1:9).
    Move ": " to Outfo(10:2).
    Compute ox = 11.
    Move "N" to NewLine.

Write-routine.
```

Figure 19.12: This COBOL module binds to the Unix-type APIs (part 2 of 3).

```
Call procedure "write"
    using by value 1
        by value OutfoAddress
        by value ox
    returning ReturnCode.
Compute ox = zero.

Read-Data.
    Call procedure "read"
        using by value 0
            by value InfoAddress
            by value 4096
        returning DataLen.
```

Figure 19.12: This COBOL module binds to the Unix-type APIs (part 3 of 3).

The Read and Write APIs each require three parameters. The first is the file descriptor, which is 0, 1, and 2 for stdin, stdout, and stderr, respectively. The second parameter is a pointer to the variable that contains the data. The third parameter is the number of bytes to be read or written. Note that all three parameters are passed by value. Both procedures return an integer value. For a read, the value is the number of bytes that were retrieved. A negative number indicates that an error occurred on the read.

Figure 19.12 shows how to read from stdin and write to stdout, but does not show how to write to stderr and set the exit status. Figure 19.13 provides an illustration of binding to those two functions.

```
process nomonoprc nostdtrunc

Identification division.
Program-ID.    Exitc.

* Write to stderr and set the exit status

* To compile:
*    CRTCBLMOD MODULE(xxx/EXITC)
*              SRCFILE(xxx/SRC)
*              SRCMBR(EXITC)
```

Figure 19.13: The Write API sends the error message to stderr. The Exit API sets the exit status to nine (part 1 of 2).

```
*       CRTPGM    PGM(EXITC)
*                 MODULE(EXITC)
*                 BNDDIR(QC2LE)

Environment division.

Data division.
Working-storage section.
01  LineFeed       pic x               value x"25".
01  Outfo          pic x(4096).
01  OutfoAddress   pointer.
01  ReturnCode     pic s9(9) binary    value zero.

Procedure division.
Main-Paragraph.

    Set OutfoAddress to address of Outfo.

* write to stderr
    String "Program EXITC ended abnormally."
        LineFeed delimited by size into Outfo.
    Call procedure "write"
        using by value 2
            by value OutfoAddress
            by value 32
            returning ReturnCode.

* set exit status to 9
    Call procedure "exit"
        using by value 9.

    Stop run.
```

Figure 19.13: The Write API sends the error message to stderr. The Exit API sets the exit status to nine (part 2 of 2).

Figure 19.14 shows the results of running the EXITC program.

```
/qsys.lib/jsmith.lib/exitc.pgm
Program EXITC ended abnormally.
/home/jsmith $
echo $?
9
/home/jsmith $
```

Figure 19.14: COBOL programs can write to stderr and set the exit status.

WRITING C AND C++ PROGRAMS FOR QSHELL

As mentioned earlier, C and C++ are good choices for writing Qshell programs, since they directly address the four requirements listed at the beginning of this chapter. C and C++ were used to implement the majority of existing Qshell utilities. In addition, the C and C++ compilers and development tools are provided for use from within the Qshell environment. Chapter 24 provides additional information about C and C++ application-development in Qshell.

Types of Available APIs

In a Qshell environment, a utility receives file-descriptors 0, 1, and 2, which represent the stdin, stdout, and stderr files. Any C or C++ application that uses those descriptors directly (using the Unix-type APIs like Read or Write) will interact with the Qshell environment. Use descriptors 0, 1, and 2 safely for standard I/O only from within a Qshell environment. In other environments (like the CL command line), those file descriptors do not represent the standard I/O files.

You can safely use all of the C and C++ standard I/O mechanisms to do input in a Qshell program. The C-standard I/O APIs are any of those that work with the stdin, stdout, and stderr standard files (either implicitly or explicitly). In C++, use standard I/O via the *cin*, *cout*, and *cerr* objects.

Qshell uses the environment variable QIBM_USE_DESCRIPTOR_STDIO to indicate that the standard I/O files should, internally, always read and write data to the file descriptors 0, 1, and 2 instead of the typical iSeries C runtime terminal. Qshell sets the QIBM_USE_DESCRIPTOR_STDIO environment variable to affect the C/C++ runtime I/O APIs.

Be careful when mixing standard I/O APIs and Unix-type APIs in the same program. The standard I/O APIs perform extensive buffering in the C and C++ runtime to optimize I/O performance. The Unix-type APIs perform buffering at a much lower layer in the operating system. Mixing the APIs on the same output streams could cause data to be intermixed because of the buffering at different layers of the APIs.

Set the exit status from a C or C++ utility using the exit() function or by returning the exit status from the main() routine.

Standard Input/Output Functions

Figure 19.15 lists the source code of a C program, *reverse*, which reverses the characters in each line read from standard input. This program is similar to the RPG program REVERSESTR, shown previously in this chapter. This example uses the fgets(), putc(), and exit() functions to access the standard I/O streams.

Here are some things to note about this program:

- The #include statements insert the definitions and function prototypes for the standard I/O and string-manipulation APIs.

- The program reads each line of input using the fgets() function.

- Instead of reversing the line in memory, the program simply writes the characters to standard output backwards, one character at a time, using the putc() function.

- After the program reads all lines of input, it returns an exit status of zero.

- The program is compiled using the Qshell utility *ixlc* (described in chapter 24).

```
cat reverse.c
#include <stdio.h>
#include <string.h>

int main(int argc, char **argv)
{
    char            buffer[4096];   // Line Buffer
    int             len = 0;        // Length
```

Figure 19.15: The reverse program reads standard input (in this case, the output of the ls command) and reverses each line before writing it to standard output (part 1 of 2).

```
    // Read a line of input. Use fgets so buffer overrun
    // does not occur if more than 4096 bytes of data is available
    while (fgets(buffer, sizeof(buffer), stdin) != NULL) {
        len = strlen(buffer);    // Length of the line we read in
        buffer[len-1] = 0;       // Remove the newline from the end
        --len;                   // Length is now one less
        // Write out each character of the string in reverse.
        while (len >= 0) {       // Process until we read the beginning.
            putc(buffer[len], stdout);   // Write the character
            --len;               // Go to the previous character.
        }
        putc('\n', stdout);      // Write the newline that we removed.
    }
    return 0;                    // Set a Qshell exit status of 0
}
/home/jsmith $
ixlc reverse.c
Program REVERSE was created in library C on 06/14/03 at 13:39:43.
/home/jsmith $
ln -s /qsys.lib/c.lib/reverse.pgm reverse
/home/jsmith $
ls -l *.[cC] | reverse
 c.ColleH 01:22  8  nuJ 701        0  HTIMSJ 1   xwrxwrxwr-
 C.ppColleH 01:228  nuJ 811        0  HTIMSJ 1   xwrxwrxwr-
 c.gnitsiL 01:22 8  nuJ 443        0  HTIMSJ 1   xwrxwrxwr-
 c.esrever 93:31 41 nuJ 689        0  HTIMSJ 1   xwrxwrxwr-
/home/jsmith $
```

Figure 19.15: The reverse program reads standard input (in this case, the output of the ls command) and reverses each line before writing it to standard output (part 2 of 2).

Figure 19.16 contains a short C++ version of the line-numbering program.

```
cat /qsys.lib/jsmith.lib/src.file/eko5.mbr
// Number lines

// To compile:
//
//      CRTBNDCPP   PGM(xxx/EKO5)
//                  SRCFILE(xxx/QCPPSRC)
//                  SRCMBR(EKO5)

#include <iostream.h>
```

Figure 19.16: This C++ reads the output of the ls command and writes numbered lines to stdout (part 1 of 2)

```
int main (int argc, char **argv)
{
    char s[4096];
    int ct = 0;

    while (1)
    {
        cin.getline(s,4096);
        if (cin.eof()) {
            break;
        }
        cout << ++ct << " =" << s << "=\n";
    }
    return 0;
}
ls b* | /qsys.lib/jsmith.lib/eko5.pgm
 1 =b2d.qsh=
 2 =b2d2.qsh=
 3 =backup.qsh=
 4 =batch01.qsh=
 5 =bscript.qsh=
 6 ==
 7 =bin:=
 8 =arglist.qsh=
 9 =ftprun.qsh=
10 =showargs.qsh=
/home/jsmith $
```

Figure 19.16: This C++ reads the output of the ls command and writes numbered lines to stdout (part 1 of 2).

IFS File-descriptor APIs

The standard stream I/O functions are often easier to use than processing data directly. However, there are some situations where it will be useful to access the file descriptors 0, 1, and 2 directly. In these situations, use the IFS file descriptor-based APIs.

Like the NBRLINES RPG example shown earlier in this chapter, Figure 19.17 outputs all input lines with line numbers. This example uses the Read and Write APIs to access the descriptors 0, 1, and 2 directly.

381

```
cat lines.c
#include <stdio.h>
#include <string.h>
#include <unistd.h>
#include <errno.h>

#define    BUF      4096

int main(int argc, char **argv)
{
    char       buffer[BUF];      // Input buffer
    char       outBuffer[BUF];   // Output buffer
    int        len = 0;          // Length of data read
    int        outLen = 0;       // Length of current out string.
    char       lineLabel[16] = {0};       // Line number label
    char       currentLine = 1;           // Current line number
    int        ndx = 0;                   // Buffer index

    sprintf(lineLabel, "%.5d: ", currentLine); // Current label
    len = read(0, buffer, sizeof(buffer));      // read a buffer
    while (len > 0) {                           // Process any data.
       for (ndx=0; ndx<len; ++ndx) {      // All bytes from start to end
         outBuffer[outLen] = buffer[ndx];      // Copy input char to output
               ++outLen;

             if (outLen >= BUF ||            // Buffer is full     OR
                 buffer[ndx] == '\n') {      // Reached a new line

                if (lineLabel[0] != 0) {    // A pending line number?
                   write(1, lineLabel,      // Write it out.
                      strlen(lineLabel));
                }
            write(1, outBuffer, outLen);       // Output the current line.
            if (buffer[ndx] == '\n') {  // New line. Create a label for
            ++currentLine;                 // the next line.
            sprintf(lineLabel, "%.5d: ",   // Pend a line number for when
                   currentLine);   // a line is written out.
                }
             outLen = 0;                          // Empty the output buffer.
            }
        }
     len = read(0, buffer, sizeof(buffer));  // Read the next input buffer
     }
     // End of all input data. Write any remaining output data
```

Figure 19.17: This program uses the Unix-type APIs to process its standard input and output. Acting as a filter, the program adds line numbers to the input data before outputting it (part 1 of 2).

382

```
        if (outLen > 0) {
            if (lineLabel[0] != 0) {      // A pending line number?
                write(1, lineLabel,       // Write it out.
                    strlen(lineLabel));
            }
            write(1, outBuffer, outLen);// Write the remaining data
            outLen = 0;
        }
        if (len < 0) {
        sprintf(outBuffer, "Error on read buffer, errno value=%d\n", errno);
            write(2, outBuffer, strlen(outBuffer));
        }
        return 0;
}
/home/jsmith $
ixlc -qifsio=64 lines.c
Program LINES was created in library C on 06/14/03 at 15:25:34.
/home/jsmith $
ls -1 | lines
00001: HelloC.c
00002: HelloCpp.C
00003: Listing.c
00004: lines
00005: lines.c
00006: newline
00007: newline.c
00008: reverse
00009: reverse.c
/home/jsmith $
```

Figure 19.17: This program uses the Unix-type APIs to process its standard input and output. Acting as a filter, the program adds line numbers to the input data before outputting it (part 2 of 2).

You Can't Teach a Newline New Tricks

When using the Unix type APIs like Read and Write, be aware of a problem that might occur with regard to the newline values. Because of a historical problem with the newline character \n in C and C++ programs, the hexadecimal value of a newline character changes depending on compilation options. At certain times, this behavior can cause significant confusion.

Using the IFS I/O compilation option on the C or C++ compiler allows C or C++ programs that use the standard C I/O routines to access IFS files instead of iSeries record-based files in the QSYS file system. In C and C++ programs that don't use IFS I/O, the newline character is EBCDIC 0x15 (hexadecimal 15). In C and C++ programs that use the IFS I/O option, the newline character is changed to EBCDIC 0x25 to maintain compatibility with data files in IFS and on other systems.

In an effort to reduce the confusion and impact on applications caused by this discrepancy, APIs and the Qshell utilities typically honor both values as a newline character. In your applications, however, you must choose to honor one or the other. In most cases, simply using the default value generated by the compilation options of the compiler will be sufficient. The IFS I/O options are recommended.

Figure 19.18 contains source code for a C program that illustrates the effect of the compiler options. A symbolic link is created that points to the location where the compiled program will be created. The C program is compiled twice—once with the default options and a second time with the *-qifsio* option. Finally, the example uses the -+ option to compile the program as a C++ program with the default options.

```
cat newline.c
#include <stdio.h>
#include <unistd.h>

// Compile this program using the IFS I/O or
// non IFS I/O to see the different values of
// the '\n' character and the support of large
// files (greater than 2 Gigabytes).
//
// CRTCMOD or CRTCPPMOD:
//          Use SYSIFCOPT(*IFSIO) or SYSIFCOPT(*NOIFSIO)
//          parameters.
//          *NOIFSIO is the default for C code
//          *IFSIO64 is the default for C++ code
//
// icc: Use -zIFSIO or -zNOIFSIO parameters.
```

Figure 19.18: This program demonstrates the possible confusion that can result from the historical feature of an EBCDIC newline value at code point 0x15, when the application is not using the IFS I/O compilation options (part 1 of 2).

```
//          -zIFSIO is the default for C code
//          -zIFSIO64 is the default for C++ code
//
// ixlc: Use -qifsio or -qifsio=64 or -noifsio
//          -qnoifsio is the default for C code
//          -qifsio=64 is the default for C++ code
//
// NOIFSIO   Newline = 0x15  Size of offset structure = 4
// IFSIO     Newline = 0x25  Size of offset structure = 4
// IFSIO64   Newline = 0x25  Size of offset structure = 8
int main(int argc, char **argv)
{
    printf("Newline: 0x%x\n", (int)'\n');
    printf("Size of the IFS offset structure off_t: %d\n",
           sizeof(off_t));
    return 0;
}
/home/jsmith $
ln -s /qsys.lib/c.lib/newline.pgm newline
/home/jsmith $
ixlc newline.c
/home/jsmith $
Program NEWLINE was created in library C on 06/14/03 at 15:00:52.
/home/jsmith $
newline
Newline: 0x15
Size of the IFS offset structure off_t: 4
/home/jsmith $
ixlc -qifsio newline.c
Program NEWLINE was created in library C on 06/14/03 at 15:01:56.
/home/jsmith $
newline
Newline: 0x25
Size of the IFS offset structure off_t: 4
/home/jsmith $
ixlc -+ newline.c
Program NEWLINE was created in library C on 06/14/03 at 15:01:29.
/home/jsmith $
newline
Newline: 0x25
Size of the IFS offset structure off_t: 8
/home/jsmith $
```

Figure 19.18: This program demonstrates the possible confusion that can result from the historical feature of an EBCDIC newline value at code point 0x15, when the application is not using the IFS I/O compilation options (part 2 of 2).

WRITING JAVA PROGRAMS FOR QSHELL

The Java language serves as another excellent mechanism for writing Qshell programs. Like the C and C++ languages, Java has built-in support for the main requirements of Qshell applications.

The first users of the Qshell environment were Java developers using the Java runtime environment. Command-line-based utilities for Java development and command-line Java applications have a common user interface across all of the platforms that they run on; Qshell is no exception.

IBM implements the iSeries Java product directly in OS/400. Not all Java development tools and utilities are available from the CL command line, however. Implementing some of the Java development and runtime utilities only within the Qshell environment provides a cost savings and a consistent command-line interface to Java application developers.

In Java, Qshell integration with your application happens automatically and is intrinsic to the Java runtime. The iSeries Java runtime environment creates and manages a Qshell terminal for the Java application if that application uses the standard mechanisms to access the input/output terminal.

Use the standard I/O objects (directly or indirectly) to access the Qshell standard input, output, and error streams for the I/O processing in your Java program:

- System.in
- System.out
- System.err

You can also use any I/O object created using one of the above objects.

The System.exit() API updates the Qshell exit status with the return code of the Java program.

386

By default, Java source code must be in an ASCII file, and Java programs read and write ASCII files. Therefore, extra steps are taken to change the expected file encoding to EBCDIC. Chapter 23 provides more information about these steps.

Figure 19.19 lists the source code of a Java program, *com.mcpress.qshell.Reverse*, which reverses the characters in each line read from standard input. This program is similar to the RPG and C examples earlier in this chapter. It uses the System.in and System.out objects in conjunction with some of the other standard file I/O mechanisms. This example is written in a procedural fashion to aid in comparison with the C and RPG examples.

```
cat com/mcpress/qshell/Reverse.java
package com.mcpress.qshell;

import java.io.LineNumberReader;
import java.io.InputStreamReader;
import java.io.IOException;

class Reverse {
   public static void main(String args[]) {
      LineNumberReader        in = null;
      String                  line = null;
      StringBuffer            reverser = new StringBuffer();

      try {
         in = new LineNumberReader(new
            InputStreamReader(System.in));
      line = in.readLine();        // Read all lines from input
      while (line != null) {       // Until the end of the input
            reverser.setLength(0); // Reset the string buffer.
            reverser.append(line);
            reverser.reverse();
            System.out.println(reverser.toString());
            line = in.readLine();  // Read the next line of input
         }
         in.close();
      }
      catch (IOException e) {
```

Figure 19.19: The com.mcpress.qshell.Reverse program reads its standard input (in this case, the output of the ls *command) and reverses each line before writing it to standard output (part 1 of 2).*

387

```
        // Write the exception message and the call stack describing
        // where it happened to standard error.
        System.err.println("An IO Error occurred");
        System.err.println(e.getMessage());
        e.printStackTrace();
        System.exit(1);
    }
    System.exit(0);
    }
}
/home/jsmith $
javac com/mcpress/qshell/Reverse.java
/home/jsmith $
ls -l
total: 56 kilobytes
drwxrwsrwx  2 JSMITH  0          8192 Jun 14 15:18 c
-rw-rw-rw-  1 JSMITH  0          6961 Jun  6 01:40 classes.jar
drwxrwsrwx  3 JSMITH  0          8192 Jun  4 21:22 com
-rwxrwxrwx  1 JSMITH  0          1073 Jun  4 21:21 goodoleboys.sql
-rw-rw-rw-  1 JSMITH  0           845 Jun  4 21:21 goodoleboys.txt
drwxrwsrwx  2 JSMITH  0          8192 Jun  5 23:05 perl
/home/jsmith $
ls -l | java com.mcpress.qshell.Reverse
setybolik 65 :latot
c                81:51 41  nuJ 2918     0 HTIMSJ 2  xwrswrxwrd
raj.sessalc      04:10 6   nuJ 1696     0 HTIMSJ 1  -wr-wr-wr-
moc              22:12 4   nuJ 2918     0 HTIMSJ 3  xwrswrxwrd
lqs.syobelodoog  12:12 4   nuJ 3701     0 HTIMSJ 1  xwrxwrxwr-
txt.syobelodoog  12:12 4   nuJ 548      0 HTIMSJ 1  -wr-wr-wr-
lrep             50:32 5   nuJ 2918     0 HTIMSJ 2  xwrswrxwrd
/home/jsmith $
```

Figure 19.19: The com.mcpress.qshell.Reverse program reads its standard input (in this case, the output of the ls command) and reverses each line before writing it to standard output (part 2 of 2).

Here are some things to note about this program:

- This Java class is part of the com.mcpress.qshell package. The import statements make the imported class definitions available to the class.

- The program wraps the standard InputStream object *System.in* with another object that provides a more desirable access mechanism to the object.

- Among many other objects and APIs, the rich and robust Java class library provides a StringBuffer class that supports a reverse() API. The resulting string is output to the standard output PrintStream object *System.out*.

- After the program reads all lines of input, it returns an exit status of zero.

- If the program fails at any time, it outputs exception information and returns an exit status of one, indicating failure.

- The program is compiled using the javac utility. This utility, and the rules for package and directory naming, are described in detail in Chapter 23.

It is seldom useful to process data directly from descriptors 0, 1, and 2 in a Java program. When it is, those file descriptors should still be accessed in standard I/O objects to provide a better API interface. In Java, the resulting program looks almost identical to one that does not use the file descriptors.

Like the *lines* C program and the NBRLINES RPG example shown earlier, Figure 19.20 outputs all input lines with line numbers. This example, however, uses objects constructed over the top of the file descriptors 0, 1, and 2 directly. As noted, this exercise is rather fruitless; in most cases, the System.in, System.out, and System.err objects can be used to construct whichever objects are desired.

```
cat com/mcpress/qshell/LineCounter.java
package com.mcpress.qshell;

import java.io.LineNumberReader;
import java.io.IOException;
import java.io.FileDescriptor;
import java.io.FileReader;
import java.io.FileWriter;
import java.io.PrintWriter;

class LineCounter {
 public static void main(String args[]) {
 // FileDescriptor.in, FileDescriptor.out, and FileDescriptor.err
 // represent descriptors 0, 1 and 2 respectively.
 LineNumberReader      in = null;
 PrintWriter           out = null;
 PrintWriter           err = null;
 String                line = null;
 StringBuffer          LineCounterr = new StringBuffer();
```

Figure 19.20: The com.mcpress.qshell.LineCounter application uses the FileDescriptor classes to assign I/O objects to the descriptors 0, 1, and 2. Acting as a filter, the program adds line numbers to the input data before outputting it (part 1 of 2).

```
try {
  err = new PrintWriter(new FileWriter(FileDescriptor.err));
  in = new LineNumberReader(new FileReader(FileDescriptor.in));
  out = new PrintWriter(new FileWriter(FileDescriptor.out));
  line = in.readLine();           // Read all lines from input
  while (line != null) {          // Until the end of the input
        int lineNumber = in.getLineNumber();
        out.print(lineNumber);
        out.print(": ");
        out.println(line);
        line = in.readLine();
  }
  in.close();
  out.flush(); // flush the output, ensuring its written.
}
catch (IOException e) {
  // Write the exception message and the call stack describing
  // where it happened to standard error.
  err.println("An IO Error occurred");
  err.println(e.getMessage());
  e.printStackTrace(err);
  System.exit(1);
}
System.exit(0);
}
}
/home/jsmith $
javac com/mcpress/qshell/LineCounter.java
/home/jsmith $
ls -1
c
classes.jar
com
goodoleboys.sql
goodoleboys.txt
perl
/home/jsmith $
ls -1 | java com.mcpress.qshell.LineCounter
1: c
2: classes.jar
3: com
4: goodoleboys.sql
5: goodoleboys.txt
6: perl
/home/jsmith $
```

Figure 19.20: The com.mcpress.qshell.LineCounter application uses the FileDescriptor classes to assign I/O objects to the descriptors 0, 1, and 2. Acting as a filter, the program adds line numbers to the input data before outputting it (part 2 of 2).

OPTION PARAMETERS

Chapter 11 presents the convention used by Unix shells for passing command-line arguments: option arguments come first, followed by non-option arguments. If an option requires an argument of its own, the argument immediately follows the option.

This stands in contrast to the way the CALL commands of CL, RPG, and COBOL pass parameters to other routines. In those languages, the order of a parameter, not its value, determines its meaning. For example, the following two CALL commands are not equivalent:

```
CALL    PGM(MYPGM)    PARM(&CUSTNBR &INVOICE)
CALL    PGM(MYPGM)    PARM(&INVOICE &CUSTOMER)
```

When you write programs for the purpose of running them within Qshell, you must decide whether you will use one of these two conventions, or some other convention for processing parameters.

Passing Parameters to C Programs

The C language is better for processing parameters according to the Unix convention. Qshell passes two arguments to the main function: the number of arguments and an array of pointers to the arguments. By convention, many C programmers refer to these as *argc* and *argv*, respectively. Programmers typically process the array of parameter pointers in a For loop, handling one parameter with each iteration. This technique is illustrated in Figure 19.21.

```
#include <stdio.h>

main(int argc, char *argv[])
{
    int ndx;
    for (ndx = 1; ndx < argc; ndx++)
```

Figure 19.21: C handles parameters as an array, regardless of the number of arguments that are passed to the program. This program lists the arguments to stdout (part 1 of 2).

391

```
    {
        printf("Arg %2d is \"%s\"\n", ndx, argv[ndx]);
    }
    return(0);
}
```

Figure 19.21: C handles parameters as an array, regardless of the number of arguments that are passed to the program. This program lists the arguments to stdout (part 2 of 2).

Passing Parameters to Java Programs

The Java language provides slightly more convenient support for processing parameters than C. Java gets a single array argument that contains all of the parameters and indicates the number and length of those arguments.

By convention, many Java programmers refer to this as the *args* array. Programmers typically process the array of String objects in a *for* loop, handling one parameter with each iteration. This technique is illustrated in Figure 19.22.

```
package com.mcpress.qshell;

class Args {
  public static void main(String args[]) {
    for (int i=0; i<args.length; ++i) {
        System.out.println("Arg " + (i+1) + " is \"" + args[i] + "\"");
    }
    System.exit(0);
  }
}
```

Figure 19.22: Java handles parameters as an array, regardless of the number of arguments that are passed to the program. This program lists the arguments to System.out.

Passing Parameters to RPG Programs

RPG and COBOL programs receive parameters in a parameter list. Each passed parameter value is a null-terminated string. Unpassed parameters cannot be addressed. Additional parameters, beyond the number declared, are ignored.

To extract the value of a parameter, use the %STR built-in function. Figure 19.23 lists an RPG program that accepts up to 12 parameters and extracts their values. The %STR function is used in the ExtractParm subprocedure. ExtractParm accepts a pointer to a parameter and passes that pointer to the %STR built-in function to access a null-terminated parameter value. If a parameter value begins with a hyphen, the remainder of the parameter is processed as a string of options. A parameter value that does not begin with a hyphen is assumed to be the argument of the last option that was found.

In this example, the options are printed to a spooled file. In a real-world situation, you would use the extracted options to control processing, of course.

```
H option(*srcstmt: *nodebugio)
H dftactgrp(*no) actgrp(*new)

Fqsysprt    o    f   132         printer oflind(*inof)

D Main                  pr                  extpgm('PRINTARGS')
D    Parm01                      48a
D    Parm02                      48a
D    Parm03                      48a
D    Parm04                      48a
D    Parm05                      48a
D    Parm06                      48a
D    Parm07                      48a
D    Parm08                      48a
D    Parm09                      48a
D    Parm10                      48a
D    Parm11                      48a
D    Parm12                      48a

D Main                  pi
D    Parm01                      48a
D    Parm02                      48a
D    Parm03                      48a
D    Parm04                      48a
D    Parm05                      48a
D    Parm06                      48a
D    Parm07                      48a
D    Parm08                      48a
```

Figure 19.23: Use the %STR built-in function to access a null-terminated parameter value (part 1 of 4).

```
D    Parm09                              48a
D    Parm10                              48a
D    Parm11                              48a
D    Parm12                              48a

D ParmCount          s                  10i 0

D PreviousOption     s                  1a
D Option_lc_b        s                   n
D Option_lc_c        s                   n
D Option_uc_c        s                   n
D Option_lc_f        s                   n
D Option_2           s                   n

D option_b_val       s                  48
D option_f_val       s                  48

D ExtractParm        pr
D    ParmPtr                          *     value

 /free
     ParmCount = %parms;
     if ParmCount >= 1;
        ExtractParm (%addr(Parm01));
     endif;
     if ParmCount >= 2;
        ExtractParm (%addr(Parm02));
     endif;
     if ParmCount >= 3;
        ExtractParm (%addr(Parm03));
     endif;
     if ParmCount >= 4;
        ExtractParm (%addr(Parm04));
     endif;
     if ParmCount >= 5;
        ExtractParm (%addr(Parm05));
     endif;
     if ParmCount >= 6;
        ExtractParm (%addr(Parm06));
     endif;
     if ParmCount >= 7;
        ExtractParm (%addr(Parm07));
     endif;
     if ParmCount >= 8;
        ExtractParm (%addr(Parm08));
     endif;
```

Figure 19.23: Use the %STR built-in function to access a null-terminated parameter value (part 2 of 4).

```
      if ParmCount >= 9;
          ExtractParm (%addr(Parm09));
      endif;
      if ParmCount >= 10;
          ExtractParm (%addr(Parm10));
      endif;
      if ParmCount >= 11;
          ExtractParm (%addr(Parm11));
      endif;
      if ParmCount >= 12;
          ExtractParm (%addr(Parm12));
      endif;
      except OptionList;
      *inlr = *on;
    /end-free

Oqsysprt    e        OptionList    2   1
O                                             'Option selection'
O           e        OptionList    1
O                                                'b:'
O                    option_lc_b      +0001
O                                     +0001 '"'
O                    option_b_val     +0000
O                                     +0000 '"'
O           e        OptionList    1
O                                                'c:'
O                    option_lc_c      +0001
O           e        OptionList    1
O                                                'C:'
O                    option_uc_c      +0001
O           e        OptionList    1
O                                                'f:'
O                    option_lc_f      +0001
O                                     +0001 '"'
O                    option_f_val     +0000
O                                     +0000 '"'
O           e        OptionList    1
O                                                '2:'
O                    option_2         +0001


P ExtractParm        b
D                    pi
D   ParmPtr                      *    value

D index              s          10i  0
```

Figure 19.23: Use the %STR built-in function to access a null-terminated parameter value (part 3 of 4).

```
D ParmValue        s          48a      varying
D option           s          1a

/free
    ParmValue = %str(ParmPtr: 48);
    if %subst(ParmValue:1:1) = '-';
       for index = 2 to %len(ParmValue);
           option = %subst(ParmValue: index: 1);
           select;
               when option = 'b';
                   Option_lc_b = *on;
               when option = '2';
                   Option_2 = *on;
               when option = 'f';
                   Option_lc_f = *on;
               when option = 'c';
                   Option_lc_c = *on;
               when option = 'C';
                   Option_uc_c = *on;
               endsl;
               PreviousOption = Option;
       endfor;
    else;
       select;
           when PreviousOption = 'b';
               option_b_val = ParmValue;
           when PreviousOption = 'f';
               option_f_val = ParmValue;
       endsl;
    endif;
/end-free
P                      e
```

Figure 19.23: Use the %STR built-in function to access a null-terminated parameter value (part 4 of 4).

Since the options may be passed into the program in any sequence, all of the following commands are equivalent and will produce the same output:

```
/qsys.lib/jsmith.lib/printargs.pgm -b bval -c -f fval -2
/qsys.lib/jsmith.lib/printargs.pgm -2cb bval -f fval
/qsys.lib/jsmith.lib/printargs.pgm -f fval -c2b bval
```

The output of the program in Figure 19.23 is shown in Figure 19.24.

```
Option selection

b: 1 "bval                                          "
c: 1 "
C: 0 "
f: 1 "fval                                          "
2: 1 "
```

Figure 19.24: The program derives the same option settings, regardless of how options are ordered in the command line.

Passing Parameters to COBOL Programs

Like RPG programs, COBOL programs receive parameters as null-terminated strings in a parameter list, and unpassed parameters cannot be addressed. Use the "address of" function to determine whether or not a parameter was passed to the program. This function returns a value of null if a parameter is not passed.

Figure 19.25 is a roughly equivalent COBOL version of the RPG program in Example 19.23.

```
        Identification division.
        Program-ID.    ArgsC.

        Environment division.

        Data division.

        Working-storage section.
        01  Ndx                  pic s9(9) binary.
        01  ParmValue            pic x(48).
        01  Option               pic x.
        01  PreviousOption       pic x.
        01  Option-lc-b          pic x      value "N".
        01  Option-lc-c          pic x      value "N".
        01  Option-uc-C          pic x      value "N".
        01  Option-lc-f          pic x      value "N".
        01  Option-2             pic x      value "N".
        01  Option-b-value       pic x(48).
        01  Option-f-value       pic x(48).
```

Figure 19.25: The COBOL program uses the "address of" expression to determine whether or not a parameter has been passed to it (part 1 of 4).

```
Linkage section.
01  Parm01     pic x(48).
01  Parm02     like Parm01.
01  Parm03     like Parm01.
01  Parm04     like Parm01.
01  Parm05     like Parm01.
01  Parm06     like Parm01.
01  Parm07     like Parm01.
01  Parm08     like Parm01.
01  Parm09     like Parm01.
01  Parm10     like Parm01.
01  Parm11     like Parm01.
01  Parm12     like Parm01.

Procedure division
    using Parm01 Parm02 Parm03 Parm04 Parm05 Parm06
          Parm07 Parm08 Parm09 Parm10 Parm11 Parm12.

Main-paragraph.
    if address of Parm01 not equal null
       move Parm01 to ParmValue
       perform Extract-Options
    end-if.
    if address of Parm02 not equal null
       move Parm02 to ParmValue
       perform Extract-Options
    end-if.
    if address of Parm03 not equal null
       move Parm03 to ParmValue
       perform Extract-Options
    end-if.
    if address of Parm04 not equal null
       move Parm04 to ParmValue
       perform Extract-Options
    end-if.
    if address of Parm05 not equal null
       move Parm05 to ParmValue
       perform Extract-Options
    end-if.
    if address of Parm06 not equal null
       move Parm06 to ParmValue
       perform Extract-Options
    end-if.
    if address of Parm07 not equal null
       move Parm07 to ParmValue
```

Figure 19.25: The COBOL program uses the "address of" expression to determine whether or not a parameter has been passed to it (part 2 of 4).

```
            perform Extract-Options
        end-if.
        if address of Parm08 not equal null
            move Parm08 to ParmValue
            perform Extract-Options
        end-if.
        if address of Parm09 not equal null
            move Parm09 to ParmValue
            perform Extract-Options
        end-if.
        if address of Parm10 not equal null
            move Parm10 to ParmValue
            perform Extract-Options
        end-if.
        if address of Parm11 not equal null
            move Parm11 to ParmValue
            perform Extract-Options
        end-if.
        if address of Parm12 not equal null
            move Parm12 to ParmValue
            perform Extract-Options
        end-if.
        Stop run.

    Extract-options.
        If ParmValue (1:1) = "-"
            perform varying ndx from 2 by 1
                    until ndx > 48
                        or ParmValue (ndx:1) = x"00"
                move ParmValue(ndx:1) to Option
                evaluate Option
                    when "b"
                        move "Y" to Option-lc-b
                    when "2"
                        move "Y" to Option-2
                    when "f"
                        move "Y" to Option-lc-f
                    when "c"
                        move "Y" to Option-lc-c
                    when "C"
                        move "Y" to Option-uc-C
                end-evaluate
                move Option to PreviousOption
            end-perform
        else
            evaluate PreviousOption
```

Figure 19.25: The COBOL program uses the "address of" expression to determine whether or not a parameter has been passed to it (part 3 of 4).

399

```
              when "b"
                  unstring ParmValue delimited by x"00"
                      into Option-b-value
              when "f"
                  unstring ParmValue delimited by x"00"
                      into Option-f-value
          end-evaluate
      end-if.
```

Figure 19.25: The COBOL program uses the "address of" expression to determine whether or not a parameter has been passed to it (part 4 of 4).

SUMMARY

Although existing Qshell utilities and scripting are powerful enough for most tasks, you can write programs to handle tasks that Qshell can't. The language processors included with the iSeries are powerful and easy to use in a Qshell environment.

Chapter 20

Accessing OS/400-Specific Objects

OS/400 is quite different from Unix. One difference is that OS/400 is an object-based operating system, whereas to Unix, everything is a file. For example, Unix-based systems provide message queues or memory-mapped files. OS/400 provides the same APIs for message queues and memory-mapped files, but it also provides a broad and robust set of OS/400-specific objects that can be used for similar tasks. The OS/400 data-queue and data-area objects have long provided similar services to those provided by Unix-based message-queue and memory-mapped files.

Qshell includes non-Unix utilities that allow it to access OS/400-specific objects like the data queue and the data area. This chapter serves two functions: to make you aware of the Qshell interfaces to OS/400 objects, and to serve as a reference to those utilities.

SYSTEM

The *system* utility allows you to run a CL command within Qshell. Because Qshell executes commands in batch mode, the CL command must be able to run under the QCMDEXC API in batch mode. To determine whether or not a CL command meets this criterion, use CL's Display Command (DSPCMD) command

and look for the values *BATCH and *EXEC in the "Where allowed to run" description. To enable a user-written command to run under the *system* utility, specify ALLOW(*BATCH *EXEC) in the CL command Create Command (CRTCMD) or Change Command (CHGCMD).

In Figure 20.1, a user tries to start the Programming Development Manager (PDM) within Qshell. However, PDM is an interactive application, so *system* fails, and error messages are sent to stderr. Notice that the *n* option can be used to suppress the message ID of the error.

```
system strpdm
CPD0031:   Command STRPDM not allowed in this setting.
CPF0001:   Error found on STRPDM command.
/home/jsmith $
system -n strpdm
Command STRPDM not allowed in this setting.
Error found on STRPDM command.
/home/jsmith $
```

Figure 20.1: Only batch commands can run under the system utility.

By default, the *system* utility copies spooled files to stdout and deletes them. Error messages are written to stderr. Like any other Qshell utility, this behavior makes the *system* utility suitable for use with Qshell filters, command substitution, and redirection. The *system* utility, then, serves as an ideal mechanism to incorporate not only CL commands into Qshell, but your existing applications, as well.

Figure 20.2 shows the Display Database Relations (DSPDBR) command run under Qshell. When DSPDBR runs in a batch job, the output is written to a spooled file. For that reason, the output in Figure 20.2 is sent to stdout.

Routing spooled data is not limited to the execution of IBM-supplied commands. This behavior occurs for any source of spooled output. For example, Figure 20.3 contains the DDS for an externally described printer file that defines a listing of customers.

402

```
system dspdbr jsmith/customer
   5722SS1 V5R2M0  020719          Display Data Base Relations

   DSPDBR Command Input
       File . . . . . . . . . . . . . . . . . . . . . :  FILE     CUSTOMER
         Library . . . . . . . . . . . . . . . . . . :           JSMITH
       Member  . . . . . . . . . . . . . . . . . . . :  MBR      *NONE
       Record format . . . . . . . . . . . . . . . . :  RCDFMT   *NONE
       Output  . . . . . . . . . . . . . . . . . . . :  OUTPUT      *
  Specifications
       Type of file  . . . . . . . . . . . . . . . . :           Physical
       File  . . . . . . . . . . . . . . . . . . . . :           CUSTOMER
         Library . . . . . . . . . . . . . . . . . . :           JSMITH
         Member  . . . . . . . . . . . . . . . . . . :           *NONE
         Record format . . . . . . . . . . . . . . . :           *NONE
         Number of dependent files . . . . . . . . . :           3
  Files Dependent On Specified File
       Dependent File      Library      Dependency JREF        Constraint
           CUSTOMER2       JSMITH       Data
           CUSTOMER1A      JSMITH       Data
           CUSTOMER3       JSMITH       Data
```

Figure 20.2: The output from a CL command is written to stdout.

```
     A                                         REF(CUSTOMER)
     A
     A          R H1                           SKIPB(1)
     A            H1REPORTID    10             1
     A                                         24'Customer List'
     A                                         52DATE EDTWRD('  -  - ')
     A                                           SPACEA(2)
     A                                          7'Cmp'
     A                                         +3'Nbr'
     A                                         +1'Name'
     A                                        +17'City'
     A                                        +13'State'
     A                                           SPACEA(1)
     A                                          7'==='
     A                                         +1'====='
     A                                         +1'==================='
     A                                         +1'================'
     A                                         +1'====='
     A
     A          R D1                           SPACEB(1)
     A            D1COUNT        5   0         1EDTCDE(4)
```

Figure 20.3: The source member CUSLISTP defines a report (part 1 of 2).

```
A               D1COMPANY R              +1REFFLD(COMPANY)
A               D1CUSTNBR R              +1REFFLD(CUSTNBR)
A               D1CUSTNAMER              +1REFFLD(CUSTNAME)
A               D1CITY    R              +1REFFLD(CCITY)
A               D1STATE   R              +1REFFLD(CSTATE)
A
A         R T1                              SPACEB(2)
A                                        1'** End of report **'
```

Figure 20.3: The source member CUSLISTP defines a report (part 2 of 2).

Figure 20.4 contains the RPG program that produces the customer-listing report.

```
Fcustomer  if   e           k disk
Fcuslistp  o    e             printer oflind(Overflow)

D forever        s              n   inz(*on)
D Overflow       s              n
D PSDS          sds
D   ProcName          *proc

 /free

     h1ReportID = ProcName;
     write h1;

     dow forever;
        read custrec;
        if %eof;
           leave;
        endif;
        d1count += 1;
        d1company = company;
        d1custnbr = custnbr;
        d1custname = custname;
        d1city = ccity;
        d1state = cstate;
        if OverFlow;
           write h1;
           Overflow = *off;
        endif;
        write d1;
     enddo;

     write t1;
     *inlr = *on;

 /end-free
```

Figure 20.4: Program CUSLIST1 builds a report.

In Figure 20.5, *system* is used to run the CUSLIST1 program from Figure 20.4. Notice that printed output is sent to stdout.

```
system call cuslist1
   CUSLIST1                     Customer List                    12-25-03
          Cmp Nbr     Name                      City              State
          === =====   ====================      =================  =====
        1 001 00044   Joe's Shoes               Duluthe           GA
        2 001 10001   Sue's Bridle Shop         Saltillo          MS
        3 001 20002   Bank of Steele            Medina            PA
        4 001 30003   Snowman Heat & Air        Lexington         OH
        5 002 00001   Xolomon Solutions         Tulsa             OK
        6 002 00003   Donaldson Electric        Whittier          CA
        7 002 00345   Gretta's Gifts            Saddle Brook      NJ
        8 003 00001   Ames Wholesale            Tupelo            MS
        9 003 00003   Army Surplus              Brunswick         OH
       10 003 00056   Jak's Liver Emporium      Mexico            OH
       11 004 40004   Grayson Paul              Little City       ND
       12 007 00222   Sardine Paradise          Happah Palloolah  CA
       13 007 00777   Pretty Boy's Gym          Lost Angeles      NY
       14 008 00001   48% of Nothing            Klondike          FL
       15 008 00002   Robert R. Roberts IV      New Yolk          CA
       16 008 00003   Sal Monella
   ** End of report **
```

Figure 20.5: Printed output has been routed to stdout.

Qshell sends the output to stdout after the program closes the printer file. If a program builds more than one spooled file, those spooled files are written to stdout one at a time. That is, the output of two spooled files is not intermingled.

The output of the program may remain in an output queue in addition to, or instead of, being routed to stdout. Three options, described in Table 20.1, control the treatment of printed output.

Table 20.1: Options that Control Spooled Output

Option	Description
s	Do not write printed output to stdout. (Suppress output.)
k	Keep spooled files.
K	Keep spooled files and the job log.

Table 20.2 shows the effect of these options if used with the preceding example.

Table 20.2: Effects of System Options

Command	Route Report to Stdout?	Save Report in Output Queue?
system call cuslist1	Yes	No
system -s call cuslist1	No	No
system -k call cuslist1	No	Yes
system -sk call cuslist1	Yes	Yes

Using the CL CALL command is not the only way to call a program object. You will usually call the program object directly, by typing the name of the program in IFS format, as in the following example:

```
/qsys.lib/jsmith.lib/cuslist1.pgm
```

However, the two methods are not equivalent. Using *system* to call a program object lets the *system* utility process the spooled file data and error messages. Calling a program by entering its name in IFS format does not give Qshell any control of the output. Since the two methods are not interchangeable, use whichever one is appropriate for the program that you're calling.

LIBLIST

Qshell inherits the library list of the job that started it. You can change the library list within Qshell, but the change only affects the Qshell session and the jobs that are created when you use Qshell utilities and commands.

When Qshell ends, the job's library list will be as it was before Qshell started. Also, if you press the F19 key from within Qshell to access an OS/400 command line, you will find that the library list does not reflect any changes that were made by running *liblist* within Qshell. This behavior exists because the library list is a job-level resource. (The job-and-process model of Qshell is described in chapter 2.)

If you do not specify any options with *liblist*, Qshell displays the library list. To modify the library list, use the options shown in Table 20.3.

Table 20.3: Options for the Liblist Utility

Option	Description
a *lib* or af *lib*	Add *lib* to the top of the library list.
al *lib*	Add *lib* to the bottom of the library list.
c *lib*	Set the current library to *lib*.
cd	Unset the current library.
d *lib*	Delete library *lib* from the library list.

In Figure 20.6, the user displays the library list, unsets the current library, and adds library QGPL to the end of the library list. The last *liblist* command displays the library list after modification.

```
liblist
QSYS          SYS
QUSRSYS       SYS
QHLPSYS       SYS
QSHELL        PRD
JSMITHS       CUR
QTEMP         USR
JSMITHO       USR
JSMITHS       USR
JSMITHD       USR
liblist -cd
/home/JSMITH $
liblist -al qgpl
/home/JSMITH $
/home/JSMITH $
```

Figure 20.6: The liblist utility displays and modifies the library list within Qshell (part 1 of 2).

```
liblist
QSYS        SYS
QUSRSYS     SYS
QHLPSYS     SYS
QSHELL      PRD
QTEMP       USR
JSMITHO     USR
JSMITHS     USR
JSMITHD     USR
QGPL        USR
```

Figure 20.6: The liblist utility displays and modifies the library list within Qshell (part 2 of 2).

You may specify more than one library when changing the library list. The libraries are processed in order, as shown in Figure 20.7.

```
# remove 2 libraries from the library list
liblist -d jsmitho jsmithd

# add 4 libraries to the beginning of the library list
# QGPL becomes the first library because it is added last
liblist -a jsmithq jsmitho jsmithd qgpl

# add 4 libraries to the end of the library list
# QGPL becomes the last library because it is added last
liblist -al jsmithq jsmitho jsmithd qgpl
```

Figure 20.7: You may add or remove multiple libraries with one command.

In Figure 20.8, the name of the current library is written to stdout. The *liblist* utility pipes the library list to *grep*, which extracts the line ending with the letters *CUR*. This finds the line containing the name of the current library, if there is one, but ignores lines that contain *CUR* within a library name. The stream editor, *sed*, removes all blanks preceding *CUR*, as well as the value *CUR* itself.

```
liblist
QSYS        SYS
QUSRSYS     SYS
QHLPSYS     SYS
QSHELL      PRD
JSMITHS     CUR
```

Figure 20.8: This compound command extracts the name of the current library (part 1 of 2).

```
QTEMP          USR
JSMITHO        USR
JSMITHS        USR
JSMITHD        USR
CURYR          USR
ARCURRENT      USR
TOCCUR         USR
QGPL           USR
/home/JSMITH  $
liblist | grep 'CUR$' | sed 's/ *CUR$//'
JSMITHS
/home/JSMITH  $
```

Figure 20.8: This compound command extracts the name of the current library (part 2 of 2).

SYSVAL

An OS/400 system value is a named value of a specific data type. System values provide the ability to read or modify a broad range of system configuration settings. Use the CL command Display System Value (DSPSYSVAL) to display system values outside of Qshell. Use the CL command Change System Value (CHGSYSVAL) to modify system values outside of Qshell.

The Qshell *sysval* utility provides a way to retrieve system values and network attributes. The output of *sysval* is written to stdout. For example, Figure 20.9 displays the system value QDAYOFWEEK. Without the *p* option, only the value is displayed. With the *p* option, the name and value of the system value are displayed in the form of an equation.

```
sysval qdayofweek
*SAT
/home/JSMITH  $
sysval -p qdayofweek
QDAYOFWEEK=*SAT
/home/JSMITH  $
```

Figure 20.9: The sysval utility can retrieve system values.

In Figure 20.10, the *n* option is used to display the name of the iSeries system.

```
sysval -n sysname
MY400
/home/JSMITH $
sysval -np sysname
SYSNAME=MY400
/home/JSMITH $
```

Figure 20.10: The sysval utility can retrieve network settings.

DATAREA

An OS/400 data area is a named, persistent object of a specific size and data type. Data areas can contain generic data of your choosing. A data area is like a one-record file, but it's not a file—it is a special OS/400 object type. Use CL's Display Data Area (DSPDTAARA) command to display a data area outside of Qshell. Use the Change Data Area (CHGDTAARA) command to change a data area outside of Qshell

The Qshell *datarea* utility, new in V5R2, allows you to retrieve and change the contents of data areas. Notice that the final *a* of *data* and the first *a* of *area* have been fused to form the name of this utility.

You may specify the names of data areas in either of two forms. First, you may specify the name in full-path form, as the following example shows:

```
/qsys.lib/mylib.lib/mydtaara.dtaara
```

Alternatively, you may use a relative path, which is simply the data area name. If you specify a relative name, you must include the *l* ("ell") option, unless the data area is in the current library.

Table 20.4 briefly describes the options that you may use with *datarea*.

410

Table 20.4: Datarea Options

Option	Description
l (ell)	Use the library list to find the data area.
r	Read.
s	Read or write only a portion (substring) of the data area.
w	Write.

The following command writes the contents of data area PLANTINFO, in library JSMITHS, to stdout:

```
datarea -r /qsys.lib/jsmiths.lib/plantinfo.dtaara
1250Lost Angeles, New Yolk    020NN-NNYYNYYY
/home/JSMITH $
```

The data area name is given in full-path form. Notice that *dtaara* is the extension for data areas.

The command below also writes the contents of data area PLANTINFO to stdout, but uses a relative format:

```
datarea -r plantinfo
1250Lost Angeles, New Yolk    020NNNNNYYNYYY
/home/JSMITH $
```

Since PLANTINFO is given in relative form and the *l* option is not specified, PLANTINFO must be in the current library.

The command in the following example again writes the contents of data area PLANTINFO to stdout, using the *r* option to read a data area:

```
datarea -rl plantinfo
1250Lost Angeles, New Yolk    020NNNNNYYNYYY
/home/JSMITH $
```

411

Since PLANTINFO is given in relative form and the *l* option is specified, the system finds PLANTINFO by scanning the library list.

To place a value into a data area, use the *w* option. In Figure 20.11, the value of the first parameter is copied into data area PLANTINFO, replacing the previous contents.

```
print \"$1\"
"1901Chicargo, Old Mexico"
/home/JSMITH $
datarea -wl plantinfo $1
/home/JSMITH $
datarea -rl plantinfo
1901Chicargo, Old Mexico
/home/JSMITH $
```

Figure 20.11: Use the w *option to write to a data area.*

Use the *s* option to retrieve part (a substring) of a data area. The argument to *s* indicates a range of positions to retrieve. The first position of a data area is position 1. The argument may be one of the following:

- A single whole number
- A whole number followed by a hyphen
- Two whole numbers separated by a hyphen
- A hyphen followed by a whole number

These alternatives are explained in Table 20.5. The letters *m* and *n* in the table represent the numbers in the range argument.

Table 20.5: Possible Arguments for the *s* Option

Positions	Description
m or *m-*	Retrieve all characters from position *m* to the end of the data area.
m-n	Retrieve characters in positions *m* through *n* of the data area.
-n	Retrieve characters in positions one through *n* of the data area.

Figure 20.12 shows how to read part of a data area. In this example, the *s* option is used to retrieve portions of PLANTINFO.

```
datarea -rl plantinfo
1250Lost Angeles, New Yolk     020NNNNNYYNYYY
/home/JSMITH $
datarea -r -s 5-29 plantinfo
Lost Angeles, New Yolk
/home/JSMITH $
datarea -r -s 5 plantinfo
Lost Angeles, New Yolk     020NNNNNYYNYYY
/home/JSMITH $
datarea -r -s 5- plantinfo
Lost Angeles, New Yolk     020NNNNNYYNYYY
/home/JSMITH $
```

Figure 20.12: Use the s option to retrieve a portion of a data area.

Figure 20.13 shows how to change part of a data area. A hyphen is placed in position 35 of PLANTINFO, which is in the current library.

```
datarea -r -s 33-43 plantinfo
NNNNNYYNYYY
/home/JSMITH $
datarea -w -s 35-35 plantinfo -
/home/JSMITH $
datarea -r -s 33-43 plantinfo
NN-NNYYNYYY
/home/JSMITH $
```

Figure 20.13: The s option allows you to change part of a data area.

When you are working with data areas, it might be helpful, or even necessary, to find the names of data areas from within Qshell. Use the *ls* utility for this purpose, as shown in Figure 20.14. Data area objects have an extension of .DTAARA. Be sure to specify the wildcard portion of a path name in all-capital letters when accessing the library file system.

```
ls /qsys.lib/js.lib/*.DTAARA
/qsys.lib/js.lib/HOLDPAGES.DTAARA
/qsys.lib/js.lib/HOLDPAGES2.DTAARA
/qsys.lib/js.lib/NEXTORDKEY.DTAARA
```

Figure 20.14: Use the ls utility to retrieve the names of data areas (part 1 of 2).

```
/qsys.lib/js.lib/PLANTINFO.DTAARA
/qsys.lib/js.lib/QQUPRFOPTS.DTAARA
/qsys.lib/js.lib/JSMITH.DTAARA
/home/JSMITH $
ls -l /qsys.lib/js.lib/plantinfo.dtaara
?rwx---rwx 1 JSMITH 0 4096 Dec 25 02:38 /qsys.lib/js.lib/plantinfo.dtaara
```

Figure 20.14: Use the ls utility to retrieve the names of data areas (part 2 of 2).

DATAQ

An OS/400 data queue is a named, persistent queue object used to communicate between programs or jobs. Data queues hold messages and have a multitude of processing characteristics and configuration options. They can be local or remote, and the messages in them can be persistent. Use CL's Create Data Queue (CRTDTAQ) command to create a data queue outside of Qshell. Use the Delete Data Queue (DLTDATAQ) command to delete a data queue outside of Qshell. Use the OS/400 data queue API's Receive Data Queue (QRCVDTAQ) or Send Data Queue (QSND-DTAQ) command to send and receive messages to a data queue outside of Qshell.

The *dataq* utility is also new in V5R2. This utility allows you to read messages on, write messages to, and remove messages from a data queue. Table 20.6 lists the defined options for *dataq*.

Table 20.6: Dataq Options

Option	Description
c	Clear the data queue.
l (ell)	Use the library list to find the data area.
n *number*	Read/write *number* messages.
p	Peek. (Read messages without deleting them.)
r	Read from the data queue.
t *seconds*	When reading, wait no more than seconds for a message to arrive on the data queue.
w	Write to the data queue.

If you read a data queue, you may remove the read messages or leave them on the queue. You may specify a data queue name in either of two formats: full path or relative path.

To send a message to a data queue, use the *w* option, as in the following example:

```
dataq -w /qsys.lib/jsmith.lib/xacts.dtaq "$mycmd"
```

This command places the value of variable *mycmd* on data queue XACTS in library JSMITH.

To receive a message from a data queue, use the *r* option. Specify the number of seconds to wait until timing out in the *t* option. Use the *n* option to specify the number of messages to receive.

By default, *dataq* removes the message from the data queue. You may leave the message on the queue by including the *p* ("peek") option. The *dataq* utility writes the message to stdout.

Figure 20.15 illustrates the process of receiving data-queue messages. The first *dataq* command receives a two-byte message from data queue XACTS in JSMITH without removing the message. The second *dataq* receives the same message again, but removes it from the queue. The last *dataq* waits two seconds for a command and, receiving none, ends.

```
dataq -rp -t 2  /qsys.lib/jsmiths.lib/xacts.dtaq
GO
/home/JSMITH $
dataq -r -t 2  /qsys.lib/jsmiths.lib/xacts.dtaq
GO
/home/JSMITH $
dataq -r -t 2  /qsys.lib/jsmiths.lib/xacts.dtaq
/home/JSMITH $
```

Figure 20.15: Use the r *option to read data queue messages.*

415

If the data queue is in the current library, you may use a relative path for its name. If the data queue is in another library in the library list, you may use a relative path by adding the *l* ("ell") option. When using a relative path, type the data queue's name in all-capital letters.

For example, in Figure 20.16, the data queue XACTS is in the current library. For that reason, the queue's name can be in relative-path form.

```
dataq -w XACTS '/home/mydir/file345.txt'
/home/JSMITH $
dataq -r XACTS
/home/mydir/file345.txt
```

Figure 20.16: The XACTS data queue is in the current library.

In Figure 20.17, the data queue is not in the current library. Instead, it is in a library in the library list. The *l* option is needed to tell *dataq* to search the library list.

```
dataq -w XACTS '/home/mydir/file345.txt'
dataq: 001-2113 Error found getting information for object
   XACTS. No such path or directory.
/home/JSMITH $
dataq -wl XACTS '/home/mydir/file345.txt'
/home/JSMITH $
dataq -r XACTS
dataq: 001-2113 Error found getting information for object
   XACTS. No such path or directory.
/home/JSMITH $
dataq -rl XACTS
/home/mydir/file345.txt
/home/JSMITH $
```

Figure 20.17: The l ("ell") option causes dataq to search the library list for the XACTS data queue.

The *dataq* utility can receive more than one message at a time, as shown here:

```
dataq -r -n3 XACTS
/home/mydir/file345.txt
/home/mydir/file346.txt
/home/mydir/file347.txt
/home/JSMITH $
```

416

Use the *c* option to clear a data queue of all messages. For example, the following command clears data queue XACTS, which is found by scanning the library list:

```
dataq -cl XACTS
```

DB2

Qshell includes two utilities that provide access to the DB2 UDB/400 database: *db2* and *Rfile*.

There are many user interfaces to DB2 UDB/400 that are officially supported and recommended (by IBM). The Qshell *db2* utility is not one of those, however, so if you find an error in it, you might or might not be able get IBM support to address the problem. Still, *db2* is available in the /usr/bin directory, so if it works for your purposes, you can certainly take advantage of it.

This section discusses the db2 utility as of some significant fixes and enhancements made by IBM in V5R2, PTF 5722SS1-SI07040. (A PTF is a Program Temporary Fix, which contains bug fixes for OS/400.) Table 20.7 lists the

Table 20.7: Db2 Options

Option	Description
d	Terminate statements with an exclamation point ("bang"); shorthand for -*T!*.
f *file lib*	Read SQL statements from *file*, using *lib* as the default library for queried files.
i	Run SQL in an interactive mode.
p	Use with the r option to supply a password for a remote database.
r *rdb*	Connect to the remote database *rdb*.

Table 20.7: Db2 Options, *continued*

Option	Description
S	Suppress spaces and padding.
t	Terminate statements with a semicolon; shorthand for -*T;*.
T	Set the following character as the statement terminator.
u	Use with the r option to supply a user ID for a remote database.
v	Echo the SQL statement to stdout.

options available with the *db2* utility, as of this PTF in release V5R2. Earlier versions of *db2* might work differently and support different options.

The *db2* utility enables you to run SQL commands within Qshell. Table names must be specified in *SQL format (library name, period, table name). If the library name and period are not specified, the table is assumed to be in a library with the same name as the user profile that is running Qshell. The output of SQL select statements is routed to stdout. Error messages are also routed to stdout.

The *db2* utility requires that the SQL statement be quoted, with either strong (single) or weak (double) quotes, so that the SQL command is treated as one argument. In Figure 20.18, *db2* routes the output of a simple SELECT statement to stdout.

Add the *v* option if you want *db2* to echo the SQL command to stdout. This is especially useful when part of the SQL command comes from a Qshell variable, and also when SQL commands are read from a file.

In Figure 20.19, the records to be selected are indicated by the value in the Qshell variable *company*. Notice that the SQL statement is enclosed in weak quotes, so that the $company token will be replaced by the variable's current value. Because of the *v* option, the *db2* utility shows the resolved SQL command.

418

```
db2 'select company,custnbr,custname,ccity,cstate from jsmiths.customer'

COMPANY   CUSTNBR   CUSTNAME                CCITY             CSTATE
--------  --------  ----------------------  ----------------  -------
      1        44   Joe's Shoes             Duluthe           GA
      1     10001   Sue's Bridle Shop       Saltillo          MS
      1     20002   Bank of Steele          Medina            PA
      1     30003   Snowman Heat & Air      Lexington         OH
      2         1   Xolomon Solutions       Tulsa             OK
      2         3   Donaldson Electric      Whittier          CA
      2       345   Gretta's Gifts          Saddle Brook      NJ
      3         1   Ames Wholesale          Tupelo            MS
      3         3   Army Surplus            Brunswick         OH
      3        56   Jak's Liver Emporium    Mexico            OH
      4     40004   Grayson Paul            Little City       ND
      7       777   Pretty Boy's Gym        Lost Angeles      NY
      7       222   Sardine Paradise        Happah Palloolah  CA
      8         1   48% of Nothing          Klondike          FL
      8         2   Robert R. Roberts IV    New Yolk          CA
      8         3   Sal Monella

  16 RECORD(S) SELECTED.
```

Figure 20.18: The db2 utility routes SQL output to stdout.

```
print $company
3
/home/JSMITH $

db2 -v "select company,custnbr, custname, ccity, cstate
>
from jsmiths.customer
>
where company=$company"

EXECUTING: select company,custnbr, custname, ccity, cstate
from jsmiths.customer
where company=3
DONE!

COMPANY   CUSTNBR   CUSTNAME                CCITY             CSTATE
--------  --------  ----------------------  ----------------  -------
      3         1   Ames Wholesale          Tupelo            MS
      3         3   Army Surplus            Brunswick         OH
      3        56   Jak's Liver Emporium    Mexico            OH

   3 RECORD(S) SELECTED.

/home/JSMITH $
```

Figure 20.19: The v option displays the resolved SQL command.

Since *db2* writes to stdout, Qshell can manipulate the output of SQL commands as it would any other data. In the next-to-last Qshell command in Figure 20.20, the output of the SQL command is routed into the stream editor, *sed*. The stream editor looks for a line containing two hyphens, which is the line that separates a column heading from the first line of data. When it finds the line of hyphens, it reads the next record, which contains the customer name, and prints the customer name to stdout. The output of *sed*—the customer name—is directed by means of command substitution into the variable *custname*.

```
print $comp; print $cust
3
56
/home/JSMITH $
db2 "select custname
>
from jsmiths.customer
>
where company=$comp and custnbr=$cust"

CUSTNAME
--------------------
Jak's Liver Emporium

  1 RECORD(S) SELECTED.

/home/JSMITH $
custname=$(
>
db2 "select custname
>
from jsmiths.customer
>
where company=$comp and custnbr=$cust"  |
>
sed -n '/--/{n; p;}')
/home/JSMITH $
print $custname
Jak's Liver Emporium
/home/JSMITH $
```

Figure 20.20: The output of an SQL statement is stored in a Qshell variable.

The preceding examples used the SELECT command, but the *db2* utility can process any SQL command that can run interactively. The following lines show the three basic file maintenance processes—changing a record, deleting a record, and adding a record:

```
db2 "update companies set conam='Lizzy''s Livery Stable' where
    company=1"
db2 "delete from companies where company = 1"
db2 "insert into companies values(3, 'Jack''s Java Palace')"
```

SQL SCRIPTS

Use the *f* option to execute SQL scripts (SQL commands stored in a file). Here are some things to keep in mind when creating SQL scripts:

- If the file is a database file member in the QSYS.LIB file system, you must specify the member name in IFS format.

- You may store more than one SQL statement in the file.

- You can enter only one statement per record.

- You must enter a complete statement in a single record unless you specify a delimiter using the *d*, *t*, or *T* options. If you specify a delimiter, a single statement may span multiple records.

- Your SQL command cannot contain references to Qshell variables.

- You may use the double-hyphen syntax to include comments in the file.

Several of these points are illustrated in Figure 20.21. The script file is CustListNbr01.sql, and the first two lines contain comments. The SQL command itself spans four lines. This is allowable because of the semicolon delimiter in the last line.

Figure 20.22 provides an example that uses Qshell I/O and the *db2* utility. The file datain.csv contains comma-separated data received via some sort of EDI mechanism. The edi210.qsh Qshell script reads the CSV data and inserts new rows into the database.

```
cat CustListNbr01.sql
-- to run: db2 -tvf CustListNbr01.sql <LIBRARY>
-- library name must be specified in -f option
select cstate, custname,company,custnbr
from customer
where company=3
order by 1,2;
/home/JSMITH $
db2 -tvf CustListNbr01.sql jsmiths

EXECUTING: select cstate, custname,company,custnbr from customer where
          company=3 order by 1,2
DONE!

CSTATE   CUSTNAME              COMPANY    CUSTNBR
-------  --------------------  --------   --------
MS       Ames Wholesale          3          1
OH       Army Surplus            3          3
OH       Jak's Liver Emporium    3          56

   3 RECORD(S) SELECTED.

/home/JSMITH $
```

Figure 20.21: The db2 utility can execute SQL script files.

```
cat datain.csv
 2260,A192287,A-195,4
 2260,A192287,C-267,12
 2260,A192287,B-332,101
 2260,A192287,N-271,5
 2260,A192287,N-105,35
 2260,A192287,D-328,17
/home/JSMITH $
cat edi210.qsh
IFS=','
while read custnbr ponbr itemnbr qty
 do
   db2 "insert into jsmiths.ediin values ($custnbr, '$ponbr', '$itemnbr',
     $qty)"
done  <datain.csv
/home/JSMITH $
edi210.qsh
DB20000I  THE SQL COMMAND COMPLETED SUCCESSFULLY.
DB20000I  THE SQL COMMAND COMPLETED SUCCESSFULLY.
```

Figure 20.22: The db2 utility can be used to update a database table (part 1 of 2).

```
DB20000I  THE SQL COMMAND COMPLETED SUCCESSFULLY.
DB20000I  THE SQL COMMAND COMPLETED SUCCESSFULLY.
DB20000I  THE SQL COMMAND COMPLETED SUCCESSFULLY.
DB20000I  THE SQL COMMAND COMPLETED SUCCESSFULLY.
/home/JSMITH $
db2 "select * from jsmiths.ediin"

CUST     PONBR      ITEM     QTY
-------  --------   ------   ----
2260     A192287    A-195      4
2260     A192287    C-267     12
2260     A192287    B-332    101
2260     A192287    N-271      5
2260     A192287    N-105     35
2260     A192287    D-328     17

  6 RECORD(S) SELECTED.

/home/JSMITH $
```

Figure 20.22: The db2 *utility can be used to update a database table (part 2 of 2).*

DB2 IN INTERACTIVE MODE

The *i* option allows you to run *db2* interactively. This differs from repeatedly running the *db2* command in the following ways:

- The *db2* utility is loaded once and remains active between command executions.

- Execution of SQL statements is similar to the way SQL scripts are executed, and is limited in the same ways. For example, interactive SQL statements cannot reference Qshell variables.

- You can use transactions consisting of multiple SQL statements, all of which can be committed or rolled back in their entirety.

- You can use *db2* as if it were a filter, accepting a stream of commands and outputting the results as appropriate.

When you enter interactive mode, *db2* responds with the *DB2>* prompt. The continuation prompt, for incomplete SQL commands, is *?>*.

When you run *db2* in interactive mode, you are communicating directly with the *db2* utility, not with Qshell. Therefore you must use *db2* subcommands, rather than Qshell commands. The first *db2* subcommand you should learn is *help*, which may be entered as the complete word "help," or as a single question mark. As Figure 20.23 shows, the *db2* utility responds with a "crib sheet."

```
/home/JSMITH $
db2 -i
DB2>
help
Enter any of the following built-in commands:
  help or ?          Show this brief help
  -- anything        Comment line
  exit or quit       End the DB2 session
  echo               Echo the text listed
  connect            Currently ignored
  terminate          Currently ignored
  !qshcommand        Run a QSH command or utility
  @clcommand         Run a CL command
  OTHER              Run the statement as SQL, reporting results
Current options specified are:
  Connected with default user to *LOCAL database
  Processing interactive statements
  Statements delimited by newline
  Verbose echo of statements is OFF
Misc
    - If using delimited SQL (-t, -d or -T), end lines with \ to avoid
      inserting a space (for example, in SQL literals)
    - If using a user specified SQL delimiter character (-T or -d
      option), be careful that the delimiter (if its the first character
      on a line) doesn't match the special built-in command modifiers
      (comment, CL or QSH command)
DB2>
exit
/home/JSMITH $
```

Figure 20.23: The db2 utility includes brief, online help text in interactive mode.

Figure 20.24 shows a more extensive *db2* session. Here, the user queries data and inserts a row into a table. Notice that the *db2* command includes the *t* switch. Without it, *db2* would try to execute an SQL command every time the Enter key was pressed. Thanks to the *t*, the semicolon delimits the commands, allowing the operator to continue commands across multiple lines of input.

```
db2 -it
DB2>
select cstate,custname,company,custnbr
  ?>
from jsmiths.customer
  ?>
order by 1,2;

CSTATE   CUSTNAME                COMPANY  CUSTNBR
-------  --------------------    -------- --------
         Sal Monella             8        3
CA       Donaldson Electric      2        3
CA       Robert R. Roberts IV    8        2
CA       Sardine Paradise        7        222
FL       48% of Nothing          8        1
GA       Joe's Shoes             1        44
MS       Ames Wholesale          3        1
MS       Sue's Bridle Shop       1        10001
ND       Grayson Paul            4        40004
NJ       Gretta's Gifts          2        345
NY       Pretty Boy's Gym        7        777
OH       Army Surplus            3        3
OH       Jak's Liver Emporium    3        56
OH       Snowman Heat & Air      1        30003
OK       Xolomon Solutions       2        1
PA       Bank of Steele          1        20002

  16 RECORD(S) SELECTED.
DB2>
insert into jsmiths.customer
  ?>
 (cstate,custname,company,custnbr)
  ?>
values ('TX','Ben Dover',2,44);
DB20000I  THE SQL COMMAND COMPLETED SUCCESSFULLY.
DB2>
select company,custnbr,custname,state
  ?>
from jsmiths.customer where company=2;

  **** CLI ERROR *****
         SQLSTATE: 42703
NATIVE ERROR CODE: -206
Column STATE not in specified tables.
DB2>
```

Figure 20.24: The db2 utility, not Qshell, converses with the user in this example (part 1 of 2).

```
select company,custnbr,custname,cstate
  ?>
from jsmiths.customer where company=2;
```

COMPANY	CUSTNBR	CUSTNAME	CSTATE
2	1	Xolomon Solutions	OK
2	3	Donaldson Electric	CA
2	44	Ben Dover	TX
2	345	Gretta's Gifts	NJ

```
 4 RECORD(S) SELECTED.

DB2>
quit
/home/JSMITH $
```

Figure 20.24: *The* db2 *utility, not Qshell, converses with the user in this example (part 2 of 2).*

RFILE

The *Rfile* (Record File) utility copies data between the standard I/O devices and the database or device files. Some of the same things you can do with the *db2* utility you can do with *Rfile,* while other things you cannot. Unlike an SQL statement with a WHERE clause, *Rfile* reads or writes all records, not subsets of records. Also, the *Rfile* utility doesn't do data conversion of non-character fields into displayable text, so results displayed in the terminal might not be what you'd expect. The *Rfile* utility does, however, allow you to access device files, which SQL cannot access.

Table 20.8 lists the options acceptable to the *Rfile* utility.

Table 20.8: Rfile Options

Option	Description
a	Append to, rather than clear, the database file.
b	Process as binary data.
c *command*	Execute the CL command *command* before copying.

Table 20.8: Rfile Options, *continued*

Option	Description
C *command*	Execute the CL command *command* after copying.
h	Display help message to stderr.
K	Keep a job log.
l (ell)	Allow long text lines.
q	Suppress warning messages.
Q	Specify QSYS.LIB file names in qualified format.
r	Read a database table and write to stdout.
s	Process SRCSEQ and SRCDAT fields of source physical files.
w	Write to a database table from stdin.

The following *Rfile* examples use the data file numbers in the JSMITHS library. The data file is shown by the *db2* utility in Figure 20.25. It contains a four-byte integer column and a 10-byte character column, with the numbers 1 through 5 in each column.

```
db2 'select * from jsmiths.numbers'

COL1         COL2
-----------  -----------
    1        One
    2        Two
    3        Three
    4        Four
    5        Five

    5 RECORD(S) SELECTED.
/home/JSMITH $
```

Figure 20.25: This data file is used in the following examples to illustrate Rfile.

Figure 20.26 shows that when the *Rfile* utility is used to read data from a table, it doesn't perform conversion on the data. Instead, it simply outputs the record,

427

unchanged, to standard output. Although the *b* option indicates data should be processed as binary, all that really means is that newline characters do not separate records.

The first *Rfile* command does not show both columns. Attempting to use the *b* option in the second *Rfile* command to use binary data simply removes the new lines between records; it doesn't generate the desired output.

As a means of debugging, the *od* command displays the hexadecimal data that *Rfile* outputs. From it, you can see the binary data for the four-byte integers 1 through 5 that are generated. You can then use another Qshell filter (perhaps the *tr* utility) to process that binary data. In Figure 20.26, *tr* converts the binary data—octal 000 (zero) through octal 011 (nine)—to the matching character digits.

```
rfile -r /qsys.lib/jsmiths.lib/numbers.file/numbers.mbr
    One
    Two
    Three
    Four
    Five
rfile -br /qsys.lib/jsmiths.lib/numbers.file/numbers.mbr
    One            Two            Three          Four           Five
/home/JSMITH $
rfile -r /qsys.lib/jsmiths.lib/numbers.file/numbers.mbr | od -txlc
0000000   000 000 000 001 0d6 095 085 025 000 000 000 002 0e3 0a6 096 025
          000 000 000 001   O   n   e 045 000 000 000 002   T   w   o 045
0000020   000 000 000 003 0e3 088 099 085 085 025 000 000 000 004 0c6 096
          000 000 000 003   T   h   r   e   e 045 000 000 000 004   F   o
0000040   0a4 099 025 000 000 000 005 0c6 089 0a5 085 025
            u   r 045 000 000 000 005   F   i   v   e 045
0000054
/home/JSMITH $
rfile -r /qsys.lib/jsmiths.lib/numbers.file/numbers.mbr | tr '/[\000-
    \011]/' '/[0-9]/'
0001 One
0002 Two
0003 Three
0004 Four
0005 Five
/home/JSMITH $
```

Figure 20.26: Binary data output from Rfile can be accessed in Qshell.

The *Rfile* utility can also be used to write records to a database file. If the database file has non-character fields, however, the issue with binary becomes somewhat problematic. The Qshell utility that generates the data needs to generate binary data appropriately for the table.

Figure 20.27 builds on the previous example. It shows an *Rfile* command that appends the binary data from an existing stream file into the JSMITHS/NUMBERS database file. The database file is specified using OS/400 library-naming convention via the *Q* option. The binary datafile.dat file matches the required record format of the database file, and can as easily come in a pipeline from a utility that generates it as from a data file. The resulting JSMITHS/NUMBERS file, containing all the records, is displayed in both hexadecimal and converted text format.

```
cat datafile.dat
     Six
     Seven
     Eight
     Nine
/home/JSMITH $
cat datafile.dat | od -txlc
0000000   000 000 000 006 0e2 089 0a7 025 000 000 000 007 0e2 085 0a5 085
          000 000 000 006   S   i   x 045 000 000 000 007   S   e   v   e
0000020   095 025 000 000 000 008 0c5 089 087 088 0a3 025 000 000 000 009
            n 045 000 000 000 010   E   i   g   h   t 045 000 000 000 011
0000040   0d5 089 095 085 025
            N   i   n   e 045
0000045
/home/JSMITH $
Rfile -awQ JSMITHS/NUMBERS < datafile.dat
/home/JSMITH $
rfile -rQ JSMITHS/NUMBERS | od -txlc
0000000   000 000 000 001 0d6 095 085 025 000 000 000 002 0e3 0a6 096 025
          000 000 000 001   0   n   e 045 000 000 000 002   T   w   o 045
0000020   000 000 000 003 0e3 088 099 085 085 025 000 000 000 004 0c6 096
          000 000 000 003   T   h   r   e   e 045 000 000 000 004   F   o
0000040   0a4 099 025 000 000 000 005 0c6 089 0a5 085 025 000 000 000 006
            u   r 045 000 000 000 005   F   i   v   e 045 000 000 000 006
0000060   0e2 089 0a7 025 000 000 000 007 0e2 085 0a5 085 095 025 000 000
            S   i   x 045 000 000 000 007   S   e   v   e   n 045 000 000
```

Figure 20.27: The *tr* utility can translate binary data into a human-readable format (part 1 of 2).

```
0000100   000 008 0c5 089 087 088 0a3 025 000 000 000 009 0d5 089 095 085
          000 010   E   i   g   h   t 045 000 000 000 011   N   i   n   e
0000120   025
          045
0000121
/home/JSMITH $
rfile -rQ JSMITHS/NUMBERS | tr '/[\000-\011]/' '/[0-9]/'
00010ne
0002Two
0003Three
0004Four
0005Five
0006Six
0007Seven
0008Eight
0009Nine
/home/JSMITH $
```

Figure 20.27: The tr *utility can translate binary data into a human-readable format (part 2 of 2).*

In addition to database files, you can use *Rfile* to access other device files in the operating system. OS/400 printer files are used to generate print output. For example, the following *Rfile* command copies the stream file FTPBUILD.QSH to the QSYSPRT printer file:

```
cat -n ftpbuild.qsh |
>
Rfile -w /qsys.lib/qsysprt.file
/home/JSMITH $
```

The *n* option of the *cat* utility numbers the lines as they are printed.

The following is equivalent in function to the preceding command:

```
cat -n ftpbuild.qsh |
>
Rfile -wQ qsys/qsysprt
/home/JSMITH $
```

In this example, however, the printer file QSYSPRT is written in the traditional OS/400 library-qualified naming in the *Rfile* command, because of the *Q* option.

430

SUMMARY

In V5R2, IBM has done a good job of creating utilities that permit access to OS/400-specific objects. The *system* utility accesses existing CL command and programs. *Rfile* and *db2* permit access to database files. The *datarea* utility reads and writes data areas, while *dataq* reads and writes data queue messages.

Chapter 21

Application Development Tools

Programmers are familiar with various integrated development environments. Many of these environments run on a client workstation and provide a superb level of features and robustness. Still, many problems lend themselves simply to an editor plus a robust command-line development environment. In addition, some programmers actually prefer a powerful editor plus a robust command-line environment for programming. (Gasp!)

If you would like to use Qshell for your Java, C, or C++ development environment, you're in luck. IBM has moved support for various compiler technologies and tools into the Qshell environment.

You have many choices for a source-code editor. On the server side, you can use the Edit File command (EDTF), covered in chapter 3. There are many more client-side alternatives, ranging from simple programs like Notepad to industrial-strength editors such as SlickEdit's Visual SlickEdit (www.slickedit.com). Regardless of which editor you choose, you need to know some basics about the compiler utilities and tools provided in Qshell to get started.

Although this chapter cannot cover all the amazing things you can do with the various compiler and build tools available in Qshell, it will provide you with enough information to write simple applications. From there, you will be able to move to larger projects.

This chapter also provides a foundation for the Perl, Java, and C/C++ development techniques that are presented in chapters 22 through 24. Those chapters provide example programs to illustrate how development in Qshell works. Some of the examples use an input data file, goodoleboys.txt, which is shown in Figure 21.1.

```
cat goodoleboys.txt
Name          Born       Phone      Dog       Wife         Shotgun   Paid
=========  ========  ========  ========  =========  =======  =====
Chuck         Dec 25     444-2345  Blue      Mary Sue     12        $2.50
Bubba         Oct 13     444-1111  Buck      Mary Jean    12
Billy Bob   June 11    444-4340  Leotis    Lisa Sue     12
Amos          Jan 4      333-1119  Amos      Abigail      20
Otis          Sept 17    444-8000  Ol'Sal    Sally        12        $5
Claude        May 31     333-4340  Blue      Etheline     12
Roscoe        Feb 2      444-2234  Rover     Alice Jean   410
Arlis         June 19    444-1314  Redeye    Suzy Beth    12        $10.75
Junior        April 30   BR-549    Percival  Lilly Faye   12
Bill          Feb 29     333-4444  Daisy     Daisy        20
Ernest T.   ??         none      none      none         none
```

Figure 21.1: The goodoleboys.txt file is used in examples in the remaining chapters of this book.

The SQL script in Figure 21.2 is used to create database data for the example programs. Run the script using the iSeries Client Access "Run SQL Scripts" action from the popup menu associated with the DataBase object in the navigation tree.

THE ISERIES TOOLS FOR DEVELOPERS

The iSeries Tools for Developers product (product number 5799-PTL) includes many useful open-source Qshell and PASE utilities. PASE utilities are AIX binary utilities that run in the Portable Application Solution Environment (product number 5722-SS1, option 30). Some of the iSeries Tools for Developers utilities are most useful for C and C++ development, but others are general-purpose tools.

```
cat goodoleboys.sql
CREATE SCHEMA JSMITHQ;

CREATE TABLE JSMITHQ.CUSTOMERS
    (NAME CHAR(15), PHONENUMBER CHAR(8), WIFE CHAR(15));
DELETE FROM JSMITHQ.CUSTOMERS;
INSERT INTO JSMITHQ.CUSTOMERS VALUES('Chuck',      '444-2345',  'Mary Sue');
INSERT INTO JSMITHQ.CUSTOMERS VALUES('Bubba',      '444-1111',  'Mary Jean');
INSERT INTO JSMITHQ.CUSTOMERS VALUES('Billy Bob',  '444-4340',  'Lisa Sue');
INSERT INTO JSMITHQ.CUSTOMERS VALUES('Amos',       '333-1119',  'Abigail');
INSERT INTO JSMITHQ.CUSTOMERS VALUES('Otis',       '444-8000',  'Sally');
INSERT INTO JSMITHQ.CUSTOMERS VALUES('Claude',     '333-4340',  'Etheline');
INSERT INTO JSMITHQ.CUSTOMERS VALUES('Roscoe',     '444-2234',  'Alice Jean');
INSERT INTO JSMITHQ.CUSTOMERS VALUES('Arlis',      '444-1314',  'Suzy Beth');
INSERT INTO JSMITHQ.CUSTOMERS VALUES('Junior',     'BR-549',    'Lilly Faye');
INSERT INTO JSMITHQ.CUSTOMERS VALUES('Bill',       '333-4444',  'Daisy');
INSERT INTO JSMITHQ.CUSTOMERS VALUES('Ernest T.', NULL,         NULL);
```

Figure 21.2: Use this script to create the example database.

You can order iSeries Tools for Developers or its source code from IBM for a nominal price. Its Web page is www-1.ibm.com/servers/enable/site/porting/tools.

To use the Tools for Developers utilities described in this chapter from Qshell, use CL's Start Tools for Developers command (STRPTL) before you run Qshell. In the following examples, the client workstation is named "elmstreet." The user is running a free, open-source window manager (XFree86) to display the graphics generated by applications started in Qshell. You do not need a window manager if you are not going to run graphical X-windows applications (discussed later in this chapter). For now, all you need to know is that the CLIENT parameter of the STRPTL command requires the workstation's host name or IP address followed by a colon and a zero, :0, as shown here:

```
STRPTL CLIENT('elmstreet:0')
```

Although the STRPTL command is the IBM-supported way to initialize the iSeries Tools for Developers, it simply sets some environment variables and, optionally, allows you to run utilities from a menu. If you prefer, you can perform a similar setup for command-line access to the iSeries Tools for Developers by adding appropriate Qshell commands to your $HOME/.profile file. If you want to enable access to the developer tools for all Qshell users on the system, add the lines to the /etc/profile file instead.

Figure 21.3 provides an example of commands added to a startup script file to provide the same type of functionality as STRPTL. If you have problems, use the STRPTL command and start Qshell after invoking the command.

```
# Add the Qshell binary locations to the path
export PATH="$PATH:/QIBM/ProdData/DeveloperTools/qsh/bin"
# Add the PASE binary locations to the path
export PATH="$PATH:/QIBM/ProdData/DeveloperTools/pase/bin"
# Add the Andrew Toolkit settings that will allow use of
# the graphical applications
export ANDREWDIR=/QIBM/ProdData/DeveloperTools/atk
export ALTMACROPATH=/QIBM/ProdData/DeveloperTools/atk/sample/macro
export ATKSHELL=/QOpenSys/usr/bin/sh
# Add other miscellaneous settings as set by STRPTL CL command
export QIBM_IFS_OPEN_MAX=33000
# Individual users must set DISPLAY to be the location of
# their X-Windows display (this example uses a system of elmstreet
# and display number 0 on elmstreet)
export DISPLAY="elmstreet:0"
```

Figure 21.3: Inserting these statements in your Qshell resource file ($HOME/.profile or /etc/profile) will enable access to the Tools for Developers utilities in a Qshell resource file, similarly to the STRPTL *CL command.*

The Tools for Developers product contains a large number of utilities, including command-line compiler utilities, open-source scripting and build utilities, and X-windows graphical utilities. There is even a graphical editor.

Yes, you read that correctly: Your iSeries has a graphical editor and other graphical tools.

QSHELL AND ASCII DATA

One very important thing to remember is that PASE applications are ASCII applications that deal with ASCII files. With the appropriate steps, you can deal with ASCII data in files easily from Qshell.

Qshell automatically translates data from the CCSID of the IFS file to the CCSID of the job when reading the data. The result is that, in many cases, Qshell and Qshell applications will deal natively with ASCII files and data. However, some applications, like the Andrew Toolkit discussed later in the next section, open files in binary mode, disabling the automatic translation. Those applications therefore require ASCII files.

The following command uses a PASE utility called *perl* (described in more detail in chapter 22):

```
perl -e 'perl-commands-here' customers.txt
```

Since perl is a PASE application, it expects ASCII files. Therefore, this command would not work if the customers.txt file were EBCDIC.

When using PASE applications from inside Qshell, you can take advantage of some of the built-in support in the system to translate EBCDIC to ASCII. If you are going to run PASE applications, you should learn some strategies for working with ASCII data.

One strategy is to use the QIBM_CCSID variable, which became available in V5R2. The QIBM_CCSID variable tells Qshell which CCSID should be used to translate data from the CCSID of the job. The following example illustrates this strategy of converting an EBCDIC file to an ASCII file using Qshell statements:

```
export QIBM_CCSID=819
cat customers.txt > ascii-customers.txt
perl -e 'perl-commands-here' ascii-customers.txt
```

A second strategy, shown in the following example, is to use the -C option for the *touch* utility:

```
# Remove the ASCII file (touch only sets the CCSID on file creation)
rm ascii-customers.txt
touch -C 819 ascii-customers.txt
cat customers.txt >> ascii-customers.txt
perl -e 'perl-commands-here' ascii-customers.txt
```

The append operator (>>) is used here to translate the data to the CCSID of the target file. Some other utilities, such as *nohup* and *rexec*, also support a -*C* option for setting the CCSID.

Alternatively, you can rely on the fact that the PASE runtime support automatically converts standard input and output as appropriate for ASCII-based PASE applications:

```
cat customers.txt | perl -e 'perl-commands-here'
```

GRAPHICAL UTILITIES

A set of graphical utilities from the *Andrew Toolkit* (*ATK*) is part of the iSeries Tools for Developers. Most of these utilities are PASE utilities, because the ATK is a UNIX-based set of applications. With the proper configuration (with STRPTL or the setup described at the beginning of this chapter), those utilities can also be used transparently from Qshell.

The Andrew Toolkit (also known as the *Andrew User Interface System*, or *AUIS*) was created in 1982 by a joint venture of IBM and Carnegie Mellon University. The goal of the venture was to form an advanced, distributed computing environment. The full ATK consists of many diverse applications, including advanced mail, document, editing, and help facilities, and a distributed file system. Transarc Corporation eventually took over the now-famous Andrew File System (AFS).

The set of modified graphical ATK utilities included with the iSeries Tools for Developers remains small and focused on application development. The following sections explain how to run these graphical applications from the iSeries.

Getting an X-Windows Server

If you run a Unix- or Linux-based workstation with a graphical user interface, you probably already run an X-Windows server (*X-Server*) on your workstation.

438

If you run Windows or another operating system, various commercial and free X-Servers are available. Choose one that fits your budget and your usage characteristics. The following two might be of interest:

- Hummingbird Exceed is a full-blown, commercial X-Server that comes packaged with many other networking tools. It is very easy to use and quite full-featured, but its price might put you off if you are just experimenting. As of the writing of this book, prices for a full version of Hummingbird Exceed 8.0 are around $300–$350.

- If you would like to invest a little time and energy instead of money, XFree86 is an open-source X-Server software package that might fit your needs. It is free software, packaged with Cygwin utilities for windows. Cygwin is an open-source, Linux-like environment for Windows, composed of a shell, compilers, many utilities, and programming APIs. Cygwin can give you an almost full Linux-like environment on your Windows platform. The XFree86 X-Server is completely customizable, but also has some potentially complex setup requirements as part of that customization.

If you choose to use XFree86, be prepared to do some research at www.cygwin.com/. To get started, read the FAQ and the *Users Guide*, and then run the Cygwin setup program. Choose to install the applications from the XFree86 category. When setup is finished, simply start your newly installed Cygwin bash shell and use the following command to start your X-Server:

```
startx &
```

On the iSeries, set the environment variables (including the DISPLAY environment variable) as shown in Figure 21.3, and give the iSeries Tools for Developers graphical application a test drive.

Using an X-Windows Server

An X-Windows server runs on your workstation and allows remote applications (the X-Windows clients) to display their graphical interfaces on your workstation.

439

Typically, on the remote system (your iSeries), the only setup required (beyond having the X-Windows client runtime) is setting the DISPLAY environment variable to point to your X-Windows display system. Figure 21.4 illustrates this process. Note that the third invocation of *ez* fails because DISPLAY was set to a host that was not present or not running an X-Windows server. The systems must be running an X-Server.

```
export DISPLAY=elmstreet:0
ez /home/jsmith/customers.txt
Starting ez...
export DISPLAY=11.22.33.44:0
ez /home/jsmith/notes.txt
Starting ez...
export DISPLAY=blah:0
Starting ez...
Xlib: connection to "blah:0.0" refused by server
Xlib: No protocol specified
Could not open the display; this program will not run without a window
    system.
Could not create new window.
exiting.
```

Figure 21.4: In Qshell, set the DISPLAY variable so that two separate Qshell X-Windows applications (both ez) show their graphical user interface on different client systems (host name elmstreet and host 11.22.33.44).

Using VNC

Virtual Network Computing (VNC) is open-source software that provides remote access to graphical environments. VNC is an alternative to running an X-Server on your workstation.

The VNC software consists of two parts: the VNC server and the VNC viewer. The VNC server, the X-Windows session (the window manager), and the graphical applications are run on a host computer—in this case, the iSeries. The iSeries Tools for Developers provides a VNC server and window manager that run in PASE.

The graphical applications (PASE- or Qshell-based) display their user interfaces on that X-Windows session directly on the iSeries. From your workstation, you run the VNC viewer application to provide a view of the graphical user interfaces on your workstation. These graphical applications may be Qshell or PASE.

First, configure and start the VNC server on the iSeries, as shown here:

```
MKDIR '/home/<user>/.vnc'
QAPTL/VNCPASSWD PASSWORD(yourpassword) VERIFY(yourpassword)
USEHOME(*NO) PWDFILE('/home/<user>/.vnc/passwd')
```

Configure the VNC Server password using these CL commands. You only need to do this one time. The X-Server manages the graphical applications you are going to run.

You can start the VNC server and the X-Windows desktop using the STRPTL CL command, as shown in Figure 21.5. Alternatively, start the VNC server and X-windows desktop using a Qshell command. Figure 21.6 shows the start of a graphical edit session (*ez*).

```
STRPTL CLIENT(*VNC)
No running Xvnc jobs found for jsmith, exiting -1...
Could not find running server, starting new server...

New 'X' desktop is CORP1.RCHLAND.IBM.COM:1

Creating default startup script /home/jsmith/.vnc/xstartup
Starting applications specified in /home/jsmith/.vnc/xstartup
Log file is /home/jsmith/.vnc/CORP1.RCHLAND.IBM.COM:1.log

Returned from starting vncserver...
Running Xvnc job found, exiting 1...
DISPLAY=CORP1:1
Press ENTER to end terminal session.
```

Figure 21.5: Use this CL command to start the VNC server and the X desktop, in addition to setting up the iSeries Tools for Developers environment variables.

You can safely start the graphical application before running the viewer. The graphical application will wait for user input. A major usability feature of VNC is that the connection between the VNC server and the display (the VNC viewer) is not permanent. Therefore, you can end and restart the viewer as many times as you like, even on different workstations, while leaving your server-side applications up and active.

```
/QIBM/ProdData/DeveloperTools/pase/bin/vncserver
New 'X' desktop is CORP1.RCHLAND.IBM.COM:1

Starting applications specified in /home/jsmith/.vnc/xstartup
Log file is /home/jsmith/.vnc/CORP1.RCHLAND.IBM.COM:1.log
export DISPLAY=corp1:1
ez test.txt
Starting ez...
```

Figure 21.6: Use these Qshell commands to start the VNC server and then run a graphical application. Note that if directory /QIBM/ProdData/DeveloperTools/pase/bin were in the PATH variable, the user would not need to type the full path in the command. Use the value for the "export DISPLAY" command that is output from the vncserver command.

At this point, you have started an X-Windows desktop and one or more graphical applications. The graphical applications use the value of DISPLAY to find the X desktop. The graphical applications will continue to run until ended. You will use the value of DISPLAY (or the X desktop value shown) and the VNC password when you run the VNC viewer on your workstation to view the graphical applications. The VNC password is required, to protect your application sessions from access by other users.

Next, connect your VNC viewer on your workstation to the VNC server so you can view the iSeries graphical applications. If you do not have a VNC viewer, download one from www.realvnc.com. You can also download the VNC server for your client platform if you want to enable remote access to that workstation from another system running the VNC viewer (your home machine, for example).

When you run the VNC viewer on your workstation, you will be prompted for the VNC server and the VNC password. Enter the value for the DISPLAY variable that you were shown when the VNC server started (in the previous examples, "corp1:1"), and the password you configured when you used the VNCPASSWD CL command. The result is that your VNC viewer session should connect to the server and show you the X-Windows desktop, as in Figure 21.7.

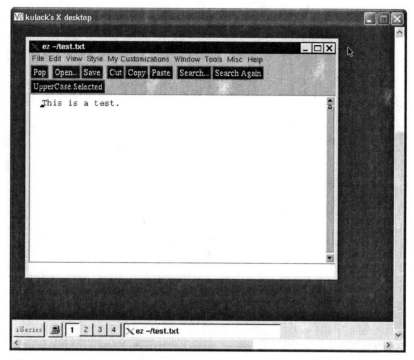

Figure 21.7: The VNC viewer shows the X-Windows desktop that was configured and started in this section.

Closing the VNC viewer window will not end the window manager and graphical applications. To end, click the iSeries button in the taskbar and select LogOut. You will still need to end the VNC server that is running on the iSeries. Use the *-kill* option of the *vncserver* utility to do this:

```
/qibm/proddata/developertools/pase/bin/vncserver -kill :1
Killing Xvnc process ID 21240
```

THE EZ UTILITY

The ez editor is an X-Windows text and document editor provided with the Andrew Toolkit. This graphical editor extends a simple text editor with some features usually found in higher-cost editors or development environments.

443

The *ez* utility is a PASE application, and therefore creates ASCII files. In many cases, using ASCII files in Qshell will be transparent to Qshell applications; Andrew applications however, require ASCII files.

Key Bindings

The *ez* utility really shows its Unix heritage when considering the key bindings available for use. There are many key bindings in a standard *ez* session, and you may add still more. Many of these key commands are multi-key combinations, and are case-sensitive. In some cases, however, a command in lowercase will also work in uppercase.

Use the Ctrl-b-K key combination to list all of the current key bindings. Table 21.1 shows the key bindings associated with *ez* menu choices.

Table 21.1: Ez Key Bindings

Key Sequence	Description
Esc ?	Describe a key binding. A description of the next key you hit will be displayed.
Ctrl-g	Cancel the current operation. Many ez operations, such as a search, result in a prompt. Press Ctrl-g to cancel the operation.
?	Prompt. In many cases, when being prompted for a value in the status bar, typing a question mark will display a list of acceptable values or more information. For example, press Ctrl-b Ctrl-v to open a new file, then type a question mark to list the files that might match the name currently being entered.
Esc - (Escape Dash)	Show the current list of editor procedures. Editor procedures can be bound to keys, menu items, or toolbar items.
Ctrl-b-K	Show the current key-binding list. Describe the current key-combination mnemonics and the editor procedures to which they are assigned.

Table 21.1: Ez Key Bindings, *continued*

Key Sequence	Description
Ctrl-b Ctrl-s	Save the current file.
Ctrl-b Ctrl-x	Exit the current ez session.
Ctrl-b Ctrl-v	Open (visit) a new file.
Ctrl-b Ctrl-w	Save (write) the current edit buffer as a new file.
Ctrl-b Ctrl-m	Save all (many) open files.
Ctrl-w	Cut the selected text to the current "cut buffer."
Esc-w	Copy the selected text to the current cut buffer.
Ctrl-y	Paste from the current cut buffer.
Esc-y	Move (cycle) to the previous cut buffer. Ez maintains separate buffers for copied and cut text.
Ctrl-b Tab	Insert the contents of a file at the cursor.
Esc-q	Query (search) and replace a regular expression.
Esc-' Esc-p	Remove one style from some stylized text.
Esc-' Esc-P	Remove all styles from some stylized text.
Esc-l	Convert the selected text to lowercase.
Ctrl-B-v	Compose a character.
Esc-r	Redo all styles. Use this to beautify source code that isn't formatted correctly.
Tab	If the cursor is at the beginning of a line or multiple lines of text are selected, indent the text appropriately for source code formatting; otherwise, insert a tab.
Esc-^R	Format a line or region appropriately for source code.
Esc-Q	Rename an identifier in the selected region of source code.
Ctrl-b-2	Open a second window for the same file.
Ctrl-b Ctrl-d	Close the current window.

Table 21.1: Ez Key Bindings, *continued*

Key Sequence	Description
Ctrl-b Ctrl-b	List all of the currently open buffers.
Ctrl-b-b	Switch to a different open buffer.
Ctrl-b-k	Delete (kill) the current buffer. (Close the currently open file.)
Ctrl-b-d	Open a directory for browsing
Esc-^D	Start graphical difference (ezdiff) processing on the current buffer. Switch buffers (with Ctrl-b-b) and then use Esc-^D again in the second buffer to continue.
Esc-^N	Highlight the next difference in the two ezdiff buffers.
Esc-^P	Highlight the previous difference in the two ezdiff buffers.
Esc-^U	Change the selected difference in the current buffer to the contents of the difference in the other buffer.
Ctrl-b-u	Highlight the URL at the current cursor position.

When you have found a match with the query (search) and replace command (Esc-q), the editor will look like it's not doing anything. In fact, *ez* is waiting for your commands. Type a question mark to be prompted for a response to your query-matching string. Table 21.2 shows the responses.

Table 21.2: Ez Query and Replace Responses

Response	Description
Space	Replace the current match and find the next match.
. (period) or - (dash)	Replace the current match and quit searching.
n or , (comma)	Do not replace the current match and find the next match.
Q or = (equal)	Quit searching immediately; do not replace the current match.
!	Replace the current and subsequent matches.

446

Editor Customization

At startup, the *ez* editor searches for several initialization files, listed here:

```
$HOME/.ezinit
/QIBM/ProdData/DeveloperTools/atk/lib/global.ezinit
$HOME/.atkinit
/QIBM/ProdData/DeveloperTools/atk/lib/global.atkinit
```

Ez executes the first initialization file it finds.

All ATK applications follow the same initialization model. By using the appropriate initialization file, you set options for an ATK application (in this case, *ez*) with the corresponding scope:

- Using $HOME/.ezinit sets options for only one user of that application.

- Using global.*ezinit* sets options for any user of that application.

- Using $HOME/.atkinit sets options for only one user of any ATK application.

- Using global.*atkinit* sets options for any user of any ATK application.

An initialization file can perform many different customization steps, but the most important step may be the "include" initialization step. Each time you create a $HOME/.ezinit file (or an init file for other applications), the first thing you should do is include the global version of that file. Failure to do this will remove required system-wide customization.

The recommended initial steps when customizing *ez* or other ATK applications are to create user-specific files that do nothing but include the global files. First, create the user-specific application-initialization file. For *ez*, the $HOME/.ezinit file should start with these two statements:

```
include $HOME/.atkinit
include /QIBM/ProdData/DeveloperTools/atk/lib/global.ezinit
```

447

Add *ez* customizations after these two include statements.

Next, create the user-specific ATK initialization file. The $HOME/.atkinit file starts with this include statement.

```
include /QIBM/ProdData/DeveloperTools/atk/lib/global.atkinit
```

Add customizations intended for all ATK applications after this statement.

The most common *ez* customizations are those that change the behavior of keys, add menu choices, and add buttons to the button bar.

When creating your own customizations, be sure to use the global initialization files as representative customization examples. Similarly, use On Keys and On Procs in the Help menu to get a list of the keys you can bind and the procedures you can bind to those keys.

The first keys that you will probably want to change will be those for cutting, copying, and pasting, as shown here:

```
# Use Ctrl-C for copy
addkey   textview-copy-region ^c
# Use Ctrl-x for cut
addkey   textview-zap-region ^x
# Use Ctrl-v for paste
addkey   textview-yank ^v
```

Add key bindings in ATK applications using the addkey customization statement in the initialization file ~/.ezinit or ~/.atkinit. The addkey statement takes the procedure and a textual representation of the key to be changed.

Adding menu choices and buttons to the button bar is also an easy task. The addmenu and addbutton statements are similar to the addkey statement. Use the third parameter for the addmenu and addbutton statements to both name and position the menu or button. Position an item in a menu or toolbar using a positioning number separated from the item name by a ~ (tilde) character. Use lower numbers to move the item to the left or upward. Use higher numbers to move the item to the right or downward.

The following example creates a menu item and buttons in ATK applications using the addmenu and addbutton customization statements in the initialization file ~/.ezinit. The third parameter names the menu or toolbar that the button is added to:

```
# Create a menu and a button on the button bar to uppercase
    selected text.
addmenu textview-uppercase-word "My Customizations~45,UpperCase
    Selected~10"
addbutton textview-uppercase-word "ez.toolbar,UpperCase
    Selected~90"
```

After the customizations, end and restart the *ez* session. The new *ez* session will have new menu choices, toolbar button, and key bindings, as shown in Figure 21.8.

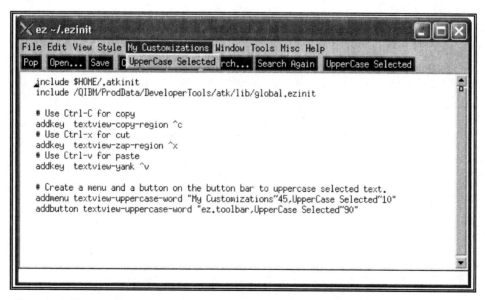

Figure 21.8: The ez editor customizations have been applied to the session.

File Formats

The *ez* editor supports many file formats, so it is useful for editing text files, Web pages, source code, and even word-processing documents. You can customize or browse the initialization files that control the way *ez* treats various files. The file /QIBM/ProdData/DeveloperTools/atk/lib/global.filetypes describes the file types that the editor supports.

The global.filetypes file (or one of your personal initialization files) sets up associations between file extensions, the type of file, and the template used to edit the text. The association can also include parameters that override the behavior of the editor.

The first parameter to the addfiletype initialization statement indicates the file extension. The second parameter indicates the general file type. The third parameter is the interesting one because it indicates which template file should be used. Template files control the color, fonts, and formatting that is used to display parts of the file (for example, keywords versus variables in source code). You can also use the third parameter to override specific settings for that template.

Figure 21.9 is a partial excerpt from the ATK global.filetypes file, these lines set up an association between file extensions, the type of text, and the template used to edit the test. The first statement in Figure 21.9 sets all files to rawtext, and the subsequent statements specialize file types.

```
addfiletype *       rawtext   "template=rawtext"
addfiletype .txt    rawtext   "template=rawtext"
addfiletype .c      ctext     "template=c"
addfiletype .cpp    ctext     "template=c"
addfiletype .h      ctext     "template=h"
addfiletype .hpp    ctext     "template=h"
addfiletype .java   xxxxx     "template=java;ctext-use-tabs=0"
addfiletype .d      text      "template=default"
addfiletype .doc    text      "template=default"
```

Figure 21.9: These lines set up an association between file extensions, the type of text, and the template used to edit the test.

ATK applications use template files to determine formatting characteristics of displayed files. The global template files are stored in the /QIBM/ProdData/ DeveloperTools/atk/tpls directory, while user-customized template files are stored in the $HOME/tpls directory. Change a template file to control the font, size, color, or other display characteristics of your *ez* sessions. Here are some possible customizations:

```
cp /QIBM/ProdData/DeveloperTools/atk/tpls/java.tpl $HOME/tpls
ez $HOME/tpls/java.tpl
```

When you edit a template file, the *ez* utility presents you with a style editor session. A style in the template file represents a name for a category of text. The ATK applications associate displayed text with a particular style, and then display it according to the formatting characteristics defined for that style. The template file contains a global style that applies to all text in the edited document. In addition, there are many other styles in the template file.

To configure a style in the template file, select the style that you would like to change in the upper frames of the window. Use the lower frames to set the formatting characteristics of that style.

In the image in Figure 21.10, the *ez* session is editing the $HOME/tpls/java.tpl file. Selecting the menu card of "no menu" and the name-on-menu-card value of "global," displays the global characteristics for all styles described in the file.

The style editor selects the attributes that represent the current characteristics of the global style. The style editor in Figure 21.10 shows a font of "AndyType," and enables the "tab by spaces," "fixed width," and "continue indent" characteristics. The justification is "left flush," and the default color is "midnightblue." Modify the characteristics used for the style by selecting the appropriate attributes from the center frames. Deselect the attribute by clicking on the attribute again.

The bottom frame of Figure 21.10 shows the content of the file when creating a new Java file. Take note of the special template parameters in the file-content

451

frame at the bottom of the window. You automatically enter data into a newly created file using text or template parameters in the new file.

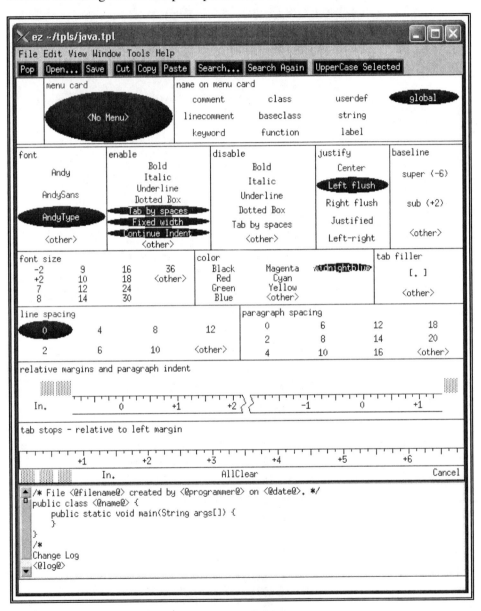

Figure 21.10: You can use the ez editor to edit a template file.

Table 21.3 describes the available template parameters.

Table 21.3: Ez Template Parameters ("Tags")

Parameter	Description
<@filename@>	The <@filename@> tag expands to the full filename of the newly created file, for example, CustomerClass.java.
<@name@>	The <@name@> tag expands to the name without the extension of the newly created file, for example, CustomerClass.
<@programmer@>	The <@programmer@> tag expands to the name of the programmer as taken from the USER environment variable. You might have to manually set the USER environment variable.
<@date@>	The <@date@> tag expands to the current date.
<@time@>	The <@time@> tag expands to the current time.
<@log@>	The <@log@> tag expands to a recursive "change log" entry. The recursive nature inserts a new log entry each time the file is edited.The <@log@> entry expands to another <@log@> tag, plus the expanded values for the <@date@>, <@time@>, and <@programmer@> tags. In addition, the <@log@> tag inserts a brief placeholder for a reason, a version, and a description of the changes.

Figures 21.11 and 21.12 provide examples of the use of template parameters. In Figure 21.11, the template parameters automatically insert replacement text into the file when it is created or opened. Figure 21.12 shows the results in a Java file.

```
/* File <@filename@> created by <@programmer@> on <@date@>. */
public class <@name@> {
    public static void main(String args[]) {
    }
}
/*
Change Log
<@log@>
*/
```

Figure 21.11: This is an example of template parameters in the file-content frame of the java.tpl template.

```
/* File Customer.java created by John Smith on Mon May 19 2003. */
public class Customer {
    public static void main(String args[]) {
    }
}
/*
Change Log
<@log@>

Mon May 19 2003  21:22:05  by John Smith
<reason><version><Brief description and why change was made.>
*/
```

Figure 21.12: This is an example of a newly created Java file after ez expands the template parameters.

The *ez* editor recognizes many source-code languages and formats the displayed text using color and indenting. As Figure 21.13 shows, you can use Qshell's *ls* command to find the supported formats.

```
ls /QIBM/ProdData/DeveloperTools/atk/tpls
ald.tpl              dialog.tpl              m3.tpl
asm.tpl              filecmplistview.tpl     mod.tpl
bufferlist.tpl       findall.tpl             pascal.tpl
c.tpl                h.tpl                   perl.tpl
changes.tpl          hpp.tpl                 rawtext.tpl
compile.tpl          html.tpl                review.tpl
contents.tpl         htmltag.tpl             rexx.tpl
cpp.tpl              i3.tpl                  rxm.tpl
cwn.tpl              java.tpl                symbol.tpl
def.tpl              jde.tpl                 typescript.tpl
default.tpl          lisp.tpl
```

Figure 21.13: Use the Qshell ls command to list the names of the source-code language templates supported by the ez editor. The editor uses some of the displayed templates for other document types.

Figure 21.14 shows a newly created, empty Java file named Customer.java. The file shows the default text formatting and color, and the expanded template parameters from the java.tpl file. The View->Line Display menu item enables the display of line numbers in the edit session.

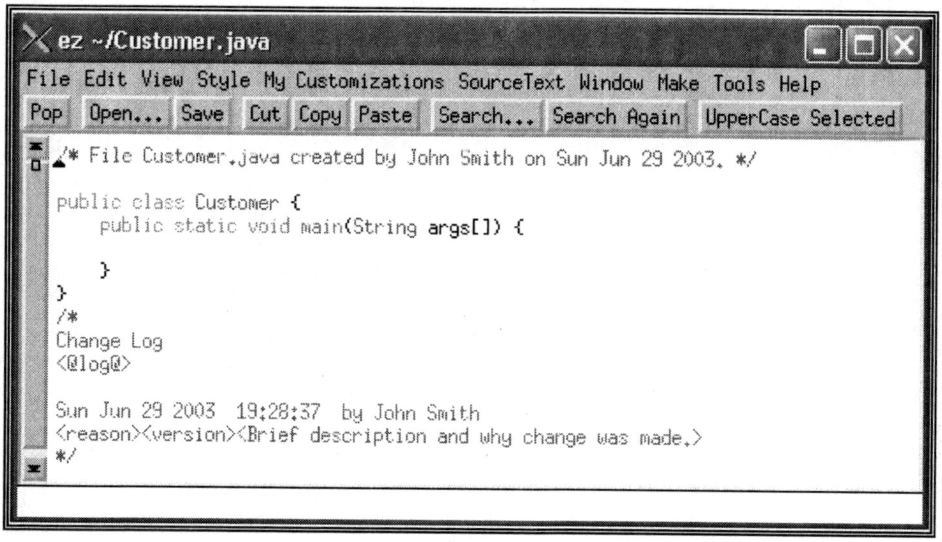

Figure 21.14: Ez has applied customization to an empty Java source file.

Directory Browsing

The *ez* editor can also serve as a graphical directory browser. Using the *ez* utility, specify a directory name as the parameter. For example, the following command edits a directory named *src*, where source files are typically stored:

```
ez /home/jsmith/src
```

When editing a directory, double-click an object to open it, or right-click it and choose Edit. As shown in Figure 21.15, use the Pop button on the toolbar to move back to the previous (higher-level) directory.

Hex Edit

Use the View->Hex Edit menu choice to open a hexadecimal editor view of the current buffer. This view supports both ASCII or EBCDIC files; choose View->ASCII or View->EBCDIC to switch between them. *Ez* disables some capabilities in a hex editor session, as shown in Figure 21.16.

455

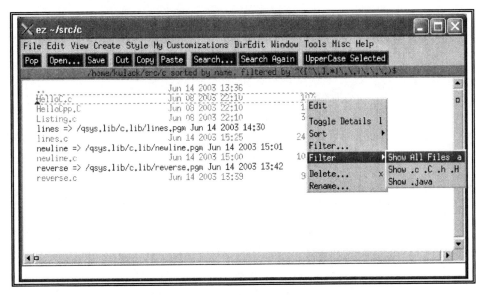

Figure 21.15: Here, ez is being used as a graphical directory browser.

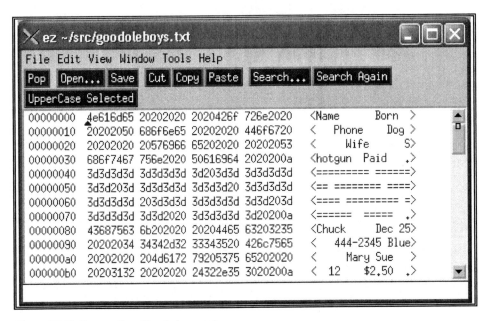

Figure 21.16: Ez permits editing in hex mode.

The *mrhex* utility is a shortcut for creating an *ez* session and starting the hexadecimal edit mode.

Undo Capability

The *ez* editor has no undo capability, so changes you make accidentally or intentionally are permanent. It does, however, create checkpoint files to help you recover from crashes or unsaved edit sessions. Look for files named *OriginalName.CKP* in the same directory as the original file you were editing. In some cases, you can use the CKP files to recover lost data.

SUMMARY

The iSeries Tools for Developers product provides basic command-line and graphical utilities that enable application development in a Qshell environment. Some initial setup is required to run the tools. After the setup is complete, Qshell's command-line, graphical, or PASE applications run as if they were built into the Qshell environment.

Chapter 22

The Perl Utility

As mentioned in the previous chapter, the perl utility provided by the iSeries Tools for Developers product is a PASE utility. Qshell provides direct support to run PASE utilities without starting a PASE environment or leaving the Qshell environment.

Perl is a truly popular piece of scripting/programming software (covered by the GNU General Public License) that can be used to do just about anything. Larry Wall originally released perl in 1987 as a Unix system-administration tool. It has now reached version 5.8, and runs on dozens of platforms.

Some of perl's many strengths include the following:

- Broad standard library and third-party libraries
- Powerful string-processing operators
- Automatic memory management
- An eclectic syntax, which provides perl programmers many ways to accomplish the same task

Many books, tutorials, and Web resources are available for learning perl. Start at the perl home page, www.perl.com, and the Comprehensive Perl Archive Network, www.cpan.org, for downloads of perl distributions and modules to do just about anything you could think of.

Perl has also been ported to iSeries as an ILE application (i.e., outside of PASE), but the PASE application is much newer, and the ILE version appears to be less frequently used. The perl utility shipped with iSeries Tools for Developers is version 5.005_03 for AIX. The current version available on CPAN in the OS/400 section is "5.8.0@18380."

RUNNING PERL

If you examine the series of directories that were added to the PATH variable in Figure 21.3 of the previous chapter, you will see the following statement:

```
# Add the PASE binary locations to the path
export PATH="$PATH:/QIBM/ProdData/DeveloperTools/pase/bin"
```

This statement sets the path to enable access to Tools for Developers PASE utilities, including perl, in a Qshell resource file. After you have run it to update your path, you can run the perl utility.

Alternatively, you can allow all users on the system to access perl from a standard location by adding a link to perl in the /usr/bin directory. Figure 22.1 shows how to create the link and start perl. The *v* option shows the version of perl.

```
ln -s /QIBM/ProdData/DeveloperTools/pase/bin/perl /usr/bin/perl
perl -v
This is perl, version 5.005_03 built for aix

Copyright 1987-1999, Larry Wall

Perl may be copied only under the terms of either the Artistic
    License or the GNU General Public License, which may be
    found in the Perl 5.0 source kit.

Complete documentation for Perl, including FAQ lists, should be
    found on this system using 'man perl' or 'perldoc perl',  If
    you have access to the Internet, point your browser at
    http://www.perl.com/, the Perl Home Page.
```

Figure 22.1: Create a symbolic link to allow all users on the system access to perl from the standard location at /usr/bin/perl.

Perl is an ASCII application. Use *ez* to edit perl scripts in ASCII and to edit perl data files. See chapter 21 for other strategies for dealing with ASCII files in Qshell.

The Perl Command

The syntax of the perl command has two forms:

```
perl [options] [--] ProgramFile arguments ...
perl [options] [-e commands] [--] arguments ...
```

You will use one or the other of these forms, but not both, in one command. You can write perl script (program code) either from the command line or in a text program file. Alternatively, write the perl program as a series of script files using the magic number (#!) syntax. Examples in this chapter use perl scripts.

Perl Options

Table 22.1 shows some of the more commonly used command-line options for perl.

Table 22.1: Perl Command-line Options

Option	Description
-w	Warn of possible errors. Always use this parameter.
-a	Automatically split the input lines on white space into array @F. The -a parameter is used with -n or -p.
-e	Perl commands follow on the command line instead of in a script file. Multiple -e options may be used.
-F/*pattern*/	This is the pattern used for the -a option (auto split). The default is to split on white space.
-i[*extension*]	Edit files in place. If an extension is specified, make a backup copy of the file to the file extension specified.
-I*directory*	Add the directory given to the list of directories processed for included perl scripts and modules.

Table 22.1: Perl Command-line Options, *continued*

Option	Description
-n	Implicitly add a While (<>) loop around the script, automatically reading lines into the $_ special variable.
-p	The same as -n, but the line is automatically printed to simulate the behavior of sed.
-v	Show perl version information.

PERL SYNTAX

Perl is a large and complex language, so this chapter only presents highlights of it. The tables describing the language in this chapter are not complete. Instead, they focus on the most frequently used perl constructs.

Variables

All variables in perl are prefixed with a special character, depending on the treatment of the variable. Variables prefixed with a dollar sign are *scalar variables* (numbers or strings). Variables prefixed with an "at" sign are array values. In general, arrays are indexed by numbers starting with zero, but variables prefixed with a percent sign are associative arrays, which are indexed by strings. When indexing into an array, indicate you want the result to be a scalar value by using the dollar-sign prefix.

Like Qshell, perl uses predefined special variables to represent common information. Table 22.2 shows some of the more commonly used perl special variables and arrays.

Table 22.2: Special Variables and Arrays

Variable	Description
$_	The current input record, which typically represents one line of input. See $/ to change this behavior.
$.	The input line number of the last input record that was read.

Table 22.2: Special Variables and Arrays, *continued*

Variable	Description
$/	The input record separator, which controls how records are delimited for reading into the $_ variable. By default, the value is newline. You may set this to a multi-character value.
$,	The value used for the output field separator by the print operator. When multiple arguments are passed to the print operator, they are, by default, separated by commas.
$\	The output record separator for the print operator.
$"	The separator that joins elements of arrays that are interpolated in strings.
$[	The index used for the first element of an array or the first character of a string. The default value is zero. You may set this to one, but beware of included library dependencies on zero-indexed arrays.
$ARGV	The name of the current file when reading from <>.
$&	The string that matched the last pattern match.
$`	The string that preceded what was matched by the last pattern match.
$'	The string that followed what was matched by the last pattern match.
$|	If set to non-zero, forces a flush after every write. The default value is zero.
$1, $2, $3, etc...	The strings that matched sub-expressions (parentheses groupings) of the last pattern match completed. $1 represents the group starting with the first left parenthesis, $2 the group starting with the second left parenthesis, etc.
$#array	The last index (the length) of the array named.
@ARGV	The array containing the command-line arguments for the script. $ARGV[0] contains the first argument.
@_	The array containing the parameter values passed to subroutines. @_[0] contains the first parameter passed to the subroutine.
%ENV	The associative array representing the current set of environment variables. Strings index associative arrays. The array %ENV will likely contain an entry for the HOME environment variable. Use $ENV{"HOME"} to access HOME.

Figure 22.2 shows usage patterns of perl variables, demonstrated by a simple lookup facility. Comments in the perl script explain details about individual steps.

```
cat lookupExample.pl
#!/usr/bin/perl -w
# These are simple variable assignments and substitutions.
$firstName = "Billy";
$lastName = "Bob";x
$number = "444-4340";
$fullNameAndNumber = "$firstName $lastName" . " at " . $number;
print "Name and number: $fullNameAndNumber\n";

# Simple array assignment. Indexes 0 to 4
@names = ("Billy Bob", "Chuck", "Bubba", "Amos", "Claude");
for ($i=0; $i<$#names; $i++) {
    print "Name #$i:  $names[$i]\n";
}
# Simple associative array of phone numbers  Indexed by name.
%phoneNumbersByName = ("Billy Bob", "444-4340",
                       "Chuck",     "444-2345",
                       "Bubba",     "444-1111",
                       "Amos",      "333-1119",
                       "Claude",    "333-4340");
# List all of the keys (indexes) of the associative array.
@keys = keys(%phoneNumbersByName);
# About to output an array as a string, set the output field
# separator to a comma plus a space.
$" = ", ";
print "Indexes of phone list: @keys\n";

# Retrieve a phone number
$target = "Billy Bob";
if (defined $phoneNumbersByName{$target}) {
    $lookup = $phoneNumbersByName{'Billy Bob'};
}
else {
    $lookup = "Not found";
}
print "Lookup of phone number for $target is $lookup\n";
lookupExample.pl
Name and number: Billy Bob at 444-4340
Name #0:   Billy Bob
Name #1:   Chuck
Name #2:   Bubba
Name #3:   Amos
Indexes of phone list: Amos, Bubba, Claude, Chuck, Billy Bob
Lookup of phone number for Billy Bob is 444-4340
```

Figure 22.2: This example perl code (plus comments) declares and uses perl variables to demonstrate a simple lookup capability using an associative array.

Operators

In addition to the traditional mathematical operators found in many languages, perl has operators for the manipulation, comparison, and construction of strings. Table 22.3 shows the more commonly used operators.

Table 22.3: Perl Operators

Operator	Description
<>	Read from standard input or the files specified in the @ARGV array.
<STDIN> <STD-OUT> <STDERR>	Read from the standard file specified.
<ARGV>	Read from the list of files specified in the @ARGV array.
<FILEHANDLE>	Read from a FILEHANDLE that was opened with the perl *open* API.
+ - * / %	These are traditional addition, subtraction, multiplication, division, and modulo operators.
& | ^	These are bitwise AND, OR, and XOR operators.
X	Create an array (or string) consisting of the operand on the left (which is an array or string) repeated the number of times specified by the operand on the right, for example, *$nine9s = "9" x 9;*
. (dot)	Concatenate two strings, for example, *$fullname = $firstname . " ". $lastname.*
|| &&	These are logical OR and AND operators.
== != < > <= >=	These are numeric comparison operators: equal; not equal; less than; greater than; less than or equal; greater than or equal.
eq ne lt gt le ge	These are string comparison operators: equal; not equal; less than; greater than; less than or equal; greater than or equal.
<=>	The numeric-ordering operator returns -1 if the left operand is greater than the right operand, zero if they are equal, and one if the right operand is greater than the left operand.

465

Table 22.3: Perl Operators, *continued*

Operator	Description
Cmp	The string-ordering operator returns -1 if the left operand is greater than the right operand, zero if the operands are equal, and one if the right operand is greater than the left operand.
=~	The search operator targets the left operand with the search, substitution, or translation function in the right operand.
!~	The negated search operator targets the left operand with the search, substitution, or translation function in the right operand.

Functions

Perl provides a standard set of built-in functions for string and array manipulation. Perl also provides a large set of functions that provide interaction with and access to operating-system services. Table 22.4 shows some commonly used functions.

Table 22.4: Perl Functions

Function	Description
m/*pattern*/*flags*	The match operator matches a pattern. Use flags to modify the match behavior. If the =~ or !~ operators are not used, the target for the match is the $_ variable.
s/*pattern*/*newpattern*/*flags*	The substitution operator substitutes the replacement text (or pattern) for the matched pattern in the original. Use flags to modify the substitution. If the =~ or !~ operators are not used, the target for the substitution is the $_ variable.
tr/*list*/*replacementlist*/*flags*	Somewhat similar to the substitution operator but more specialized, the translation operator translates characters found in the list to those in the replacement list. Use flags to modify the translation. If the =~ or !~ operators are not used, the target for the translation is the $_ variable.
print(*file list*)	The print function prints a string- or comma-separated list of strings (fields). If FILEHANDLE is not specified, the output goes to stdout.

466

Table 22.4: Perl Functions, *continued*

Function	Description
time()	The time function returns the number of seconds since January 1, 1970. Use this as input to localtime().
localtime(*time*)	The localtime function converts the time returned from the time function to a nine-element array. The array contents are typically retrieved using the following notation: *($sec, $min, $hour, $monthday, $month, $year, $weekday, $yearday, $isDST) = localtime(time());*
chomp(*string*)	The chomp function safely removes end-of-line characters (represented by the $/ variable). If no end-of-line characters are present, the variable is unchanged. If no parameters are specified, the target is the $_ variable.
index(*string, substring, offset*)	The index function returns the position of a substring in the string, starting at offset. If an offset is not specified, it searches for the substring at the beginning of the string. This function returns -1 if the substring is not found.
length(*expression*)	The length function returns the length of the expression in characters.
rindex(*string, substring, offset*)	The rindex function returns the position of the last substring at or before an offset. If no offset is specified, it starts at the end of the string. This function returns -1 if the substring is not found.
substr(*string, offset, length*)	The substr function extracts a string of *length* characters starting at the offset in the original string. If no length is specified, substr returns the characters to the end of the string.
split(*pattern, expression, limit*)	The split function separates an expression at the occurrences of the pattern into an array of strings, and returns the array. Optionally, use the limit parameter to limit the number of array elements returned. If the expression is omitted, split the $_ special variable. If all parameters are omitted, split the $_ special variable on white space.
join(*expression, list*)	The join function joins a list into a single string, separated by the value of the expression. It returns the string.
pop(*@array*)	The pop function removes and returns the last value of the array, and decreases the length of the array by one.

Table 22.4: Perl Functions, *continued*

Function	Description
push(*@array, list*)	The push function adds the values of the list onto the end of the array, and increases the length of the array by the length of the list.
shift(*@array*)	The shift function removes and returns the first value of the array, and decreases the length of the array by one. If an array is not specified, shift works on @ARGV.
unshift(*@array, list*)	The unshift function adds the values of list to the beginning of the array. The unshift function increases the length of the array by the length of the list.
keys(*%array*)	The keys function returns a normal array containing all of the keys (indexes) of the associative array.
values(*%array*)	The values function returns a normal array containing all of the values of the associative array.
defined	The defined function returns true if the variable passed as an argument has already been defined.
sub *functionname* { *code;* }	The sub function defines a subroutine with the specified function name.
undef	The undef function removes a variable definition.
local	The local function declares variables locally to the enclosing code block.

Use flags to modify the match and substitution functions:

- The *m* flag enables a multiline match. In a multiline match, the newline character is not a special character. Match it with the \n character.

- The *g* flag matches as many times as possible (globally).

- The *i* flag matches in a case-insensitive fashion.

- The *o* flag expands variables only once.

In addition to the flags supported by the match function, the substitution function accepts an additional flag, *e*, to interpret the replacement string as an expression.

You can also use flags to modify the translation function:

- The *c* flag complements the search list.

- The *d* flag deletes all characters not found in the search list.

- The *s* flag "squeezes" all sequences of characters in the search list, replacing them with the single target character.

Regular Expressions

The perl language supports an extensive regular-expression language for specifying patterns. All characters match themselves except for the special characters explained in Table 22.5. Group a series of expressions into a single expression.

Table 22.5: Special Characters in Regular Expressions

Character	Description
. (dot)	Match any single character, but not a newline character.
+	Match the preceding element one or more times.
?	Match the preceding element zero or one times.
*	Match the preceding element zero or more times.
{N, M}	Match the preceding element a minimum of *N* times, and a maximum of *M* times. Use {N} to match exactly *N* times. Use {N,} to match at least *N* times.
[...]	Use the bracket grouping to match any of a group of characters. Use a group of [^...] to negate the match.
(...|...|...)	The | operator is an OR operator. Match one of the individual expressions.
\w	Match a single alphanumeric.
\W	Match a single non-alphanumeric.
\b	Match a single word boundary.
\B	Match a single non-word boundary.

469

Table 22.5: Special Characters in Regular Expressions, *continued*

Character	Description
\s	Match a single whitespace character.
\S	Match a single non-whitespace character.
\d	Match a numeric character.
\D	Match a nonnumeric character.
\n \r \f \t	Match the newline, carriage-return, formfeed, or tab characters, respectively.
\1, \2, \3, etc.	Match a previously matched subexpression group. The \1 represents the group starting with the first left parenthesis, \2 the group starting with the second left parenthesis, etc. These are similar to the special variables $1, $2, $3... described in Table 22.2.

PERL EXAMPLES

The first examples in this section are constructed simply, while subsequent examples use more complex constructs. Examples for phone-number lookup, PTF status, and database access are repeated in C, Java, and perl, for comparison purposes. The data for all of the exercises is the goodoleboys.txt file, which was shown in the previous chapter, in Figure 21.1.

Figure 22.3 demonstrates how to use a command in the perl language on the command line, with the *e* option. The match operator implicitly matches the current input line. The *n* option implicitly loops the script around all standard input.

```
perl -wne 'if (m/444/) { print "$_"; } ' < goodoleboys.txt
Chuck      Dec 25   444-2345 Blue      Mary Sue    12   $2.50
Bubba      Oct 13   444-1111 Buck      Mary Jean   12
Billy Bob June 11   444-4340 Leotis    Lisa Sue    12
Otis       Sept 17  444-8000 Ol' Sal   Sally       12   $5
Roscoe     Feb  2   444-2234 Rover     Alice Jean  410
Arlis      June 19  444-1314 Redeye    Suzy Beth   12   $10.75
```

Figure 22.3: This example searches for the string 444 in the input. Use the -e option to write perl program code on the command line. The -n option loops the program over all lines in the input.

470

Where Figure 22.3 uses the *-n* operator, Figure 22.4 uses the <> operator. This example explicitly iterates through all lines of standard input. The <> operator sets the $_ variable to the input line, and returns true if there are still lines remaining in the input. The *chomp* function removes the newline from the input stream, requiring you to add it again if you print the $_ variable.

```
cat showLocalBoys.pl
#!/usr/bin/perl -w
while (<>) {
    chomp;
    if (m/444-/) {
        print "line $.:   $_\n";
    }
}
showLocalBoys.pl < goodoleboys.txt
line 3:   Chuck     Dec 25   444-2345 Blue     Mary Sue    12  $2.50
line 4:   Bubba     Oct 13   444-1111 Buck     Mary Jean   12
line 5:   Billy Bob June 11  444-4340 Leotis   Lisa Sue    12
line 7:   Otis      Sept 17  444-8000 Ol' Sal  Sally       12  $5
line 9:   Roscoe    Feb 2    444-2234 Rover    Alice Jean  410
line 10:  Arlis     June 19  444-1314 Redeye   Suzy Beth   12  $10.75
```

Figure 22.4: Use Qshell to run this perl script, which shows all records in the input file that match a local dialing prefix.

In Figure 22.5, the *match* function tells perl to search for strings that have the format of a telephone number. For a more explicit match, the match expression includes word boundaries (\b) around the telephone number. The match specifically matches three occurrences of the *4* character, a dash, and four occurrences of any numeric character (\d).

Enclosing the entire phone number inside parentheses creates a sub-expression. The special variable $1 holds the value of the first sub-expression after a match. If the *match* function returns true, the substr() function removes the first 10 characters and assigns them to the name variable. The script then prints out the name of the phone number's owner and uses the special $1 variable to print out the number.

In Figure 22.6, telephone numbers that end in 2300 through 9999 in local exchange 444 are updated to be part of a new local exchange, 445.

```
cat showLocalBoyDialList.pl
#!/usr/bin/perl -nw
chomp;
if (m/\b(4{3}-\d{4})\b/) {
    $name = substr($_, 0, 10);
    $phone = $1;
    print "$name\t$phone\n";
}
showLocalBoyDialList.pl goodoleboys.txt
Chuck          444-2345
Bubba          444-1111
Billy Bob       444-4340
Otis           444-8000
Roscoe         444-2234
Arlis          444-1314
```

Figure 22.5: This perl example uses a complex regular expression to match a phone-number format. It uses the $1 variable to retrieve the previously matched sub-expression group from the match function.

```
cat newLocalPrefix.pl
#!/usr/bin/perl -nwei.backup
chomp;
if (m/\b(4{3}-(\d{4}))\b/) {
    $last4phone = $2;
    if ($2 >= 2300) {
        s/\b(4{3}-(\d{4}))\b/445-$last4phone/;
        print STDERR "Updating 444-$last4phone\n";
    }
}
print "$_\n";
newLocalPrefix.pl goodoleboys.txt
Updating 444-2345
Updating 444-4340
Updating 444-8000
ls good*
goodoleboys.txt          goodoleboys.txt.backup
cat goodoleboys.txt
```

Name	Born	Phone	Dog	Wife	Shotgun	Paid
=========	========	========	========	=========	=======	=====
Chuck	Dec 25	445-2345	Blue	Mary Sue	12	$2.50
Bubba	Oct 13	444-1111	Buck	Mary Jean	12	
Billy Bob	June 11	445-4340	Leotis	Lisa Sue	12	
Amos	Jan 4	333-1119	Amos	Abigail	20	
Otis	Sept 17	445-8000	Ol' Sal	Sally	12	$5
Claude	May 31	333-4340	Blue	Etheline	12	
Roscoe	Feb 2	444-2234	Rover	Alice Jean	410	
Arlis	June 19	444-1314	Redeye	Suzy Beth	12	$10.75
Junior	April 30	BR-549	Percival	Lilly Faye	12	
Bill	Feb 29	333-4444	Daisy	Daisy	20	
Ernest T.	??	none	none	none	none	

Figure 22.6: This perl script updates a phone list using the -i option to perform an in-place edit with a backup.

Always use a backup file extension with the *i* parameter. It is very easy to make mistakes, and if you tell it to, perl with gladly throw away your original data and leave you with the corrupted data remnants resulting from a buggy script. The *i* parameter is used to update the input files in place. Backup files are created with a .backup extension. Perl uses all text output to the stdout file handle as replacement for the lines in the original file. Text output to the stderr file handle is not assumed to be part of the edited file.

This example demonstrates the ability to interchange strings and numeric values. The special variable $2 receives the four final digits of the telephone number. That value is used in a numeric comparison with 2300. If the value is greater than or equal to 2300, the substitution function changes the exchange to 445. The script prints a status message to stderr.

Building on the previous examples, Figure 22.7 uses the data file from Figure 22.6 to demonstrate a functioning, interactive phone-number lookup application. The application uses two associative arrays to provide lookup services based on the data file. Compare and contrast this perl application to the similar Java example in Figure 23.6 and C example in Figure 24.5. From a perl perspective, the associative array provides exactly the right functionality for a lookup program of this type. The robust and flexible regular expressions that perl provides are only used slightly in this example because the data file is composed of fixed-length fields. If the fields were delimited or needed some additional processing, the regular expression capabilities would make perl a much more attractive solution for this program.

When developing perl programs that interact with Qshell, you can use Qshell utilities to perform tasks while processing input or output for the utilities with perl. Interacting with Qshell commands in this fashion lets you reuse the broad set of utilities for their functions.

```
cat phoneList.pl
#!/usr/bin/perl -w
if ($#ARGV < 0 || $ARGV[0] eq '-h') {
    print "Usage:  phoneList [-h] <data-file>...\n";
    exit(1);
}
# An associative array that allows lookup of the phone number
# by the good ole boy's name
%numberByOleBoy = ();
# An associative array that allows lookup of the good ole boy
# by his wife's name.
%oleBoyByWife = ();
# Read input from all the data files passed on the command line
while (<ARGV>) {
    chomp;
    if ($. == 1 || $. == 2) {
      # The first 2 lines of each data file represent
      # header lines.
      next;      # Go to the next input line.
     }
    # For each field:
    # - Take the characters from the correct column for the field
    #   into a variable.
    # - Remove any trailing spaces at the end of the variable
    $oleboy = substr($_, 0, 10);
    $oleboy =~ s/\s+$//g;

    $oleboyswife = substr($_, 37, 10);
    $oleboyswife =~ s/\s+//g;

    $phonenumber = substr($_, 19, 8);
    $phonenumber =~ s/\s+//g;

    # Build an associative array so that we can lookup phone
    # number based on the ole boy's name.
    $numberByOleBoy{$oleboy} = $phonenumber;
    # Build an associative array so that we can lookup the
    # ole boy's name based on the wife's name.
    if ($oleboyswife ne "none") {
  $oleBoyByWife{$oleboyswife} = $oleboy;
     }
 }
# Set the output to be unbuffered.
$| = 1;
# Get the user's input.
```

Figure 22.7: This example shows a functioning, interactive phone-number lookup interface (part 1 of 2).

```perl
print "Enter 'exit' or a name to lookup:\n";
while (<>) {
   chomp;
   if ($_ eq "exit" || $_ eq "quit") {
      last;
    }
   # Is the name a good ole boy?
   if (defined $numberByOleBoy{$_}) {
     # Yes, print out the number.
     print "Found good ole boy's number at $numberByOleBoy{$_}\n";
    }
   # Otherwise, is the name a good ole boy's wife?
   elsif (defined $oleBoyByWife{$_}) {
# Yes, print out the number.
print "Found good ole boy's number using his wife at
   $numberByOleBoy{$oleBoyByWife{$_}}\n";
    }
   else {
   print "Didn't find number (the lookup is case sensitive)\n";
    }
   print "Enter 'exit' or a name to lookup:\n";
}
phoneList.pl goodoleboys.txt
Enter 'exit' or a name to lookup:
Bill
Found good ole boy's number at 333-4444
Enter 'exit' or a name to lookup:
Daisy
Found good ole boy's number using his wife at 333-4444
Enter 'exit' or a name to lookup:
Claude
Found good ole boy's number at 333-4340
Enter 'exit' or a name to lookup:
Etheline
Found good ole boy's number using his wife at 333-4340
Enter 'exit' or a name to lookup:
Fred
Didn't find number (the lookup is case sensitive)
Enter 'exit' or a name to lookup:
exit
```

Figure 22.7: This example shows a functioning, interactive phone-number lookup interface (part 2 of 2).

Figure 22.8 shows a simple version of running Qshell commands and processing their output from perl. Since perl is a PASE utility, the PASE qsh utility is used to execute a Qshell command.

```
cat qshellFromPerl.pl
#!/usr/bin/perl -w
if ($#ARGV != 0 || $ARGV[0] eq "-h") {
    print "Usage:  qshellFromPerl [-h] <QshellCommand>\n";
    print "  Run a qshell command using PASE perl utility\n";
    exit(1);
}

# Create a file handle connected to the output
# of a Qshell process
# A first character of "|" would be used to create
# a file handle that could be written to, in order
# to send input to the created process.
open(QSH, "qsh -c \"$ARGV[0]\" |")
    || die "Couldn't open the Qshell command";

while (<QSH>) {
    chomp;
    print "QSHOUT: $_\n";
}
exit(0);
qshellFromPerl.pl "ls -S"
QSHOUT: 819 lookupExample.pl
QSHOUT: 819 newLocalPrefix.pl
QSHOUT: 819 phoneList.pl
QSHOUT: 819 phoneListDB.pl
QSHOUT: 819 ptfStatus.pl
QSHOUT: 819 qshellFromPerl.pl
QSHOUT: 819 showLocalBoyDialList.pl
QSHOUT: 819 showLocalBoys.pl
```

Figure 22.8: Use the perl utility to process the output from any Qshell utility. Process the output in whichever way is appropriate.

Building on the ability to invoke a Qshell command, Figure 22.9 uses the Qshell *system* utility to interact directly with a CL command. Invoking the *system* utility like this is a shortcut to processing that may use a temporary file to hold the output from a Qshell or CL command or utility.

When running CL commands, the *system* utility processes temporary spooled files and job-log data created by the command.

In the case of a native Qshell command, no temporary file is created. The APIs read or write directly to the running application via an interprocess communication mechanism called a *pipe*. As the program runs, it runs at the same time as the started application, reading data from or writing it to the pipe. The pipe buffers the data as appropriate, but there is never a single complete copy of all of the data.

Compare and contrast the perl code in Figure 22.9 to the Java example in Figure 23.8 and the C example in Figure 24.7. The advanced functions available with perl regular expressions start to become more important in this example, enabling us to easily pick out the PTF number from the data stream that is produced by the Qshell command. Very little programming is needed to start and process the output from a Qshell utility; it almost happens naturally.

```
cat ptfStatus.pl
#!/usr/bin/perl -w
if ($#ARGV < 0 || $ARGV[0] eq "-h") {
    print "Usage:  ptfStatus [-h] <ptf>\n";
    print "  Query the status of a list of PTFs\n";
    exit(1);
}

$debug = 0;
# Create a file handle connected to the output
# of a process running the system command to process
# the CL command DSPPTF.
open(DSPPTF, 'system "DSPPTF OUTPUT(*PRINT)" |')
    || die "Couldn't open DSPPTF command";

while (<DSPPTF>) {
    chomp;
    # PTF list in the output is a 7 character name,
    #      2 alpha, 5 digits         or
    #      3 alpha, 4 digits
    # prefixed by one space on each line.
    print "<$_>\n" if $debug;
    if (m/^\s((\D{2}\d{5})|(\D{3}\d{4}))\s/) {
        # Use the PTF that we just matched in the parenthesis
        $ptf = "$1";
        # Grab the PTF status from the line.
        $status = substr($_, 13, 19);
        # Remove trailing whitespace from status.
        $status =~ s/\s*$//g;
        $ptfList{$ptf} = $status;
        print "OUT:$ptf    $status\n" if $debug;
    }
```

Figure 22.9: This perl example uses the system utility to run a CL command, and then processes the output (part 1 of 2).

```
}

print "-------\t--------------------\n";
print " PTF  \t       Status      \n";
print "-------\t--------------------\n";
for ($i=0; $i<=$#ARGV; $i++) {
    $ptf = $ARGV[$i];
    if (defined $ptfList{$ptf}) {
        print "$ptf\t$ptfList{$ptf}\n";
    }
    else {
        print "$ptf\tNot Loaded\n";
    }
}
exit(0);
ptfStatus.pl SI06971 SI06972 SI06973 SI06974 SI06975 SI06976 SI06977
-------  --------------------
 PTF         Status
-------  --------------------
SI06971 Temporarily applied
SI06972 Superseded
SI06973 Not Loaded
SI06974 Not Loaded
SI06975 Temporarily applied
SI06976 Temporarily applied
SI06977 Superseded
```

Figure 22.9: This perl example uses the system utility to run a CL command, and then processes the output (part 2 of 2).

Since perl is a PASE application, the PASE system utility is executed in this example, not the Qshell system utility. The PASE and Qshell system utilities both work similarly. Use the PASE utility qsh to execute a Qshell utility from within perl (or other PASE applications). The output from the CL command is processed into an associative array. The associative array serves as the lookup mechanism for a list of randomly selected PTFs (Program Temporary Fixes).

The perl language provides a standard way to access a database using the perl DBI module. Provided with the perl implementation on iSeries is the DB2 implementation of perl database (DBI) access. Figure 22.10 demonstrates a more realistic phone-number lookup application than the example shown in Figure 22.7. The names and phone numbers reside in the relational database on the iSeries. Compare and contrast this perl database example to the Java example in Figure 23.8 and the C example in Figure 24.8.

Using the perl || operator along with the *die* or *warn* function lets a concise error-handling model take shape in this program. The database functions used by this program are designed to be similar to the Java and C models, which helps developers who program in multiple languages. The strength of automatic memory-management and automatic conversion of data types shows here. The program doesn't need to concern itself about the size or type of data parameters, or with allocating storage for them.

```
cat phoneListDB.pl
#!/usr/bin/perl -w
use DBI;
use DBD::DB2;
use DBD::DB2::Constants;

if (defined $ARGV[0]) {
    print "Usage:  phoneList [-h]\n";
    exit(1);
}

# Create the database connection and the statement to use.
$hdbc = DBI->connect("dbi:DB2:*LOCAL") || die "Couldn't connect";
$ps = $hdbc->prepare("SELECT PHONENUMBER FROM QSHELLDATA.CUTOMERS " .
                    "WHERE NAME = ? OR WIFE = ?") || die "Couldn't
                        prepare, err=$hdbc->err";

# Set the output to be unbuffered.
$| = 1;
# Get the user's input.
print "Enter 'exit' or a name to lookup:\n";
while (<>) {
    chomp;
    if ($_ eq "exit" || $_ eq "quit") {
        last;
    }

    # Set the input parameters
    $ps->bind_param(1, $_);
    $ps->bind_param(2, $_);
    $ps->execute() || warn "Couldn't execute, err=$hdbc->err";
    # retrieve the first row
    @row = $ps->fetchrow;
```

Figure 22.10: Use perl to access the iSeries database. The additional modules for database access are provided with the implementation of perl. This example does the phone-number lookup demonstrated in Figure 22.7, but uses the database for input, instead of a text file (part 1 of 2).

```
        if (!defined $row[0]) {
            print STDERR "Didn't find customer: $_\n";
        }
        else {
            print STDOUT "Found $_ at $row[0]\n";
        }
        $ps->finish();
        print "Enter 'exit' or a name to lookup:\n";
}
$hdbc->disconnect();
exit(0);
phoneListDB.pl
Enter 'exit' or a name to lookup:
Bill
Found Bill at 333-4444
Enter 'exit' or a name to lookup:
Daisy
Found Daisy at 333-4444
Enter 'exit' or a name to lookup:
Claude
Found Claude at 333-4340
Enter 'exit' or a name to lookup:
Etheline
Found Etheline at 333-4340
Enter 'exit' or a name to lookup:
Fred
Didn't find customer: Fred
Enter 'exit' or a name to lookup:
exit
```

Figure 22.10: Use perl to access the iSeries database. The additional modules for database access are provided with the implementation of perl. This example does the phone-number lookup demonstrated in Figure 22.7, but uses the database for input, instead of a text file (part 2 of 2).

SUMMARY

The perl language provides a powerful text-processing environment. You can use perl to access Qshell and iSeries services, creating simple yet powerful scripts or applications.

Chapter 23

Java Development Tools

In addition to the substantial integration with Qshell that the Java runtime provides, application development can be done in Java directly from a Qshell environment.

Three Java command-line utilities stand out above all the others in terms of importance: the *java* utility, the *javac* utility, and the *jar* utility.

THE JAVA UTILITY

Java developers on iSeries can provide Java applications with CL command interfaces, Qshell command interfaces, or other server-side, command-line user interfaces. Java applications range from simple stand-alone applications to large and complex applications that run within a Java server environment like Websphere Application Server.

You use the *java* utility to run stand-alone Java applications. The utility creates a Java runtime environment (including the Qshell terminal), loads a Java application, and runs it.

Here are two versions of the *java* syntax that start the execution of a Java class:

```
java [options] class-name [parameters]...
java -jar [options] jar-file-name [parameters] file...
```

Java Options

Depending on the version of the java command that you use, different option parameters are available. Table 23.1 shows the more commonly used options.

Table 23.1: Java Options

Option	Description
-classpath *<path>*	Specifically set the CLASSPATH environment variable of the Java runtime environment created. The value of this parameter overrides the current setting of CLASSPATH.
-cp *<path>*	The -cp parameter is short notation for -classpath.
-D*<property=value>*	Set the value of the Java system property named *property* to *value*. A Java system property is a global parameter available to all Java application code in the new Java runtime environment.
-verbose	Log information that explains when and from where each class is loaded.
-verbosegc	Cause the garbage collector to output messages for each garbage collection.
-opt	Change the optimization level.

Running Java

To run the java utility, the Java executable code (classes) and the CLASSPATH environment variable need to be set up correctly. Setting CLASSPATH correctly requires an understanding of some of the fundamentals of Java application-development and packaging. You must know the packaging of the applications and third-party libraries you are using. A frequent problem when doing Java development involves difficulties with setting the CLASSPATH variable (or parameter) correctly.

Java Files

A Java *class* defines one of the most basic units of application development in a Java program. Most commonly, a single Java compilation unit (an ASCII .java file) defines a single java class. After compilation, the class is contained within a .class file. The .class file is the binary representation of the Java class consisting of Java byte-code instructions. The class file is binary, and is compatible with existing Java implementations on any platform.

The Java language also supports units of application development other than the class, and allows more than one of these structures in a single file. For further reading, study Java interfaces, abstract classes, inner classes, and private or protected classes. A good place to start might be the book *Thinking in Java* by Bruce Eckel. The electronic form of this book is available for free at www.bruceeckel.com. Another alternative might be a book *The Java Tutorial* by Mary Campione, also available for free, at www.thejavatutorial.com.

As a beginner, put one Java class in each ASCII .java file. Create Java applications using one or more of those java classes. The classes might or might not access third-party library code. Each class definition includes a statement describing the package that contains the class.

Java Packages

The Java package name serves multiple purposes. The package fully qualifies a class name, allowing it to be uniquely distinguished from other classes. The package also identifies and groups one or more Java classes. Java classes inside a package have privileged access to some of the internals of other Java classes in the same package. The package also describes the physical packaging structure of the Java class.

Use a package and put your .java files and the resulting .class files in a directory structure matching the package name. When you refer to the package or the fully qualified class name, use the Java notation for the package name, with dots separating the elements. When you refer to the file or directory name, use Qshell notation for the package name, with slashes separating the elements.

You can deliver Java applications and classes as stand-alone files, or as part of a jar or zip file. (Jar files are created with the jar utility, discussed later in this chapter.) The classes in the jar or zip file must be contained within a directory entry in the archive file that matches the package name.

Java class files and archive files are binary files, so you cannot modify them with an editor. Similarly, you cannot successfully upload or download them with an ASCII-mode file transfer (in FTP, for example).

Java System Properties

Use the *-D* option to set Java system properties that control the behavior of the Java runtime environment. Each Java application usually has a unique set of Java system properties that it uses to control its behavior.

The iSeries JVM (Java Virtual Machine) uses Java system properties to affect its internal behavior. Table 23.2 describes some of the more commonly used system properties.

Table 23.2: Java System Properties

Properties	Description
-Djava.version=1.2	Set the version of the Java runtime environment to 1.2. The valid values of this property depend on which JDK versions are currently installed on the iSeries.
-Dos400.stdin=*value*	Assign stdin to a specific file or TCP/IP connection. For example, *use file:/path/file.txt, port:<hostname>:21,* or *port:<ipaddress>:21* to write data to file.txt or an Internet host at port 21.

Table 23.2: Java System Properties, *continued*

Properties	Description
-Dos400.stdout=*value*	Assign stderr to a specific file or TCP/IP connection. For example, *use file:/path/file.txt, port:<hostname>:21,* or *port:<ipaddress>:21* to write data to file.txt or an Internet host at port 21.
-Dos400.stderr=*value*	Assign stdout to a specific file or TCP/IP connection. For example, *use file:/path/file.txt, port:<hostname>:21,* or *port:<ipaddress>:21* to write data to file.txt or an Internet host at port 21.
-Dos400. stdio.convert=*value*	Use this property to modify the data conversion that is performed on the stdin, stdout, and stderr file streams. The default value is *N*, no conversion. Other valid values are as follows: ■ Y-All standard I/O data is converted to/from the job CCSID. ■ 1—Stdin data is converted. ■ 2—Stdout data is converted. ■ 3—Stdin and stdout data is converted. ■ 4—Stderr data is converted. ■ 5—Stdin and stderr data is converted. ■ 6—stdout and stderr data is converted. ■ 7—All standard I/O data is converted.
-Dos400. runtime.exec=*value*	Use this property to modify the behavior of Runtime.exec(). **Note:** The behavior of Runtime.exec() changed between iSeries Java versions 1.2 and 1.3. Set this property to a value of EXEC to get the version 1.3 behavior, which executes a program or utility directly. Use a value of QSHELL to get the old behavior (1.2 and prior), which allows Runtime.exec() to execute a Qshell command.

THE JAVAC UTILITY

The *javac* utility compiles Java source code contained in an ASCII file into a Java executable, composed of binary class files. The resulting binary class files can be used on any Java platform; transfer them in binary mode to the target system.

When the *javac* command compiles source files, it uses the current CLASSPATH setting to find classes that the source files are *dependent* on. The *javac* utility provides a limited dependency-checking capability to assist in building Java projects. If javac finds source files for *dependent* classes before it finds the class files, it compiles the source files to get the *dependent* classes. Similarly, if *javac* finds both the source files and the class files for the *dependent* classes, but the class files are older than the source files, the source files for the *dependent* classes are recompiled.

The syntax of the *javac* command to compile Java source code is as follows:

```
javac [options] <java-source-files>...
```

Depending on the version of the *javac* command that you use, different option parameters are available. Table 23.3 shows the more commonly used javac options.

Table 23.3: Javac Options

Option	Description
-classpath <path>	Specifically set the CLASSPATH environment variable of the Java runtime environment created. The value of this parameter over-rides the current setting of CLASSPATH.
-O	Enable optimization.
-g	Enable debugging of the resulting class files.
-verbose	Use the -verbose option to log information about various compilation steps and when and from where each class is loaded.
-deprecation	Output detailed messages about deprecated APIs. Java marks an API as deprecated when a more appropriate API has replaced the original one. Try to avoid using deprecated APIs.
-d <directory>	Output the class files to a directory other than the directory in which the source files are located. Directories that match the packages defined in the Java classes are created as required.
-encoding	Specify the character encoding used by the Java source files.

THE JAVADOC UTILITY

The *javadoc* utility provides a standard mechanism by which a Java developer can provide API documentation for the classes that they develop. Delivering documentation is a critical step in developing classes and APIs in a team, department, or corporate environment. Other developers need to be able to understand the services provided.

In a hectic development environment, it is very easy for documentation and APIs to become hopelessly out of date in relation to each other. The Java language addresses this problem by combining source code and documentation in a simple and standard way. It defines the syntax of the source-code comments, and the tags used in those comments, to define detailed descriptions of the code.

The *javadoc* utility parses Java source code similar to the javac compiler. Instead of generating binary code from the source statements, however, the *javadoc* utility focuses on the Java comments. It looks at packages, class declarations, and method declarations, and is very tolerant of Java source code that does not compile.

The *javadoc* utility uses the comments and tags to generate HTML documentation describing the APIs. If run against a group of Java source files, the HTML documentation automatically generates a table of contents and an index. The group of files and the classes and methods contained within are automatically cross-referenced in a way that enables even the simplest documentation to become fairly professional and useful. However, the *javadoc* utility supports a varied and robust set of tags (in addition to HTML tags and links), so that a developer can generate as detailed and feature-rich a set of documentation as desired.

You can generate useful *javadoc* documentation without using any of the special *javadoc* tags that are inserted into those comments. Simply use the *javadoc* comment immediately preceding each class, variable, and method that you declare. Regular multiline Java comment start with /* and end with */. A *javadoc* comment starts with /** and ends with */.

The *javadoc* utility will even generate documentation for Java source with no comments. The generated documentation will still have the class, interface, method names, and types. The documentation will also have an index and cross-references generated in a very useful fashion.

Running the Javadoc Utility

The *javadoc* utility is a bit more flexible in the type of parameters it accepts than other Java utilities. *Javadoc* accepts Java package names, source file names, individual Java class names, or text files that contain lists of option parameters or Java package names.

Here is the syntax of the *javadoc* command to generate documentation from Java source code:

```
javadoc [options] [packages] [sourcefiles] [classnames] [@files]
```

Javadoc Options

Table 23.4 describes some of the basic *javadoc* options.

Table 23.4: Javadoc Options

Option	Description
-help	Show help for options and parameters.
-sourcepath <path>	Find the java source files associated with a list of classes or packages passed on the command line.
-classpath <path>	Set the CLASSPATH of the javadoc environment created. Individual CLASSPATH entries are separated by colons. The CLASSPATH is used to assist in the lookup of Java source files for those classes and packages specified on the command line.
-d <directory>	Output the HTML files to a specific directory. Many HTML files and subdirectories, matching packages defined in the Java classes, are created as required.

Table 23.4: Javadoc Options, *continued*

Option	Description
-windowtitle *"title"*	Set the title that will be used in the HTML browser when browsing the documentation.
-public	Show only the public classes and methods in the generated documentation. Use this option for generating external documentation
-protected	Show protected and public classes and methods in the gener- ated documentation. This is the default. Use it for generating external documentation.
-private	Show all classes and methods regardless of the access specification. Use this to generate internal documentation.
-stylesheetfile *<file>*	Use this option to specify your own style sheet for customization of the javadoc style.
-version	Include @*version* tags in the documentation.
-author	Include @*author* tags in the documentation.

Javadoc Tags

Table 23.5 describes some of the more commonly used *javadoc* documentation tags.

Table 23.5: Javadoc Documentation Tags

Tag	Description
@author *<text>*	Use this tag to copy all subsequent text to the docu- mentation. Commas separate contents from multiple author tags.
@deprecated *<text>*	Use this tag to indicate that the class or method is old and should no longer be used. The first sentence is copied to the summary section of the documentation. Subsequent sentences/lines can describe more details.

Table 23.5: Javadoc Documentation Tags, *continued*

Tag	Description
@exception *classname* *text*	The same as the @*throws* tag.
@param *name text*	Add a parameter and its description to the "parameters" section of the documentation. The text description describes the parameter, and can be multiple lines.
@return *text*	Describe the return value of the method. The text description can be multiple lines.
@see *target*	Create a reference to another piece of documentation. Among other values, specify target as a package, class, interface, field or method, followed by optional text that you want to display for the link. The target doesn't need to be fully qualified if its referenced in the code, but you can fully qualify it as in the following: *package.Class#method(Class,Class,...)*
@throws *classname text*	The same as the @*exception* tag. Generate a "throws" subheading to the documentation and a reference to the class name. The text should describe the error condition as appropriate, and it may be multiple lines.
@version *text*	Adds a "version" subheading to the generated documentation.

A Javadoc Example

Figure 23.1 illustrates the *javadoc* utility. The documentation is output to the "doc" directory, and is then archived into a single file using the *jar* utility. The archive can be moved to a workstation or distributed as appropriate.

The doc.jar file from Figure 23.1 is transferred to a client workstation and extracted. Figure 23.2 shows what the documentation looks like when a browser displays the doc/index.html file. Because the set of classes used in Figure 23.1 only defines one package, there is a table of contents for the individual classes, but not for the packages.

```
cat com/mcpress/qshell/JavaDocExample.java
package com.mcpress.qshell;

/**
 * This class represents a simple example for
 * using javadoc comments. The first line of
 * every javadoc comment is a summary of the class
 * or method, while the subsequent lines of the
 * comments are used for the detailed description
 * that the javadoc utility generates.
 *
 * @author Joe Smith
 * @version 1.0
 */
public class JavaDocExample {
    /**
     * The internally maintained application name
     */
    private String  name = null;
    /**
     * The name of the database table used to lookup
     * the customer
     */
    private String  customerDatabase = null;
    /**
     * The getApplicationName() method returns the name
     * of the application. The name of the application
     * is generated randomly based on the time of
     * day.
     *
     * @return String representing the application name
     * @see com.mcpress.qshell.JavaDocExample#getName
     * @deprecated
     */
    public String getApplicationName() {
        return null;
    }
    /**
     * The getName() method returns the true name of
     * the application. The name of the application is
     * the full name of the class containing the main
     * method.
     *
     * @return String representing the application name
     * @since 1.1
     */
    public String getName() {
```

Figure 23.1: This example demonstrates using the javadoc command on a group of classes (part 1 of 3).

491

```
        return null;
    }
    /**
     * The lookupCustomer() method looks up a customer
     * based on customer ID. The customer ID is the ID
     * that we print on all invoices and use in database
     * tables to uniquely identify a customer.
     *
     * @param number Unique customer ID
     *
     * @return The customer name or null if the
     * customer wasn't found
     */
    public String lookupCustomer(int number) {
    }
}
mkdir doc
ls com/mcpress/qshell/*.java
com/mcpress/qshell/Args.java
com/mcpress/qshell/CustomerDBLookup.java
com/mcpress/qshell/CustomerList.java
com/mcpress/qshell/CustomerLookup.java
com/mcpress/qshell/HelloJava.java
com/mcpress/qshell/JavaDocExample.java
com/mcpress/qshell/LineCounter.java
com/mcpress/qshell/PtfStatus.java
com/mcpress/qshell/Reverse.java
javadoc -d doc -private -windowtitle "Qshell javadoc example"
    com/mcpress/qshell/*.java
Loading source file com/mcpress/qshell/Args.java...
Loading source file com/mcpress/qshell/CustomerDBLookup.java...
Loading source file com/mcpress/qshell/CustomerList.java...
Loading source file com/mcpress/qshell/CustomerLookup.java...
Loading source file com/mcpress/qshell/HelloJava.java...
Loading source file com/mcpress/qshell/JavaDocExample.java...
Loading source file com/mcpress/qshell/LineCounter.java...
Loading source file com/mcpress/qshell/PtfStatus.java...
Loading source file com/mcpress/qshell/Reverse.java...
Constructing Javadoc information...
Building tree for all the packages and classes...
Building index for all the packages and classes...
Generating doc/overview-tree.html...
Generating doc/index-all.html
Generating doc/deprecated-list.html...
Building index for all classes...
Generating doc/allclasses-frame.html...
Generating doc/index.html...
Generating doc/packages.html...
```

Figure 23.1: This example demonstrates using the javadoc command on a group of classes (part 2 of 3).

```
Generating doc/com/mcpress/qshell/Args.html...
Generating doc/com/mcpress/qshell/CustomerDBLookup.html...
Generating doc/com/mcpress/qshell/CustomerList.html...
Generating doc/com/mcpress/qshell/CustomerLookup.html...
Generating doc/com/mcpress/qshell/HelloJava.html...
Generating doc/com/mcpress/qshell/JavaDocExample.html...
Generating doc/com/mcpress/qshell/LineCounter.html...
Generating doc/com/mcpress/qshell/PtfStatus.html...
Generating doc/com/mcpress/qshell/Reverse.html...
Generating doc/serialized-form.html...
Generating doc/package-list...
Generating doc/help-doc.html...
Generating doc/stylesheet.css...
ls doc
allclasses-frame.html    index-all.html             packages.html
com                      index.html                 serialized-form.html
deprecated-list.html     overview-tree.html         stylesheet.css
help-doc.html            package-list
jar cf doc.jar doc
```

Figure 23.1: This example demonstrates using the javadoc command on a group of classes (part 3 of 3).

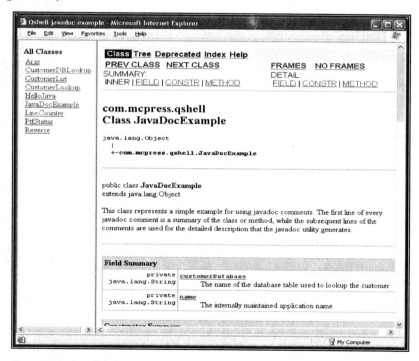

Figure 23.2: Javadoc documentation may be viewed with a Web browser.

493

THE JAR UTILITY

The *jar* utility provides support for creating and extracting Java archives. A Java archive is a zip-format file that typically contains java class files, although a jar file may contain any file type. The Java archive also contains additional information (meta-information), added by the *jar* utility to describe the contents of the archive file and attributes of the Java classes or applications in the file. Use a jar file as part of the CLASSPATH to allow the java runtime access to the classes or other resources in the jar file.

The syntax of the *jar* utility, shown below, is unique compared to other Qshell utilities:

```
jar <action-option>[options] <jar-file> <manifest-file> <-C
directory> <files-or-directories>...
```

Note that the option parameters must be grouped together, and they do not require leading dashes (except for the *-C* parameter). The *jar* utility accepts option parameters (*m* and *f*) that require file names, but those file names are not specified immediately following the parameter. The utility recursively processes any directories named on the command line.

Table 23.6 shows values for the action option. At least one of the values in Table 23.6 must be specified.

Table 23.6: Jar Action Options

Key Sequence	Description
c	Create the jar file specified as a new archive file.
t	List the contents of the jar file specified.
x	Extract the contents of the jar file specified.
u	Update the contents of an existing jar file.

Table 23.7 shows other options for the *jar* utility. If the *f* and *m* options are both used, specify the jar-file and manifest-file parameters in the same order as the options parameters.

Table 23.7: Additional Jar Options

Key Sequence	Description
v	Process the files verbosely, generating additional output for each file processed.
f	Specify the java archive file is specified. Always use the f parameter. If the m option is also specified, use the associated jar-file and manifest-file parameters in the same order as the f and m options.
m	Specify a manifest file. If the f option is also specified, use the associated jar-file and manifest-file parameters in the same order as the f and m options.
0 (zero)	Store the files in the Java archive without using zip compression.
M	Don't automatically create a manifest file at META-INF/MANIFEST.MF in the archive file.
i	Generate index information for the jar files specified.
-C *dir*	Change to the directory name specified before archiving the target file or directory names.

In Figure 23.3, the *jar* utility is used to zip the java source and class files. The output is produced due to inclusion of the *v* option.

Jar files are compatible with the WinZip and PKZip utilities, so you can also use *jar* as a convenient command-line zip/unzip utility to manipulate zip archives, if no other archive tool is present. Using the *M* option, as in Figure 23.4, ensures that no manifest files are added to the archives. Adding the *v* option to the *t* option generates a listing that contains information about the files' sizes and dates.

```
pwd
/home/jsmith/src
jar cvf sourceAndBinaries.jar com
added manifest
adding: com/(in = 0) (out= 0)(stored 0%)
adding: com/mcpress/(in = 0) (out= 0)(stored 0%)
adding: com/mcpress/qshell/(in = 0) (out= 0)(stored 0%)
adding: com/mcpress/qshell/CustomerList.class(in = 2091)
   (out= 1173)(deflated 43%)
adding: com/mcpress/qshell/CustomerList.java(in = 1710)
   (out= 587)(deflated 65%)
adding: com/mcpress/qshell/CustomerLookup.class(in = 2791)
   (out= 1557)(deflated 44%)
adding: com/mcpress/qshell/CustomerLookup.java(in = 3967)
   (out= 1214)(deflated 69%)
adding: com/mcpress/qshell/HelloJava.class(in = 599) (out= 367)
   (deflated 38%)
adding: com/mcpress/qshell/HelloJava.java(in = 197) (out= 144)
   (deflated 26%)
adding: com/mcpress/qshell/CustomerDBLookup.class(in = 2879)
   (out= 1671)(deflated 41%)
adding: com/mcpress/qshell/CustomerDBLookup.java(in = 4097)
   (out= 1350)(deflated 67%)
adding: com/mcpress/qshell/PtfStatus.class(in = 2401)
   (out= 1333)(deflated 44%)
adding: com/mcpress/qshell/PtfStatus.java(in = 3434) (out= 1062)
   (deflated 69%)
```

Figure 23.3: Use the jar utility from your base source-file directory to zip the java source and class files.

```
jar cfM classes.jar com/mcpress/qshell/*.class
jar tvf classes.jar
2879 Thu Jun 05 02:51:20 UTC 2003 com/mcpress/qshell/CustomerDBLookup.class
2091 Thu Jun 05 02:47:58 UTC 2003 com/mcpress/qshell/CustomerList.class
2791 Thu Jun 05 02:47:58 UTC 2003 com/mcpress/qshell/CustomerLookup.class
599  Thu Jun 05 02:47:58 UTC 2003 com/mcpress/qshell/HelloJava.class
2401 Fri Jun 06 05:36:52 UTC 2003 com/mcpress/qshell/PtfStatus.class
```

Figure 23.4: Use the jar utility to create and list the contents of an archive. The M option prevents a META-INF/MANIFEST.MF file from being created in the archive file.

JAVA EXAMPLES

Starting with a typical "Hello World" example and working up to more complex techniques, the code samples in this section show various ways that your Java application can interact with Qshell. The examples for phone-number lookup, PTF status, and database access are very similar to those coded in perl in chapter 22, and in C in chapter 24. These implementations of similar programs in three different languages provide you with a good basis for comparing perl, Java, and C.

The example in Figure 23.5 shows Java source code and an appropriate directory structure for Java application development. It demonstrates the *javac* utility and the java utility. The CLASSPATH environment variable is set to the base location of classes. The package name further qualifies the classes stored in that location by modifying both the full class name and the java/class file location. The Java application sets a Qshell exit status.

```
pwd
/home/jsmith/src
find /home/jsmith/src
/home/jsmith/src
/home/jsmith/src/com
/home/jsmith/src/com/mcpress
/home/jsmith/src/com/mcpress/qshell
/home/jsmith/src/com/mcpress/qshell/HelloJava.java
cat com/mcpress/qshell/HelloJava.java
package com.mcpress.qshell;

import java.lang.*;

class HelloJava {
    public static void main(String args[]) {
        System.out.println("Hello Java");
        System.exit(5);
    }
}

export CLASSPATH=/home/jsmith/src
javac com/mcpress/qshell/HelloJava.java
find /home/jsmith/src
/home/jsmith/src
/home/jsmith/src/com
/home/jsmith/src/com/mcpress
/home/jsmith/src/com/mcpress/qshell
```

Figure 23.5: This example shows Java source code and an appropriate directory structure for Java application development (part 1 of 2).

```
/home/jsmith/src/com/mcpress/qshell/HelloJava.class
/home/jsmith/src/com/mcpress/qshell/HelloJava.java
java com.mcpress.qshell.HelloJava
Hello Java
echo $?
5
unset CLASSPATH
java -classpath /home/jsmith/src com.mcpress.qshell.HelloJava
Hello Java
```

Figure 23.5: This example shows Java source code and an appropriate directory structure for Java application development (part 2 of 2).

Figure 23.6 demonstrates a customer list in Java. This example is used as a building block for the more complex examples that follow.

```
cat com/mcpress/qshell/CustomerList.java
package com.mcpress.qshell;

import java.util.Hashtable;

public class CustomerList {
    public final static String  NONE = "none";
    Hashtable        table;
    public CustomerList() {
        table = new Hashtable();
        table.put("Chuck",      "444-2345");
        table.put("Bubba",      "444-1111");
        table.put("Billy Bob",  "444-4340");
        table.put("Amos",       "333-1119");
        table.put("Otis",       "444-8000");
        table.put("Claude",     "333-4340");
        table.put("Roscoe",     "444-2234");
        table.put("Arlis",      "444-1314");
        table.put("Junior",     "BR-549");
        table.put("Bill",       "333-4444");
        table.put("Ernest T.",  NONE);
    }
    public String lookup (String name) {
        return (String)table.get(name);
    }
    public static void main(String args[]) {
```

Figure 23.6: This example demonstrates a simple command-line lookup utility. This application has the data written directly into the Java application. Expanding this example to read in the data would produce a more flexible application (part 1 of 2).

```
        if (args.length == 0) {
            System.err.println("Usage: java CustomerList
                [name-to-lookup]");
            System.exit(1);
        }
        CustomerList      list = new CustomerList();
        String            item;

        for (int i=0; i<args.length; ++i) {
            item = list.lookup(args[i]);
            if (item == null) {
                System.err.println("Didn't find customer:" +
                    args[i]);
            }
            else {
                if (item == NONE) {
                    System.err.println("No listing for" +
                        args[i]);
                }
                else {
                    System.out.println("Found" + args[i] +
                        "at" + item);
                }
            }
        } // end of for (i=0 < args.length)
        System.exit(0);
    } // end of main
}
export CLASSPATH=/home/jsmith/src
javac com/mcpress/qshell/CustomerList.java
java -cp /home/jsmith/src com.mcpress.qshell.CustomerList Chuck Bubba
Found Chuck at 444-2345
Found Bubba at 444-1111
```

Figure 23.6: This example demonstrates a simple command-line lookup utility. This application has the data written directly into the Java application. Expanding this example to read in the data would produce a more flexible application (part 2 of 2).

Using the goodoleboys.txt data file (from Figure 21.1), Figure 23.7 demonstrates a functioning, interactive phone-number lookup application. This application uses two Hashtable objects to provide lookup services based on the data file. Compare and contrast this code with the similar perl example in chapter 22 (Figure 22.7) and the C example in chapter 24 (Figure 24.5).

Several things in this example are worth noticing:

- Built-in string-manipulation functions that are used.

- The LineNumberReader object named *in* is an example of the tendency in Java to wrap one object in another object, and perhaps still another. Java developers frequently do this.

- In Java, the large standard class library almost always has just the right interface for the particular job.

- Although the Java example appears somewhat longer than the perl example, this is primarily due to the comments and structural aspects we used when writing it.

The programmer always needs to create a Java class, but this example is also different because we took a more object-oriented approach to the problem. We provided a CustomerLookup object that performed the work in a rather abstract way. The main routine simply creates a CustomerLookup object based on a file, and then uses the *lookup* method without concern for its internals.

That additional work can be viewed as pure overhead, or as good software design. In the case of this small example, it is probably more overhead. You can probably just as easily write a small program in perl or C as in Java. Because of its object-oriented nature, however, you might find it easier to write Java software that isolates its internal structures from other parts of the application.

```
pwd
/home/jsmith/src
cat com/mcpress/qshell/CustomerLookup.java
package com.mcpress.qshell;

import java.util.Hashtable;
import java.io.*;

public class CustomerLookup {
    public final static String          NONE = "none";

    // Two Hashtables mapping one object to another
```

Figure 23.7: This fully functioning Java example reads in data from a file and provides a lookup of a customer's phone number by the customer name or the name of his wife (part 1 of 4).

```
Hashtable       numberByOleBoy = new Hashtable();
Hashtable       oleBoyByWife = new Hashtable();

public CustomerLookup(String filename) throws IOException {
    // Use a LineNumberReader on top of a FileInputStream object.
    LineNumberReader in =
        new LineNumberReader(
        new InputStreamReader(
        new FileInputStream(filename)
        ));
    // Read each line and split into its components.
    String     line = in.readLine();
    while (line != null) {
        String  oleBoy = line.substring(0,10);
        oleBoy = oleBoy.trim();

        String  oleBoysWife = line.substring(37, 47);
        oleBoysWife = oleBoysWife.trim();

        String  phoneNumber = line.substring(19, 27);
        phoneNumber = phoneNumber.trim();
        if (phoneNumber.equals("none")) {
            phoneNumber = NONE;
        }

        numberByOleBoy.put(oleBoy, phoneNumber);
        oleBoyByWife.put(oleBoysWife, oleBoy);
        line = in.readLine();
    }
}
/**
 * Lookup a phone number based on the name of the customer or
 * his wife. Return CustomerLookup.NONE if the customer has no
 * phone, Return the phone number string if found. Return null
 * if not found.
 */
public String lookup(String name) {
    String  phoneNumber = (String)numberByOleBoy.get(name);
    if (phoneNumber == null) {
        String oleboy  = (String)oleBoyByWife.get(name);
        if (oleboy != null) {
            phoneNumber = (String)numberByOleBoy.get(oleboy);
        }
    }
    return phoneNumber;
```

Figure 23.7: This fully functioning Java example reads in data from a file and provides a lookup of a customer's phone number by the customer name or the name of his wife (part 2 of 4).

```
        }
        public static void main(String args[]) {
            if (args.length != 1) {
          System.err.println("Usage: java CustomerLookup data-file");
                System.exit(1);
            }
            try {
              CustomerLookup      list = new CustomerLookup(args[0]);
                 String                item;
                 String                name;

        // Get a 'nicer' interface over the System.in object
        // that represents standard input. We'll use LineNumberReader
        // just for fun.
        LineNumberReader     in =
            new LineNumberReader(new InputStreamReader(System.in));

        while (true) {
            System.out.println("Enter 'exit' or a name to lookup:");
            // Read the next name from standard input, any input
            // class (API) that could be constructed from System.in
            // could be used here.
            name = in.readLine();
            if (name == null) {
                // All done.
                break;
            }
            if (name.equals("exit") || name.equals("quit")) {
                break;
            }

            // Lookup the name
            item = list.lookup(name);
            if (item == null) {
                System.err.println("Didn't find customer:" + name);
            }
            else {
                if (item == NONE) {
                    System.err.println("No listing for" + name);
                }
                else {
                    System.out.println("Found" + name + "at" + item);
                }
            }
        }
    }
```

Figure 23.7: This fully functioning Java example reads in data from a file and provides a lookup of a customer's phone number by the customer name or the name of his wife (part 3 of 4).

```
        // Exit successfully.
        System.exit(0);
    }
    catch (Exception e) {
        System.err.println("Error occurred" );
        e.printStackTrace();
        // Exit in error condition.
        System.exit(2);
    }
  } // end of main
}
export CLASSPATH=/home/jsmith/src
javac com/mcpress/qshell/CustomerLookup.java
java com.mcpress.qshell.CustomerLookup /home/jsmith/src/goodoleboys.txt
Enter 'exit' or a name to lookup:
Bill
Found Bill at 333-4444
Enter 'exit' or a name to lookup:
Daisy
Found Daisy at 333-4444
Enter 'exit' or a name to lookup:
Claude
Found Claude at 333-4340
Enter 'exit' or a name to lookup:
Etheline
Found Etheline at 333-4340
Enter 'exit' or a name to lookup:
Fred
Didn't find customer: Fred
Enter 'exit' or a name to lookup:
exit
```

Figure 23.7: This fully functioning Java example reads in data from a file and provides a lookup of a customer's phone number by the customer name or the name of his wife (part 4 of 4).

Like perl, Java provides the ability to invoke a Qshell command. Figure 23.8 uses the Qshell *system* utility to interact directly with a CL command. Recall from chapter 22 that invoking the utility like this is a shortcut, which may use a temporary file to hold the output from a Qshell or CL command or utility.

Figure 23.8 uses the Runtime.exec() API to process the output from a Qshell command. The Qshell *system* utility is used to execute a CL command. The output is used to build a Hashtable containing the PTF (Program Temporary Fix) names and their statuses. The Hashtable serves as the lookup mechanism for the status of each randomly selected PTF. Compare and contrast this Java example with the similar perl example in Figure 22.9 and the C example in Figure 24.7.

Notice, in this example, that running a Qshell utility from within Java is almost as simple as in the perl program. You have to do a bit more processing related to the code page of the data sent back from the program, but the difficulty is minimal. Also, notice that the regular expression features of perl are missing (in Java 1.3). Although the method used here might perform better for this example, regular expressions would be a useful alternative to this model for finding a PTF in a line of text. Regular expression support is present in Java 1.4.

```
pwd
/home/jsmith/src
cat com/mcpress/qshell/PtfStatus.java
package com.mcpress.qshell;

import java.util.*;
import java.io.*;

public class PtfStatus {
    public final static boolean debug = false;

    Hashtable        ptfs;
    public PtfStatus() throws Exception {
        ptfs = new Hashtable();
        String        commandArray[] =
            new String[]{
            "/usr/bin/system",
                "DSPPTF OUTPUT(*PRINT)"
        };
        Runtime             run = Runtime.getRuntime();
        Process             proc = run.exec(commandArray);
        // Since we're running a Qshell command, the process
        // will output EBCDIC data. We'll use an encoding of
        // Cp037 to read US English EBCDIC (CCSID 37)
        LineNumberReader      in =
                new LineNumberReader
                (new InputStreamReader(proc.getInputStream(), "Cp037"));
        // Read each line.
        String              line = in.readLine();
```

Figure 23.8: This Java example demonstrates using the Runtime.exec() API to run a Qshell command and process the output (part 1 of 3).

```
        while (line != null) {
            if (debug) {
                System.out.println("<" + line + ">");
            }
            // PTF list in the output is a 7 character name,
            //    2 alpha, 5 digits          or
            //    3 alpha, 4 digits
            // prefixed by one space on each line.
            boolean isAPtf = true;
            isAPtf = isAPtf && Character.isSpace(line.charAt(1));
            isAPtf = isAPtf && Character.isLetter(line.charAt(2));
            isAPtf = isAPtf && Character.isLetter(line.charAt(3));
            isAPtf = isAPtf && Character.isLetterOrDigit(line.charAt(4));
            isAPtf = isAPtf && Character.isDigit(line.charAt(5));
            isAPtf = isAPtf && Character.isDigit(line.charAt(6));
            isAPtf = isAPtf && Character.isDigit(line.charAt(7));
            isAPtf = isAPtf && Character.isDigit(line.charAt(8));
            isAPtf = isAPtf && Character.isSpace(line.charAt(9));

            if (isAPtf) {
                String  ptf = line.substring(2, 9);
                String  status = line.substring(14, 33);
                if (debug) {
            System.out.println("OUT: <" + ptf + ">, <" + status + ">");
                }
                ptfs.put(ptf, status);
            }
            line = in.readLine();
        }
    }
    public String getStatus(String name) {
        String status = (String)ptfs.get(name);
        if (status == null) {
            status = "Not Loaded";
        }
        return status;
    }
    public static void main(String args[]) {
        if (args.length == 0) {
          System.err.println("Usage: java PtfStatus <ptf-to-lookup>...");
            System.exit(1);
        }
        try {
            PtfStatus               ptfs = new PtfStatus();
            String                  status;
```

Figure 23.8: This Java example demonstrates using the Runtime.exec() API to run a Qshell command and process the output (part 2 of 3).

```
            System.out.println("-------\t--------------------");
            System.out.println("  PTF  \t        Status       ");
            System.out.println("-------\t--------------------");
            for (int i=0; i<args.length; ++i) {
                status = ptfs.getStatus(args[i]);
                System.out.print(args[i]);
                System.out.print("\t");
                System.out.println(status);
            } // end of for (i=0 < args.length)
        }
        catch (Exception e) {
            e.printStackTrace();
            System.exit(2);
        }
        System.exit(0);
    } // end of main
}
java com.mcpress.qshell.PtfStatus SI06971 SI06972 SI06973 SI06974 SI06975
SI06976 SI06977
------- --------------------
  PTF          Status
------- --------------------
SI06971 Temporarily applied
SI06972 Superseded
SI06973 Not Loaded
SI06974 Not Loaded
SI06975 Temporarily applied
SI06976 Temporarily applied
SI06977 Superseded
```

Figure 23.8: This Java example demonstrates using the Runtime.exec() API to run a Qshell command and process the output (part 3 of 3).

The Java language provides a standard way to access a database using *JDBC* (*Java Database Connectivity*) APIs. Figure 23.9 uses these APIs to demonstrate a more realistic phone-number lookup application than in Figure 23.7. The names and phone numbers reside in the relational database on the iSeries; Java is used to access this database. Compare and contrast this Java example with the similar perl example in Figure 22.10 and the C example in Figure 24.8.

Except for the need to load the JDBC driver before accessing the database, this example looks similar to the perl program. The database-access APIs are object-based in both perl and Java, so they are very similar.

The Java program has some requirements with regard to exception-handling that aren't present in the other languages. Java exceptions eliminate some of the need for error-checking in the mainline program path. At times, handling exceptions for possible or expected error conditions can be slightly more complex in Java than error-checking in other languages.

The commands shown in Figure 23.9 also demonstrate the type of error that can occur if the CLASSPATH variable is not set up correctly:

```
java.sql.SQLException: No suitable driver
```

Fixing the CLASSPATH variable enables the example program to run successfully.

```
pwd
/home/jsmith/src
cat com/mcpress/qshell/CustomerDBLookup.java
package com.mcpress.qshell;

import java.util.Hashtable;
import java.io.*;
import java.sql.*; // Get the JDBC classes

public class CustomerDBLookup {
    public final static String       NONE = "none";
    Connection                       conn;
    PreparedStatement                ps;

    static {
        // Load the JDBC driver that we're going to use.
        // JDBC drivers register themselves when loaded.
        try {
            Class.forName("com.ibm.as400.access.AS400JDBCDriver");
        }
        catch (Exception e) {
            System.err.println("Didn't load the toolbox driver");
        }
    }
    public CustomerDBLookup() throws SQLException {
        conn = DriverManager.getConnection("jdbc:as400:localhost");
        ps = conn.prepareStatement
```

Figure 23.9: Use the database to perform the phone number lookup previously demonstrated using a Hashtable (part 1 of 4).

```java
            ("SELECT PHONENUMBER FROM JSMITHQ.CUSTOMERS" +
             "WHERE NAME = ? OR WIFE = ?");
    }
    public String lookup(String name) throws SQLException {
        // Everything is already created. Just set the parameters
        // and execute the statement.
        ps.setString(1, name);
        ps.setString(2, name);
        ResultSet rs = ps.executeQuery();
        String   phoneNumber = null;
        if (rs.next()) {
            // Get the first column from the first row of the result set.
            phoneNumber = rs.getString(1);
            if (phoneNumber == null) {
                // Found the customer, but no phone number
                phoneNumber = NONE;
            }
        }
        rs.close();
        return phoneNumber;
    }
    public void close() {
        if (conn != null) {
            try {
                conn.close();
            }
            catch (Exception e) {
                e.printStackTrace();
            }
        }
        conn = null;
        ps = null;
    }
    public static void main(String args[]) {
        if (args.length != 0) {
            System.err.println("Usage: java CustomerDBLookup");
            System.exit(1);
        }
        CustomerDBLookup    list = null;
        try {
            String              item;
            String              name;

            list = new CustomerDBLookup();
            // Get a 'nicer' interface over the System.in object
            // that represents standard input. We'll use
```

Figure 23.9: Use the database to perform the phone number lookup previously demonstrated using a Hashtable (part 2 of 4).

```
            LineNumberReader
            // just for fun.
            LineNumberReader    in =
                new LineNumberReader(new InputStreamReader(System.in));

        while (true) {
            System.out.println("Enter 'exit' or a name to lookup:");
            Read the next name from standard input, any input
            // class (API) that could be constructed from System.in
            // could be used here.
            name = in.readLine();
            if (name == null) {
                // All done.
                break;
            }
            if (name.equals("exit") || name.equals("quit")) {
                break;
            }

            // Lookup the name
            item = list.lookup(name);
            if (item == null) {
                System.err.println("Didn't find customer:" + name);
            }
            else {
                if (item == NONE) {
                    System.err.println("No listing for" + name);
                }
                else {
                    System.out.println("Found" + name + "at" + item);
                }
            }
        }
        // Exit successfully.
        System.exit(0);
    }
    catch (Exception e) {
        System.err.println("Error occurred");
        e.printStackTrace();
        // Exit in error condition.
        System.exit(2);
    }
    finally {
        // Be sure to clean up any DB resources that were allocated.
        if (list != null) {
            list.close();
```

Figure 23.9: Use the database to perform the phone number lookup previously demonstrated using a Hashtable (part 3 of 4).

```
            }
         }
      } // end of main
}
export CLASSPATH=/home/jsmith/src
java com.mcpress.qshell.CustomerDBLookup
Didn't load the toolbox driver
Error occurred
java.sql.SQLException: No suitable driver
    java/lang/Throwable.<init>(Ljava/lang/String;)V+4
        (Throwable.java:90)
    java/sql/SQLException.<init>(Ljava/lang/String;Ljava/lang/String;)V+1
        (SQLException.java:60)
    java/sql/DriverManager.getConnection(Ljava/lang/String;Ljava/util/
        Properties;Ljava/lang/ClassLoader;)Ljava/sql/Connection;+
243 (DriverManager. java:537)
java/sql/DriverManager.getConnection(Ljava/lang/String;)Ljava/sql/
        Connection;+12  (DriverManager.java:199)
com/mcpress/qshell/CustomerDBLookup.<init>()V+0
        (CustomerDBLookup.java:22)
        com/mcpress/qshell/CustomerDBLookup.main([Ljava/lang/String;)V+0
(CustomerDBLookup.java:58)
export CLASSPATH=/QIBM/ProdData/HTTP/Public/jt400/lib/jt400.jar:
    $CLASSPATH
java com.mcpress.qshell.CustomerDBLookup
Enter 'exit' or a name to lookup:
Bill
Found Bill at 333-4444
Enter 'exit' or a name to lookup:
Daisy
Found Daisy at 333-4444
Enter 'exit' or a name to lookup:
Claude
Found Claude at 333-4340
Enter 'exit' or a name to lookup:
Etheline
Found Etheline at 333-4340
Enter 'exit' or a name to lookup:
Fred
Didn't find customer: Fred
Enter 'exit' or a name to lookup:
exit
```

Figure 23.9: Use the database to perform the phone number lookup previously demonstrated using a Hashtable (part 4 of 4).

SUMMARY

The Qshell environment is an integral part of Java application development. Java applications have built-in support for interacting with Qshell, and many Java commands are only accessible from within Qshell. The Java *jar* utility can serve as a general-purpose archive and file-compression utility.

Chapter 24

C and C++
Development Tools

The C and C++ languages provide substantial integration to Qshell with the
standard I/O functions described in chapter 19. In addition, Qshell provides
direct ILE C and C++ compiler support so that you can develop your application using Qshell.

COMPILING C AND C++

The *icc* utility is provided by the iSeries Tools for Developers (product number
5799-PTL). It is located in the /QIBM/ProdData/DeveloperTools/qsh/bin directory. The *icc* utility is a wrapper program for accessing the CL commands used
for C and C++ application development.

In addition, *icc* creates *soft links* in the file system, allowing a development
process that simulates placing binary objects like modules and programs in the
IFS (Integrated File System), instead of in the QSYS.LIB file system.

Use EBCDIC source files with *icc*. Internally, *icc* simply uses the CRTCMOD
(Create C Module), CRTCPPMOD (Create C++ Module), and CRTPGM (Create
Program) CL commands to process the source files.

The syntax of the *icc* command is shown here:

```
usage: icc [-cgs+v] [-D name[=value]]... [-I directory]...
[-O [optlevel]]  [-o outfile]  [-q value]  [-M dependfile]...
[-P listingfile] [-L directory] [-l<key.] [-z ifsIOoption]
operand
```

Table 24.1 shows values for *icc* options.

Table 24.1: Icc Compiler Options

Option	Description
-c	Compile only; don't link the module object(s) into a program object.
-g	Generate debugging information in the resulting module.
-+	Treat the source files as C++ source code, regardless of the file extension.
-v	Print the CL commands used for the compilation steps.
-D *name=value*	Define *name* as *value*, as if it were defined in a C/C++ #define directive. If a value portion is not specified, name=1 is used by default.
-I *dir*	Search in directory *dir* for included files that are not specified with a full path.
-O*optlevel*	Specify an optimization level of one, two, three, or four, corresponding to the system optimization level of 10, 20, 30, or 40 on the CRTCMOD or CRTCPPMOD commands.
-o *outfile*	Use *outfile* as the name of the resulting executable program instead of the default name (a.out).
-q option=*value*	Specify advanced option settings for the C/C++ CL command.
-M *dependfile*	Generate a make description file into *dependfile*.
-P *listingfile*	Generate listing information into *listingfile*.
-L *directory*	Search for the library files specified with the -l option in the directory named.

Table 24.1: Icc Compiler Options, *continued*

Option	Description
-lname	Link modules in the specified library file. An icc library file is a symbolic link to an iSeries Binding Directory (*BNDDIR) object. The value *name* would search for library files named libname.a.
-zifslOoption	Specify the IFS I/O value for the SYSIFCIO keyword on the CRTCMOD or CRTCPPMOD CL commands. The default value is IFSIO. Other acceptable value are NONE, ALL, NOIFSIO, and IFS64IO.

The *icc* utility determines the appropriate action for input files based on the file extensions. Files with extensions of *.CPP*, *.cpp*, *.CC*, *.cc*, or *.C* are treated as C++ source files. Files with an *.o* extension are symbolic links to module or service program objects. Files with an *.a* extension are symbolic links to binding directory objects.

The *icc* utility uses a library to hold the iSeries objects it creates that cannot be placed in the IFS directory. Modules and programs are inserted into the library with the same name as the directory containing the source. Use the OUTPUTDIR environment variable to override the name of the library used for the creation of those objects.

Figures 24.1 and 24.2 illustrate program creation using *icc*. Figure 24.1 uses the printf() API for generating output, and returns the exit status from the main routine. If desired, you could set the exit status using the exit() API instead.

```
pwd
/home/jsmith/src/c
ls -lS
total: 16 kilobytes
37 -rw-rw-rw-  1 JSMITH  0        107 Jun  8 15:04 HelloC.c
37 -rw-rw-rw-  1 JSMITH  0        116 Jun  8 15:04 HelloCpp.C
cat HelloC.c
#include <stdio.h>

int main(int argc, char **argv)
```

Figure 24.1: This simple C example sends output to the Qshell runtime terminal and sets the exit status (part 1 of 2).

```
{
    printf("Hello From C\n");
    return 4;
}
icc -gv HelloC.c
command = CRTCMOD MODULE(c/HelloC) SRCSTMF('HelloC.c')
    DBGVIEW(*ALL)
TEXT('/home/JSMITH/src/c/HelloC.o') SYSIFCOPT(*IFSIO)
    OPTION(*LOGMSG)
command = CRTPGM PGM(c/a) MODULE(c/HelloC )
    TEXT('/home/JSMITH/src/c/a.out')
ls -l
total: 24 kilobytes
-rw-rw-rw-  1 JSMITH  0        107 Jun  8 15:04 HelloC.c
lrwxrwxrwx  1 JSMITH  0         29 Jun  8 15:06 HelloC.o ->
    /qsys.lib/c.lib/HelloC.module
-rw-rw-rw-  1 JSMITH  0        116 Jun  8 15:04 HelloCpp.C
lrwxrwxrwx  1 JSMITH  0         21 Jun  8 15:06 a.out ->
    /qsys.lib/c.lib/a.pgm
./a.out
Hello From C
echo $?
4
```

Figure 24.1: This simple C example sends output to the Qshell runtime terminal and sets the exit status (part 2 of 2).

In Figure 24.2, the *cout* object generates output and returns the exit status from the main routine. Again, the exit status could be set using the exit() API, instead.

```
cat HelloCpp.C
#include <iostream.h>

int main(int argc, char **argv)
{
    cout << "Hello from C++" << endl;
    return 5;
}
icc -gv -o HelloCpp HelloCpp.C
command = CRTCPPMOD MODULE(C/HELLOCPP) SRCSTMF('HelloCpp.C')
    DBGVIEW(*ALL)
TEXT('/home/JSMITH/src/c/HelloCpp.o')
command = CRTPGM PGM(C/HELLOCPP) MODULE(C/HELLOCPP)
    TEXT('/home/JSMITH/src/c/HelloCpp')
```

Figure 24.2: This simple C++ example, built with the icc utility, sends output to the Qshell runtime terminal and sets the exit status (part 1 of 2).

```
ls -l HelloCpp*
lrwxrwxrwx  1 JSMITH  0              28 Jun  8 15:18 HelloCpp ->
    /qsys.lib/c.lib/HelloCpp.pgm
-rw-rw-rw-  1 JSMITH  0             118 Jun  8 15:18 HelloCpp.C
lrwxrwxrwx  1 JSMITH  0              31 Jun  8 15:18 HelloCpp.o ->
    /qsys.lib/c.lib/HelloCpp.module
./HelloCpp
Hello from C++
echo $?
5
```

Figure 24.2: This simple C++ example, built with the icc utility, sends output to the Qshell runtime terminal and sets the exit status (part 2 of 2).

The Ixlc Utility (V5R2)

The *ixlc* utility represents a fully supported C and C++ compiler that runs in Qshell in V5R2. Unlike *icc*, which is a simple wrapper program with limited documentation, the full documentation for the *ixlc* compiler is found in the V5R2 ILE compiler's reference manual. Also unlike *icc*, *ixlc* supports ASCII source files. Using ASCII source files enables a set of useful iSeries Tools for Developers utilities and workstation tools. Additionally, *ixlc* allows compilation of source files in the QSYS.LIB file system (files and members in libraries).

Since the *ixlc* command is fully supported, it should be used for development under V5R1 and beyond. The syntax of the command is shown here:

```
ixlc [-c+] source-file [compiler-options] [-B'binder-command']
```

The *ixlc* compiler has an extensive and robust set of compilation options. The compilation options are based on the keywords and options that would be used with the CRTCMOD and CRTCPPMOD CL commands. The *ixlc* utility uses the last specified option if multiple incompatible or conflicting options are specified.

The V5R2 ILE compiler reference fully documents all of the options. Table 24.2 describes some of the most common ones, and those related directly to Qshell development. Table 24.2 groups closely related options together; keep in mind that only one of a set of closely related options is usually used.

Table 24.2: lxlc Compiler Options

Option	Description
-c	Compile only; do not link the generated module object into a program object.
-+	Treat the source files as C++ source code regardless of file extension.
-olib/*object*	Name the output object something other than the default name. The default object name used is the same as the source file. The default library used is the current library specified in the user profile, or QGPL if no current library is set. Set the current library on the user profile using the Qshell system utility, for example: *system "CHGUSRPRF USRPRF(JSMITH) CURLIB(C)"*
-I*dir*	Use the -I option to specify directories searched for include files. The values specified with the -I option override any values specified in the INCLUDE environment variable. The default include path is /QIBM/Include.
-B'*binder command*	Use the -B option to specify a different binder command than the default. A binder command usually consists of the CL command CRTPGM or CRTSRVPGM, and is used to link modules in ways other than the default. Use the -B option to provide nonstandard options to CRTPGM or CRTSRVPGM, or to link multiple modules together.
-qifsio=64 -qnoifsio -qifsio	Set IFS I/O options. IFS I/O options are used to affect the way C/C++ applications access files using the C and C++ standard I/O routines. Specifying IFS I/O means that those routines access files in IFS, while specifying no IFS I/O indicates that those routines access files and members in libraries. The default value is -qifsio=64 (64-bit IFS I/O) for C++ applications, and -qnoifsio for C applications.
-g -qdbgview=none -qdbgview=stmt -qdbgview=source -qdbgview=list -qdbgview=all	Generate debug information. The -g option generates debug information equivalent to -qdbgview=all. Different types of debug views allow different debug capabilities: ■ A stmt-level debug view allows debugging using statement numbers and symbolic names, in conjunction with a separate listing file (not generated by this parameter).

Table 24.2: lxlc Compiler Options, *continued*

Option	Description
	■ A source-level debug view allows source level debugging using the source code (which must remain on the system in the same location). ■ A list-level debug view uses the various listing options to affect the listing that is presented while using the debugger. ■ The -qdbgview=none is the default debug option.
-qtext=*descrip-tion*	Add a description to the resulting object. If the description contains spaces, use single or double quotes on the Qshell command.
-qnoprint -qprint -qoutput=*filename*	Generate a listing. The -qprint option generates a compile listing to a spooled file. The -qoutput option generates a compile listing to an IFS file. The -qnoprint option is the default option.
-qgen -qnogen	Stop the compilation process after the compiler performs syntax-checking. The -qgen option is the default option.
-qlonglong -qnolonglong	Disable the explicit 64-bit "long long" data type. The -qlonglong option is the default value, enabling the "long long" data type.
-qnoshowinc -qshowinc	Show user and system includes. Use the -qshowinc option to expand user and system include files in the listings generated using the listing options. The -qnoshowinc option is the default.
-qnoshowsys -qshowsys	Show system includes. Use the -qshowsys option to expand system include files in the listings generated using the listing options. The -qnoshowsys option is the default.
-qnoshowusr -qshowusr	Show user includes. Use the -qshowusr option to expand user include files in the listings generated using the listing options. The -qnoshowusr option is the default option.
-qnofull -qfull	Use the -qfull option to turn on all optional listing categories of output in the listings generated using the listing options. Typically, use the -qfull option with the individual -qno*xxxx* option to turn off listing categories that are not desired. The -qnofull option is the default.

Table 24.2: lxlc Compiler Options, *continued*

Option	Description
-qnoexpmac -qexpmac	Use the -qexpmac option to expand macros in the listings generated using the listing options. The -qnoexpmac option is the default.
-qnoagr -qagr	Use the -qagr option to generate an aggregate listing category showing the sizes and offsets of fields within structures in the listings generated using listing options. The -qnoagr option is the default.

Choosing lxlc or lcc

The *ixlc* utility has some differences from the *icc* utility that will affect your decision to use one or the other in production development within Qshell:

- The *ixlc* utility does not create symbolic links to other development objects, like modules and programs in the IFS. The *icc* utility, on the other hand, creates some of these objects automatically.

- Production build scripts and configuration files for the *make* utility typically depend on objects in the file system. The utilities or scripts use the objects to check whether source code should be recompiled. You will need to address these issues on your own if you use *ixlc*.

- The *ixlc* utility provides parameters for the full set of functions provided by the compiler, while *icc* provides a smaller set of direct parameters.

- If you do complex or very customized builds, you might find that some of the parameters you need are not available or are too complex to specify *icc*.

- The *icc* utility is part of the iSeries Tools for Developer PRPQ (product 5799PTL), while *ixlc* is part of the Websphere Development Toolset (product 5722WDS).

- If you experience errors with either of these tools, you'll probably get better support and fixes from IBM with the utilities from the Websphere product. Alternatively, use the *-v* option on *icc*, then try the CL command that *icc* displays directly and see if you can recreate the problem before calling IBM support.

- The iSeries Tools for Developers PRPQ delivers some other Unix-based utilities that help address building multiple-module service programs or similar programs. The *ixlc* utility provides no such features from within Qshell, but instead provides the *-B* parameter. The *-B* parameter takes a CL command that can be used to create the resulting objects, but it doesn't provide any help for the IFS build process or for automatically using IFS objects in that step.

- The *icc* utility provides some automatic mapping from long IFS file names to shorter names that can be used for the resulting library objects. The *ixlc* utility provides no such mapping; in some cases, your personal build scripts or source files might need to be changed. Figure 24.3 shows a way to provide mapping from long to short names using *ixlc*.

```
icc -v HelloLongCpp.C
command = CRTCPPMOD MODULE(C/HELLOLONGC) SRCSTMF('HelloLongCpp.C')
   TEXT('/home/jsmith/src/c/HelloLongCpp.o')
command = CRTPGM PGM(C/A) MODULE(C/HELLOLONGC )
   TEXT('/home/jsmith/src/c/a.out')
ls -l a.out
lrwxrwxrwx 1 JSMITH 0 21 Jul 28 10:06 a.out -> /qsys.lib/c.lib/a.pgm
ixlc HelloLongCpp.C
Value 'HELLOLONGC' for PGM exceeds 10 characters.
Errors occurred in command.
ixlc -c -ojsmith/Hello HelloLongCpp.C
Module HELLO was created in library JSMITH on 06/29/03 at 14:59:44.
```

Figure 24.3: The icc *utility handles long file names, but* ixlc *requires manual intervention to handle long file names.*

EXAMPLES

Figure 24.4 is a typical "Hello World" programming example. Subsequent examples in this chapter show various ways that your C or C++ application can interact with Qshell. The Java and perl examples for phone-number lookup, PTF status, and database access in chapters 22 and 23 are similar to those examples in this chapter. This is done to provide you with a good basis for comparing the three languages.

```
cat HelloCpp.C
#include <iostream.h>

int main(int argc, char **argv)
{
    cout << "Hello from C++" << endl;
    return 5;
}
ixlc HelloCpp.C
Program HELLOCPP was created in library QGPL on 06/29/03 at 14:13:54.
system "CRTLIB JSMITH"
CPC2102:  Library JSMITH created.
system "CHGUSRPRF USRPRF(JSMITH) CURLIB(JSMITH)"
CPC2205:  User profile JSMITH changed.
ixlc HelloCpp.C
Program HELLOCPP was created in library JSMITH on 06/29/03 at 14:14:35.
/qsys.lib/jsmith.lib/hellocpp.pgm
Hello from C++
echo $?
5
```

Figure 24.4: This simple C++ example, built with the ixlc utility, sends output to the Qshell runtime terminal and sets the exit status. It uses the cout object for generating output and returns the exit status from the main routine. If desired, you could set the exit status with the exit() API, instead.

Using the goodoleboys.txt data file from Figure 21.1, Figure 24.5 demonstrates a functioning, interactive phone-number lookup application. This application uses two list-data structures to provide lookup services based on the data file. Compare and contrast the complexity of this C example with the relative simplicity of the Java and perl examples (Figures 23.7 and 22.7, respectively). Java has a very rich and robust class library, while perl is well-suited (and intended for) text processing. In C, the programmer frequently has to resort to writing additional program code for solving minor problems unrelated to the main program. This example needed to include memory-management, list-manipulation, and string functions. Those features can sometimes be provided with third-party class libraries.

```
cat phoneList.C
#include <stdio.h>
#include <stdlib.h>
#include <string.h>

// This example doesn't handle lines longer than
// BUFSIZE characters.
#define BUFSIZE   256

typedef struct {
    int     listCurrentSize;
    int     listMaxSize;
    char    **itemKeys;
    char    **items;
} list_t;

void listAllocate(list_t *l, int maxSize);
void listAdd(list_t *l, char *key, char *item);
char *listFind(list_t *l, char *key);
void rtrim(char *variable, int maxSize);

int main(int argc, char **argv)
{
    list_t    numberByOleBoy;
    list_t    oleBoyByWife;
    char      buffer[BUFSIZE];
    char      oleBoy[16];
    char      oleBoysWife[16];
    char      phoneNumber[16];
    int       len;
    char      *theItem;

    if (argc < 2 || strcmp(argv[1], "-h") == 0) {
        printf("Usage: phoneList [-h] <data-file>...\n");
        exit(1);
    }
    // Allocate a large list that needs no extending for
    // this simple example (this example doesn't handle
    // extending the list size).
    listAllocate(&numberByOleBoy, 128);
    listAllocate(&oleBoyByWife, 128);

    // Read input from all the data files passed on the
    // command line.
```

Figure 24.5: Like the perl and Java examples in chapters 22 and 23, this phone-list example shows a functioning, interactive phone-lookup utility (part 1 of 5).

```
for (int i=1; i<argc; ++i) {
    FILE *argvFile = fopen(argv[i], "r");
    if (argvFile == NULL) {
        fprintf(stderr, "Error opening file %s\n", argv[i]);
        exit(1);
    }
    // The first 2 lines of each data file represent
    // header lines
    fgets(buffer, BUFSIZE, argvFile);
    fgets(buffer, BUFSIZE, argvFile);

    while (fgets(buffer, BUFSIZE, argvFile) != NULL) {
        // For each field:
        // - Take the characters from the correct column for
        //   the field into a variable.
        // - Remove any trailing spaces at the end of the variable
        memset(oleBoy, 0, sizeof(oleBoy));
        memset(oleBoysWife, 0, sizeof(oleBoysWife));
        memset(phoneNumber, 0, sizeof(phoneNumber));

        memcpy(oleBoy, &buffer[0], 10);
        memcpy(oleBoysWife, &buffer[37], 10);
        memcpy(phoneNumber, &buffer[19], 8);

        rtrim(oleBoy, sizeof(oleBoy));
        rtrim(oleBoysWife, sizeof(oleBoysWife));
        rtrim(phoneNumber, sizeof(phoneNumber));

        listAdd(&numberByOleBoy, oleBoy, phoneNumber);
        if (strcmp("none", oleBoysWife) != 0) {
            listAdd(&oleBoyByWife, oleBoysWife, oleBoy);
        }
    } // while (fgets)
    fclose(argvFile);
} // for i loops each argument

// Get the user's input.
printf("Enter 'exit' or a name to lookup:\n");
fflush(stdout);
while (fgets(buffer, BUFSIZE, stdin)) {
    len = strlen(buffer);
    buffer[len-1] = 0;
    if (strcmp(buffer, "exit") == 0 ||
        strcmp(buffer, "quit") == 0) {
        break;
    }
```

Figure 24.5: Like the perl and Java examples in chapters 22 and 23, this phone-list example shows a functioning, interactive phone-lookup utility (part 2 of 5).

```
        // Is the name a good ole boy?
        theItem = listFind(&numberByOleBoy, buffer);
        if (theItem != NULL) {
            // Yes, print out the number
            printf("Found good ole boy's number at %s\n",
                    theItem);
        }
        else {
            // Otherwise, is the name a good ole boy's wife?
            theItem = listFind(&oleBoyByWife, buffer);
            if (theItem != NULL) {
                // Yes, print out the number.
                theItem = listFind(&numberByOleBoy, theItem);
                printf("Found good ole boy's number using his wife at %s\n",
                        theItem);
            }
            else {
              printf("Didn't find number (the lookup is case sensitive)\n");
            }
        }
        printf("Enter 'exit' or a name to lookup:\n");
        fflush(stdout);
    }
    exit(0);
}

// Allocate a new list.
void listAllocate(list_t *l, int maxSize) {
    l->listCurrentSize = 0;
    l->listMaxSize = maxSize;
    // Create array of strings, size=maxSize
    l->itemKeys    = (char**)malloc(sizeof(char*)*maxSize);
    l->items       = (char**)malloc(sizeof(char*)*maxSize);
}

// Add an element by key to the list
// (making a dynamic copy of the element and the key)
void listAdd(list_t *l, char *key, char *item) {
    char   *newKey  = strdup(key);
    char   *newItem = strdup(item);
    int     ndx = l->listCurrentSize;
    // Note this simple example doesn't expand the list.
    if (!(ndx < l->listMaxSize)) {
        fprintf(stderr, "Hit the maximum list size. Exit with status=1\n");
        exit(1);
    }
```

Figure 24.5: Like the perl and Java examples in chapters 22 and 23, this phone-list example shows a functioning, interactive phone-lookup utility (part 3 of 5).

```
        // printf("Add: <%s> at <%s>(%d)\n", newItem, newKey, ndx);
        l->itemKeys[ndx] = newKey;
        l->items[ndx] = newItem;
        l->listCurrentSize = ndx+1;
}

char *listFind(list_t *l, char *key) {
        // Note: this simple example uses a poor search mechanism
        // (a linear search). See the standard C qsort() and qsearch()
        // functions.
        // printf("Find: <%s>\n", key);
        for (int i=0; i<l->listCurrentSize; ++i) {
            if (strcmp(key, l->itemKeys[i]) == 0) {
                return l->items[i];
            }
        }
        return NULL;
}

// Remove spaces from the end of the variable
// given the maximum size of the variable.
void rtrim(char *variable, int maxSize) {
        for (int i=maxSize-1; i>=0; --i) {
            if (variable[i] == 0 ||
                variable[i] == ' ') {
                variable[i] = 0;
            }
            else {
                // done
                break;
            }
        }
}
```

```
ixlc phoneList.C
Program PHONELIST was created in library JSMITH on 06/29/03 at 16:16:08.
/qsys.lib/jsmith.lib/phonelist.pgm /home/jsmith/src/data/goodoleboys.txt
Enter 'exit' or a name to lookup:
Bill
Found good ole boy's number at 333-4444
Enter 'exit' or a name to lookup:
Daisy
Found good ole boy's number using his wife at 333-4444
Enter 'exit' or a name to lookup:
Claude
Found good ole boy's number at 333-4340
Enter 'exit' or a name to lookup:
```

Figure 24.5: Like the perl and Java examples in chapters 22 and 23, this phone-list example shows a functioning, interactive phone-lookup utility (part 4 of 5).

Etheline
Found good ole boy's number using his wife at 333-4340
Enter 'exit' or a name to lookup:
Fred
Didn't find number (the lookup is case sensitive)
Enter 'exit' or a name to lookup:
exit

Figure 24.5: Like the perl and Java examples in chapters 22 and 23, this phone-list example shows a functioning, interactive phone-lookup utility (part 5 of 5).

The C runtime library provides the ability to invoke a Qshell command. Figure 24.6 uses the Qshell *system* utility to interact directly with a CL command. As mentioned in previous chapters, invoking *system* like this is a shortcut.

The popen program in Figure 24.6 demonstrates the simple implementation of an API that acts similar to the Unix-standard popen() API, using the spawn() interface. This program is necessary because the iSeries does not provide the popen() API natively, but instead provides only the constituent parts. Use this simulated API to run Qshell utilities or other C/C++ programs while having access to the program's input or output data. After being compiled, the popen program is used to invoke the compound Qshell statement 'echo "hi\nbye" | while read i; do echo $i; done'. The example uses a *while* loop in the compound statement to add complexity and demonstrate the capability of the program.

```
cat popen.H
#ifndef __POPEN_H
#define __POPEN_H
#include <stdio.h>
#include <stdlib.h>
#include <string.h>

#ifdef __cplusplus
extern "C" {
#endif

// A close simulation of the popen() and pclose() APIs
// with slight differences.
FILE *popen(const char *pgm, char **pgmArgs);
int   pclose(FILE *fp);
```

Figure 24.6: The capability to start Qshell commands and programs while processing the input to and output from programs is a powerful Qshell programming feature (part 1 of 6).

```
#ifdef __cplusplus
}
#endif

#endif
cat popen.C
#include <stdio.h>
#include <stdlib.h>
#include <string.h>
#include <ifs.h>
#include <errno.h>
#include <fcntl.h>
#include <sys/wait.h>
#include <sys/types.h>
#include <spawn.h>
#include <sys/socket.h>
#include "popen.H"

#define   POPEN_MAX_ARGS 32

extern char **environ;

// Allow the NO_MAIN preprocessor directive to remove
// the main() entry point. Its used for testing, but
// not when this module is used by other programs.
#ifndef NO_MAIN
int main(int argc, char **argv)
{
    FILE   *fp;
    int    rc;
    char   i;
    char   *popenchild;
    char   buffer[256];
    char   **args;

    if (argc < 2) {
        printf("usage: popen <program> [args]\n");
        printf("          or\n");
        printf("          popen -c <qsh-command-line>\n");
        printf(" Execute a program or qshell command, piping\n");
        printf(" its output back to the caller\n");
        printf(" Example:\n");
        printf("   popen /usr/bin/ls /home /qibm\n");
        printf("   popen -c 'echo \"hi\\nbye\" | while read i;
          do    echo $i; done"\n");
        exit(1);
```

Figure 24.6: The capability to start Qshell commands and programs while processing the input to and output from programs is a powerful Qshell programming feature (part 2 of 6).

```
    }

    // Qshell command?
    if (strcmp(argv[1], "-c") == 0) {
        // Yes. Run the qshell program with the
        // -c parameter and pass it along plus all subsequent
        // arguments.
        popenchild = "/usr/bin/qsh";
        args = &argv[1];
    }
    else {
        // Nope, just a program object itself.
        popenchild = argv[1];
        args = &argv[2];
    }

    fp = popen(popenchild, args);
    if (fp == NULL) {
        printf("Failed to start a child, err=%d\n", errno);
        exit(0);
    }

    while(fgets(buffer, sizeof(buffer), fp) != NULL) {
        fprintf(stdout, "%s", buffer);
    }

    pclose(fp);
    exit(0);
}
#endif


// popen() like interface. Always returns a FILE * that can
// be used for both reading and writing from and to the child.
FILE *popen(const char *pgm, char **pgmArgs)
{
    // Data/variables for the spawn API
    int                 fdCount=3;
    int                 fdMap[3];
    struct inheritance  inherit;
    // Arguments plus 1 for program name and 1 for NULL terminator.
    int                 argCount;
    char                *cargv[POPEN_MAX_ARGS+2] = {
        (char *)pgm, NULL
    };
    // NOTE: Could pass all current environment variables too.
    int                 envCount;
```

Figure 24.6: The capability to start Qshell commands and programs while processing the input to and output from programs is a powerful Qshell programming feature (part 3 of 6).

```
char                    **env;
char                    *stdioEnvironmentVariable =
    "QIBM_USE_DESCRIPTOR_STDIO=Y";
// File descriptor data and variables used to setup
// file descriptors for this job and the child jobs.
int                     fdToClose;

int                     pipeFd[2];
// The FILE pointer that will be returned to the caller
FILE                    *fp;
int                     rc;
char                    *junk;
int                     i;
pid_t                   pid;
```

```
// Pipe creates a descriptor for reading only and a descriptor
// for writing only. Socketpair creates two descriptors, each that
// can be used for both reading AND writing.
// socketpair() is more useful in this example.
    // rc = pipe(pipeFd);
    rc = socketpair(AF_UNIX, SOCK_STREAM, 0, pipeFd);
    if (rc != 0) {
        printf("pipe() failed, %d\n", errno);
        return NULL;
    }

    // Set up the fdMap to map file descriptors in the child
    // to a copy of pipeFd[0] from this job.
    fdMap[STDIN_FILENO]  = pipeFd[0];
    fdMap[STDOUT_FILENO] = pipeFd[0];
    fdMap[STDERR_FILENO] = pipeFd[0];

    // Setup the default spawn inheritence parameters
    memset(&inherit, 0, sizeof(inherit));
    // Add the desired options.
    inherit.pgroup = SPAWN_NEWPGROUP;
    inherit.flags |= SPAWN_SETTHREAD_NP;

    // Copy the arguments if there are any.
    for (int i=0; i<POPEN_MAX_ARGS; ++i) {
        if (pgmArgs[i] == NULL) {
            argCount = i;
            break;
        }
        cargv[i+1] = pgmArgs[i];
    }
```

Figure 24.6: The capability to start Qshell commands and programs while processing the input to and output from programs is a powerful Qshell programming feature (part 4 of 6).

```
    cargv[argCount+1] = NULL;

    // Create the environment variable array (we're adding
    // a variable so we can't just directly use environ.
    envCount = 0;
    while (environ[envCount] != NULL) { ++envCount; }
    // Add room for the NULL terminator and the new variable
    env = (char **)malloc((envCount+2) * sizeof(char *));
    for (int i=0; i<envCount; ++i) {
        env[i] = environ[i];
    }

    // Add the stdio environment variable if its not present
    // (because we're not running from QSHELL) and the null
    // terminator.
    if (getenv("QIBM_USE_DESCRIPTOR_STDIO") != NULL) {
        env[envCount]    = NULL;
    }
    else {
        env[envCount]    = stdioEnvironmentVariable;
        env[envCount+1]  = NULL;
    }

    // Create the child.
    pid = spawn(pgm, fdCount, fdMap, &inherit, cargv, env);
    if ((int)pid < 0) {
        printf("Failed to start child %s, err=%d\n", pgm, errno);
        free(env);
        return NULL;
    }

    // Open a stream FILE over the file descriptor connected
    // to the parent.
    fp = fdopen(pipeFd[1], "r+");
    if (fp == NULL) {
        printf("Creating stream failed, errno=%d\n", errno);
        free(env);
        return NULL;
    }

    // Close the file descriptor that we're not going to use
    // in our process.
    close(pipeFd[0]);
    free(env);
    return fp;
}
```

Figure 24.6: The capability to start Qshell commands and programs while processing the input to and output from programs is a powerful Qshell programming feature (part 5 of 6).

```
int pclose(FILE *fp) {
    fclose(fp);
    return 0;
}
ixlc -g popen.C
Program POPEN was created in library JSMITH on 07/02/03 at 15:19:17.
ln -s /qsys.lib/jsmith.lib/popen.pgm popen
./popen -c 'echo "hi\nbye" | while read i; do echo $i; done'
hi
bye
```

Figure 24.6: The capability to start Qshell commands and programs while processing the input to and output from programs is a powerful Qshell programming feature (part 6 of 6).

Figure 24.7 uses the simulated popen() API introduced in Figure 24.6 to process the output from a Qshell command. Like the similar Java and perl examples, this example displays the status of the PTFs passed on the command line. Since the API implementations for the popen(), pclose(), and list-related APIs have been shown previously in this section, they are not shown again here.

Compare and contrast this PTF example with the Java code in Figure 23.8 and the perl code in Figure 22.9. The output from the CL command is processed in a list_t structure that acts rather like a perl associative array or a Java Hashtable object. The list_t structure serves as the lookup mechanism for a list of randomly selected PTFs. The resulting C example looks quite similar to the perl and Java examples, but depends on quite a bit of hand-written code. The Java and perl examples, on the other hand, depend only on the runtime services for those languages.

```
cat ptfStatus.C
#include <stdio.h>
#include <stdlib.h>
#include <string.h>
#include <ctype.h>
#include <errno.h>
#include "list.H"
#include "popen.H"
```

Figure 24.7: This C example demonstrates using the spawn() API to run a CL command and process the output (part 1 of 4).

```c
// This example doesn't handle lines longer than
// BUFSIZE characters.
#define BUFSIZE    256

int debug = 0;

int isAPtfLine(char *buffer);


int main(int argc, char **argv)
{
    list_t        ptfList;
    FILE          *DSPPTF;
    char           buffer[BUFSIZE];
    char          *pgm = "/usr/bin/qsh";
    char          *pgmArgs[] = {
        "-c", "system \"\DSPPTF OUTPUT(*PRINT)\""
    };

    if (argc < 2 || strcmp(argv[1], "-h") == 0) {
        printf("Usage: phoneList [-h] <ptf>...\n");
        printf("  Query the status of a list of PTFs\n");
        exit(1);
    }

    listAllocate(&ptfList, 4096);

    // Create a file handle connected to the output
    // of a process running the system command to process
    // the CL command DSPPTF.
    DSPPTF = popen(pgm, pgmArgs);
    if (DSPPTF == NULL) {
        printf("Failed to start a child, err=%d\n", errno);
        exit(0);
    }

    // Process all of the output of the Qshell command
    while(fgets(buffer, sizeof(buffer), DSPPTF) != NULL) {
        char *ptf = NULL;
        char *status = NULL;
        if (debug) {
            fprintf(stdout, "<%s>\n", buffer);
        }
        if (isAPtfLine(buffer)) {
            // Use the PTF that we just matched in the parenthesis
            ptf = &buffer[2];
```

Figure 24.7: This C example demonstrates using the spawn() API to run a CL command and process the output (part 2 of 4).

```
            buffer[9] = 0;
            // Grab the PTF status from the line.
            status = &buffer[14];
            buffer[49] = 0;
            // Remove trailing whitespace from status.
            rtrim(status, 35);
            if (debug) {
                printf("OUT:<%s> <%s>\n", ptf, status);
            }
            listAdd(&ptfList, ptf, status);
        }
    }
    pclose(DSPPTF);

    printf("-------\t--------------------\n");
    printf("  PTF \t          Status        \n");
    printf("-------\t--------------------\n");
    for (int i=1; i<argc; ++i) {
        char  *ptf = argv[i];
        char  *status = NULL;

        status = listFind(&ptfList, ptf);
        if (status != NULL) {
            printf("%s\t%s\n", ptf, status);
        }
        else {
            printf("%s\tNot Loaded\n", ptf);
        }
    }
    exit(0);
}


// PTF list in the output is a 7 character name,
//     2 alpha, 5 digits            or
//     3 alpha, 4 digits
// prefixed by two spaces on each line.
int isAPtfLine(char *buffer) {
    if (buffer[0] == ' ' &&
        buffer[1] == ' ' &&
        isalpha(buffer[2]) &&
        isalpha(buffer[3]) &&
        isalnum(buffer[4]) &&
        isdigit(buffer[5]) &&
        isdigit(buffer[6]) &&
        isdigit(buffer[7]) &&
```

Figure 24.7: This C example demonstrates using the spawn() API to run a CL command and process the output (part 3 of 4).

534

```
        isdigit(buffer[8])) {
        return 1;
    }
    return 0;
}
ixlc -c -g -DNO_MAIN popen.C
Module POPEN was created in library JSMITH on 07/08/03 at 13:46:39.
ixlc -c -g list.C
Module LIST was created in library JSMITH on 07/08/03 at 13:46:46.
ixlc -g -c -B"CRTPGM PGM(JSMITH/PTFSTATUS) MODULE(JSMITH/POPEN
    JSMITH/LIST JSMITH/PTFSTATUS)" ptfStatus.C
Module PTFSTATUS was created in library JSMITH on 07/08/03 at 13:46:59.
Program PTFSTATUS created in library JSMITH.
/qsys.lib/jsmith.lib/ptfstatus.pgm SI06971 SI06972 SI06973
    SI06974 SI06975 SI06976 SI06977
------- --------------------
 PTF         Status
------- --------------------
SI06971 Temporarily applied
SI06972 Superseded
SI06973 Not Loaded
SI06974 Not Loaded
SI06975 Temporarily applied
SI06976 Temporarily applied
SI06977 Superseded
```

Figure 24.7: This C example demonstrates using the spawn() API to run a CL command and process the output (part 4 of 4).

Although a standard database access mechanism is not built into the C or C++ languages, the *ODBC (Open Database Connectivity)* APIs are available. Java's JDBC APIs are very similar to ODBC APIs; Java designers modeled JDBC based on ODBC. The same can be said for the perl database APIs. The iSeries provides an API set that is very similar to ODBC called the *CLI (Call Level Interface)*. CLI is used to access the native relational database on the local or a remote iSeries system.

Figure 24.8 demonstrates a more realistic phone-number lookup application then the example in Figure 24.5. The names and phone numbers reside in the relational database on the iSeries.

```
cat phoneDB.C
#include <stdio.h>
#include <stdlib.h>
#include <string.h>
#include <sqlcli.h>

#define BUFSIZE     256

void checkForSQLError(int rc, char *errorMessage) {
    if (rc != SQL_SUCCESS) {
        fprintf(stderr, "Error: %s\n", errorMessage);
        exit(1);
    }
}

int main(int argc, char **argv)
{
    char            buffer[BUFSIZE];
    long            bufferLen;
    long            bufferLen2;
    char            oleBoy[16];
    char            oleBoysWife[16];
    char            phoneNumber[16];
    long            phoneNumberLen = 0;
    int             len;
    char            *theItem;

    // Variables for basic SQL access
    int             rc;
    SQLHENV         henv = SQL_INVALID_HANDLE;
    SQLHDBC         hdbc = SQL_INVALID_HANDLE;
    SQLHSTMT        ps = SQL_INVALID_HANDLE;
    char            *sqlText;
    long            attr;
    // Variables for demonstrating SQL diagnostic data
    int             sqlCode = 0;
    char            sqlState[10];
    char            sqlErrorMessage[256];
    int             sqlErrorMessageLen = 256;
    SQLSMALLINT     sqlErrorMessageLenOut = 0;


    if (argc != 1) {
        printf("Usage: phoneList [-h]\n");
        exit(1);
    }
```

Figure 24.8: Use C and the CLI APIs to access the iSeries database (part 1 of 5).

```
// First create the SQL environment
 rc = SQLAllocHandle(SQL_HANDLE_ENV, SQL_NULL_HANDLE, &henv);
 checkForSQLError(rc, "allocate SQL environment");

// Use SQL_ATTR_SERVER_MODE for multi-connection, multi-user, or
// multi-threaded SQL CLI applications.
//
// iSeries DB access is typically optimized for single connection
// programs accessing a local DB under the currently running user.
// In that environment, DB access and DB engine work occurs directly
// within the calling process, providing significant optimizations.
//
// If we're using a multi-user, multi-connection or multi-threaded SQL
// application, it may be beneficial to use CLI's server mode for SQL.
// This causes each connection to be serviced by a backend agent (the
// server). The backend agent for one connection is more isolated
// from the front end application job and the other SQL connections.
// Using server mode for SQL provides significant portability
// improvements in some environments.
//
// attr= SQL_TRUE;
// rc = SQLSetEnvAttr(henv, SQL_ATTR_SERVER_MODE, &attr, 0);
// checkForSQLError(rc);

// Create a handle for an SQL connection object
rc = SQLAllocHandle(SQL_HANDLE_DBC, henv, &hdbc);
checkForSQLError(rc, "creating connection handle");

// Connect to the local iSeries database (NULL is allowed for
// specifying the *LOCAL database with the current user and password
rc = SQLConnect(hdbc, NULL, SQL_NTS, NULL, SQL_NTS, NULL, SQL_NTS);
checkForSQLError(rc, "connecting to local DB");

// Create a statement handle to be used for a prepared statement
rc = SQLAllocHandle(SQL_HANDLE_STMT, hdbc, &ps);
checkForSQLError(rc, "allocating statement handle");

// Prepare the statement (a prepared statement can be reused)
sqlText = "SELECT PHONENUMBER FROM JSMITHQ.CUSTOMERS WHERE NAME = ?
  OR WIFE = ?";
rc = SQLPrepare(ps, sqlText, SQL_NTS);
// If prepare fails, retrieve diagnostic data (diagnose typo's or
      problems
// with the SQL tables and the statement we're using)
if (rc != SQL_SUCCESS) {
    rc = SQLError(henv, hdbc, ps, sqlState, (SQLINTEGER *)&sqlCode,
                 sqlErrorMessage, sqlErrorMessageLen,
```

Figure 24.8: Use C and the CLI APIs to access the iSeries database (part 2 of 5).

```
                        &sqlErrorMessageLenOut);
        fprintf(stderr, "Error on SQLPrepare: rc=%d, "
                "sqlState=%5.5s, sqlCode=%d, msg=%s\n",
                rc, sqlState, sqlCode, sqlErrorMessage);
        exit(1);
}

// Output character data for column 1 to the phoneNumber variable
rc = SQLBindCol(ps, 1, SQL_CHAR, (SQLPOINTER)&phoneNumber,
                sizeof(phoneNumber), &phoneNumberLen);
checkForSQLError(rc, "bind output column");

// Get the user's input.
printf("Enter 'exit' or a name to lookup:\n");
fflush(stdout);
while (fgets(buffer, BUFSIZE, stdin)) {
    len = strlen(buffer);
    buffer[len-1] = 0;
    if (strcmp(buffer, "exit") == 0 ||
        strcmp(buffer, "quit") == 0) {
      break;
    }

    // Is the name a good ole boy?

    // Set both the first and the second parameters to
    // the input NTS (null terminated string).
    bufferLen = SQL_NTS;
    rc = SQLBindParam(ps, 1, SQL_CHAR, SQL_CHAR,
                      strlen(buffer)+1, 0, buffer, &bufferLen);
    checkForSQLError(rc, "binding parameter 1");

    // This parameter is modified by the API at execute time.
    // Using a second variable for the second call avoids effecting
      the first
    bufferLen2 = SQL_NTS;
    rc = SQLBindParam(ps, 2, SQL_CHAR, SQL_CHAR,
                      strlen(buffer)+1, 0, buffer, &bufferLen2);
    checkForSQLError(rc, "binding parameter 2");

    // Execute the statement using the values set
    rc = SQLExecute(ps);
    checkForSQLError(rc, "execute the statement");

    // After execution, retrieve the data
    rc = SQLFetch(ps);
    if (rc != SQL_SUCCESS && rc != SQL_NO_DATA_FOUND) {
```

Figure 24.8: Use C and the CLI APIs to access the iSeries database (part 3 of 5).

```
        // Error condition.
        checkForSQLError(rc, "fetching data");
    }

    if (rc == SQL_NO_DATA_FOUND) {
        printf("Didn't find customer: %s\n", buffer);
    }
    else {
        // Yes, print out the number
        printf("Found %s at %s\n", buffer, phoneNumber);
    }

    // close the open cursor (releases locks and resources when unused)
    rc = SQLCloseCursor(ps);
    checkForSQLError(rc, "closing cursor");

    printf("Enter 'exit' or a name to lookup:\n");
    fflush(stdout);
}

// Cleanup for good measure and building good habits.

// Close the statement and free the statement handle
rc = SQLFreeStmt(ps, SQL_DROP);
ps = SQL_INVALID_HANDLE;
checkForSQLError(rc, "closing statement");

// Disconnect from the DB
rc = SQLDisconnect(hdbc);
checkForSQLError(rc, "disconnect");

// Free the connection handle
rc = SQLFreeConnect(hdbc);
hdbc = SQL_INVALID_HANDLE;
checkForSQLError(rc, "free connection handle");

rc = SQLFreeEnv(henv);
henv = SQL_INVALID_HANDLE;
checkForSQLError(rc, "free environment handle");
exit(0);
}
ixlc -g phoneDB.C
Program PHONEDB was created in library JSMITH on 07/12/03 at 16:31:34.
/qsys.lib/jsmith.pgm/phonedb.pgm
Error on SQLPrepare: rc=0, sqlState=42704, sqlCode=-204, msg=CUSTOMERS
    in JSMITHQ type *FILE not found.
```

Figure 24.8: Use C and the CLI APIs to access the iSeries database (part 4 of 5).

```
db2 -f /home/jsmith/src/data/goodoleboys.sql
DB20000I   THE SQL COMMAND COMPLETED SUCCESSFULLY.
DB20000I   THE SQL COMMAND COMPLETED SUCCESSFULLY.

**** CLI ERROR *****
          SQLSTATE: 02000
NATIVE ERROR CODE: 100
Row not found for DELETE.
DB20000I   THE SQL COMMAND COMPLETED SUCCESSFULLY.
DB20000I   THE SQL COMMAND COMPLETED SUCCESSFULLY.
DB20000I   THE SQL COMMAND COMPLETED SUCCESSFULLY.
DB20000I   THE SQL COMMAND COMPLETED SUCCESSFULLY.
DB20000I   THE SQL COMMAND COMPLETED SUCCESSFULLY.
DB20000I   THE SQL COMMAND COMPLETED SUCCESSFULLY.
DB20000I   THE SQL COMMAND COMPLETED SUCCESSFULLY.
DB20000I   THE SQL COMMAND COMPLETED SUCCESSFULLY.
DB20000I   THE SQL COMMAND COMPLETED SUCCESSFULLY.
DB20000I   THE SQL COMMAND COMPLETED SUCCESSFULLY.
DB20000I   THE SQL COMMAND COMPLETED SUCCESSFULLY.
/qsys.lib/jsmith.pgm/phonedb.pgm
Enter 'exit' or a name to lookup:
Bill
Found Bill at 333-4444
Enter 'exit' or a name to lookup:
Daisy
Found Daisy at 333-4444
Enter 'exit' or a name to lookup:
Claude
Found Claude at 333-4340
Enter 'exit' or a name to lookup:
Etheline
Found Etheline at 333-4340
Enter 'exit' or a name to lookup:
Fred
Didn't find customer: Fred
Enter 'exit' or a name to lookup:
exit
```

Figure 24.8: Use C and the CLI APIs to access the iSeries database (part 5 of 5).

Compare and contrast this code with the similar Java example in Figure 23.8 and the perl example in Figure 22.9. For example, note that this C program is significantly longer than the Java and perl equivalents. This is due, in part, to the resource cleanup and error-checking required in C. The C database APIs have more parameters and more stringent requirements on the size, type, and storage model of the parameters than either the perl or Java programs. The fundamental concepts of database access and the general APIs remain quite consistent between this C example and the perl and Java programs, but these complexities might initially cause more errors in your application code as you learn the programming model.

The commands shown in Figure 24.8 demonstrate the error that might occur if database setup has not been completed. Running the goodoleboys.sql script with the *db2* utility corrects the problem, and the phoneDB program runs successfully.

SUMMARY

The C and C++ compilers and languages are not as integrated with the Qshell environment as the Java language. Extra steps during the development and build stage are required. Multiple versions of the C and C++ compilers provide flexibility to help you choose a solution that matches the requirements of your application. Writing special-purpose APIs might require that you focus more on testing and reusing C/C++ application code in order to keep productivity high.

Appendix A

Summary of Changes by Release

This appendix summarizes the changes made to Qshell in each release of OS/400.

V5R2

In V5R2, many utilities, variables, and operators were added or modified. These are listed in the following tables. In addition, support was added for CCSIDs 425, 905, 1026, 1097, and 1155.

New Utilities	
attr	Get or set a file's attributes.
builtin	Run a built-in utility.
dataq	Send or receive data queue messages.
datarea	Read or write a data area.
declare	Declare variables and set attributes.
help	Display help for a built-in utility.
iconv	Convert characters from one CCSID to another.

New Utilities, *continued*

ipcrm	Remove the interprocess communication ID.
ipcs	Report the interprocess communication status.
locale	Get locale-specific information.
mkfifo	Make special files FIFO.
nohup	Run a utility without a hangup.
printenv	Display the values of environment variables.
ps	Display the process status.
rexec	Run a remote command.
rexx	Run a Rexx procedure.
Rfile	Read or write record files.
source	Run commands in the current shell. (This is the same as the "dot" command.)
tar	Archive files.
type	Find the type of command.
typeset	Provide an alternative form of declare.
ulimit	Set or display resource limits.

Modified Utilities

exec	Added -c option
hash	Added -p option
trap	Added -l option
uname	Added -m option
xargs	Added -E, -e, -L, and -l options

New Predefined Variables

EGUID	Holds the effective primary group ID
EUID	Holds the effective user ID
GID	Holds the primary group ID
HOSTID	Holds the IP address of the host
HOSTNAME	Holds the name of the host
HOSTTYPE	Holds the type of host
MACHTYPE	Holds the type of machine
OSTYPE	Holds the type of operating system
PS3	Provides the prompt used by the select command
QIBM_CCSID	Holds the CCSID for translation
QIBM_QSH_CMD_ESCAPE_MSG	Sends escape messages from QSH CL command
QIBM_QSH_CMD_OUTPUT	Controls output of QSH CL command
QIBM_QSH_INTERACTIVE_CMD	Provides the initial interactive command
QIBM_QSH_INTERACTIVE_TYPE	Holds the type of interactive session
QIBM_SYSTEM_ALWMLTTHD	Allows multithread capable job
UID	Holds the user ID

Operators
Extended conditional construct [[ ]]
New syntax for functions
Select construct added
Substring word expansion
Substitute string for pattern word expansion
Tilde expansion updated

V5R1

The following tables list the utilities that were added or modified in V5R1. In addition, the TRACEFILE predefined variable was added to hold the path name of a trace file.

New Utilities	
cmp	Compare files.
compress	Compress data.
dspmsg	Send output from a message catalog.
file	Determine the file type.
od	Provide a file dump.
pax	Run the portable archive exchange.
sed	Run the stream editor.
setccsid	Set a file's CCSID attribute.
sysval	Retrieve system values or network attributes.
tr	Translate characters.
uncompress	Expand compressed data.
wc	Count words, lines, or characters.
zcat	Expand and concatenate data.

Modified utilities

getconf	Four new operands were added:	
	CCSID	Coded character-set ID
	PAGE_SIZE, PAGESIZE	Hardware page size
	PIPE_BUF	Maximum number of bytes that can be written automatically to a pipe
getjobid	-s option added to display qualified job name in a short format	
ls	-S option added to display a file's CCSID attribute	

V4R4

The following tables list the changes to utilities, variables, APIs, and operators that were made in V4R4. In addition, the *system* utility was modified with the addition of options *n* and *q*.

New Utilities

ajar	Create an alternative Java archive.
basename	Return the non-directory portion of a path name.
cat	Concatenate and print files.
chmod	Change file modes.
chgrp	Change file group ownership.
chown	Change file ownership.
clrtmp	Clear the /tmp directory.
cp	Copy files.
date	Print the date and time.
dirname	Return the directory portion of a path name.
env	Set the environment for command invocation.
expr	Evaluate arguments as an expression.

New Utilities, *continued*

find	Search a file hierarchy.
getjobid	Display job information.
grep	Search files for a pattern.
head	Copy the first part of files.
hostname	Display the name of the host system.
id	Return user identifiers.
let	Evaluate an arithmetic expression.
ln	Link files.
logger	Log messages to QHST.
logname	Display the user's login name.
ls	List directory contents.
mkdir	Create a directory.
mv	Move or rename a file.
pr	Print files to standard output.
pwdx	Print the working directory, expanded, to standard output.
rmdir	Remove a directory.
rm	Remove a link.
split	Split files into pieces.
tail	Copy the last part of files.
tee	Duplicate standard input.
touch	Change file-access and modification times.
uname	Display the system name on the standard output device.
uniq	Report or filter out unique names in a file.
whence	Determine how a command is interpreted.

New Predefined Variables	
QSH_REDIRECTION_CODE-PAGE	Code page for file redirection
QSH_REDIRECTION_TEXTDATA	Data processed as text for file redirection

New APIs	
QzshSystem()	Run a Qshell command.
QzshCheckShellCommand()	Find a Qshell command.

Operators
Parameter expansion operators #, ##, %, %% added
Greatly enhanced arithmetic expressions
Support for floating-point arithmetic

V4R3

In V4R3, the following changes were made:

- The *liblist* utility was added to manage library lists.

- The *test* utility was modified with the addition of the –*N* option to check for native objects.

- The QSH_VERSION predefined variable was added for the current Qshell version.

- The QSH_USE_PRESTART_JOBS predefined variable was added to give the ability to use prestart jobs when available.

- National language support was added for CCSIDs 1140-1149, for Euro currency.

Appendix B

Qshell versus DOS

This reference is provided for the benefit of those who have used the DOS batch language and need to learn Qshell.

CASE-SENSITIVITY

Although Unix shell commands are case-sensitive, that is not true of Qshell. For example, to get a directory listing, you can use either form of the List directory contents *(ls)* shown here:

```
ls -l
LS -l
```

However, options *are* case-sensitive, so the following command is *not* equivalent to the previous two commands under Qshell:

```
LS -L
```

OPTIONS (SWITCHES)

DOS options are preceded by the forward slash. Qshell options are preceded by a hyphen, or in some cases, by a plus sign. For example, in DOS, you would add an option to the directory command like this:

```
C:\WINDOWS> dir /p
```

In Qshell, you would do this:

```
ls -l
```

SEPARATION OF TOKENS

Qshell requires that command-line tokens be separated from one another by white space. DOS permits tokens to immediately follow one another when no confusion arises. So, the following would be acceptable in DOS:

```
C:\WINDOWS> cd\
C:\>
```

In Qshell, however, it would lead to an error:

```
/home/THOLT $
cd/
qsh: 001-0014 Command cd/ not found.
```

Instead, you would need to enter the command as follows:

```
/home/THOLT $
cd /
/ $
```

COMPARISON OF COMMANDS

The following table gives a list of corresponding DOS and Qshell commands. Keep in mind that these are not exact equivalents—the Qshell commands do not behave exactly like their DOS counterparts.

Corresponding DOS and Qshell Commands

Dos	Qshell	Function
assign	ln	Link file.
attrib	chmod	Change file attributes.
call *file*	file	Execute a batch file (script).
cd	echo $PWD	Display the current directory.
cd, chdir	cd	Change the current directory.
cls	F13 key	Clear the display.
command	qsh, sh	Invoke a command shell.
copy	cp	Copy a file.
copy ... con	cat	Copy the contents of a file to stdout.
date	date	Display the date.
del	rm	Remove (delete) a file.
deltree	rm -r	Delete a directory and its contents.
dir	ls -l	Show directory contents.
dir /w	ls	Show directory contents.
echo	echo, print	Display text.
erase	rm	Remove (delete) a file.
find	grep	Search a file.
for	for	Execute a loop.
goto	None	Branch to an instruction
md,mkdir	mkdir	Create (make) a directory.
move	mv	Move a file to another directory.
path	echo $PATH.	Display the path.
pause	sleep	Suspend execution.
print	pr	Print to stdout.

Corresponding DOS and Qshell Commands, *continued*

Dos	Qshell	Function
prompt	PS1=value	Set the prompt string.
rd, rmdir	rmdir	Remove (delete) a directory.
prompt	PS1=value	Set the prompt string.
rem	#	Ignore a line. (In other words, include a comment.)
ren, rename	mv	Rename a file.
sort	sort	Sort stdin.
type	cat	Display the contents of a file.
xcopy	cp	Copy files.

Qshell and CL Commands for the IFS

The tables in this appendix list CL and Qshell commands that reference the Integrated File System.

QSHELL COMMANDS FOR IFS OBJECTS

The following table lists useful Qshell commands for working with files in the IFS.

Directory Commands	
cd	Change the working directory.
ls	List the directory contents.
mkdir	Make a directory.
pwd	Get the name of the present working directory.
pwdx	Print the name of the present working directory, expanded.

Directory Commands, *continued*

rm	Remove directory entries.
rmdir	Remove a directory.

Object Commands

attr	Get or set a file's attributes.
basename	Get the non-directory portion of a path name.
cat	Print files to standard output (stdout).
compress	Reduce the size of one or more files.
dirname	Get the directory portion of a path name.
cp	Copy files.
file	Determine the file type.
find	Find files.
getconf	Get POSIX configuration values.
head	Copy the first part of files.
ln	Link files.
mkfifo	Make a FIFO special file.
mv	Move files.
od	Dump file contents.
pax	Create a portable archive exchange.
pr	Print files.

Object Commands, *continued*

setccsid	Set the CCSID attribute.
tail	Copy the last records of a file.
tar	Create a file archive.
touch	Change file access and modification times, or create a file.
umask	Get or set the file-mode creation mask.
uncompress	Expand a compressed file.
zcat	Expand and concatenate data.

Authority Commands

chgrp	Transfer file ownership to another group.
chmod	Change file modes.
chown	Transfer ownership of a file.

CL COMMANDS FOR THE IFS

The following table lists useful CL commands for working with files in the IFS.

Directory Commands

GO FSDIR	Display the Directory Commands menu.
CRTDIR, MKDIR, MD	Create a directory.
RMVDIR, RMDIR, RD	Remove a directory.
CHGCURDIR, CHDIR, CD	Change the current working directory.
DSPCURDIR	Display or print the name of the current working directory.

Object Commands

GO FSOBJ	Display the Object Commands menu.
WRKLNK	Work with object links.
DSPLNK	Display object links.
EDTF	Edit a stream file or database file member.
CPY	Copy an object or a group of objects.
RNM, REN	Rename an object.
MOV	Move an object to a different directory.
ADDLNK	Add a link to (the name of) an object.
RMVLNK, DEL, ERASE	Remove a link to (the name of) an object.
SAV	Save an object to backup media.
RST	Restore an object from backup media.
CHGATR	Change an attribute of an object or group of objects.
CHKOUT	Check out an object. This prevents other users from modifying the object.
CHKIN	Check in an object.
CPYTOSTMF	Copy a database file member or save file to a stream file in the IFS.
CPYFRMSTMF	Copy a stream file to a database file member or a save file.
CPYTOIMPF	Copy a database file member to a file to be used for exchanging data with other applications.
CPYFRMIMPF	Copy an import file to a database file.

Authority Commands

GO FSSEC	Display the menu of IFS security commands.
WRKAUT	Allow modification of users' authority to IFS objects.
DSPAUT	Display a user's authority to IFS objects.
CHGAUT	Change a user's authority to an IFS object.
CHGOWN	Transfer ownership of an IFS object to another user.
CHGPGP	Change an object's primary group, or specify that there is no primary group for the object.
CHGAUD	Set up or change auditing on an object.

Index